Sex and the Citizen

NEW WORLD STUDIES

J. Michael Dash, *Editor*

Frank Moya Pons and
Sandra Pouchet Paquet,
Associate Editors

Sex and the Citizen

Interrogating the Caribbean

Edited by Faith Smith

University of Virginia Press

Charlottesville and London

University of Virginia Press

© 2011 by the Rector and Visitors of the University of Virginia

All rights reserved

Printed in the United States of America on acid-free paper

First published 2011

9 8 7 6 5 4 3 2 1

Library of Congress Cataloging-in-Publication Data

Sex and the citizen : interrogating the Caribbean / edited by Faith Smith.
    p. cm.   —   (New World studies)
  Includes bibliographical references and index.
  ISBN 978-0-8139-3112-8 (cloth : acid-free paper) —
  ISBN 978-0-8139-3113-5 (pbk. : alk. paper) — ISBN 978-0-8139-3132-6 (e-Book)
    1. Caribbean fiction—History and criticism. 2. Gender identity—Caribbean Area.
3. Identity (Psychology)—Caribbean Area. 4. Sex role in literature. I. Smith, Faith,
1964-
  PN849.C3S49 2011
  809'.897290904—dc22

                                                                2010044992

Contents

Desiring Subjects and Modernity

Reimagining Pasts and Futures

Acknowledgments

THIS BOOK has been a long time in the making, so first I must express my gratitude to the contributors who stayed the course and those who did not for their patience and goodwill. Audiences at Duke University, the University of Massachusetts at Boston, the "Conversations on Caribbean Transnational and Diasporic Feminisms" seminar organized by York and Toronto universities, the "Re-routing Diaspora" seminar at the University of Pennsylvania, and the "Black Love" symposium at DePaul University gave valuable feedback. I thank the Student Scholar Partnership of the Women's Studies Research Center, the Theodore and Jane Norman Award, and the Program in Latin American and Latino Studies' Jane's Award travel grants, all of Brandeis University, as well as Lauren Holm Ellis, Samantha Miller, Samuel Nicolosi, and Lisa Pannella. Supportive colleagues at the W. E. B. Du Bois Institute at Harvard University gave me the will to take this project up again, and the space at 40 Concord Avenue allowed me to complete it. M. Jacqui Alexander, Bernadette Brooten, Belinda Edmondson, Lyndon Kamal Gill, Thomas Glave, Sue Houchins, Florence Ladd, Sue Lanser, Patricia Mohammed, Patricia Powell, Rhoda Reddock, Marjorie Salvodan, Mark Schafer, Thandeka, and the Small Axe collective encouraged and inspired me. Once again, Cathie Brettschneider kept the faith. Joanne Allen's patience and meticulousness have made this a better book. The comments of two anonymous reviewers were invaluable. Finally, Donette Francis, Tracy Robinson, and Michelle Rowley first showed me the connections between sexuality and citizenship in the region: thank you.

Sex and the Citizen

Introduction

Sexing the Citizen

Faith Smith

WHAT DOES it mean to be *Caribe, Antillais, West Indian, Kréyol, Kwéyòl, Créole, Creole,* and why are responses to this question tied so insistently to the sexed bodies, practices, and identities of the region's people? The contributors to this volume address this question by looking across the Caribbean, including its extended diasporic and coastal parameters. They examine parliamentary legislation, novels, film, and the visual arts. They speak from within but also challenge the assumptions of feminism, literary and cultural studies, queer studies, and anthropology. Literary texts, ethnographic interviews, and scenes from the classroom test claims made about agency, the reach of the law, and the uneven power dynamics between "over there" and "here." The contributors discuss the sexual practices, identities, and desires that have violated what many people in the region deem to be Caribbean norms of heterosexual respectability, though not all focus on the specifically same-sex aspects of the perceived transgressions that have been repudiated so insistently in some of the region's territories in recent years. Ultimately, they show that Caribbean discourses of sexuality constitute a still understudied topic that can be illuminated by regional, local, diasporic, and multidisciplinary lenses and also, crucially, that these discourses mark a paradigmatic shift in the way the Caribbean is demonstrating to itself and to the world what it means to live in and with the present moment of globalization.[1]

Since the early 1990s, events across the Caribbean and discussions about them within and outside of the region have been *languaged by sex* as public discussions about political and cultural sovereignty have taken shape around the issue of "legitimate" sexualities and as the intensity of the flow of goods and ideas and the shifts in tastes and values that are associated with globalization have raised the stakes about just who Caribbean people are and who they can be. The contributors to this volume are interested in the present moment or in events of a century ago, which we shall provisionally assume can be defined by the Caribbean's response to, respectively, the *taboo of homosexuality* and the *taboo of miscegenation*. They show that these taboos are at once useful structuring signposts—our present does seem to be marked by one in particular, and it is useful to keep in mind that other taboos of sexuality were significant in the past—but also limiting. That is, these taboos overlap in time but also epistemologically and discursively. They create anxieties differently (or not at all) in different parts of the region or among different constituencies, and other taboos may complement or supersede them in significance.

We shall see how notions of sexuality are deeply inflected by colonial and imperial inheritances that have framed nationalism's discourses and silences and continue to inform, more or less, the structures of feeling of the region's people. On the other hand, over the last two decades or so, political, economic, and cultural developments in the global arena have necessitated trade-offs in the Caribbean that are deemed to have jeopardized, even as they have enabled, notions of sovereignty and autonomy for Caribbean nations, colonies, associated territories, and overseas departments. To quote M. Jacqui Alexander, "Not just anybody can be a citizen," and if the essays that follow are for the most part focused on notions of citizenship only in the very broadest sense of affiliation with one of the region's territories, we nevertheless see how specific contexts of sex and sexuality have informed feelings of belonging or disaffection.[2] These essays show that for a very long time there have been as many forms of sexual expression as there have been ways to break the codes conferred by law and by custom and that the full range of these can illuminate what appear today to be new infractions—and new possibilities—of what it means to be "authentically" attached to the region.

What It Means to Be Languaged by Sex
Sovereignty and the Taboo of Miscegenation

To speak of the *taboo* of miscegenation might seem odd, because if the region has answered to the charge of the sin of the improper mixture of blood, it has also scoffed at or celebrated this perceived sin. Over and over, the impurity of blood or the mixture of races has been the reason for the region's being understood to be inferior to Europe, and later also the United States, and thus incapable of morality or not ready for political autonomy. The response has been to show proof of purity or to repudiate purity as a virtue. In the eighteenth and nineteenth centuries, for example, colonial planter-historians and planter-statesmen in the Americas, such as Bryan Edwards (England, Jamaica), Edward Long (England, Jamaica), and Thomas Jefferson (United States), worried about white degeneracy and unnatural combinations of species, such as "mulattoes" and "albinos," and debated polygeneist and monogeneist theories, even while some of their contemporaries, such as the plantation bookkeeper Thomas Thistlewood, were more forthcoming about the less philosophical aspects of the sexual combinations in which all of them were engaged (K. Brathwaite, *Development*; Carnegie; D. Hall).

We can see implicit or explicit responses to the charge of racial impurity ("mixed blood" or an unseemly cohabitation of racial groups) in the discourses of nineteenth-century Caribbean nationalists. The Cuban José Martí, reporting from New York on the recently convened International Monetary Conference in 1891, critiques Puritan ethnocentrism and says of North Americans: "They believe that the nations of Hispanoamerica are primarily made up of Indians and Negroes." "As long as the United States knows no more about Hispanoamerica than this," he asks, how could those nations have a union with the United States that was to their benefit? (306). John Jacob Thomas, of Trinidad (one of Martí's "Negroes"), responds to Victorian metropolitan ideas that Caribbean people could not participate in their political systems because whites would not work with blacks by noting that in Trinidad British governors consorted with dusky "Ethiopian damsels" (J. Thomas 116; F. Smith, *Creole Recitations* 163). Racial (heterosexual) "combination" becomes a way to prove something about political capacity.

The Haitian Anténor Firmin marvels at the "sick mind" "singing a hymn of desolation" when Count Gobineau in his *Essai* anticipates the end of the white species because of "the promiscuous relations among the different ethnic groups" (Firmin, *Equality* 438–39). But Firmin has his own ideas about which groups mix well. In repudiating Gobineau's ideas about mixing races, he hails the "contrast of colors" that makes the mulatress more "radiant" than the Ethiopian woman and more "sharply nuanced" than the white woman; having "all the qualities of her mother," she is generous, selfless, intelligent, sweet, "devoted and accommodating," and all this and more lights up her eyes and brows (200). On the other hand, the handsome features of her male counterpart, the mulatto, are "neutralized" by "his affected, effeminate, studied, or pretentious manners . . . he rarely exhibits that melange of abandon, freedom, and vigor in movement which are characteristic of male beauty, . . . a fact which can be verified not only in Haiti but also in the Dominican Republic and in the European colonies, keeping in mind the many outstanding exceptions to the rule" (*Equality* 199; *De l'égalité* 181).

The most beautiful in this hierarchy are black men. Firmin writes, for example, "[In Port-au-Prince in 1883 I saw] a young Black man so mesmerizingly handsome one could not take one's eyes off his face" (*Equality*

197–98; *De l'égalité* 178–79). Another man is "regular" featured, well pro-
portioned, well mannered, and well educated, and visitors used to "gaze
admiringly at this man whose handsome features were enhanced by his
black skin." Yet another "tall," "handsome" Haitian general visiting Paris
"could show himself on the city's boulevards next to the handsome European males with only his black skin as a differentiating trait" (*Equality* 198;
De l'égalité 179). "Handsome Black men are a common sight in Haiti";
they are "lithe" with "well-toned muscles" and the "proud expressions"
that reflect the "Ethiopian's sense of being free, independent and equal to
everyone else, and one will have a clear idea of these men whose forefathers
showed such heroism that history will always remember" (*Equality* 197; *De
l'égalité* 178).

Here military bearing, freedom, and revolutionary heroism are key ingre-
dients of black men's beauty. Firmin reproduces longstanding clichés about
"mulattoes," such as their supposed sterility, and is particularly critical of
men who are male but not masculine. Thus, although these nationalists
have their specific discursive contexts, they agree that "racial combinations"
prove something about "us," that they gender us, sex us, mark us in particular ways. For colonial subjects, the refutation of racial slander is also a
contestation over how the group being spoken for is sexed. Racial combinations become a way to assign or refute inferiority and to prop up racial and
masculine honor. Sex—or at least heterosexual, reproductive sex—proves
something about the success or failure of political rule, and written into the
nationalist text are these refutations and affirmations.

Furthermore, it is not only the mixing of *this* "blood"—colonizing European and colonized nonwhite—that causes anxiety. When the Victorian
historian J. A. Froude declares that "the African and Asiatic will not mix"
(65), a statement that Thomas does not refute in his response to Froude,
he reminds us how deeply invested the colonizing power is in this taboo,
with his willed pitting of two labor pools against each other in order to
forestall economic and political alliances that would undermine British rule.
Nationalist honor in the region has entailed negotiating anxiety about mixing between these two colonized groups, in terms of competing for political
and economic power but also for fear of diasporic degeneration caused by
relocation to and inappropriate mixing in the Caribbean.[3]

Robert J. C. Young notes that eighteenth- and nineteenth-century Europeans' discussions of hybridity constituted "an implicit politics of heterosexuality" (25) and that these discussions of the mixing of various genres
of plants and people were "covertly" stories about desire. Young points
out that for these men it was never simply a matter of their being repulsed
by their colonial and racial subordinates. In the work of Count Gobineau,
to whom, as we have already seen, Anténor Firmin's text was a response,

blood mixture is at once the source of both degeneration of the superior Aryan race and its compulsion. The so-called superior race is drawn to sexual conjugality with yellow and brown races, who in turn show their savage tendencies by being repulsed by such mixing. For Young's Gobineau, the white man's irresistible attraction to yellow and black rejuvenates him and is a mark of his civilization, since it means that he is open to change.[4]

In pointing out the drive to hybridity, which would seem to go against the grain of colonial superiority and domination, Young discusses Bryan Edwards's celebratory eighteenth-century poem "The Sable Venus: An Ode," in praise of an enslaved "Angolan" woman. Yet the same text is read by the historian Barbara Bush (11) and the literary critic Jenny Sharpe (47–51) as white male investment in exoticizing black women and an instance of the "anti-conquest" narrative as outlined by Mary Louise Pratt, in which, in a disingenuous disavowal of power, it is African women rather than white males who are depicted as the colonizers. Similar critical readings of pre-revolutionary Saint Domingue (Garraway) and of Cuba (Kutzinski) remind us that hybridity and creolization in and of themselves do not guarantee the removal of hierarchies and can in fact enshrine them (Bolland).

Indeed, there are numerous examples of poets, novelists, and theorists in the region who rely on heterosexual desire to represent the violation of the region's landscape, a landscape that has to be spoken for and rescued from the colonial violator, without, however, risking the violation of the male warrior-artist (Edmondson; I. Rodríguez). Or sex in a feminized Caribbean landscape or with the Caribbean woman is naturalized as a way of understanding something about the region, so that [Edward] Kamau Brathwaite says of its history that "it was in the intimate area of sexual relationships where the most significant (and lasting) inter-cultural creolisation took place" (*Development* 303). Veronica Gregg sees in this passage the use of women as the unacknowledged sexual underpinning of the new arrangements of early Creole societies that Brathwaite examines and how his statement simultaneously assumes and overlooks "the constructions of sex, gender and race in terms of power" (149).

Viewed this way, the theorists who are so admired for their repudiation of Enlightenment binarism and roots and their openness to routes, rhizomes, *verrition,* and chaos are as dependent on reproductive, heterosexual relations as the blood purists they abjure (Arnold, "Erotics"; Césaire, *Notebook;* Clifford), and this accounts for their invocations of traitorous women (Fanon; Paz), womblike slave ships delivering dead souls (Glissant 6; B. Thomas 26), and black women's thighs, which will save us from the apocalypse (Benítez-Rojo 10). Discourses of creolization and hybridity, then, far from being liberatory, can enshrine notions of inside and outside and of who is authentically Caribbean and who is not.

Sovereignty and the Taboo of Homosexuality

The taboo of homosexuality would seem to define the present moment in the region, what with opposition to gay cruises, the pronouncement of one nation in the region as "possibly the most homophobic place on earth" (Padgett), dancehall reggae lyrics' infamous calls for violent extermination of gays and lesbians, and the repudiation of the installation of homosexual church leaders in Europe and North America. Yet here we might discern historical contexts for what appear to be such recent developments.

The Firmin passages cited earlier, for instance, remind us that as much as the discourses of nineteenth-century nationalists naturalize heterosexual sex, they can also affirm homosocial and perhaps also homosexual desire. This is in line with Michelle Stephens's contention about a later generation of Caribbean nationalists who in defiance of a willed heterosexuality give us "rebellious meanings and constructions of masculinity which, precisely in engagement with and in defiance of a heterosexual politics, create more homosocial desires for community and more homoerotic forms of national longing" (Stephens 288n35; see also Braziel). It is important to add that this longing might very well repudiate (male or female) "femininity" as extraneous to or disruptive of liberatory nationalist dreams.

It is tempting to speculate that Firmin's mulattoes have to be effeminate and pretentious because they are the political rivals of black men. In the discourses of European men, black and mulatto men are represented as pretentious and pedantic parrots in their bid for a share in political rule.

The taboo of homosexuality first "languaged" the region much earlier than the nineteenth century. The Caribbean and its people have long defined external or internal threats to the body politic in terms of sexual transgression, even as the Caribbean—as part of the so-called New World or in its own right—has been regarded by the rest of the world as the very epitome of excessive sexuality. Fifteenth- and sixteenth-century travelers concluded that they had come to a region inhabited by unnatural consumers of human flesh: "For these [Caribs] . . . are wilder men. When conquering and eating those [Arawak] Indians, they may have committed that extreme offence [of sodomy] out of spite."[5] The anagrammatic connection between *Carib* and *cannibalism* exemplified by Caliban in Shakespeare's *Tempest* and explored by so many of the region's writers shows us the power of discourse to produce knowledge.[6] Indeed, Michel Foucault has noted that "it is in discourse that power and knowledge are joined together" (*History*, 100).

Let us pause for a moment to consider the reference to sodomy in the above quotation about Arawaks and Caribs. Foucault proposes that before the nineteenth century, "the sodomite had been a temporary aberration" and "sodomy was a category of forbidden acts," eliciting both horrific punishment by fire and, inconsistently, no punishment at all (43). Beginning in the nineteenth century, various knowledge-producing disciplines have engaged in both a frenzied classification of and a clamping down on this "sin," even as a "reverse discourse" has used these new classifications and subclassifications to claim "legitimacy" for homosexuals. From the nineteenth century on, a certain kind of sexuality has been stamped into the sodomite's soul and "written immodestly onto his [*sic*] face and body because it was a secret that always gave itself away" (43). This insight is very helpful, because it points our attention to the way different eras decide that a particular event or behavior is or is not transgressive and what punishment or other consequence ought to be applied. What is "seen" and then condemned or defended becomes a function of a set of laws, statements, categories. Sex is produced from discourse, rather than discourse merely describing or reflecting some "fact" about sex.

Given the history of the Caribbean as one of the first sites of European conquest in the Americas, we can surmise that a "Carib sodomite" did not have the privilege, albeit dubious, of waiting to be found out in the nineteenth century, and not just because of the almost wholesale decimation of the region's indigenous population. His body, her body, was already visibly something that was comprehensible to the European viewer as unnaturally and thoroughly *other*. As Michael Horswell shows for the Andean and Iberian contexts and Jonathan Goldberg *(Sodometries* and *Tempest)* shows for Renaissance England and the Anglophone Caribbean, discourses of sodomy reflected changing notions about what distinguished sexual intercourse without procreation, bestial desire, inhuman desire and activity, and cannibalism as sinful; about heterosexual and homosexual monogamy; about sexual exertion and the proper conduct of the body; and about the proper place of the androgynous and feminine relative to the masculine.

These and other anxieties were part of the self-fashioning of various Euro-Christian identities and helped to make conquered populations in Ireland, South America, and the Caribbean legible as pathological. European notions of being improperly sexed, then, became part of the way that colonized populations were stigmatized as inferior. Thus it is necessary to discern how sex, as noted in Foucault's passage, is racialized. M. Jacqui Alexander points out that colonialism entailed both "racializing and sexualizing the population, which also meant naturalizing whiteness. There could really be no psycho-social codices of sexuality that were not simultaneously raced" ("Not Just (Any) *Body*" 11–12). As scholars in postcolonial studies and other fields have concurred, it is important to be attentive to the intersection of race, sexuality, and colonial and imperial domination.[7]

Commenting on Foucault's distinction, cited above, between "temporary aberration" and permanent disclosure, Marlon Ross notes:

> Foucault's scientists can script their human subjects as total homosexual compo-
> sitions only because those bodies are *not* already marked as Negroid or Oriental;
> that is, in other words, because they are silently, invisibly already marked as
> unspecified Anglo-Saxons. Likewise, Foucault himself can script the formation of
> homosexuality as a totalized identity only by leaving unremarked the racial ideol-
> ogy undergirding these emerging sciences. ("Beyond the Closet" 167, emphasis
> in original)

Since *race* is deemed to be stable, that is, scientists can claim to ferret out *sexual* difference, whether this is scientific or psychological. But by virtue of being indigenous, African, or Asian, and even by residing in the tropics, one is probably already marked as deviant, queer, or perverse. This is also why, for Ross, the theorization of the closet in relation to being either visible or not yet visible, or to being on the journey from repression to public disclo-sure and liberation, hues too closely to narratives of progress, modernity, and (under)development—"evolutionary notions of the uneven develop-ment of the races from primitive darkness to civilized enlightenment" (163).

The importance of attending to race and sexuality simultaneously is reinforced by Roderick Ferguson's reminder that in the North American context, "women of color feminist theorizations of racialized sexuality" necessarily attended to specificities of geography and history and often preceded Foucault's theorizations, though they are not credited as having done so ("Normative Strivings" 86). At the same time, he points out that anxieties about respectability in the face of racial terror and social discrimi-nation produced silences around sexuality for feminists of color. Kamala Kempadoo addresses reticence about sexuality in the context of the Carib-bean when she urges that "we cannot simply view [hypersexuality] as a fabrication of the European mind and imagination, or dismiss it as colonial discourses or metaphors"; we must also recognize it "as a lived reality that pulses through the Caribbean body." In addition, states Kempadoo, today's Caribbean states are "incorporating sexuality into their national strategies for competing in the globalized economy" (*Sexing the Caribbean* 2–3).

Certainly it is Caribbean feminists' engagement with discourses of nation-alism, popular culture, reproductive and waged labor, and domestic violence that has laid the groundwork for much recent scholarship on sexuality.[8] Yet precisely because of the intersection of race, nationalism, and sexual pro-priety, regional feminist agendas have largely omitted nonheteronormative sexuality. In this anthology Tracy Robinson and Yasmin Tambiah allude to the painful silences and trade-offs that have marked Caribbean feminists' activism, so that lobbying for laws against domestic violence, for instance, has meant sacrificing the same-sex erotic autonomy of the region's female citizens.[9]

Attending to the silences in Foucault's text and in various feminist discourses, we can hear another inflection in the discourse of sodomy. We have seen that for Foucault and in the text of at least one fifteenth-century commentator, *sodomite* is gendered male. When the dancehall reggae artiste Beenie Man declares that it is "right" to "bun" (burn) "chi chi man" (the Jamaican term of contempt for a man perceived to be effeminate or homosexual, from *chichi,* the name of the termite that burrows into and destroys wood, and its "chichi dust," or fecal matter) and "sodomite," in effect he genders *sodomite* female, as opposite to and equal in perversion to male homosexuality in the Creole grammar of at least one Caribbean territory. Makeda Silvera notes that for women in the region, *sodomite* has been a "dread" designation: "In Jamaica, the words used to describe many of these women would be 'Man Royal' and/or 'Sodomite.' Dread words. I heard sodomite whispered a lot. . . . and tales of women secretly having sex, joining at the genitals, and being taken to the hospital to be 'cut' apart were told in the school yard. Invariably, one of the women would die" (15).

We need multiple perspectives, then, to read and hear the discourses and silences of the region's relationship to this taboo, including Iberian and Elizabethan contexts for the fullest interpretations of what "Caribs" allegedly did to "Arawaks," the sexual "secret" that Foucault sees first, and the racialization of his insights. Of course, we should not allow Silvera's racial identity as an Afro-Caribbean-Canadian woman to obliterate or undermine her identity as a lesbian. Specifying other "local" and "authentic" conjugations is also important. We see that neither Creole languages' much-vaunted "indigenous" "authenticity" nor the challenge posed by "dread talk" to the linguistic and social status quo (Chevannes; Pollard) can mitigate a hard truth. Silvera learns that the endpoint of women's erotic desire for other women narrated on her mother's verandah in the rural heartland can only mean death, a truth confirmed by Beenie Man's Creole grammar. In this volume Omise'eke Natasha Tinsley shares with Odile Cazenave a suspicion about the liberatory capacity of Creole speech in the region, and while it has been used to draw the line between fluent insiders and clueless outsiders (Cooper, "Lyrical Gun"), Creole speech is a repository for sexual slurs and sexual violence. A vocabulary of local, insider's names—*battyman, chichi man, tek man, maricon, makome, masisi, sodomite, Man Royal, Aunty/ Anti-Man*—is a rich source of abusive terms for women and men who diverge from the procreative trajectories of national or ethnic collectivities and encodes a range of sexual and political desires. These are all local names reflecting local propensities for (at least) rhetorical violence, just as there are many Creole names for "pounding" a woman during violent sex with her (Rey 80). Creole grammars are as likely to police and authenticate as they are to affirm and liberate. The local names for things do not inherently promise liberation.[10]

Sovereignty and Package Deals

These taboos, then, suggest the inheritances that define the parameters of identities, desires, and silences, which must be squared with pragmatic choices in the present. The designations "possibly the most homophobic place on earth" and "familiar to [North] Americans primarily as a laid-back beach destination" (Padgett) are two truths about the region: it is both violently homophobic and available for servicing the global North (Younge). It is wrongly sexed when it protests gay cruises and nude weddings and murders homosexual Caribbean residents, and it is rightly sexed when it offers itself fully to the pleasure of foreign visitors who, temporarily fleeing the pressures of the hardworking modernity of the North, are in search of a "laid-back" "Paradise" (Alexander, *Pedagogies;* Binnie; Puar, "Circuits"). Sex attaches to the region both when it repudiates sex and when it affirms it.

To agree with "the West" that the region is violently homophobic, or even that homophobia is reprehensible, is to risk yielding the hard-won sovereignty of a region historically subject to the whims of colonizers and foreign military and financial institutions. It is to concede the spectacular and exceptional nature of the region's violence and its not quite modern character. The continuing legacies of slavery, indenture, and colonialism and the attendant threat to the integrity of the Caribbean (particularly nonwhite) body and psyche dictate that any departure from a wholesome, clean, straightforward sexuality would risk a return to the scene of colonial degradation.

Viewed this way, postcolonial liberation and autonomy become the freedom to assert control over one's sexual autonomy, defined as wholesome, normative, straight. Every affirmation of sovereignty is part of a package deal that includes the assumption of heterosexuality as the best or only way to be Caribbean.

Two small examples, both from the territory that has most recently been at the center of the more heated debates about homosexuality in the region, might suffice here. When the Jamaican prime minister tells his BBC interviewer that there will be no homosexuals in his cabinet, he is reassuring party supporters in the context of local speculations about videotapes and the character of the other party's composite masculinity: not only will there be no homosexuals but there will be none in *his* cabinet (Golding). But he is also signaling to his compatriots and to the world that patriotism is incompatible with admitting to any deviation from a heterosexual norm. When Oprah Winfrey informs her audience that her Jamaican guest is fleeing the homophobic terror of her homeland, "a place we [in North America] call Paradise" ("Gay Around the World"), she is reinforcing the choice between Paradise and a place of homophobic violence as the options available for thinking about the region, perpetuating the idea of the region as premodern and repressive but also marking it as thoroughly *other,* since the discussion does not include instances of homophobic violence in the United States. These cannot be spoken of in the same program. Repudiating these ideas about the Caribbean, on the other hand, also means denying that homophobia exists, or that it is a plausible cause for concern in the region, or that the discussion of homosexual desire is appropriate.

Events and affiliations have become linked to one another in "package deals" that we can take apart, examine, and perhaps reassemble. Prime Minister Golding's response to his BBC interviewer was a knee-jerk reaction to a package deal represented by, for example, the nonwhite Indian and Jamaican guests on Winfrey's program, whose appearance reinforced their respective global locations as places from which to escape and the United States as a haven from tyranny. The juxtaposition of the descriptors "laid-back" and "most homophobic on earth" encodes a package deal in which a nonhomophobic Caribbean is taken to mean something like "available for servicing the global North." It is precisely against such "package deals" that M. Jacqui Alexander protests when she asserts, "I provide a sobering note on the dangers of offering up sexual freedom alone on the broken platter of U.S. democracy in order to secure or ostensibly guard the boundaries of modernity, and ultimately I urge queer studies and queer movements to take up questions of colonialism, racial formation, and political economy simultaneously" (*Pedagogies* 12).

BUT IF these things have always been true, is it just an illusion that rhetoric on sexuality has become more virulent in some Caribbean territories? The last two decades or so have witnessed the impact on the region of HIV/AIDS, as well as the structural adjustment programs mandating the shrinking of public services in order to conform to International Monetary Fund and World Bank demands, the attenuation of agricultural and other sources of revenue in favor of the expansion of tourism (and thus the intensification of the region's association with particular kinds of services), and the flooding of Caribbean markets with cable television and other media. Except for HIV/AIDS, these developments are associated with globalization, which has increased concerns about how to meet new expectations and acquire new tastes while remaining true to "who we are."

Feminist theorists have shown us how the global restructuring of labor and capital associated with globalization affects personal choices and notions of national sovereignty, such as why someone traveling from Manila to Rome to clean offices is helping to solve her country's debt crisis, and the Caribbean has provided rich examples, including specifically in the arena of sexuality.[11]

Alexander calls Caribbean governments' ceding of authority to the World Bank and the IMF in the last two decades of the twentieth century a "crisis of legitimation," given the promises they made to their electorates in the wake of independence, and she points out that in order to compensate for losing face in the economic arena, governments have exerted heightened surveillance in the moral arena, with legislation tightening restrictions around homosexuality since the early 1990s. She is very interested in the extent to which, as she puts it, "the archetypal source of state legitimation is anchored in the heterosexual family, the form of family crucial in the state's view to the founding of the nation." "*Some* bodies," as she puts it, "are not productive enough for the nation" ("Not Just (Any) *Body*" 20, emphasis in original). Whereas governments have clamped down even harder on what she terms "non-procreative" sexualities, they have given a hypocritical nod and a wink to the sexual servicing of tourists that brings in foreign exchange ("Erotic Autonomy" and "Not Just (Any) *Body*").

As tourism and sex have become even more closely identified with the Caribbean's place in the global arena, there has been increasing anxiety about what it means to participate in a global discussion and a global marketplace that present themselves as equitable. How do small Caribbean states fare, and to what foreign tastes are they expected to cater in this economic order, when the region's participation in the global marketplace seems to have been marked out so clearly as servicing foreign visitors? If Stephanie Black's *Life and Debt* stages one modality of what it means to look and sound and feel sovereign under siege—natural milk displaced by powdered substitutes, the de-nationalization of bauxite and bananas by the World Bank and the IMF, all to the soundtrack of "conscious" reggae music—then the dancehall reggae lyrics that are so reviled for the absence of a seventies-style political and ethical "authenticity" and/or for their homophobia register and affirm another modality. Patricia Saunders notes that contrary to the assumption that dancehall lyrics are amoral, they indicate a deep investment in "values," though, ironically, the musicians who write and perform them find that they give offense in the putatively value-free global circulation of music, which turns out to have rules after all. She analyzes how such songs link the acquisition of "foreign" sexual tastes to the buying power of tourists and local women, both of whom exert unreasonable demands on working-class Caribbean men ("Is Not Everything Good to Eat").

Long a powerful site for registering anxieties about sexuality, race and ethnicity, and diaspora, this music and its musicians have become a site of contestation over who may speak for, indeed who may be counted part of, the constituency designated "Jamaican people" or, more generally, "Caribbean people." This is in part because it is one of the few arenas of expression for a dispossessed social constituency and thus is endowed with, some might say burdened by, the weight of authenticity. The oppositional vein historically associated with reggae music, its medium of Creole speech—which is still heavily frowned upon in public respectable discourse, while also, paradoxically, claimed as a national product—and the powerful libidinal energies that it harnesses and releases make it absolutely compelling.

In the denunciation of songs as homophobic and the repudiation of this denunciation as racist or heavy-handed, we can see a contestation over "our" values or "who we really are." As (local) commentators accuse foreign journalists of mistranslation and (diasporic) scholars and activists accuse (resident) scholars of misguided nationalism, they reveal the pressure points of belonging, sovereignty, and authenticity, setting parameters of outside and inside (T. Chin; Cooper, "Lyrical Gun"; Noel). Those who object to the songs are disrespectful or clueless outsiders, or inauthentic insiders, or diasporic subjects who have forgotten their true-true name. In this volume Gillespie and Agard-Jones show what happens when this music travels throughout the region; they show, for example, that it becomes folded into conversations already in progress in Barbados, Martinique, and elsewhere. In an interesting twist, Gillespie shows that when one of its dance companies travels to Barbados, Jamaica becomes the site of a worrying homoerotic masculinity and not just the notorious source of the repudiation of such masculinity.

Dancehall reggae is not the only music to have been a highly charged site of sexual anxiety in the region's recent history. When she performed in the calypso tent in Trinidad in the late 1980s and early 1990s, Drupatee Ramgoonai produced anxieties about translation and interpretation, about insiders and outsiders, about who was listening to and laying eyes on her and where they were doing so (S. Hall, "Worlds Apart"; Puri, "Facing the Music"). Both examples suggest not only anxiety but also the deep yearning for community and filiation that music can bring, as it serves to represent the nation itself, a constituency's claim on or disaffection with a nation, or a diasporic community. Here it is useful to think about the nostalgic claims made on these musical traditions and their performers by critics or the warnings against making such claims.

Kobena Mercer has proposed that the finger-pointing in response to the homophobia of musicians and other performers of black diasporic popular culture and of black intellectuals is ultimately unproductive, because it presumes the fiction of a coherent, stable subject, who is then clearly culpable. For Mercer, Frantz Fanon's work, with its own homophobic resonances, offers insights into the unstable, incoherent self that is "rarely the master of its own house (121)." Attending to this incoherence and instability rather than simply condemning or ignoring it might get us closer to a more thoroughgoing examination and ultimately liberation of all constituencies touching on and touched by the Caribbean, a liberation not necessarily achieved by conceptions of (post)colonial freedom that have bypassed sexuality as a key area of concern or even by the fight for legislative sexual rights, important as these are and have been.

It may very well be in the arena of performance—the dancehall reggae stage, with its sequins and spectacular, gender-bending gestures; the Vodou *hounfort*, the Revival table, and the Santería *bembe*, where deities seem to embrace the androgyny that their Catholic and Protestant counterparts spurn; or the Carnival stage—that sexual desires are given a wider range and reign than they are in other areas of life, and attending to this might show us that regional conversations about the affirmation of all sorts of desires predate our present moment and therefore exceed the imprisoning limitations of defending or impugning the region's honor against charges of homophobia. In this volume Rosamond S. King discusses nineteenth-century Carnival performances in terms of new sexualities and citizenship, whereas others, such as Pamela Franco, are decidedly more doubtful about the emancipatory possibilities of the same constituency of *jamets* and *jamettes*. The region's performances ought not to be read merely as antithetical to notions of respectability, whether one does so approvingly or disapprovingly, but as a repository for the sensual, the erotic, the playful: a "truth" about "who we are" that stands beside rather than replaces (with all the attendant contradictions) other "truths." Certainly the region's creative writers have been exploring such desires for a long time, and literary analysis is thus as key to current conversations about sexuality as are discussions of popular music (see in this volume Francis and Donnell; elsewhere see, e.g., Glave, *Our Caribbean,* and Rahim).

Theories of performance and performativity are helpful in stressing contingency, play, and desire and in unmooring notions of identity from a one-to-one relationship with political and linguistic representation. On the other hand, they are necessarily the subject of critique for not always making clear the consequences to specific constituencies of performance in particular situations (Braziel; Butler, *Gender Trouble*; Foucault, *History;* Hennessy, *Materialist Feminism* and "Queer Visibility").

Indeterminacy and not-quite-ness are often heralded in such theories as the antidote to imprisoning, binaristic notions of identity, just as theorists have used the Caribbean itself to challenge binarism. Indeterminacy can be used to affirm the ways in which the Caribbean is identified with a range of erotic desires; think of fictional characters who hover above or inhabit multiple genders in Lawrence Scott's *Witchbroom,* Michelle Cliff's *No*

Telephone to Heaven, and Shani Mootoo's *Cereus Blooms at Night.* But it can also be used to suggest that homosexual desire is alien to Caribbeanness or is better left ambiguous and unnamed. "Coming out leaves no space or room for blissful ignorance of one's sexual preference. It allows no uncontested space for role play," writes Cooper ("Lyrical Gun" 440). In privileging "play" and repudiating binaries, as well as, importantly, in wanting to strategize safe ways to escape possible violence, does Cooper also foreclose and police, suggesting that particular desires, practices, and identifications are not quite or not at all Caribbean?

In this volume Antonia Macdonald-Smythe cautions against using terminology from outside the region to make visible a continuum of erotic desire between women in the region and thus flattening out the complexity of its meanings. Omise'eke Natasha Tinsley also cautions against imposed terminology and offers the working-class yard as an alternative to the closet in her discussion of desire between women that is affirmed by them and has been present in their daily lives in the region for generations. It is worth noting that Tinsley's analysis, as well as Agard-Jones's interviews, refutes both those who contend that it is impossible to live in the Caribbean as a queer subject and those who would use the fact of queer subjects' residing in the Caribbean to deny that homophobia exists.[12]

Both inheritances, then—what came before the present moment and helps to explain or justify choices—and the present-day package deals or trade-offs, associated more recently with the specific implications of the sex tourism associated with globalization, can help us to frame what it means for the territories in the region to claim, refute, or accept their place at the global table as the provider of particular services that cater to "foreign" tastes. It is these trade-offs—what many deem to be Faustian bargains with apocalyptic consequences—that are being discussed so heatedly in the region and its many diasporas today.

Notes

1. For this formulation and for others in the following two paragraphs, I am indebted to the anonymous reviewers of this anthology. Within and sometimes across the linguistic divisions of the region, much scholarship on gender, nationalism, Carnival, tourism, spirituality, reproduction, labor, family life, law, race, slavery, indenture, and other areas bears on sexuality. Recent texts that address Caribbean discourses of sexuality specifically deal with AIDS, human rights, sex work, same-sex identities, desire, practices, legislation, sexual violence, medicine, spirituality, literary discourses, creative writing, and popular music. A small sample of already published discussions of Caribbean sexuality includes Alexander, *Pedagogies;* Balderston and Guy; Barrow, de Brujin, and Carr; Bergmann and Smith; Brennan, *What's Love;* Chávez-Silverman and Hernández; Donnell, "Sexing the Subject"; Douglas; Glave, *Our Caribbean* and *Words to Our Now;* K. Kempadoo, *Sexing*

the Caribbean; La Fountain-Stokes, *Queer Ricans;* L. Lewis; Maurer; O'Callaghan, "Compulsory Heterosexuality"; Quiroga; Reddock, *Interrogating;* Rey; Saunders; Silvera; F. Smith, "Genders and Sexualities"; and Wekker, *Politics of Passion.*

2. On citizenship and sexuality for the Caribbean, see Alexander, "Not Just (Any) *Body*"; Francis, *Fictions;* Robinson, "Fictions"; and Sheller, *Citizenship from Below* and "Work That Body." For elsewhere, see, e.g., Berlant; Cruz-Malavé and Manalansan; Evans; Luibhéid; Luibhéid and Cantú; Seidman; and Somerville, "Queer History."

3. As Niranjana reminds us in this collection, Indian nationalists worried about a debased modernity for indentured laborers crossing the *kala pani,* the vast, strange body of water that promised both possibility and contamination. In the West African context, the slave trade has been represented as producing ghosts doomed to search in vain for a home and a name (Aidoo; Cobham; Hartman, *Lose Your Mother*), with infertility as the price of participation in the slave trade (Aidoo 55–124). Hortense Spillers theorizes a process of ungendering in the Middle Passage that continues in the Americas. On the Caribbean side, fear of African-Indian combinations has been discussed, often heatedly (see, e.g., Puri, "Race, Rape"; and Reddock, "Douglarisation"), and it is interesting that novelists such as Shani Mootoo and Ramabai Espinet suggest that *intra*racial sexual violence is at least as problematic as *inter*racial relationships (see Espinet; Mootoo, *Cereus;* and Donnell in this volume). Gayatri Gopinath and Sean Lokaisingh-Meighoo ask us to imagine the interactions of indentured laborers, both on board ship crossing the *kala pani* and on Caribbean plantations, in terms of erotic same-sex desire and thus diasporic filiations that bypass the imperative of procreation. On this point for Afro-Surinamese shipmates see Tinsley in this volume.

4. Power's erotic charge is underlined when Foucault notes that "through a tactical reversal of the various mechanisms of sexuality," we must "counter the grips of power with the claims of bodies, pleasures, and knowledges, in their multiplicity and their possibility of resistance" (*History,* 157). Responding to this formulation, Rosemary Hennessy asks about a potential theoretical fuzziness in which the body, both "agent and object," is the site on which power inscribes itself, as well as the means by which such power is resisted (*Materialist Feminism* 44).

5. Michele di Cuneo, letter of 28 October 1495, cited in Trexler 65, 214n6.

6. In many parts of the Caribbean, the term *Taino* is used instead of *Arawak* or *Carib.* For connections between *Carib, cannibal,* and *Caliban,* see Hulme; for the specifically sexual aspects of these terms, see Goldberg, *Tempest.* Many Caribbean and Latin American writers have used *The Tempest* as a point of departure for discussions of national and sexual sovereignty, political and gendered domination, and the hierarchies implicit in references to "good" Arawaks and "bad" Caribs. See K. Brathwaite, "Caliban" and "Dream Sycorax Letter"; Césaire, *Une Tempête;* Cliff, "Caliban's Daughter"; Lamming; Marshall; Nixon; Retamar; and Wynter, "Beyond Miranda's Meanings."

7. See Abdur-Rahman; Arondekar; Cruz-Malavé and Manalansan; Eng; R. Ferguson, *Aberrations* and "Normative Strivings"; Findlay; Gopinath; Hawley; Heng and Devan; N. Hoad; Gunkel; Johnson and Henderson; La Fountain-Stokes, "1898"; McClintock; Patton and Sánchez-Eppler; Reid-Pharr, "Tearing the Goat's Flesh"; Sarah Salih, "Focus on Queer Postcolonial"; Somerville, *Queering the Color Line;* Stockton; and Stoler, *Carnal Knowledge, Haunted by Empire,* and *Race.*

8. See Bailey and Leo-Rhynie; E. Barriteau, *Confronting Power, Theorizing Gender;* Barrow; Mohammed, *Rethinking;* Reddock, *Women, Labour;* and Springfield.

9. See also Calhoun, on Anglo-American feminism's uneasiness with the lesbian; Hammonds, on African American women and respectability; Jenkins, on African Americans and the taboo of sexuality; Robinson, "Fictions"; and Rowley, "Caribbean In/Humanities," noting that if gender is the means by which one is recognized as human, and if the achievement of women's studies was to "excavate woman as a category," then this has produced a silence around heterosexuality that makes the project of women's or gender studies complicit with the state and with a masculinist nationalism. See also Rowley, "Whose Time is It?"

10. On terminology and homosexuality, see also King; Leap and Boellstorff; and Provencher.

11. See Ehrenreich and Hochschild; Enloe; Grewal and Kaplan, "Global Identities" and *Scattered Hegemonies;* Kaplan, Alarcon, and Moallem; and Mullings. For the Caribbean, see Basch, Glick Schiller and Szanton Blanc; and Freeman. On Caribbean sexuality specifically, see Brennan, *What's Love;* Fusco; K. Kempadoo, *Sexing the Caribbean;* and Stout.

12. Besides Agard-Jones in this volume, J. Allen and Gill demonstrate the power of ethnography to tease out the complex subjectivities of citizens who fail to conform to the terms of national and regional belonging and of first-world queer activist belonging.

Contemporary Package Deals

Buyers Beware, "Hoodwinking" on the Rise

Epistemologies of Consumption in Terry McMillan's Caribbean

Patricia Saunders

IN *Consuming the Caribbean* Mimi Sheller analyzes the patterns and ethics involved in consuming commodities from the Caribbean. She argues that the ethics of consumerism has far-reaching implications that stretch from the tables of Europeans to sugar plantations in the Caribbean and to the countries in Africa where human beings were stolen and brought to the shores of the Americas. In Sheller's view, the bodies being consumed to produce goods for the British Empire and the bodies involved in consuming these goods are more intricately bound than we have cared to admit. She notes that

> in relation to the Caribbean, food consumption became a particularly powerful point of ethical critique both because it so intimately entered the body of the consumer, and because it so violently impinged upon the bodies of plantation labourers enslaved to feed the consumer markets. Contrary to the assumption that it was only the pursuit of gold and other precious metals that drove European exploration, it was as much the desire to acquire new edible, pleasurable, and pharmaceutical substances, *things that had direct and powerful effects on the bodies of those empowered to consume them.* (76–77, emphasis in original)

This analysis of the routes (and roots) of consumption is particularly insightful, because it demands that we pay attention to the privileges that were (and still are) integral to global trade. Then as now, the privilege of mobility, whether for goods, services, or people, is always defined through the needs and demands of the largest economic systems in the global marketplace.

The significance of disseminated images of the Caribbean for patterns and modalities of consumption is central to my analysis in this essay. Consumer patterns in the global marketplace depend increasingly on images that shape our desires for services, commodities, and even expectations of pleasure. Music, films, literature, commercials, photography, fashion, and other cultural artifacts shape our expectations of places, people, and experiences.

In *An Eye for the Tropics* Krista Thompson maps the production and dissemination of the Caribbean region as a "picturesque" landscape.

In my analysis of "market goods" (which include sex, food, medicine, fashion, and music) in Terry McMillan's novel *How Stella Got Her Groove Back* (1996), I look at how visual economies of desire inform the cultural and political palates of consumers, particularly in the United States. The Caribbean region has been produced—some would argue overproduced—as a paradise. In McMillan's novel, which was turned into a film in 1998, two years after it was published, the Caribbean is a place of luxury, excess, mystery, and sensuousness. At the other end of the spectrum of visual images, there are films like Wes Craven's *The Serpent and the Rainbow*, which depicts Haiti as a place of poverty, disease, underdevelopment, violence, and corruption. Somewhere in the midst of these representations lies a far more complex region. Despite the differences in these representations of the Caribbean, they have thoroughly penetrated consumers' desire for the region as a vacation destination and, at the same time, fed their fears of it as an unsafe place for visitors.

Jamaica, in particular, has become a trope for the entire region, a signifier that is both loaded and empty. Jamaica's reggae and dancehall cultures have been heralded as the voice of the region, leaving behind (at least in terms of market sales, "branding," and "visibility") equally relevant cultural traditions such as calypso, zouk, and soca, to name a few. When most Americans make the effort to "place" or locate the Caribbean within their imaginations, Jamaica is the starting point and the measuring stick for the entire region. Some would argue that this is because of the country's proximity to the United Sates geographically, but only if you ignore Cuba, as Americans have been encouraged to do by the U.S. government. Others might point to the world-renowned artist and icon Bob Marley and argue that the success of reggae music has emblazoned Jamaica's iconography onto the minds of people the world over. My concern here is not which explanation is most accurate. I am more interested in the ironies of consumerism and capitalism, particularly where cultural commodities are concerned. In the end, regardless of the motivation, what is heralded as "Jamaican," or more broadly, "Caribbean," is a fabricated ideal designed to reflect the cultural, social, and political values and institutions that Americans can digest within their "low-calorie" (read "low-tolerance"), "high-fashion" (read "high-cultural-capital") consumer diets.

The connection between how the Caribbean is viewed and how it is consumed is not merely discursive. Building on Sheller's critique of ethical consumption, Krista Thompson's *An Eye for the Tropics* traces a complex cartography of shifts in the "visual economy" of the Caribbean. The Caribbean region became a desirable destination for tourists at precisely the same moment that consumer goods from the region were becoming increasingly sought after. Thompson charts the processes involved in turning what had been viewed/seen as a zone of "tropical death" into a location where the mercantile elite could both increase their wealth and flaunt it, at the same time acquiring a tremendous amount of cultural capital. Ironically, foods, or more specifically fruits, were an essential element in this shift in the visual economy of the region.

In 1871 Captain Lorenzo Dow Baker introduced bananas, a previously unknown fruit, to consumers in the United States. By 1899 Baker's Boston Fruit Company, which at its peak shipped more than 16 million stems of the fruit to the United States, had become the United Fruit Company, a major player not only in the fruit-export business but also in the tourism industry (Thompson 48–49). The company's aim was twofold: to sell exotic fruits (bananas, pineapples, oranges, etc.) to U.S. consumers and to sell the visual image of the Caribbean as a safe, clean, exclusive, comfortable place of natural beauty. These two aims had surprising results:

> The United Fruit Company's reach also extended to the tourist trade, as their steamships doubled as passenger ships for tourists. The company also acquired two hotels on the island [Jamaica]. It built the Titchfield Hotel in Port Antonio in 1897 and assumed ownership of the Myrtle Bank Hotel in Kingston in 1918. Subsequently, the American company controlled a significant percentage of both the fruit and tourism trades. (Thompson 49)

This small development contributed not only to how the Caribbean would be seen but also to how it would be consumed. As Thompson notes, no expenses were spared by the mercantile elites to remap the visual terrain of the Caribbean. The space had to be made more readily consumable for investors and tourists alike. Fast-forwarding to the twentieth century, the argument could well be made that the efforts of the United Fruit Company and its British counterpart, Elder Dempster and Company, represent one of the most extensive and successful marketing campaigns of the late nineteenth and twentieth centuries. Few vacation destinations are as popular as countries in the Caribbean.

You Are What You Eat: The "All-Inclusive," "Authentic" Vacation Experience

Laurent Cantet's film *Heading South* (2005) manages to combine both characterizations of the Caribbean—that of a highly sought after vacation destination and that of a place that is unsafe. In the film, this lack of safety proves to be far more detrimental to local residents than to tourists. Adapted from three short stories by Danny Leferrière, the film presents Haiti as a proverbial sexual playground for three middle-aged white women on holiday. All three women seem to have found their heaven on earth among the gods who roam Haiti in the 1970s—Legba, played by Ménothy César, and Neptune, a local fisherman. This film has not received the critical attention it deserves, and unfortunately, space does not permit a full critique here. My critique of the film is aimed specifically at linking the patterns of visual consumption developed during the colonial era to contemporary manifestations of what Thompson refers to as the "visual economy" that informs consumer expectations, desires, and experiences in the Caribbean.

That Cantet's film features white women as the new consumers of exotic black bodies in the Caribbean is symbolic of changing patterns of consumption. The three middle-aged women speak directly to the camera, describing their participation in sex tourism in Haiti in candid monologues. In one of the most revealing accounts, Brenda, a divorcee from Savannah, Georgia, describes first meeting Legba:

> The first time I came here was with Mark, my husband. It all started when Mark took pity on this young boy who hadn't eaten in two days, he invited him to eat at our table. Albert [the restaurant manager] wasn't too happy about it. The boy didn't look a day over fifteen. Mark told him he could order anything he wanted. You should have seen him, I've never seen anyone eat so much in my life. (Cantet)

Brenda notes that Legba seemed to take their "adoption" for granted, then immediately recalls inviting him to go swimming with her.

> He took me to a secluded beach. We were lying in our bathing suits on a big rock basking in the sun. His body fascinated me: long, lithe, muscular; his skin glistened. I couldn't take my eyes off him. The later it got the more I was losing my mind. I remember every move I made as if it were yesterday. I edged my hand over and placed it on his chest. Legba opened his eyes and immediately closed them again. That encouraged me and I moved my hand down his body. Such soft young skin, he was motionless. Then I slid two fingers into his bathing suit and touched his cock. Almost immediately it started getting hard growing in the palm of my hand until it just popped out. He breathed faintly, but very regularly. I looked around to see that no one was coming and I threw myself on him. I literally threw myself on him. It was so violent I couldn't help but scream—I think I never stopped screaming. It was my first orgasm. I was forty-five.

The proximity of Brenda's descriptions of the magnanimous act of feeding this young boy who "hadn't eaten in two days" and her sexually assaulting him on the beach is significant.[1] The magnanimous "I" of the opening statement disappears, and an all-consuming "I" that devours the previously malnourished young black male assumes control of both the act and the narrative. We never hear Legba's account of his experiences with these women; he is referred to only in the third person.

In Haitian Vodou culture, Legba is the master of the crossroads, controlling the gates between the mortals and the loas. He is also known as a trickster figure who walks with a limp, some say from the difficult work of navigating these pathways. In the film, Legba skillfully maneuvers between the world of the streets of Haiti, where corrupt police take advantage of the poor, and the world of the resort, where tourists attempt to do the same. However, as the balance between these worlds is compromised, both he and his young girlfriend are violently reminded by the "gods" (the henchmen of the colonel, presumably Duvalier, given the time period) that the pathways of power are governed by powers far greater than them and far, far greater than American or Canadian tourists. When the sea spits up their dead bodies, the American women can only look on in horror and pity, still ignorant of the realities of life in a country they have visited year after year.

If what we ingest—food, spirits, pharmaceuticals, and so on—is one point of entry for ethical debates about power, mobility, and consumption, then sex should be examined as another point of ethical critique for visitors and "natives" alike. We would do well to ask what "inside information" sexual intimacy provides and how it is decoded, disseminated, and valued as cultural capital in the marketplace. Do sexualized bodies signify, or perform, a kind of strategic withholding during these intimate exchanges? And if so, how might this withholding function as a kind of labor taxation occasionally exercised by those being exploited?

Contemporary imaginings of the Caribbean rarely represent Haiti as a place of relaxation, fun, and exotic "natives." However, *Heading South* succinctly captures the emerging preference for the "all-inclusive" as the preferred choice in vacation experiences, because it allows travelers to avoid thinking about cost while they consume. While globalization has transformed the appetites and patterns of consumption, the "dietary" preferences for cultural and sexual goods and services have become more complex. The desire for new "dietary supplements" to feed the ever-growing appetites of global markets can be mapped through the shift in the palates of consumers. The "all-inclusive" provides "all you can eat," but the menus rarely feature local, Caribbean cuisine. American tourists prefer foods they identify with, tastes they are familiar with. Their appetite for "spicy," "exotic" experiences is satisfied by extracurricular activities in the resorts and journeys into less familiar places and even experiences.

In "Globalization, Tourism and the International Sex Trade," Beverly Mullings asserts that the desire for truly "authentic" vacation experiences has led to the production and consumption of "far off" places: "Particularly since the 1980s an increasing number of travelers have begun to demand travel experiences that are closely tailored to individual tastes. The 'new middle classes,' as these travelers are often described, emerged in the 1980s as new cultural intermediaries initiating and transmitting new consumption patterns, including the search for 'authentic' holidays in developing countries" (59).

Although "adventure seeker" vacations are in no way unique to the Caribbean region, the desire for sexual adventure in "stable" political environments makes the Caribbean a highly sought after vacation location (others include Africa, Latin America, and Asia). The idea of vacation as a mode of relaxation, a space to recuperate one's energies, has long since mutated into an opportunity to achieve and attain cultural capital through consumption. But as many vacationers have learned, the complex and at times dangerous social, political, and cultural milieus do not pause because they plan to vacation in areas experiencing these difficulties. The most egregious examples of this include the deaths of adventure seekers who travel to regions of the world that are in the midst of civil wars and other military disputes.

But there are also less tragic (but more ironic) examples of the new phenomenon of adventure-seeking travelers. Take, for example, the recent scandal of Terry McMillan's breakup with her Jamaican-born husband, who had announced after several years of marriage that he was gay. McMillan showed readers and moviegoers the world over how they could "get their grooves back" in exotic places like Jamaica, where beautiful, available men were waiting to meet black and white American women. McMillan's well-publicized marriage to Jonathan Plummer, a young Jamaican twenty-three years her junior, was the subject of her bestselling novel, *How Stella Got Her Groove Back*. She received more than a million dollars for the rights to her novel, which became a Hollywood film starring Angela Basset as Stella and Taye Diggs as Winston Shakespeare, her young Jamaican love interest (Sullivan). One has to wonder about McMillan's sense of humor (or maybe irony?) in naming her main protagonist. Does she see him as a poet or a gifted dramatist of his time? The story has a boy-meets-girl narrative structure, but with an interesting twist: the "boy" is not the stereotypical beach dread (a fit, dreadlocked beach bum) who sells sex and sometimes marijuana to tourists looking for "something new."[2] For white women, there is the possible thrill of experiencing "jungle fever" through sexual encounters with black men.[3] For black women, the experience is closer to the infamous stereotype of Dexter St. Jacques, made popular by the comedian Eddie Murphy.[4]

Winston is not the typical Jamaican "beach bum," searching for women/clients on the beach. When he gets the job at Windswept, his parents (who we are told once owned ten horses) send a car to pick him up so that he can come home and collect his things (150, 163). Winston is from a middle-class Jamaican family and seems to be living a rather comfortable life in Jamaica before he meets Stella, who is trying to escape the impending burnout from her corporate job. Like many other tourists, Stella travels to Jamaica in order to get away from her mundane existence and finds fun in the sun, a young lover, and her "groove."[5]

McMillan devotes a great deal of time to constructing a variety of canons to guide her audience through the terrain of conspicuous consumption that is essential to American popular-cultural identity.[6] These canons include music, books, clothes, mobility, and food. Stella's "diverse" range of music preferences provides an interesting portrait of what cultural consumption means to African Americans in this novel. As she packs for her trip to Jamaica we are introduced, through an exhaustive catalog, to the breadth of her music appreciation. She despises most hip-hop, because of its misogynist lyrics and its use of the word *niggah,* which, she is keen to point out, "we have never used and I don't allow to be used in our house" (50). Stella's eclectic taste in music, like (her son) Quincy's, suggests a "seasoned palate."

> I do appreciate some hip-hop, a little SWV TLC Xscape R. Kelly Mary J. Blige Brownstone Boy II Men Jodeci etc. etc. etc. I also like a lot of music by white people, which a lot of my friends don't understand.
>
> Quincy loves that rock group Green Day and Aerosmith and Hootie and the Blowfish and I kind of like them too and I love Seal *even though he is African but British* and mostly white people buy his music and I love Annie Lennox Diva over and over and Julia Fordham and Sting and hell good music is good music. (50, emphasis added)

Her range of musical tastes transcends the boundaries of race and national identity. However, there seems to be an incongruent or at least contradictory sentiment about black music and musicians from Africa and Britain.

There is also a peculiar, unstated confusion implicit in the statement that she loves Seal "*even though* he is African but British." There is little basis for this conditionality, so it is difficult to discern whether the contradiction lies in Seal's Africanness, his Britishness, the fact that mostly white people buy his music, or the fact that she likes his music for the same reasons that she likes music by other white European artists. It is quite possible that the contradiction lies in the suggestion that she, an African American, likes his music for the same reason that white people do: *even though* he is African, "good music is good music." The idea that race can transcend cultural boundaries appears to need qualification when racial difference emerges from a "third space" ("Third World") that is neither America nor England ("First World"). The subtexts that inform this effort to differentiate between social classes and cultural identities are not the emphasis of McMillan's novel. In fact, we are constantly distracted from asking what, in Bourdieu's terms, the "habitus" is that links Stella not only to other white people in America but also to Seal, who is "African [read "Third World"] but British." The answer to this question might become clear if we look closely at the formation of the culinary canon that informs consumption patterns in McMillan's novel (Calhoun, LiPuma, and Postone). The consumption of music and food are as intricately and intimately connected to the "body politic" as is the consumption of black inter/national culture.

After Stella returns from her "groove-getting" excursion to Jamaica, she begins to come to terms with the idea that maybe, just maybe, she is emotionally attached to her young lover. Her second trip to Jamaica involves a different kind of "retail therapy," as she seeks to separate herself from other travel companions. She decides to upgrade the three tickets (for herself, her best friend, and her son) to first class, "for a mere three thousand dollars," in order to assure her enjoyment on the flight over, in the event that she dies before realizing her dream of making love to Winston once more (285). With the tickets upgraded, she decides to load up on snack food for her trip. Her selection, coupled with her philosophical musings, provides another occasion for critical reflection on the relationship between the patterns and ethics of consumption, the expectations of consumers, and the real situations in which the goods, services, and bodies being consumed exist. When Stella is struck with a sudden fear of dying from a fatal disease, she concludes:

> If I could have another chance to press and seal my lips against Winston's just one more time which if God really is fair He or She would grant me a final pleasure before I go and if there's time an hour or two of some nuggies would be like frosting on the cake if it's not asking too much. So while I buy two packages of Oreo cookies a super-saver size Kit Kat one Three Musketeer a Butterfinger a Pay Day three bags of Lay's potato chips—plain, barbeque and sour cream and onion—I add all this stuff up and I come to the conclusion that I have earned the right to some happiness and by golly I'm going to get me some. (284–85)

As in the laundry list of music, the absence of punctuation and the emphasis on the inventory of junk food (and other commodities) highlight the fact that consumption is the yardstick by which "happiness" is measured. Given the many flavors of potato chips and kinds of candy bars, along with the uniquely American concept of the super-saver, the inclusion of sex ("nuggies") on this list of last pleasures should not be surprising. Discursively, it is merely one of the many sweet treats on the list. Arguably, sex functions much like the "frosting on the cake": it is a high-calorie intake with no nutritional value whatsoever.

McMillan's novel shares several stylistic conventions with the diaries kept by domestic servants during the Victorian era. According to Anne McClintock, in *Imperial Leather,* these diaries provide remarkable insight into the extent to which progress was measured by a growing preoccupation with commodities, the things that effectively kept the boundaries between classes solid. Writing about Hannah Cullwick's diary, McClintock asserts, "If the diary as a genre is dedicated to the idea of the individual, the syntax of Cullwick's early diaries bears witness to an erasure: the sovereign 'I' of individual subjectivity is missing" (169). Although McMillan's novel differs significantly from McClintock's work in its historical context and content, the overwhelming emphasis and accounting of things and objects in the two works draws our attention to the power of commodity fetishism during both the colonial era and the new era of globalization. There is a fundamental difference, however, between the Victorian emphasis on labor and the contemporary capitalist emphasis on consumption. The "I" of individual subjectivity, far from being erased, is now so large that it overwhelms all others in its wake. The relentless list of objects and goods gives way to the "I" that determines the meaning and value of all goods being exchanged and consumed.

This pattern of syntax is repeated time and time again as Stella goes into malls, department stores, grocery stores, music shops, and specialty stores. Ironically, it also occurs when she gets excited about seeing Winston: she begins to recount the cologne he is wearing, his clothes, the music that is playing. This emphasis on material objects, according to McClintock, is "what Marx called commodity fetishism: the central social form of the industrial economy whereby the social relations between people metamorphoses into a relation between things" (170).

Although the junk food listed and itemized is actually for Winston, neither Stella nor readers are encouraged to consider why these items are either unavailable or too expensive for Winston and other Jamaicans. Junk foods are not quite the trinkets traded with "natives" in the New World, but they function in the same way, as small objects of trade and affection meant to indicate the goodwill of the visitors. To be clear, I am not casting Winston (or other Caribbean people who participate in these kinds of relationships) as unconscious, easily fooled, naive victims of tourists. By outlining the social and political subtexts that inform the popularity of these kinds of narratives about the Caribbean, I am suggesting that they should raise questions and eyebrows but that they rarely do.

Despite losing her job upon her return home, Stella sends Winston gifts of jewelry, clothes, and sneakers, all of which he wears when he visits her at the hotel during her second trip. Although there is no explicitly stated exchange of goods for sex, the narrator draws our attention to what Winston is wearing, which certainly encourages such an interpretation. The food chain is such that Winston consumes what Stella provides, and Stella in turn consumes him, a pattern that is strikingly similar to the one in Cantet's *Heading South*. The exchange of clothes and junk food for the happiness she so desperately feels she deserves (and is intent on getting) seems to be one of "fair trade," in the global-market sense of the phrase. According to the spirit of the legal definition of fair trade, Stella is improving the quality of Winston's life by contributing to his capacity to maintain his lifestyle, while unwittingly providing him the support—a free ticket to the United States, a visa, and possibly later a green card—that will allow him to compete on the global market.

Anancy and the Tale of Dietary Caution: How Terry McMillan Lost Her Groove

Reading McMillan's novel through the lenses of colonial commodity fetishism, socioeconomic discourses of development, and global exchange highlights the complex nexus of negotiations taking place between vacationers and the workers they encounter during their stay. McMillan's novel does not operate simply as a text about sex tourism. On the contrary, *How Stella Got Her Groove Back* is an invaluable piece of popular fiction that carefully maps out emergent modes of social and economic exchange, sexual desire, market demands, and the "contact zones" in which all of these registers are fused, and at times confused, particularly when life begins to imitate art, with equally unexpected and undesirable endings.

Mullings asserts that sociologists have sought to distinguish the categories of relationships between tourists and workers with whom they develop sexual partnerships. In "For Love and Money: Romance Tourism in Jamaica," Deborah Pruitt and Suzanne LaFont (1995) have argued that "male sex workers are involved in romance rather than sex tourism, because there is often a level of emotional involvement that is not often present in sex tourism. These holiday relationships tend to be longer term, involving a much higher level of social and economic commitment on the part of both parties in the exchange." Mullings says that Pruitt and LaFont also argue that "some relationships may last for many years and result in marriage or migration" (Mullings 66).

These sexual liaisons, as Mullings suggests, are complicated by the power inequities between visitors to and residents of the Caribbean and other developing countries resulting from differences in class and culture. Exchanges and negotiations are enmeshed in these power structures and necessarily determine the tenor of relationships regardless of romantic desire, genuine affection, and sexual desire. It is virtually impossible to demarcate where desire for a better life (through migration, marriage, or both) ends and romantic desire begins, as evidenced by the very public relationship, marriage, and divorce of Terry McMillan and her young lover, who is indeed Winston Shakespeare's real-life counterpart.

As Faith Smith notes, Stella (and Terry McMillan) can now travel to the Caribbean to indulge her desire for pleasure in any way that she chooses:

> Imperialist fantasies of the Caribbean reveal themselves in the sustained focus on the body of the upper-middle-class-elite-turned-beach-bum who catches Stella's fancy. Ironically, this focus rereads the classed and gendered Jamaican in ways that are potentially liberating, but the film is less interested in local subtexts than in facilitating the America tourist's three day, two-night groove. *Black professional women now replace the succession of European and American male adventurers who traditionally consume the bodies of exotic and available Caribbean females.* (F. Smith, "You Know You're West Indian If . . . ," 47, emphasis added)

"Local subtexts" in this case refers to the loaded/empty signifier Jamaica. There is very little mention of what Jamaica is like beyond the resort environment. It is as if Jamaica does not exist beyond the people who work in the hotels, beaches, and restaurants. Stella, who apparently is falling in love with Winston, makes no effort to learn anything about Jamaican culture. Instead, she fashions him according to her own (or maybe her son's?) tastes, going to the mall and buying music, brand-name clothes, a CD player. When she stops briefly to ask herself, "What if he thinks I'm doing this to impress him or to buy his affection," she quickly follows with, "Why would he think that, Stella? And besides, this stuff doesn't even add up to my car payment" (255). We might wonder what it would mean if Stella thought about what kind of music Winston liked and whether his taste in music was different from hers. Of course, all of this assumes that the local subtexts that ground the novel—more than two-third of the novel is set in Jamaica—and the film actually matter to Stella and vacationers like her. There is an "already-known" quality about Jamaica in McMillan's novel, one that pervades most popular texts about the region. Why think about Jamaica beyond the resort if you can afford not to?

As a result of her whirlwind courtship with Jonathan Plummer and the completion of her book, McMillan became a virtual poster child for all-inclusive Jamaican vacations, which were guaranteed to rest, relax, and restore all grooves. As part of the promotion for her book and her film, McMillan traveled around the United States singing the praises of her relationship with her new-found love, who stood by her side. Similar to colonial travelers who brought back specimens (birds, fruit, fabrics, even human beings) from the New World, McMillan reveled in the spectacle of the public's response to Plummer's presence. He was the "gold" that so many black women who traveled to El Dorado (the Caribbean) hoped to lay claim to. So McMillan wanted her readers and viewers to see him shine, and at the time Plummer seemed more than willing to play his part.

McMillan's real-life romance followed a similar trajectory to what is presented in the novel, but recently the real-life marriage ended, and a new part of the drama, which seems ripped from the pages of a bestselling novel, began. McMillan and Plummer's relationship ended just as publicly and dramatically as it had begun. The end of their marriage marked the beginning of a torrent of complex negotiations for authority, ownership, rights, and citizenship, all subtexts that her novel works so very hard to ignore. McMillan recently filed for divorce in Contra Costa County, California, Superior Court, citing her husband's "fraud" as the grounds for the separation. According to McMillan, her husband, Jonathan Plummer, now thirty years old, lied about his sexual orientation when they married. Plummer recently revealed to McMillan that he was gay, a fact he only realized after several years of marriage to McMillan.

Two moments in this developing drama about the relationship between sexuality, globalization, and consumerism are instructive. McMillan's court declaration reads like a bill of sale for a product that was damaged or at least not as advertised. "It was devastating," she declared, "to discover that a relationship I had publicized to the world as life-affirming and built on mutual love was actually based on deceit, lies, and obtained by fraud. I was humiliated to realize that Jonathan was not attracted to me and possibly had never been. . . . I reacted angrily and sometimes impulsively, as many would."[7] Plummer sought a restraining order based on the allegations of acts of harassment listed in his declaration, some of which he admits are "not fit for public consumption."

> A. She came to my place of business and left:
>   a) a jar of hot pepper sauce she labeled "penis juice";
>   b) a bottle of Island Spices Seasoning where she circled the word jerk and wrote "appropriate";
>   c) a bottle of Jamaican pepper sauce on which she wrote "Fag Juice Burn Baby burn."[8]

It is almost too easy to highlight the emphasis on these consumable Jamaican goods, which are inseparable from Plummer's sexuality. And yet my earlier comments about reserving the "spicy" adventures for the resort have particular relevance. Like her protagonist, McMillan engaged in this relationship precisely because she saw the Caribbean as a place where she could free herself of any inhibitions about choosing a sexual partner. McMillan claims that she was hoodwinked and that Plummer fraudulently claimed to be something other than he was. In using the term *hoodwinked* I draw on double entendre both to signify the sense of being duped and to draw attention to the popular terminology in Jamaica for the penis, *hood*. This signification highlights how the phallus (in this instance) becomes a tool in the repertoire of the trickster (Anancy the Spider) for outwitting predators or competitors. But the pun can be extended to draw our attention to the practice of "looking under [or in this case beyond] the hood" (or sex) before buying a bill of "goods." I do not mean to suggest that on closer "inspection" McMillan would have been able to "discover" Plummer's sexual identity. This cautionary tale invites us to consider the production of hypersexualized black bodies in the Caribbean specifically and poor bodies in other parts of the world. I emphasize the physical body here because the physical and sexual "encounters" between Stella and Winston and between McMillan and Plummer were too easily scripted into the well-documented fantasies of travel, leisure, adventure, and consumption.

Plummer continues to maintain that he did not know he was gay when he met McMillan. Regardless of his sexual self-discovery, this public exhibition of consumer expectations gone awry provides an occasion to consider how and where Caribbean culture and Caribbean masculinity are interpolated into American consumer culture. More importantly, to return to Sheller's analysis, the scandal also forces us to consider the ways in which sexuality can be deployed as a tool or weapon to balance unequal power dynamics in the global marketplace:

> Against the forces of a world economy that commodified black bodies, sucked the marrow from their bones, and tried to turn them into will-less workers, *resistance took the form of taking a claim in one's own body. Using one's own sexuality for personal gain and profiting from the sexual display of oneself are ways of "turning a trick."* In contrast, to work for another, to become an object controlled by forces outsides oneself suggest a disciplined body, a body without agency, a zombie. (155, emphasis added)

This interpretation of the political economy of sexuality has a very significant cultural context that must be considered as part of this cautionary tale. What Sheller describes as "turning a trick" has long been part of the discourse of the street, of pimps, prostitutes, and patrons, who buy, sell, and trade sex in the global marketplace. There is also another subtext, one that draws on the Caribbean tradition of Anacyism. In Caribbean oral traditions, Anancy the Spider employs wit and cunning in order to succeed against other, larger predators. In a global economy in which smaller, developing countries become playgrounds for vacationers and travelers in search of "authentic" experiences, there will always be room for a hustle. Many would argue that in any developing country there is no chance of survival without some kind of hustle. Whether this involves working as a police officer by day and a bouncer by night, selling pirated versions of music, clothes, handbags, movies, or any other copyrighted objects, selling baked goods without a license, marrying for money or a green card, or selling drugs, it is part of a thriving global informal economy.

The moral of the story here is an old one, a cliché even: buyers beware; not all that glitters is gold. This is a lesson that McMillan has learned, with Plummer insisting that he deserves a share of the income earned from the sales of *How Stella Got Her Groove Back*. In Richard Allsopp's *Dictionary of Caribbean Usage*, the definition of *Anancyism* includes a brief quotation from the *Daily Gleaner*, a Jamaican newspaper, which reads: "Nowhere in the vast literature of anancyism is there an instance of Anancy paying for anything. Ananciologists have justified this attitude to life by arguing that Anancy is a small creature who . . . has to employ his wits to protect himself against much larger predators and competitors" (Allsopp 30). The legal documentation presented by McMillan includes a list of all of the monetary support McMillan provided to Plummer. The unspoken assumption here is that McMillan, not Plummer, set out the terms of the arrangement, including the prenuptial agreement and Plummer's "allowances." Based on these "agreements," McMillan understood herself to be in possession of a loyal (hetero)sexual subject. Her reaction, therefore, is as much about how people will see her as a result of Plummer's "coming out." To be sure, many have asked, and the question will continue to be asked, how she could not have known that he was gay, implying that her "gaydar" somehow malfunctioned. Or was it simply that she, like Stella, had seen the commercials describing what Jamaica had to offer and simply was not interested in anything beyond the fact that she had "earned the right to some happiness" (285).

Others might justifiably argue that if Plummer in fact had married McMillan to obtain his citizenship, had he not also worked hard (as her husband, lover, partner) and "earned" his right to happiness? The phenomenon of the black male as an "embodied commodity" was certainly realized as a lived fantasy through McMillan's novel, so much so that it sparked a new trend: "The whole tableau was so inspirational that thousands of itchy women started flocking to the Caribbean, scouring the beaches for their own special bronzed groovemakers" (Gerhart).

What lessons, if any, can be learned from vacationers who gorge themselves and then complain to the management that the food is no good, the sun is not bright enough, the groove is no longer there? Or as Sheller asks, "Does metropolitan culture in fact again reproduce its domination, reconstitute its centres of knowledge and power, and erase the (neo)colonial relations of violence that enable this proximity in the first place?" (181). These are among the questions that are not asked of popular texts that invent and reproduce the Caribbean as a place of exotic others whose reason for being is to "service" and make real the fantasies of visitors. Whether we read McMillan's narrative and real-life drama as a case of "hoodwinking" or "playing dead to catch corbeau alive," the moral of the story might well be that the shifting tides of globalization obscure the intricate international flows (and definitions) of labor, sexual identity, and capital. If nothing else, McMillan's public love affair with Jonathan Plummer, and the ease with which the public consumed it as a commodity (in film and in print), should give us pause, at least long enough to consider the cultural caloric content. These often well-advertised and well-packaged cultural narratives about the Caribbean tend not to problematize or even recognize the uneven economic and political terrain that lies between blacks in the overdeveloped world and other people of color in the developing world. There is an oversimplified representation of race and power in McMillan's novel that obscures the interstitial dynamics present in all intimate relationships. These kinds of popular-cultural narratives, when consumed by those predisposed to "silent killers" like hypertension or its cultural equivalents (stereotyping, exoticizing poverty, assuming that one's view is the only one that matters), often lead to dangerous social illness accompanied by chronic cultural deficits. Practices of consumption can and will always be interpolated into cultural and discursive registers that are beyond the reach and tastes of many consumers. This is a reality of consumerism. However, the instability of signs, economies, bodies, and identities creates opportunities for participating in acts of resistance that include redirecting and challenging what we know, or think we know, about the cultures, products, and consumer practices with which we are engaged. In short, the dynamism of interstitial identities, communities, and most definitely markets requires newly inspired epistemologies of consumption.

Notes

1. I describe Brenda's act as a sexual assault to draw attention to the unequal power relationship between a minor and an adult. What Brenda describes is actually an act of statutory rape, though *sexual assault* is the phrase most often used in legal statutes today. A key premise in statutory-rape laws to protect minors is the fact that minors are "economically, socially, and legally unequal to adults" and therefore need to be protected by adults (U.S. Department of Justice).

2. The recent film *Something New* is based on a similar theme, but the African American woman's love interest is a white working-class man. The adventure is doubly intriguing because of the interracial coupling and also because of the difference in the circumstances of the two: he is a landscaper, while she is a corporate lawyer. Both films share the motif/dilemma of successful black women who have a great career and financial stability but no love life.

3. *Jungle Fever* is the title of Spike Lee's 1991 film that explores an intimate relationship between a black middle-class protagonist (played by Wesley Snipes) and a young Italian working-class woman (played by Annabella Sciorra). In the film

Snipes leaves his (light-skinned) black wife for his lover. The interracial relationship and the circumstances of its existence draw heavily on stereotypes (sometimes to undercut, other times to advance them) about culture and class differences along racial/ethnic lines.

4. Dexter St. Jacques is a character in a skit featured on Murphy's 1987 album, *Raw,* in which a wronged wife or girlfriend gets even with her partner by taking off on a vacation to the Bahamas, where she links up with a reggae-loving, dreadlocked lady's man (see Townsend and Chernov). When she encounters Dexter, he asks why a pretty woman like her is on the beach alone. The crucial part of the skit occurs when Murphy, swinging the microphone (a stage double for Dexter's penis), throws it over his shoulder and listens while the young woman recounts her misfortune. In McMillan's novel, Stella is repeatedly asked whether "the rumor" is true about Caribbean men. In the novel we are led to believe that the rumor has to do with penis size rather than with what the skit implies, namely, that Caribbean men are good, even if opportunistic, listeners.

5. Jamaica Kincaid's book *A Small Place* focuses on this aspect of the tourist industry in Antigua. However, her critique of tourism assumes that the visitor is white, not black. McMillan's novel offers an interesting companion text that contradicts some of the assumptions made about the attitudes of white British and American tourists.

6. Colin Channer's novel *Waiting in Vain* might qualify as a more transnational, gender-conscious envisioning of the same cultural and political project.

7. The divorce papers filed in Contra County Court were posted on the website "The Smoking Gun," http://www.thesmokinggun.com/graphics/art3/0630052 bstella16.gif (accessed 6 July 2005), which focuses on celebrity scandals and run-ins with the law. The documents are now archived at http://www.thesmokinggun.com/archive/0630052cstella1.html.

8. Ibid.

"Nobody Ent Billing Me"

A U.S./Caribbean Intertextual, Intercultural Call-and-Response

Carmen Gillespie

ON THE CARIBBEAN island nation of Barbados there is a place called Farley Hill. Farley Hill is a windswept landscape perched on one of the highest points on the island. From there, unlike from most locations on the island, you cannot hear but you can see the sea. The trees of Farley Hill are never still, and it is cool and dark, even at noon. Beyond the trees, there is a cane field, the primary source of income for all of the previous owners of the Farley Hill plantation. The house, now roofless, is home only to tourists, Sunday picnics, and national celebrations and bears a plaque placed in its front wall by Queen Elizabeth during one of her visits to the island. In 1956 Hollywood chose Farley Hill as the location for shooting the film *Island in the Sun*.

This place, Farley Hill, on what the Guyanese poet Grace Nichols calls a "tiny sugar island," metaphorizes the complex multivalent identities, histories, and ideological struggles that create the fluid dynamics of Bajan (Barbadian) cultures and inform the island's historical and contemporary interactions with the rest of the world. Farley Hill is emblematic of many of the questions and crossroads that suffuse the porous and interactive ideological terrains of the island: the displacements and losses of colonialism and slavery; the realities of diasporic homelessness and the search for home; the struggle for identity, agency, and autonomy; the determinative impacts of geography; the complexities of nationalism and neocolonialism; the power of naming; the desire for and acquisition of voice, agency, and subjectivity; the ambiguities of postcolonialism and tourism; the crises of representation; and the gaze of the other.

I visited Farley Hill often when I lived in Barbados as a Fulbright scholar during the spring of 1997. During that time I witnessed with great fascination an intercultural musical exchange that reiterated some of the literal and archetypal nuances, conflicts, and complexities embedded in the symbolic geographies of Farley Hill and in the particular intricacies that form the contours of Barbados itself. Farley Hill, Barbados, and the Caribbean are all spaces marked by the cultural crosswinds of ancient and contemporary ideological conflicts rooted in well-founded post- and neocolonial anxieties about the relationships between autonomy and identity. "The past continues to dwell in the present," writes the Bajan historian Hilary Beckles, "and the resultant turbulence produces the enormous energy sources that define and propel the cultural revelation that is the Caribbean" (789). Although Barbados is technically a sovereign nation, independent from England since 1966, since it is a member of the British Commonwealth, the queen of England remains the titular head of state. As Beckles has observed, "George Lamming [an internationally celebrated Bajan writer] has consistently made the point that, with respect to the empty formality of constitutionally independent nation-states, . . . those who govern don't rule" (787). The events of the present are forever colored by the histories of these spaces.

These terrains constitute what the sociologist Ulf Hannerz has termed an *ecumene,* "a region of persistent cultural interaction and exchange" (218). In 1997, the release of the African American rhythm-and-blues song "Bill" on Bajan radio stations and the subsequent release of the response song "In De Tail," by the Bajan calypsonian Red Plastic Bag, exposed the multiple trajectories of the particular ecumene formed by the Caribbean region. This musical exchange exposed some of the extant tensions on the island with respect to the correlations between sexualities and national identity and became an unexpected and revealing tool in my efforts to explore the complicated narrative relationships between Barbados and the United States.[1]

The exploration and documentation of this exchange is significant to studies of the contemporary Caribbean, as exegesis of this cultural moment in 1997 presents a unique opportunity to "rethink and reframe the ways that state, nation, gender, and sexuality are mutually constituted," an analysis that is critical to parsing the nuances of the postmodern and dynamic realities of the island nations of the Antilles (Kim-Puri 139). This musical exchange also supports the assertion that the cultural products exported from the metropole are not consumed unilaterally, without rejoinder and intercultural discourse.[2]

Work by scholars such as the musicologist and anthropologist Thomas Turino supports close readings of individual public responses to this cultural interchange as an appropriate and uniquely illuminating methodological approach. Turino maintains that "the actual site of social and cultural dynamism resides in specific people's lives and experiences" (52). As a consequence, the constitutive elements of transnational cultural exchange may be exposed by careful examination of the microcosmic responses to this international cultural conversation (52).

DURING THE spring of 1997, the song "Bill," performed by the African American singer Peggy Scott-Adams, hit Bajan airwaves. The reaction in the Caribbean island nation to the Scott-Adams song about a woman's discovery of her husband's homosexuality[3] exemplifies the complexity of intercultural and international intertextuality, as well as the intricate and particular relationships between nationalism and sexualities in the Caribbean.[4] The lyrics of the American song "Bill" were controversial in the United States, but in Barbados the song produced a veritable storm of rhetorical contention, the essence of which appeared with regularity on the editorial pages of both major Bajan newspapers, the *Barbados Advocate* and the *Nation,* as well as in other, minor print publications.

According to cultural critics like Marlon Ross, popular musics are one of the United States' most influential and perhaps its largest export ("In Search" 599). The mass media of the United States, particularly its popular musics, travel "far more widely than any other western idiom"; however, as previously mentioned, in spite of the dominance of American music on the global stage, it is important to document the reality that its messages are not received passively and often incur cultural resistance (T. Taylor xv). Investigations of the trajectories and receptions of popular musics are paramount, as they "help raise . . . [transnational] theoretical issues better than other musics, even better, perhaps, than any other cultural form" (xv). The work of Paul Gilroy also supports the primacy of scholarly investigations in this area. Gilroy recognizes that the influences of this potent cultural expression have not been fully appreciated as a vital investigative tool, particularly within the African diaspora. He maintains that "it is ironic, given the importance accorded to music in the habitus of diaspora blacks [that those studying questions of black identity do not] take the music very seriously" (qtd. in Monson 33). Validating these observations about the influence and pertinence of popular music, the American song "Bill" created a surprisingly multifaceted set of responses in Barbados. These responses provide particularly insightful illuminations about the contemporary impacts of postcolonialism and neocolonialism on definitions of national identity and as catalysts of cultural resistance. The text of the American song and the multiple Bajan rejoinders it engendered form a fascinating postmodern, international, intercultural call-and-response.[5]

The literary and cultural critic John F. Callahan maintains that the call-and-response tradition "is a call to self, to voice, to community, to nationhood" (22). The Bajan replies to "Bill" catalyzed public contestations about the definitions of each of those identity markers. My analysis of Bajan public rejoinders to "Bill" posits that as in the United States and most other locales throughout the world, a pervasive and consistent homophobia exists on the island. Much more significantly, Bajans writing to the major local newspapers generally read the song as evidence of the corrupting influence of the outside world and concomitantly denoted homosexuality as an outside phenomenon. Following initial reactions to the song, the word *bill* gained vernacular currency and usage as a pejorative term of reference for homosexuals and homosexuality in Barbados.

The most well known public response to Scott-Adams's song in Barbados was another song, written and performed by the popular Bajan calypsonian Stedson Wiltshire, better known as RPB or Red Plastic Bag.[6] This song, "In De Tail," enjoyed even more popularity in Barbados than the original Scott-Adams song (Alleyne). As the scholar Gail-Ann Greaves has noted, the traditional role of the calypsonian is "to function as the people's newspaper, a social or political reformer, the nation's mouthpiece, or all of the above" (34). With his release of "In De Tail," Red Plastic Bag fulfilled all of these roles. "In De Tail" is a direct confrontation not only with the narrative implications of "Bill" but also with forces perceived as impeding Bajan economic and political self-determination.

"In De Tail" plays on three semantic transformations of the word *bill*. First, the catchphrase of the song, "nobody ent billing me," resonates deeply on an island dependent primarily on tourism for its income. Second, the American song and the Bajan musical response illuminate tensions about the relationship between homophobia, masculinity, and nationalism. Finally, the U.S. president Bill Clinton's visit to the island in May 1997 for a summit with the Caribbean heads of state amplified the political significances of the Bajan song and the applications of the word *bill*. As a result of the serendipitous connections, Scott-Adams's and Red Plastic Bag's songs, the president's first name, and the political circumstances surrounding Clinton's visit, "In De Tail" also became a Bajan anthem of anti-American sentiment.

The cultural critic Timothy S. Chin, in his article "'Bullers and Battymen': Contesting Homophobia in Black Popular Culture and Contemporary Caribbean Literature," outlines the controversy surrounding the release of the Jamaican singer Buju Banton's song "Boom Bye Bye" and its arguably antigay lyrics. Chin asserts that in examining the popular-cultural exchanges between the United States and the Caribbean, "we clearly need a critical practice that goes beyond simple dichotomies—us/them, native, foreign, natural, unnatural—a practice that can not only affirm but also critique" (139). Analysis of the reception of the popular American song "Bill" in both the United States and Barbados presents an opportunity to apply such theoretical practice.

The roots of this popular-cultural call-and-response sprout from the fertile soil of New Orleans with the blues singer Peggy Scott-Adams and the U.S. release of the song "Bill" on her album *Help Yourself*. As one reviewer noted in *Rolling Stone,* "Penned by Miss Butch Records owner Jimmy Lewis, the song contains a modern twist on a blues template as old as the genre itself. Mourning the loss of her husband to a love, the protagonist in 'Bill' is startled to find out that her husband's love interest isn't another woman, but a male friend, Bill" (Reece 10). The release of the novelty song spawned a comeback for Peggy Scott-Adams. In the United States, the album originally played on blues-format stations; then, as a consequence of its unexpected popularity, the song moved to the rhythm-and-blues/urban-contemporary market. It is significant that the song was performed by a blues singer and employed a blues format. "Like oral storytellers and subsequent modern writers, as performers, blues singers improvise variations on existing songs and thereby confirm and intensify bonds of kinship and experience with their listeners" (Callahan 16). By employing a familiar form to express an unexpected and potentially controversial narrative, Scott-Adams and the song's composer, Jimmy Lewis, may have instigated a conversation about the complications of sexuality by and among constituencies that might other-wise have been disinclined to participate.

From its bluesy and inviting invocation, the song exudes fluidity and multiple cultural resonances. The invocation of the song—"All of you ladies out there, turn up your radio/Girls, I'm about to tell you something you may want to know/you know things, they're not always what they appear to be/Something happened to me I don't want to happen to you" (J. Lewis)—evokes both the traditional narrative format of the blues and call-and-response traditions of the African diaspora. Scott-Adams's call received an unanticipated and vociferous response from American audi-ences. This response might be understood as a predictable response to the blues format. By embedding this story in the blues idiom, it "assume[s] some shared experience on the part of the musician and the audience and set[s] . . . those listening flowing with their own stories" (Callahan 16). One *Washing-ton Post* reporter noted, "Peggy Scott-Adams' provocative ballad is hitting radio audiences like an emotional bomb. In Washington, D.C. and other cit-ies, some listeners have called in sobbing to request 'Bill,' saying it captures their life stories. Others simply can't believe it" (Leiby). The lyrics that gen-erated such visceral reactions describe the narrator's simultaneous discovery of her husband's infidelity and his homosexuality. "He was in Bill's arms breathing hard and French kissing./I was ready for Mary, Susan, Helen, and Jane. When all the time it was Bill that was sleeping with my man." The usual trajectory of infidelity has been dramatically altered, because it is Bill who has been "sleeping with [her] man."

It is important to note that these lyrics and the responses to them oc-curred in 1996 and 1997, years before the discussion of African American men engaging in extramarital same-sex affairs was common. There had not yet been public engagement with this subject and acknowledgment of it as a relatively widespread phenomenon in African American communities. In the United States, public conversations about African American married men having secret sexual relations with men became a part of public discourse in 2003 with the publication of Benoit Denizet-Lewis's *New York Times Magazine* article "Double Lives on the Down Low," one of the first public accounts of this issue.

Because these conversations had not been a part of public discourse, reactions to "Bill" actually mark one of the first published public explorations of what would come to be called the Down Low Syndrome. According to articles in many major U.S. newspapers, including the *Washington Post,* the *Atlanta Constitution, USA Today,* the *New York Daily News,* and the *Chicago Sun-Times,* "Bill" inspired amusement and sometimes empathy from its largely African American listeners. This constituency and its attendant public discourses solidified the song's popularity by generating sales that supported the album's meteoric success on *Billboard*'s 1997 Blues Album and R&B Album charts (S. Murray).

Largely regarded as seriocomic, the negative response from U.S. audiences was minimal, according to newspaper accounts. In interviews, both Scott-Adams and Lewis expressed relief at the lack of controversy generated by the song. Scott-Adams told *Billboard* magazine, "When 'Bill' was presented to me, I was a little reluctant . . . I didn't want to be tagged with something that would create negative controversy, but once I did the vocal I was pleased with the song" (Reece 11). Similarly, in a *USA Today* interview Lewis stated, "It's a hard song to write because you have to be very careful and walk a thin line not to offend anybody. I'm not bashing anybody or promoting anything. She's just telling a story about what happened to her" (Jones). These assertions by the singer and the songwriter seem to validate their intention to create a fictional tale using African American cultural and musical syntheses to produce a neutral narrative without sociological or political ramifications. Ironically, the context for this aspiration occurred in a country that maintained serious legal prohibitions to same-sex relationships. In 1996, half of the states in the United States had laws that made sexual acts in private between two consenting adults of the same sex illegal.[7]

While Lewis's and Scott-Adams's attempts to neutralize ideologically based responses to the song "Bill" may have been, for better or worse, largely successful in the United States, such was not the case in Barbados. The song's release on the island in early spring 1997 catalyzed a flurry of public reactions. To contextualize this response, it is necessary to provide some sense of the sociopolitical climate of Barbados with regard to homosexuality (Best; Gale).

In Barbados, as in many nations in the Caribbean and throughout the world, private sexual acts between two consenting adults of the same sex are illegal. These acts were illegal in Barbados in 1997 and remain illegal in 2010 (Immigration and Refugee Board of Canada). When "Bill" was released on the island, gay and lesbian activism in the Caribbean was a relatively new phenomenon; the 1st Caribbean Conference on Gay, Lesbian, and Bisexual Issues, was held in Jamaica in August 1996, shortly before the Bajan release of the song.[8]

Bajan editorials, opinion columns, and letters to the editor appearing in national newspapers often characterize homosexuality as abhorrent and abnormal. These responses were common in the late 1990s and still occur, albeit with less frequency.[9] In 1997 the Bajan writer and activist Ndelamiko Lord wrote in an open letter to the editor of the *Barbados Advocate* that "for years I have read stories in the newspaper that foster a feeling of intolerance towards gay people. Editors seem to choose stories reporting gay people being beaten, murdered gruesomely, and ones in which the gay person is being punished for one thing or another. Very rarely are gay people painted in anything but a negative light." Other articles validate Lord's observations.

In April 1997, for example, following an appearance of the National Dance Theater of Jamaica, a rather lengthy article appeared in the *Sunday Advocate* responding to the possibility that one of the performances, a dance with two male performers, had possessed a gay subtext. According to the article's author, Lynette Taylor, many Bajans had left the performance with "somewhat of a bitter-sweet taste" in their mouths. The performance in question (which I saw) featured two male dancers, clad in minimalist costumes, in physically proximate and interactive positions. The Bajan man responsible for bringing the troupe to Barbados, Andrew Cummins, responded to the criticisms saying, "I did not see it as anything sexual. . . . West Indian Blacks easily exclude and marginalise people once they view them as being different. If you are different in this sense you are soft and if you are soft then you are gay" (L. Taylor). This equation of traditional masculinity and heterosexuality with strength and homosexuality with softness and weakness is the key to understanding some of the Barbadian response to the song "Bill." These editorials reveal the ways that "unequal economic, political, and social relations are mediated and (re)produced through cultural representations and discourses" (Kim-Puri 138).

Reacting to the song's Bajan release, a February editorial noted that "sources at the radio stations say a day doesn't pass without several women calling to say they can relate to the experiences of the song. . . . Now that really doesn't say much for Bajan men at all" ("Fitting"). Implicitly, the presence of homosexuals on the island became a threat to constructions of Bajan masculinity. The U.S. writer Essex Hemphill asserted that as a result of the legacy of historical emasculation of black men, blacks of the African diaspora often "view homosexuality as the final break with masculinity" and as a threat to the assertion of a collective and "normal" national identity (in Riggs). Throughout the diaspora, cultural nationalism often manifests as a reassertion of masculinity. Speaking specifically of the construction of the Caribbean, Supriya Nair maintains that most representations persist in "feminizing both culture and its consumption" (71). As a result, in Caribbean rhetoric there is often a perceived correlation between political agency and patriarchal masculinist modalities.[10] In this context, homosexuality can be misperceived as a threat to the efforts and ability of a marginalized group, culture, or nation to establish self-determination.

Issues of identity are of particular concern to the island nations of the Caribbean as a result of their relative marginalization on the world stage.

> Considering that most postcolonies are newsworthy to the Western media only when some natural or political disaster strikes, the popular images of the Caribbean circulated in mass media simulations in the industrialized world today . . . would have us believe, the sun and sands of the primal, edenic, archipelago promote untiring joie de vivre whether on the part of the visiting tourists or of the local populations eager to encourage the marketing of their islands as little paradises. (Nair 72)

In light of the consistent perpetuation of imperialist constructions of the Caribbean as a benign, monolithic, powerless, and cultureless entity, it is not surprising that issues of cultural identity become such contested terrain.

Debates in Barbadian newspapers about homosexuality and the song "Bill" reflect the depth of the contestations about Bajan national identity. In an anonymous letter to the columnist Al Gilkes, a self-identified gay Bajan man asserts that "the song 'Bill' has caught the imagination of the entire population, expressly because it purports to deal with homosexuality, which is still treated with an unwarranted degree of hostility by Barbadians and other Caribbean people" (Gilkes). Correspondingly, in many newspaper accounts, authors of the letters or articles I examine here characterize the homosexuality invoked in the song "Bill" as an outside phenomenon invading the Bajan cultural landscape. The anthropologist Robert J. Foster has noted that such a response is common in nations struggling with the perpetual questions of national identity: "A discourse of 'corruption,' 'pollution,' and purity characteristically accompanies attempts to imagine the national community" (239). In an attempt to protect traditional constructions of Bajan masculinity and national sexual homogeneity, one reviewer noted that lesbianism or a "Jill [is] more likely to happen here in Barbados" ("William Is That You?" 16). David A. B. Murray, in his ethnographic study of gay men in Martinique, observed a similar phenomenon. He found that many Martinican heterosexual men claimed that "homosexuality simply didn't exist in Martinique" ("Between a Rock" 263).

An incredulous Bajan reporter, Harry Mayers, recounted in the *Daily Nation* on February 12, 1997, his first experience of "Bill": "Heard Bill today. Shocking. Almost ran into the car ahead of me. Abhorrent. Abominable. Nauseating. Frightful. Turned the radio off. Didn't even hear traffic around me." Locating homosexual activity as exterior to Barbados, Mayers states that his exposure to homosexuality is limited to conversations about the television show *Melrose Place* and to reading about the jokes of a British comedian.[11] With these disclaimers, Mayers locates homosexuality not only as non-Bajan but also as a constituent element of the rubric of whiteness.[12]

One of the most involved of the newspaper reactions to "Bill" appeared in another column by Al Gilkes. There, Gilkes describes his regular Friday afternoon "lime," or gathering in the local rum shop. While Gilkes and his friends are assembled, the song "Bill" comes on the radio. With his discussion of the reaction of his friends in the rum shop, Gilkes distances the traditional Bajan man, the man welcome in the conviviality of the rum shop, from homosexuality. He suggests this distancing with the title of his article, "The 'Outside Woman' of the '90's." In Barbados, as in other places, the phrase *outside woman* describes a mistress, the sexual partner outside the marriage. Paralleling the position of the so-called outside woman, outside the legitimated home, the subtext of Gilkes's title suggests that the gay man is outside traditional constructions of Bajan masculinity—outside the collegiality and camaraderie of the rum shop. In the last lines of his column, Gilkes unapologetically reveals that gay Bajan men will be the subject of gossip and derision in the shop: "I am eagerly looking forward to next Friday's lime because I am sure that the names of quite a number of Barbadian 'Bills' will come up for discussion." With their suggestion that male homosexuality is distinct and excluded from traditional male Bajan social circles, these responses to "Bill" reveal the stakes invested by some vocal public voices in the construction of an essentialist and indigenous heterosexual masculinity and in the assertion of that definition's synonymy with the nation's identity.

Another illustration of the cultural resonance of "Bill" in 1997 Barbados is the fluid adaptation of its title as a linguistic signifier. The semantic stage was set for the ready vernacularization of "Bill" well before the song's release in the spring of 1997. In Bajan and other Caribbean colloquialisms, the word *buller* is slang for a gay man. According to an April 1997 newspaper account, "The word has now gone from 'buller' to 'biller' and married men are having to pay a terrible price because of the lousy tune about a woman who caught her husband with a man's tongue in his mouth" ("Bill Wreaking Havoc" 9). The proximate pronunciations of *bill* and *buller* enabled easy co-optation of the word in popular usage. As early as February 22, the newspaper *Sun on Sunday* reported that "one woman called in [to the radio station] and said she nicknamed her ex-husband Bill the Bull" ("Fitting"). In March one beleaguered gay man wrote to Al Gilkes to assert that "I am a 'Bill' who is not ashamed to be a 'Bill.' However, I am ashamed to be a Barbadian 'Bill' because I am forced to remain in the closet; I am forced to live with my emotions boxed. Now that song has turned my box into a coffin, and every time I hear it played on the radio, it's as if another nail is being driven into that coffin" (Gilkes, "Tough"). The anonymous letter demonstrates the extent to which the word *bill* acquired popular currency, even becoming a term of self-description by gay men. Another article, entitled "William Is That You?" predicts the redefinition of the word *bill*: "Quite a few guys are going to insist on being called 'William' for a long time to come. Yes, 'Bill' [used to be] what you'd get in the mail" ("William Is That You?" 16). Reportedly, a Bajan man even went to court to have his name legally changed (Griffith). In an article entitled "Poor Bill," the aforementioned man was said to be unable to "take the hassles from his friends since the song about Bill has become popular on the airwaves. He told friends that he is not gay and should not suffer as a result of a song" (Griffith). These accounts demonstrate the surprising impact that "Bill" had on the popular imagination.

An April 24 antigay commentary recounts a conversation in which the word *bill* is used as a verb to describe gay sexuality without any direct reference to the song. The gay man in the conversation says, "I was billing from the time I was 12 years old and I going to bill until I die" ("Rum Shops"). Oddly and significantly, the conversation is said to have taken place years earlier, even before the release of the song.

The word *bill* also became a euphemism for a person who acquires profits by taking unfair advantage of someone. According to an April 10 account entitled "Bill Wreaking Havoc," a person can bill "himself to the top of the heap" by either "'billing' bad, bad, bad, or 'theifing' [*sic*] worse, worse, worse." In addition to the cultural complexities they reveal, these responses indicate an engagement with and push against this song as an American cultural product. They reveal cultural resistance and support the assertion that "global interconnection and interdependence do not necessarily mean cultural conformity" (Holton 140). The particular definitional iteration of *bill* as equivalent with greed and usury becomes the catalyst for the use of the word as a political signifier.

One of the first commentators to make the association between former president Clinton and the slang *bill* in print was Harold Hoyte, in a speculative discussion about Clinton's 1997 knee injury.[13] The word *bill* took on yet another nuance when Hoyte used it in an article entitled "Not the Real Bill" to imply, not homosexual, but heterosexual impropriety by the then American president. "Stories are beginning to make the rounds," wrote Hoyte, "about how Bill Clinton really managed to fall and hurt his leg. I don't have to tell you what the American people are saying he was running after at 1:30 in the morning." Reinforcing this association between Bill Clinton and the Bajan semantic play on the word *bill* is an article written when the Clinton cohort James McDougal began cooperating with Whitewater prosecutors.[14] McDougal is quoted in a *Daily Nation* newspaper article as saying, "I just got sick and tired of lying for [Clinton]." Significantly, the title of the article is "The 'Billing's' Over." These articles signal the growing association between the Bajan use of the word *bill,* President Bill Clinton, and the experience of exploitation.

The Bajan calypsonian Red Plastic Bag merged the multiple connotations of the word *bill* into his musical rebuttal to Peggy Scott-Adams's "Bill." The titular double entendre of Bag's song "In De Tail" both caricatures gay sexuality and "details" the myriad intricacies inherent in this intercultural music exchange. The first stanza of the song seems simply to refer to the narrative of Scott-Adams's "Bill":

Well all the talk about billing
And the fellows it killing
It's a funny funny happening
Man ah tell you it's frightening
And the women complaining
How they dem men and husband they losing
To these men that doing the killing
Coz they billing
And they billing (repeat three times)
                                   (Wiltshire)

Bag's song equates homosexuality and violence, unconditionally associates homosexual sex with death, and characterizes the homosexual sex act as not only dangerous but murderous. The implications insinuate and reinforce a presumed connection between homosexuality and AIDS and concomitantly suggest a violent rape narrative, none of which is a part of the original Scott-Adams song.

The refrain of "In De Tail" is a frank and defensive disassociation of the narrator from "billing," a distancing that echoes the rhetorical constructions of Bajan masculinity in opposition to homosexuality:

Nobody ent billing me (not a fella)
And I ent billing anybody (not a boy)
I ent stooping so low to de bottom

They could offer a billion billion
Nobody ent billing me (not a fella)
and I ent billing anybody me (not a fella)
And I ent billing anybody (not a boy)
I want to be on the success road
But please don't put me in Billboard
No body ent billing me (not a fella)
And I ent billing anybody

While this refrain can be read as a literal and rather crude protest against homosexuality, it, like the stanza reproduced earlier, also supports a number of alternative exegetical possibilities. Of particular interest is the power dynamic in the assertive first line of the refrain, "Nobody ent billing me." This line seems to imply the need to defend oneself from an aggressor. Also of note is the implication that this individual wants to be successful but will not be bought or compromised. "I ent stooping so low to de bottom / They could offer a billion billion." The song expresses an adamant fight against victimization, as well as a refusal to be commodified in American terms, with its cry, "I want to be on the success road / But please don't put me in Billboard." Bag's particular intonation of the word *success* in his recorded performance of the song seems to allude to fellatio as he uses the word *success* to pun on the word *suck*. The artist wants success on his own terms, and not as dictated by the abject quantification and commodification of artistry that the U.S. magazine *Billboard*'s charts represent. In addition, the word *Billboard* in this context provides a simultaneous double entendre and vernacularization of a homosexual sex act that also allows the words "don't put me in Billboard" to be understood as "don't put bill's board in me." The semantic fluidity of "In De Tail" enables a shift in the subtextual nuance of this popular-music interchange from sociological to political, from commentary on homosexuality to critique on the relationship between Barbados and the United States.

In the spring of 1997, the political relationship between these two countries was in crisis, at least from the Bajan perspective, as a result of a treaty popularly called the Shiprider Agreement. The treaty instituted maritime enforcement rights for the United States in the national waters of the islands of the Caribbean. Essentially, the treaty allows U.S. ships and aircraft free access to sovereign Caribbean territorial waters when in pursuit of drug smugglers (*Weekly Compilation of Presidential Documents* 702). Given the history of U.S. involvement in the region (i.e., in Haiti, Cuba, Grenada, and other nations), some of the island nations, namely Barbados and Jamaica, saw this agreement as a potential threat to their independence and sovereignty.

Such a fear was not at all unwarranted. In an article entitled "The Shiprider Solution: Policing the Caribbean," published in the right-wing U.S. periodical *National Interest*, Elliot Abrams, a lawyer and foreign-policy expert, outlines a plan for recolonization of the islands of the Caribbean using the Shiprider Agreement as a first step. Abrams maintains that in the Caribbean, "reliance on a foreign power for security and prosperity may be the most sensible form of nationalism. And the only available foreign power is the United States" (86). It was precisely this neocolonial impulse that Barbados and Jamaica attempted to combat when their governments initially refused to acquiesce to the Shiprider Agreement.

The refusal of Barbados and Jamaica to sign the agreement created the likelihood of U.S. reprisals. The United States had then, and has now, the capacity to decertify, to withhold "approval (and hence aid) to countries that the American president does not certify to Congress as doing enough in the war against drugs" ("Uncle Sam" 45). The United States also had other means of forcing the islands to sign the agreement. As reported in both the *Nation* and the *Barbados Advocate,* many Bajans viewed the rather odd reclassification of the Barbados airport (an airport that at the time supported regular landings of the Concorde) by the U.S. Federal Aviation Administration as a grade-three airport in December 1996 as a warning against further resistance to the Shiprider Agreement. Both Barbados and Jamaica, dependent on tourism as one of their primary sources of revenue, were in the subordinate position in the power struggle, a position that resonates with the lyrics of "In De Tail."

In a satirical commentary on the agreement, Richard Hoad wrote in a March article in the *Weekend Nation* of a fictive invasion by the United States. In the account, Clinton declares war on Barbados. The president states that the invasion will be led by a rear admiral "who has been staying at [Clinton's] place since his break up with Peggy Scott-Adams" (R. Hoad). Hoad clearly equates the U.S. assertion of control over Barbados with "billing."

The Bill discourses achieved a denouement with the president's visit to Barbados in May 1997 for a summit with the Caribbean heads of state. Just hours before the president's arrival, Barbados signed a version of the controversial Shiprider Agreement. As a result, the visit itself generated much contention. One editorial written at the time begins with the lyrics from "In De Tail" and continues, "Red Plastic Bag was controlling the airwaves, his smashing hit reverberating with as much resonance as the chopper blades as they hovered overhead, as if in perfect response to the stepped up security, tantamount to an invasion of our privacy and solemn peace" (Parris). In a fascinating juxtaposition, the calypso lyrics are positioned as a powerful opposition to the symbol of U.S. military might, the invading, noisy, predatory helicopter. This rhetorical defense illustrates what Hilary Beckles has identified as a common definitional denominator for the Caribbean, a region he calls "a postcoloniality in which African and Afro-Caribbean identities and ontologies are set out in subversive opposition to imperialism" (783). The words of the song become an effective, perhaps singular weapon in the Bajan anti-imperialist defense arsenal—as Bill Ashcroft has characterized it, an instance of the empire writing back.

The most pointed criticism of the Clinton visit, however, came in another editorial, entitled "Mekking the Billing Issue Clear." The author, Kerner Garner, uses Bag's song as a springboard to comment in Bajan dialect on both the Shiprider Agreement and the excesses of the president's visit:

> Someone ask if de whole thing wid Bill didn't get overdone. He say dat he wondering if it did necessary tuh do things like close roads and shut down a whole hotel just fuh one man. He wanted tuh know who gine pay de bills fuh Bill. He say dat he sure that Bill ain't going tuh do it, and Owen [prime minister of Barbados] either, so it mean dat we Bajans gine get billed. . . . I know dat Bag nuhbody ain't billing he, but I frighten dat we done get bill already and ain't even know, so de question ain't if we getting bill is how big Bill bill be. (9)

The relationship between the United States and Barbados, between neocolonialism and sovereignty, is a tenuous one. The song "In De Tail," a response to Scott-Adams's "Bill," gave voice to the ironies of national and cultural identity and power in a country racially, economically, politically, and geographically marginalized on the world stage.

Whatever the articulated positionality, clearly the release of Scott-Adams's "Bill" in Barbados served as a mechanism for a vigorous debate on myriad subjects. The reactions to the song illustrate the power of call-and-response to catalyze individuals to "read and hear, and potentially, contribute to the still unfolding narratives that inform and influence our identities and our experiences" (Callahan 21). The song set off a veritable chain reaction in the context of a dynamic response in which *bill* became variously defined as a closet homosexual, any homosexual man, a homosexual woman (Jill), an attempt to profit unfairly, a debt, lying to protect someone, money, a record chart, forced compliance, a usurious relationship, a club, a phallus, and finally, cultural, economic, and political neocolonialism. Defying simplistic analysis, Red Plastic Bag's "In De Tail" and the fervor surrounding it evokes readings that categorize the text on a spectrum from homophobic reactionary ballad to calypsonian anthem of nationalist masculinized political resistance. In this instance, RPB, as the calypsonian man of words, may embody "the cultural paradigmatic feature of Caribbean modernity— the rise of the common citizen to institutional and cultural leadership" (Beckles 784).

The reception of and responses to the American popular song "Bill" in Barbados reveal not only intracultural homophobia and the tenuous marriage between masculinist heteronormativity and national identity but also some of the potent and circuitous permutations in the cultural, ideological, and political relationship between Barbados and the United States. Although in some ways these interactions are illuminated more fully by the attempt to retrace this postmodern call-and-response, in the end there is no neat and conclusive pronouncement to be had. Each of these transnational interactions remains as ambiguously defined as the rise at Barbados's center, the ridge known as Farley Hill, whose only certain ideological contours are as indeterminate as the sea.

Notes

1. As Homi Bhabba noted in his collection *Nation and Narration,* a dynamic and more realistic strategy for defining nations is to consider their narrative corpuses, what he calls "the complex strategies of cultural identification and discursive address that function in the name of 'the people' or 'the nation' and make them the immanent subjects and objects of a range of social and literary narratives" (292). It is this understanding of the centrality of narrative to the concept and definition of nation that informs my analysis of the songs "Bill," "In De Tail," and the published public responses to them and the issues they raise.

2. "Globalization is assumed to be a one way flow from the first world to the third" (Kim-Puri 141).

3. The labeling of sexualities is complex and problematic, particularly when framed by a cultural exchange between the United States and Barbados. Although the song's protagonist could also be described using other labels, such as *bisexual,* the songs "Bill" and "In De Tail" refer to Bill as homosexual. Consequently, I use this term to describe "Bill." I employ the term *homosexual* because it is the most consistent with the definitional frameworks of the texts I examine.

4. See, for example, Antonio Benítez-Rojo's famous (or infamous, depending on your perspective) reading of the gendered and sexualized identity of the Caribbean in *The Repeating Island:* "Let's be realistic: the Atlantic is the Atlantic . . . because it was once engendered by the copulation of Europe—that insatiable solar bull—the Caribbean archipelago; . . . Europe . . . conceived the project of inseminating the Caribbean womb with the blood of Africa, the Atlantic is today the Atlantic . . . because it was the painfully delivered child of the Caribbean, whose vagina was stretched between continental clamps, . . . all Europe pulling on the forceps . . . ; then the febrile wait through the forming of a scar: suppurating, always suppurating" (3).

5. I use here John F. Callahan's definition of call-and-response. Callahan understands call-and-response as a potentially interactive experience that is "both a fundamentally, perhaps even universal oral mode and a distinctively African and African American form of discourse in speech and story, sermons and songs" (16).

6. Red Plastic Bag is the pseudonymic appellation of the Bajan musician, producer, composer, entrepreneur, and calypsonian Stedson Wiltshire. Since his debut in 1979, Wiltshire arguably has been the most popular and best-known calypsonian on the island. His fame extends beyond Barbados to an international audience. As of the summer of 2010, Wiltshire is the only nine-time winner of the island's major

calypso competition, the Pic O' de Crop, which is the culminating musical event of the island's annual carnival, Cropover. The winner of the Pic O' de Crop competition is crowned the island's calypso king.

7. See United States Sodomy Laws, http://www.sodomy.org/laws/ (accessed 15 September 1996). Sodomy laws in the United States were struck down in 2003 by the Supreme Court case *Lawrence and Garner v. State of Texas.*

8. Since 1997 there has been a surge in awareness and activism about issues of sexuality in the Caribbean and in Barbados. See Abramschmitt; Barbados Gays and Lesbians Against Discrimination; Douglas; and Glave, *Our Caribbean* and *Words to Our Now.*

9. For examples of recent editorials in Bajan newspapers about lesbian, gay, bisexual, and transgender issues, see GlobalGayz.com, http://globalgayz.com/country/Barbados/view/BRB/gay-barbados-news-and-reports (accessed 31 August 2009).

10. The correlation between the traditional definitions of masculinity, patriarchy, and self-determination is common in rhetoric throughout the African diaspora. For example, many of the texts of the African American Black Arts Movement, of the 1960s and 1970s, connect black nationalism with the need for black men to gain patriarchal control of their communities. For complex analyses of this issue, see Belton; Harper; Ongiri; Riggs; Shin and Judson; and Yelvington.

11. The U.S. television show *Melrose Place,* which premiered on the FOX network on 8 July 1992 and remained on the air until 1999, featured a gay character named Matt Fielding, played by Doug Savant. The show, created by Darren Star and produced by Aaron Spelling, was rebroadcast on Bajan television.

12. As the educator Arthur Lipkin has noted, it is not uncommon for individuals from marginalized or minority communities to regard homosexuality not only as an issue of gender identity but also as a racialized phenomenon that derives from a particular geography. In other words, a definition of "homosexuality as white and Western" (*Understanding Homosexuality* 34).

13. On 14 March 1997 President Bill Clinton tore his quadriceps tendon when he fell down a flight of stairs (Bennet).

14. James McDougal was an Arkansas lawyer and confidant of Clinton's. He served prison time as a result of his involvement in the Whitewater scandal, which involved a 1978 real-estate deal between the Clintons and the McDougals and the subsequent activities and investigations related to that interaction. McDougal died while completing his sentence in 1998. For more information on the scandal, see http://www.washingtonpost.com/wp-srv/politics/special/whitewater/timeline.htm (accessed 5 September 2009).

Novel Insights

Sex Work, Secrets, and Depression in Angie Cruz's *Soledad*

Donette Francis

Ultimately, it does not matter what consumption possibilities the media depict and how much individuals fantasize about them: living out fantasies means having access to required resources, particularly the right passport. Otherwise, citizenship trumps transnational desires every time.
—Denise Brennan, *What's Love Got to Do with It?*

An emphasis on the sexual agency of women should not lead to a prematurely romanticized portrayal of resistance and in the process foreclose a discussion of the very real constraints that sex workers face in their daily lives, both on as well as off the job.
—Red Thread Women's Development Programme,
"Givin' Lil' Bit fuh Lil' Bit"

They had a special on women who sleep through depression. They want to die, but they don't have the courage to go that far. They said depression is anger turned inward. . . . Olivia never shows anger. She always holds it in, stuffing it inside to the deepest corners.
—Angie Cruz, *Soledad*

THIS ESSAY examines contemporary Caribbean women's writings to consider their novel insights about sexuality and female citizenship. The ethos of this fiction articulates a feminist poetics that I define as *antiromance*, which writes beyond the conciliatory happy ending by foregrounding the intimate lives of Caribbean women and girls to underscore that neither familial home, national homeland, nor immigrant nation functions as a safe space of belonging; and female characters therefore often dwell in liminal spaces of vulnerability. Centering the sexed female body, these novels demonstrate that from their very inception Caribbean states, because of not only the constraints of globalized labor demands but also their own naked violence, have exhausted whatever emancipatory promises they imagined. Thus, for many female citizens, the goal has been to craft ways to survive life's many contingencies and serial setbacks.[1]

In the world of the novels, these migratory female characters are shaped by their sexual pasts, and despite their best efforts, they cannot simply leave the past behind to chart new futures. Hence these antiromances offer no normative coupling, and coercion, wherever it is located, is vividly marked as violence and sexual abuse. The value of antiromance, then, is its reluctance to offer grand narrative closure, settlement, or any satisfaction derived from other genres, such as tragedy's "catharsis" or romance's joy of witnessing eventual agonistic triumph. Antiromance defies reconciliation: it yields no catharsis, no enlightenment, no surety of the path forward. By contrast, it exposes the folly of believing that somehow the national, the diasporic, or the intimate sphere is a privileged space for the reconciliation of otherwise impossible differences. These writers, therefore, foreground an understanding of belonging that simultaneously acknowledges both the failures and the possibilities, the contingencies and the contradictions, of female everyday experiences and thus force a more complex discussion of Caribbean women's agency.

Writers such as Patricia Powell, Nelly Rosario, Edwidge Danticat, and Elizabeth Nunez share this poetic sensibility, which rewrites various imperial, national, and diasporic romance narrative formulas. Each novel begins with a different historical signpost—emancipation, indentureship, or U.S. military intervention in one of three different national contexts—to ask how reading the moment as a crucial intimate juncture enhances our understanding of the centrality of sexual citizenship to imperial or nation-building projects, as well as how these novelists reimagine canonical narrative histories through the antiromance.

Set during the emancipation period in nineteenth-century Jamaica, Patricia Powell's book *The Pagoda* (1998) inserts the traveling Chinese woman to rewrite the romance of escape from old-world imperial China to participate in new-world adventures. Immediately, readers learn that for such women this new-world travel romance is often thwarted at sea with an act of sexual violence. The novel pursues the sexual politics of a Chinese woman's gender and sexual passing by using the Asian body as bonded laborer to represent the ambiguous terrain between enslavement and freedom. Nelly Rosario's *Song of the Water Saints* (2002) rewrites the imperial romance of the American military hero who rescues poor local women from the tyranny of their weak national patriarchs. Rosario's novel considers the violence implicit in visual images, particularly those produced for export, used to project and to produce a sexualized narrative about the availability of Caribbean people, especially its "exotic" mulatto women. Rosario recuperates visual indices such as the postcard and the photograph as counter-archival sources of subaltern history making, which enables her to challenge the romance of the American occupation.

Both Edwidge Danticat and Elizabeth Nunez rewrite nationalist romances in Haiti and Trinidad, respectively. If the nationalist romance of the 1940s Haitian indigenist movement—from whose ranks François Duvalier emerged—promised to restore black Haitians and their Afrocentric cultural practices to their rightful revolutionary place within the nation, Danticat's *Breath, Eyes, Memory* (1994) explores the ramifications of the violence of Duvalier's regime. Centering the experiences of poor black Haitian women, the novel illustrates how cultural narratives such as folklore work to replicate violence against women and to reinscribe patriarchal power. Nunez's *Bruised Hibiscus* (2000) considers what Trinidad's national motto, "Together we aspire, Together we achieve," means for this multiracial diasporic colonial outpost precisely by centering the question of *racial* hybridity. Could Trinidad, on the verge of self-rule and invested in the romance of a Creole society, successfully incorporate the various racial and ethnic groups found on the island? The novel tackles this question in the form of a love story replete with interracial sex and domestic violence and prompts readers to question why violence is at the heart of narrating national intimacy. The novel's time period and its "plural" cast of characters suggest that even on the eve of independence, signs of a failed nationalist project based on the romance of Creole societies and citizenship were already evident, especially within the intimate domain.

In this essay I focus on Angie Cruz's 2000 novel *Soledad,* as it astutely brings together timely questions of sexuality and transnational citizenship and thereby challenges an emerging diasporic romance of better fortunes and sexual freedoms abroad. *Soledad* encourages readers to measure one's intimate life against one's relationship to two nation-states to consider how transnationalism is lived when, for example, an individual's home state cannot provide the basic necessities to survive and the host society does not recognize one as a legitimate member. The novel explores how these and related circumstances impact one's sense of self, one's physical and mental well-being, as well as one's access to resources such as basic social services. The epigraphs that precede this essay capture the nuances about how both macro- and micropolitics govern individual experiences: the first reflects on the significance of legal papers—visas and passport—in structuring one's mobility and therefore one's access; the third responds to the first, in that it asks what happens when one subverts these official governmental organizational structures? Certainly one outcome might be "living happily transnationally," but another, equally compelling story is the pathos of living between two nation-states, with neither assuming the responsibility to provide for one's needs.

More specifically, *Soledad* prompts readers to question how sex workers are talked about in an era of globalization, in which economic inequities shore up distinctions between the first and third worlds. It compels readers to question whether the exchange of sex for a first-world visa or currency is best understood as the modern-day extension of slavery and bondage and is therefore a persistent narrative of coercion and domination or whether sex work is a space where laborers can sell their service for meaningful financial gain and thereby exercise empowerment in the global marketplace. While these polarities may appear overly sharp, for transnational feminists wrestling with the complexities of women's agency in the sex-work industry under conditions of global inequalities, our language remains inadequate and incomplete, in spite of our collective best efforts.[2] My analysis of *Soledad* contributes to this ongoing engagement, as it reads the sex worker's body as an archival site to center feelings as an experiential embodied reality. Examining how a woman feels about sex work and how it materializes as depression enables a consideration of its effect on the sex worker, her family, and her children. Such an embodied reading of the sex worker offers a grounded analysis of diaspora—which avoids telescoping one moment of migratory victory—to underscore the sexual restrictions of transnational citizenship.

Set principally in the Washington Heights section of New York, *Soledad* tells the story of a Dominican American family's struggle to plant roots in the United States. Readers witness how poverty and lack of opportunity push people out of their homelands and into the United States. We also discover that during this late capitalist period of female-led migration to fill service-sector jobs in northern metropoles, many women and girls sacrifice their bodies in an attempt to make a better life for themselves and their families. Through this extended family's experiences we realize how immigrants rely on one another for mutual sustenance, how such family obligations keep them tied to ethnic enclaves, how they use secrets as a mode of protection, and finally, how these various familial ties curtail their ability to pursue individual dreams. At first glance, the novel might appear to be an immigrant novel, a bildungsroman, or a portrait of an artist as a young Dominican American girl trying to escape the clutter of family and the confines of her Dominican community in Washington Heights for the hippy artistic lifestyle of the East Village. But the novel is as much about Soledad's mother, Olivia. In fact, the author seems to suggest that you cannot tell Soledad's story without Olivia's backstory and the life events that shaped her mother. It is important to know that the now thirty-six-year-old Olivia became a sex worker in Puerto Plato, Dominican Republic, when she was fifteen. This, as well as other sexual secrets that readers uncover throughout the novel, is key to understanding how these particular national subjects are formed and central to understanding the dynamics between all the characters.

In the public sphere, because Olivia makes it to the United States and actually stays there, she might appear to have successfully traded sex for a visa. But her private angst, depression, and failed relationship with her daughter tell another story. Through Olivia's character, we explore what happens when one stuffs one's insides into the deepest corners, connecting one's labor choices to one's mental health and overall well-being. While the novel and its various narrative strategies work toward making the story of sex work, secrets, and depression audible, my analysis in this essay looks at citizenship in an era of globalization, taking into account one woman's intimate life in relationship to two states, the United States and the Dominican Republic. Reading agency and resistance alongside personal and psychological pain foregrounds the limits of both articulating and protecting women's rights under such circumstances.

Disciplining Narrative

Across the disciplines, feminists grapple with the quotidian complexities of sex work for such female laborers. Where Cruz's novel shows a young Olivia at work in a sex town, Denise Brennan offers a complementary ethnography of Sosua, one specific town in the Dominican Republic whose economy is structured around sex tourism. As a town of migrants—Germans, Eastern European Jews, internal migrants from other Dominican towns, European and North American tourists—Sosua operates as a "sexscape" and a transnational "place of opportunity" within the Dominican Republic (Brennan, *What's Love* 21).[3] Brennan initially foregrounds women's agency, arguing that these sex workers distinguish between marriage *por amor* (love) and marriage *por residencia* (the visa). Yet in a closing chapter, entitled "Transnational Disappointments: Living in Europe," Brennan reflects, "I had set out to write a feminist ethnography of the sex trade to raise questions about poor women's power, control and opportunities in a globalized economy. The waters are murky when considering women's agency in the sex trade, no matter how determined and creative their efforts to get ahead" (211). Brennan's ethnography details that for poor local Dominican women, the options remain constrained, despite their best efforts to utilize sex work as an "advancement strategy" rather than simply as a means of survival. Her study offers "thick descriptions" of single mothers who engage in various strategic maneuvers, only to realize that locations like Sosua, firmly situated in the developing world, reproduce existing global inequalities (Brennan, *What's Love* 23, 45).

Precisely because of the nature of their jobs, and because housing and marriage are often the very things bartered to gain an economic foothold, distinctions between public and private are untenable. These, then, are the constraints of the circumstances under which such women and girls labor. There is a further paradox inherent in the sex worker's body, since it is simultaneously nonreproductive and productive. That is, it does not produce desirable progeny for the state, but it is fiscally productive, in that it generates foreign exchange for the national economy. Hence, these are unruly but not readily disposable bodies (Alexander, "Erotic Autonomy").

As Cruz's novel unfolds, the distinctions between marriage for love and marriage for residence become less clear. Because sex work is almost universally ascribed a negative social value, and because the negative value is internalized—even if the labor is not—distinctions between abstracted emotional labor and the separation of work and identity are not readily discrete and complicate the matter of thinking through women's agency. In following Olivia from age fifteen to thirty-six, Cruz shows the impact over time for female sex workers, even those who labor far away from home to ensure anonymity. She thus makes two clear interventions. First, one's choices are never simply about the individual but in fact impact one's entire family and future generations. Throughout the novel, Olivia struggles to come to terms with the aftermath of her labor choice and its impact on her daughter, Soledad. By being taken into their everyday lives, readers witness how women like Olivia embody their pain: in child rearing, especially in mother-daughter relationships; in maintaining spiritual lives, and in marital partnerships. We meet Olivia in an emotional coma, when she can no longer mask the pain of how her choice of sex work has propelled her into what turn out be an unfortunate series of events. Even while her body does "what it needs to survive"—she eats, drinks, and even goes to the bathroom—her spirit is somewhere else all together (67). Cruz takes readers into the mysticism of Olivia's belief system, where we witness absent and pregnant spirits and feelings of despondency and shame. Olivia's emotional coma challenges the abstraction of emotional labor as somehow separable from the rest of her social identity and world.

Cruz also shifts our gaze from the usual focus on and castigation of foreign men consuming and exploiting Dominican females to offer a more internal critique of Dominican men exploiting Dominican women. By casting a Dominican man living in New York as the predator who goes to the Dominican Republic in search of a vulnerable young girl, Cruz makes her story less a nationalist impulse to blame an imperial or imperial power; she instead relocates violence as an everyday experience to which Dominican women are subjected. In this way, Cruz pursues the national and diasporic implications of machismo in heterosexual relationships. She makes clear that sharp divisions between home and diaspora are unsustainable when one is trying to understand Dominican realities. As the story unfolds, readers understand that the fact of this Dominican New Yorker's U.S. citizenship contributes greatly to his sense of entitlement to local women on the island and, correspondingly, to their desire for him.

To plot this antiromance about the intimate issues of contemporary globalization, Cruz manipulates the conventional novel form. The narrative action moves back and forth in time and space (i.e., between the Dominican Republic and the United States) with abrupt shifts in point of view, not discerning between dialogue and omniscient third- or first-person narration; Spanglish is liberally interspersed throughout, and switches in narrative voice are marked only by an asterisk on the page (45, 47). This strategy reflects the absence of a singular authoritative position. It suggests that the truth is intelligible only through the muddle of all the tellers' various versions. Hence, the novel attempts to echo through narration the intensity and multiplicity of movement, clutter, and chaos that marks this Dominican American family. The very opening scene of the novel, in italics, immediately marks the author's experimentation with form and registers narrative difference in terms of time and consciousness. We come to realize that this italicized narration is Olivia's comatose voice, which is in sharp juxtaposition to the first fifty pages, where we learn about Olivia primarily through everyone else's narration of her, while she lies in an emotional coma (35).

Olivia's opening preface instantly charts the spatial topography of the novel: "When I close my eyes . . . I remember the way the sunset dropped into the sea at home in Dominican Republic. It's the only place I can remember outside of my apartment in Washington Heights, before Manolo, before I became a mother to Soledad" (9). This idyllic remembering of home space in the Dominican Republic—the juxtaposition of the vast openness of the sea at home and the cramped apartment in New York—shows movement from spatial openness to spatial closedness. It prompts readers to question what has rendered Olivia unable to move beyond her past to confront her present and future. Her story is not a model of diaspora that valorizes the homeland, nor does it proffer an idealized version of the American dream, or diasporic romance. Readers surmise that the ensuing story is not one of immigrant success in coming to America but rather one of entrapment both in the immigrant space of Washington Heights and in identities of wife and mother. And this is what makes the antiromance mode of emplotment clear: the innocence of childhood abruptly interrupted, attempts at romance foiled. Olivia is not a grand character acting at an epochal moment; rather hers is the story of an ordinary woman facing the intimate pressures of globalization. The novel's movement dwells on the mundane, everyday details of living with memories of the past and the self-erosion that accumulates over time as Olivia gradually disintegrates into a comatose state.

Disciplining Olivia

Olivia's very name, connoting her olive complexion, marks how she figures as "pretty and desirable" in local and international economies of heterosexual male desire. Significantly, her phenotype does not mark Iberian whiteness but rather a light-skinned mulatta, so that the racial mixing and the lightness of the mixing is what is of importance. Furthermore, as a dark-skinned Dominican New Yorker, Manuel goes to the island in search of a light-skinned woman, figuring that his American capital and citizenship can be exchanged for a pliable woman with old-world values—lack of feminist sensibilities—and what Michel-Rolph Trouillot terms "epidermic capital" (*State Against Nation*).

Throughout the novel we learn that various sociocultural institutions seek to discipline Olivia, first among them her family, specifically her father's rule of law: "Olivia's father was just waiting until she was old enough to marry her off. Things were becoming very hard for them. Olivia knew her parents were looking for ways to move to the States" (57). To avoid being a pawn in a patriarchal arrangement—being married off by her father to a Dominican man in New York for a U.S. visa—Olivia leaves home. Certainly, leaving home is an act of resistance, since she subverts an instance of patriarchal regulation, but the novel further demonstrates that such singular acts of resistance are always incomplete. Agency is not a fixed destination at which one arrives with the act being forever completed; rather, it is a continuous series of maneuvers to be enacted and reenacted. Actions under one instance of domination do not forever alter the system of dominance and therefore often have to be repeated. This scene is perhaps the first instance in which Olivia becomes aware of her sexuality, and it is where she begins to understand that her sexed body can be bartered for financial and material resources. In other words, she learns that she can trade sex for the visa, and importantly, this lesson is taught by her father.

Rejecting her father's perceived right to barter her, Olivia first opts out of the patriarchal marriage contract. As a young girl without much formal education, she does not yet realize the somber realities of her limited labor choices, and she unwittingly enters the sex trade when a Swedish agent comes to their small town and tells her that she can work as a model. In her naiveté, she chooses this employment as a better option than an arranged marriage, leaving home and telling her family that "she was going to do tourismo" (59). Her internal migration to Puerta Plata is not at all exceptional; it shows an attempt to secure autonomy from familial dictates in the homeland. Yet, one wonders if her parents knew what kind of work she was going to do, especially since, when Olivia arrives in New York and calls her sister, Gorda, to inform her of her pregnancy and marriage, the first question Gorda asks is, "Is it his?" (89). This response implies that even though Olivia did this work far away from her home community and lives in what she believes to be secrecy, her family knows exactly what kind of labor "doing tourismo" signals for a young girl working in a tourist town. Her family never speaks of her sex work, and readers must contemplate whether they keep her secret to protect her sense of self as well as their own. For while she holds what she describes as the "dirty work" inside as private transgression, and it eats away at her, she is nonetheless able to perform a public identity of intactness. Conversely, to go public with it, or even speak of it among family, would be to acknowledge how sex work has shaped not only her identity but that of her family members as well. It reflects their own shame that she had to choose this particular labor option—demonstrating that her patria/father/family could not offer her protection from this choice. This family silence around her sexual labor is akin to what Soledad describes in another context as "a part of the family code to protect each other, even if it feels wrong" (72). And keeping this labor secret inside proves to have profound disadvantages for Olivia and her family. Olivia's sex work encourages readers to think about the gendering of wage labor in an era of rapid globalization in which the men are either un- or underemployed and fathers, husbands, and boyfriends barter their women and girls as property, and as a generative source of capital (Brennan, "Women Work").

The novel necessitates an acknowledgment of the negative value assigned to sex work in most cultures, and especially in the Caribbean. Arguing that "work is a site of deep self-formation that offers rich opportunities for human flourishing or devastation," the legal theorist Vicki Schultz asserts that "to a large extent it is through our work—how it is defined, distributed, characterized, and controlled—that we develop into the men and women we see ourselves and others see us as being" (1883). Schultz's argument is relevant in the Caribbean context, as it involves a young girl making a labor choice that will follow her into adulthood. Olivia's scenario raises related questions: Given its negative cultural valuation, how does one negotiate a sense of self and cultural codes of respectability when doing sex work? Is opting out of social value systems an instance of resistance that comes at a price, especially for females? More importantly, how do women like Olivia see themselves in relation to this labor practice? Olivia cannot talk publicly about her job as a sex worker, which is in sharp contrast to her later work as an office cleaner in New York. Even if office cleaning registers as menial labor, it is still valued as a respectable day's work. Her daughter, for example, appreciates and values the magazines Olivia brings home, as they open her imagination to a world of travel. This question of the cultural value assigned to labor choice cannot be minimized. The novel reveals the secrets and lies surrounding Olivia's sexual labor and the coping strategies she devises in order to do this work. All these strategies suggest the shame Olivia herself attaches to sex work.

Scholarship on sex work acknowledges geographic distancing as one dis-associative strategy deployed by the laborers. John K. Anarfi's ethnography on Ghanian female sex workers in the Ivory Coast, for example, usefully links the question of distance to respectability. He documents that "to ensure a later life of marriage, business ownership and respectability in one's area of origin, it is necessary that the transient period as a prostitute be spent far away" (111). He also records sex workers' subjective response in viewing themselves as deviants and unworthy of going to church, which makes vis-ible the link between this labor choice and mental and spiritual well-being. In response to their moral angst, Anarfi reports that churches have sprung up to meet the psychological and spiritual needs of these women and, not coincidentally, the entrepreneurial pursuits of male capitalists (112). Show-ing the importance of cultural distance, his ethnography illustrates the seri-ous constraints of engaging in sex work: that men from other cultures are more desirable clients; that how one is viewed back home still matters to the psychic lives of sex workers; and finally, that off the job, these women wrestle with their spiritual lives. Emphasizing the active and even contradic-tory ways women navigate this labor choice underscores the complexity of interior lives and its attending vulnerabilities.

In Olivia's case, clearly the agent knew that distance from home would be crucial for her to even entertain this line of work once she really understood what she had signed up to do. The fact that these male clients too would remain at a distance after their vacation was also crucial: "She allowed the licking, kissing scratching. As long as she knew that once it was over she never had to see them again; that they were going away to Europa, far far away" (58). That geographic and psychic distancing were central shows that work does impact Olivia's sense of self and that she has to steel herself from the various acts of sexual-economic transactions. While she tries to find strategies of distancing, Olivia confirms Schultz's claim that "as human beings, we are not purely instrumental, and we cannot easily compartmen-talize the selves we learn to become during working hours" (1890). The self that Olivia becomes during work hours disassociates. Furthermore, she relies on the fact that sex will be a chance encounter with a stranger whom she will never have to see again. The novel makes readers privy to how she processes herself after engaging in this line of work and how she grapples with reemerging into "respectable" society.

Respectability becomes an important, if elusive and paradoxical, category for women. All women are sexually socialized into a hierarchical continuum of respectability and status based on sexual orientation, race, class, and nationality. As a social practice, rather than a legal mandate, respectability functions as nebulous social categorization upon which women are judged nonetheless. The novel pursues what happens when women willfully opt out of categories of respectability, and it suggests that this action often forecloses the ability to reenter. The intent here is not to essentialize respectability as a social value or identity that all women desire or aspire to but rather to show that respectability is generally a closed category into which it is often difficult to regain entrance once a woman has overtly shunned it. The desire for respectability cannot simply be dismissed as a bourgeois preoccupation or as buying into heteropatriarchy. Olivia, like other subaltern women and girls, wants room for such maneuvers and desires.

That Olivia worries about her respectability is clear when she asks Gorda, "What kind of woman do you think I am?" and when she tells her that she "prays for forgiveness for being the kind of woman who doesn't deserve God's mercy" (89, 75). Olivia's worrying over the meaning of respectable womanhood underscores the link between labor and her identity. That secrets, dissociations, and distancing are her coping strategies signals the link between work and subject formation. The novel's focus on the quotidian—especially day-to-day mental health—allows readers to see how Olivia manages her life as a sex worker and afterwards. The web of secrets and lies that both she and her family create is a fragile attempt to preserve her respectability, and while she tries to live behind the wall of her body, in the end she finds this body masking, or disassociation of mind and body, ineffective.

Olivia meets her future husband, Manolo, while she is engaged in sex work in Puerto Plato. He comes from New York in search of a local virgin. Their meeting is framed with mutual lies: informed that she is new to the trade and still maintains her virginity, he buys her for her virginity and her skin color (60); meanwhile, she does not disclose that she has been sexually involved with previous clients. That Olivia is unable to say what she has done and that they never confront this throughout their marriage, even though Manolo knows, implies that there is something unspeakable about her labor. It also highlights the difficulty of entering into a marriage union after engaging in sex work. Even if as feminists we applaud Olivia's sex work because it represents a step outside the bounds of heteronormativity, the subsequent heterosexual marital contract that she enters into illustrates the entrenchment of the heteropatriarchal gender system. This fact compels questions about the shelf life of sex workers; even if they resist heteronormativity during their tenure as sex workers, we have to address the subsequent repercussions. In fact, sex workers shore up, rather than challenge, middle-class notions of respectable womanhood.

With Manolo and Olivia, Cruz explores how a woman who has engaged in sex work finds and sustains a relationship, especially with a man from her own national culture. The visibility of racial difference in a marriage to a European almost already marks the union as concubinage and therefore an uplift from prostitution but not quite "respectable marriage." But within an intracultural marriage, racial signs do not visibly mark otherness, and the partners are left trying to pass for a "traditional" respectable couple, a performance that does not quite work. In the attempt to upgrade her from prostitution to marriage, Olivia lies and Manolo disavows. This necessity suggests that for many women and their male partners, reemergence into respectable society requires that they cover over a past labor history of sex work.

Olivia's youth and disenfranchised position and Manolo's maturity and U.S. papers structure the power dynamics in their relationship from the start. From their first meeting, Manolo actively seeks to control Olivia's body and limit her mobility: "He didn't let her speak in public. . . . He told Olivia how to wear her hair, the color to paint her nails and the way to swing her hips" (60). When he finds out that she is pregnant, she convinces him the unborn child is his; he then secures her a fake passport and an airplane ticket to New York. The uncertainty about Manolo's paternity would haunt their relationship. Engaging in sex work to provide for her children is a reason that the culture accepts for this particular labor choice. But in Olivia's case, Cruz presents readers with an unexpected but very likely outcome. What happens when one's sex work leads to pregnancy, and how is this managed?

In accepting the ticket and false passport, Olivia officially buys into a patriarchal pact, though from a constrained position. Showing physical signs of pregnancy, she cannot go back home, nor can she continue to work in that sex town. Marriage becomes the best barter she can negotiate. But in Manolo's mind, her acceptance gives him right of access to Olivia's body whenever he desires. She becomes his possession. He tests out this property right that first night: "[Olivia] didn't want to make love that night . . . but he entered her without asking. She was dry and it was painful" (76). This scene of subjection is instructive: in the context of working in a sex town, where women actively trade sex for the visa, Olivia processes the rape that night as the price of the ticket—the bodily trade for the visa. This first rape scene, which takes place when she is fifteen years old, in girlhood, becomes a central moment of subject formation and crucial to understanding Olivia's relationship to subsequent domestic and sexual violence in the novel. She believes that it is the price she now has to pay for engaging in this type of labor. Olivia provides a sharp contrast to the agential self-possessed sex worker. Popular culture and social scientific literature present these workers as exhibiting the ultimate act of self-possession in being able to sell their sexed bodies; we are therefore to understand this labor simply as a matter of commodity exchange. But these instances of sexual exchange become at once scenes of subjection and subject formation. Even as a trade for the visa, sex is not a completed service or performance but rather a continuous one; and the workers' "selves," by which I mean body *and* soul, are held as collateral to maintain this tenuous marriage status.

Olivia's process throughout the novel is to *undo* her identity as sex worker—and its repercussions—especially as she marries and moves to another country. In the laboriously static movement of the antiromance, this novel details the difficulty of such a process of unbecoming. Once they arrive in New York, Manolo continues to regulate Olivia's behavior, going so far as to take the "keys with him when he went to work." He instills fear in her by saying that "he didn't like her to be on the streets alone without him because it was unsafe" (149). Going a step further, I argue that Olivia suffers from battered-wife syndrome as she equates abuse with love: "That is how much Manolo loves me, so I won't forget, he leaves me marked" (123). "Sometimes after he hit her, she tried to seduce him. She thought it would help appease him" (150). We should remember that not only are Olivia and Manolo not officially married, and therefore there is no legal documentation of their union, but her passport is invalid. Thus, as an undocumented immigrant woman, Olivia is bound to Manolo; and she lives with the knowledge that she could be discovered and deported at any time. Manolo holds this precarious legal status over her. His various psychological ploys and physical abuse are attempts to erode her confidence in her ability not only to navigate the city on her own but also to navigate her sense of self-possession and agency.

One wonders why, since Olivia is in the United States, where there is active oppositio to domestic violence, she does not simply leave or report Manolo. But as a new immigrant woman without strong English-language skills, with limited mobility, and with a child, she remains dependent on Manolo. The legal theorist Kimberle Crenshaw points out the vulnerable position such women find themselves in as it relates to the law: "The Marriage Fraud Amendment to the 1986 Immigration Act states that a person who immigrated to the United States to marry a United States citizen or permanent resident had to remain 'properly' married for two years before applying for permanent resident status, at which time applications for the immigrant's permanent status were required by both spouses." With such strictures, says Crenshaw, many women fear deportation: "When faced with the choice between protection from their batterers or protection against deportation, many immigrant women chose the latter" (1247). She goes on to note that as a result of advocacy work, the Immigration Act of 1990 allows for "an explicit waiver for hardship caused by domestic violence" (1247). Olivia's marriage is thus a fraud on two counts: because of the domestic-violence legislation and because she and Manolo do not have legal papers.

Here two kinds of law—the law of the United States state and the law of her husband—limit her actions and destroy her sense of empowerment.

Olivia is literally trapped between two states. The Dominican Republic values the remittance dollars that women like her send back home, relieving the state of the onus of providing for them; however, it would have little to offer Olivia if she returned, especially as a deportee.[4] Similarly, U.S.-based corporations value her cheap labor in cleaning and maintaining their office buildings, but the larger public discourse decries that these illegal immigrants drain state's resources and abuse tax payers' hard-earned dollars in their bid to seek social services.

Without strong English-language skills, Olivia has little access to support systems outside her immediate family and community of Washington Heights. To compound the situation, women in her ethnic enclave perceive her life with Manolo as relatively privileged: "Olivia's life was not so bad, they say. She had a good husband who paid her rent until the day he died" (175). Again the public sees that she is housed and values the husband as a financial provider. This community response evinces the reproduction of patriarchy beyond national borders. Within the walls of their home, scenes of physical and psychological abuse, disrespect and infidelity, take place every day. From these scenes we get a more nuanced picture of how transnationalism is lived by such immigrant women and the difficulty of undoing one's identity as a sex worker. With Olivia's story, Cruz offers an antiromantic perspective on what it means to sell sex for a visa: Olivia's innocence is violently lost, her romantic quest is thwarted, and she lives an unsatisfying life at home and in the diaspora.

Narrating the Antiromance of Sexual Citizenship

One of the extreme ways in which Olivia reacts to the violence of her circumscribed condition in New York is to push her husband to his death. In the face of spousal abuse, and lacking family, community, or institutional support, Olivia kills her husband to ensure her safety, and Soledad quietly acts as a passive accomplice, since what she has learned from her mother about intimacy is that only extreme measures will guarantee her survival.

Manolo's death was supposed to rid Olivia and her family of the secrets of her past life and present abuse, yet by not confronting the truth, they continue to be haunted. Soledad, Olivia, and Gorda all feel responsible for Manolo's death, and in their supernatural world Manolo comes back to haunt their bodies and spirits. While Gorda could do nothing to stop the spousal abuse, she performed rituals to drain his spirit and "prayed every night to Santa Altagracia" for his death (142–43). Yet, when Soledad tries to speak to her aunt about her personal trauma resulting from her father's death, "Gorda covers [her] mouth with her hands and pretends the words were never spoken . . . shhing her every time she tried to speak" (144). This silencing becomes their active way of trying to avoid—unsuccessfully—their psychic and bodily pain. Other incidents of sexual abuse in the novel remain unspoken: in addition to Olivia's physical and sexual abuse, Soledad too has suffered sexual violence at the hands of Manolo, but she speaks of it to no one.

If this violation is unspeakable for Soledad, the novel is also quiet in its narration, since the scene in which Manolo sexually abuses her literally appears just pages before the novel's end. This strategy is intended to mark the commonplace nature of such violence and how a young girl like Soledad, with a family in chaos, might have no forum in which to express her violation. I quote Cruz at length from an interview with Silvio Torres-Saillant:

> I think there are things we really don't talk about, but so many of the women I know have been sexually abused. We all look like we're ok, we are not going around crying every five minutes "I was sexually abused," *but it's still part of our every day life that we know it happened.* I felt with Soledad it would be more powerful to show it that way instead of making it "the thing." Imagine this girl, on top of everything she has to deal with, she also has that, but she can't even deal with that because there's all this other stuff going on. I think in some ways by not making it the central part, it makes her less special since, in truth, *she is not an exception.* (Cruz, "Writing has to be Generous" 124, emphasis added)

Cruz notes that her writing style here is deliberate. While she wants to deal with the sexual violence that is not talked about, she does not want to make it "the thing." Like her mother, Soledad suffers in silence and isolation. She has no one with whom to share her story. Her mother is consumed with her own crisis, and her best friend, Caramel, has a bohemian nationalist vision of the Latino/a experience that does not allow the narration of compromising narratives. As a result, both Olivia's and Soledad's bodies archive unspeakably violent sexual incidents. The novel is at pains to show that this trauma gets no proper hearing or redress; instead, it leads to depression and other mental and physical distress.

With no outlet for expression, when the net result of everything takes its toll on Olivia, she spirals into a deep depression, which is the state she is in when readers first meet her, in the opening pages of the novel. Several factors lead to Olivia's depression: pressure to marry someone she does not love in order to provide her family with U.S. visas; unintended sex work; an unplanned pregnancy and uncertainty about the child's father; lying to get Manolo to marry her and take her to the United States; managing a marriage based on lies; suffering from domestic and sexual abuse; and finally, trying to manage a relationship with a daughter who reminds her of a past life she detests. Recognizing that she has been using her body as a wall to keep out the world, while internally "rotting inside" (118), Olivia withdraws into her self-protective shell. In one grand gesture, she shuts down: "I am tired of being afraid of hiding inside an apartment with gates so the burglars won't come in. I am tired of letting what other people think of me, or will discover about me, control my life. I am tired" (231). This statement shows that she has not only internalized Manolo's attempts to make her fearful of the world outside of her immediate community but also carefully guarded the secret of her prior life. The recurring memories of her sex work, her guarded secrets, and their repercussion finally lead to Olivia's emotional coma, or depression.

It is in this depressive state that Olivia begins the process of sexual denaturalization, as she grapples with the difficulty of rescuing her identity from her sexual labor. This unlearning is painful, especially as it is managed without professional help. Yet the novel encourages readers to understand Olivia's going "to sleep" as a pivotal agential act, since she is exercising "the courage to regress" in a culture where for women especially "it's a luxury to lie in bed and be taken care of" (66). While she is in this restful state, both Olivia and her family have to put the pieces of her life together. Entering into a state of depression is Olivia's way of confronting and breaking the lie, a lie that her family perceived as so ugly that they could not talk about it. Confronting the lie is the first step toward enabling her to narrate her story. I want to be careful, however, not to celebrate depression as a mere act of resistance. Olivia's depression is a resigned attempt to seek intervention. Pointedly, the novel, which opened with Olivia's depression, does not rush to a felicitous resolution. Instead, it slowly chronicles how her mental state impacts and disrupts the entire family and the various strategies they deploy.

It is while Olivia is in this comatose state that Soledad discovers her mother's past and is finally able to understand the emotional barriers that contributed to their failure to bond with each other. This attention to how children fare in the aftermath of their mother's labor shows that bodies bear archival memories that cannot be erased by simple geographic relocation. Cruz's novel provides an exploration of how trauma experienced in the homeland impacts the mother-child dynamic abroad. Soledad's body experiences and lives her mother's secrets. She says, "My skin is touched with every secret I've saved" (200). This internalization has limited her capacity for emotional connection to her own mother and to others, especially men. She is profoundly uncomfortable in her own skin, and in addition to sexual abuse, Soledad remembers Manolo's constant chiding—"She is your child"—as she was sent to the Dominican Republic "for months at a time" during the summer months (150). Olivia sent Soledad away "so the house would have less tension, be more peaceful. . . . When Soledad returned home, his outburst of rage started all over again" (150). Soledad says, "All my life I've wondered why I am the way I am . . . *mami always looked so unhappy, hiding and pretending to be so strong to save me from her pain.* It just made it worse. Every day, she pushed me farther away from her until she didn't have to push anymore. I just left" (216, emphasis added). Soledad began to plot her escape from this dysfunctional setting to her own invented stability. Olivia's inability to connect with her daughter is connected to the shame of sex work, uncertainty about her child's paternity, and the pressures both situations put on her marital relationship.

In the process of cleaning her mother's apartment to rid the family of Manolo's haunting presence, Soledad makes a transformative archival discovery. Among the family documents Olivia has saved, Soledad finds Olivia's "old and worn" paperback romance novels, most of them in Spanish. "My mother likes love stories. Maybe she thinks love is romantic, like in these books. Maybe she thinks the man of her dreams will gallop up to Washington Heights on a horse and whisk her away" (202–3). The insertion of this first archival find—romance novels—ironically critiques the genre Cruz directly writes against. In a culture of telenovelas, this escapist romance—just like storybook renditions of "selling sex for the visa"—is unsustainable, and Olivia's life experiences serve as a direct foil.

Soledad then discovers three metal boxes, labeled "Manolo," "Olivia," and "Soledad." In her own box, Soledad finds everything from her birth certificate, a lock of her baby hair, and a baby tooth to her elementary-school diploma. Manolo's, in contrast, contains only his passport. But the real archival discovery is in Olivia's box: "a matchbook from a restaurant called Puerto Plato Disco" and a notebook listing men by date (May 17–June 14), by nationality (German, French, Greek, blond American, Black American, Chinese Cuban, Argentinean, Italian, and Swiss), and by physical characteristics (drunk, cute but small, skinny, pretty, ugly teeth). The final entry, dated June 14, reads simply "Manolo." Soledad reads the list slowly and aloud; she pictures each man and comes to realize her mother's secret prior life as a sex worker. With a twist of magical realism, and unbeknownst to Soledad, in naming all these men out loud she effectively conjures all the clients her mother slept with, so that they literally appear "all naked, penises exposed con much confianza," in the living room of their Washington Heights apartment (205). For weeks Soledad lives with these men, carefully scrutinizing their features in order to discover her paternity. With Gorda's help, she gradually realizes the futility of such an endeavor and focuses instead on trying to find herself, her mother, and the context that produced them both.

Uncertain Futures

The final lesson of the novel has to do with mother-daughter bonding. It is not the heterosexual love plot that needs to be resolved. In Soledad's first attempt at rewriting her diasporic romance, she replaces what she perceives as her dysfunctional family and failed mother with the alternative art-house spaces and bohemian communities. Yet, if Soledad and Olivia are to reach individual wholeness, they must first learn from, and lean on, each other. Again Cruz comments: "Soledad and Olivia are almost the same person. It's like a cycle and the fact that one wakes up and the other sleeps sort of shows two facets of their experience. I see one side of Soledad dying and a new side being born. It's like the ultimate *limpieza* to me, with her falling into the lake and Olivia now getting a chance to being listened to" ("Writing has to be Generous" 125). Soledad and her mother have to become mutually dependent. Rather than her aunt, Gorda, or her grandmother, Dona Sosa, it is Soledad who takes her mother back to the Dominican Republic. In the course of the trip home for the cleansing, Olivia has to return to, or experience, the physical site of Puerto Plato. In this way, Olivia goes back to the physical space where she lost her childhood innocence to sex work but gained her only child.

In the final scene of ritual cleansing by water, Soledad actively confronts her fate as she immerses herself in the water and struggles against drowning. Hearing her mother's scream jolts Soledad out of her own catatonic state and enables her reemergence from the water. While Olivia was mute for the majority of the novel, this primal scream gives birth to her voice once again. She can now narrate what she previously rendered unnarratable because of her own feelings of guilt and shame. "When I open my eyes," says Soledad, "my mother is holding me. . . . I want to ask her so many questions about my father, her past, my birth. But before I even open my mouth, *she speaks,* as if all this time she has been listening, reading my mind, waiting to tell me the things I want to hear" (237, emphasis added). By revealing herself and the sexual past she tried to repress, Olivia opens the possibility of establishing a meaningful relationship with her daughter. Soledad no longer rejects her maternal line. For Olivia, this return home with her daughter breaks the grip that her past work had on her.

This potential reconciliation between mother and daughter holds out hope for future understanding, even while it remains open ended. The novel provides readers with an *antiromantic* story about the psychic and physical cost of sex work and its transgenerational impact, but it is not simply a cautionary tale. Cruz narrates this story against stereotypical representations that position young Dominican females as "hot Latina women" even though they live in homes and communities where women censor talk about sex and sexuality. Cruz nuances discussions about sexual agency within the sex-work industry by acknowledging that for many subaltern teenagers and young women it is a labor choice made out of economic necessity rather than in response to a career desire.

Angie Cruz's *Soledad* offers a window on the affective terrain. Its portrayal of the characters' interiority and the motivations and feelings behind their actions captures the effect sexual labor has on women's overall sense of well-being.[5] Such representations can help us understand the complex continuum between agency and domination. They can also help us connect emotional well-being to our feminist theorizing of labor to include the public and private domains, as well as women's physical, mental, spiritual, emotional, and aspirational well-being. In offering literature as a site that explores interior lives and the sexual dynamics of this particular story, I am by no means suggesting that fictional characters are exemplars of real people or that fiction can serve as an exemplar for the social sciences. Rather, I invoke Michel-Rolph Troullot's assertion that we should look at the multiple locations and actors who make history, since no one discipline is the sole participant in the production of history (*Silencing the Past* 25). What I am suggesting, therefore, is that literature adds affective nuances; in this way, it complements our feminist investigations of complex social issues, especially as they pertain to women's sexuality. Literature potentially offers "novel insights" that can help us attend "not only to the women's words but also to their bodies and actions as texts to be interpreted" (Red Thread Women's Development Programme 285).

Notes

1. Several critics engage the romance genre's ideological link to various colonial and national projects. Particularly helpful is Doris Sommer's analysis in *Foundational Fictions* of how nineteenth-century Latin American novels represented nonviolent consolidation through the heterosexual love plot and thus served as foundational fictions in the history of that region's nation building.

2. Arguments for the legalization of sex work and for unionizing sex workers make good sense, but they are not my specific interest here. Instead, I am trying to make sense of sex workers in the context of inequalities between the first and third worlds.

3. Brennan builds on five terms used by Arjun Appadurai—*ethnoscapes, mediascapes, technoscapes, finanscapes,* and *ideoscapes*—to explain the critical role the social imaginary plays in processes of contemporary globalization.

4. The film *My American Girls* has a scene in which the mother returns to the Dominican Republic with food to distribute to members of the local community.

5. How the dynamic of masculinity plays on male sex workers is also worthy of exploration.

Diasporic Citizenship

Against the Rules of Blackness

Hilton Als's *The Women* and Jamaica Kincaid's *My Brother* (Or How to Raise Black Queer Kids)

Rinaldo Walcott

THE TITLE of this essay pays homage in part to Eve Kosofsky Sedgwick's 1991 essay "How to Bring Your Kids Up Gay." Sedgwick's essay is a reading of revisionary psychoanalysis and psychiatry in the post–DSM III excision of homosexuality as pathology. She argues that the attempt to normalize adult homosexual bodies is simultaneously an attempt to render gay bodies not present, and she suggests that this is done through an attempt to pathologize youthful sexualities. Sedgwick's critique of "the new psychiatry of gay acceptance" (23) is cautioned by her readings of medical discourses on gender-disordered youth or youth who might be gay. The result of her against-the-rules reading and interpretation is the difficult knowledge that post–DSM III medical discourse finds so-called gender-disordered youth to be abnormal and in need of repair or fixing, even in the era of adult gay recognition.

Thus Sedgwick's reading goes against the commonsensical rules of contemporary understandings, which now appear to assume that there is such a thing as a "normal" and "proper" gay and lesbian body and thus person. The implications of her interpretation are important for making sense of the discomfort with contemporary gay and lesbian bodies and persons that continues nonetheless.

For my purposes, such a reading by Sedgwick opens up both the presence and the absence of queer discourses and subjects within the context of black diaspora discourses. Queer discourses in black diaspora studies remain against the rules, out-of-order utterances that trouble the borders of the "normal" and "proper" black body. That "normal" and "proper" black body is an imagined heterosexual black body. But the absent/present dyad that exists in black diaspora studies does not and cannot entirely eliminate what we might tentatively call a black queer diaspora. However, some of us have ventured to consider how such a black queer diaspora comes into being. Or as Sedgwick puts it in a different but related context, "There is no unthreatened, unthreatening theoretical home for a concept of gay and lesbian origins" (26).

In this essay I pursue the absented presence of a black queer body through readings of Hilton Als's *The Women* and Jamaica Kincaid's *My Brother*. These two nonfiction texts interestingly intersect with concerns around mothering, queer sexualities, and diaspora circuits and might be said to elliptically probe "black gay origins." Importantly, these two texts might be read as against the rules of blackness because of the ways in which they attempt to "normalize" queer sexualities within blackness. By this I mean that these texts write against a heterosexual mythic blackness that, when confronted with the evidence of black queers, crumbles miserably in the face of its sexual other. I read these texts as against the rules of blackness because, as Robert Reid-Pharr states, writing about Gary Fisher, "The black gay man is then an object of attack not because he represents that which is horrid but because he represents one location at which the possibility of choosing one's identity (even within the most oppressive conditions) becomes palpable" (*Black Gay Man* 16). The absented presence of the black queer body, then, is so because such a body represents a counter to the desired respectability of the heterosexual black body. Both *The Women* and *My Brother* are about much more than I read them for, but it is important to note that both texts were published at the height of the Afrocentric debates and both ignore such debates to offer us a different view of blackness. I bring all those conversations into collision.

In what follows I attempt to trouble the discourse of black mothering, both actual and symbolic, within diasporic discourse. I do so as heroic black motherhood encounters youthful queer sexualities that exist within and against blackness. Black mothers are endowed with the responsibilities of raising black heterosexual children. But how might we make sense of the context when they fail to produce the proper black subject? I respond to the interconnected discourses of heroic black motherhood postulated by Afrocentrism and the role of Mother Africa contained in such postulations. In particular, I see a link between Afrocentric discourses of motherhood and the veneration of Mother Africa. Significantly such venerations become problematic in the face of queer sexualities, especially for boys, who in such discourses must be considered as less than men. Therefore, I turn to queer theory to marshal an argument of living black queerness *as if*. Queer life is an essential element of blackness constituted both by its insistence on realizing itself and by discourses that seek to render it not present, which in fact work to acknowledge its presence. To demonstrate the *as if* of black queer life, I turn to Hilton Als and Jamaica Kincaid, who retrospectively show how queer childhoods are an essential element of blackness. Recalling such childhoods from the place of adulthood complicates calls for thinking differently about black motherhood and ultimately Mother Africa. Does black motherhood fail when queer kids appear? Can normative notions of black motherhood account for black mothers' rearing of black queer kids? Further, I suggest and show that some discourses of blackness make such a possibility a problem for black mothering. Thus, discourses of black mothering in normative narratives refuse the possibility of queer childhoods. This essay refutes such claims.

Sedgwick's essay challenges us to conceive of social, cultural, and medical discourses that would allow for the healthy rearing of gay youth. She wants an "erotically invested affirmation of many people's felt desire or need that there be gay people in the immediate world" (26). At the least, such a challenge takes queerness outside of the pathologizing discourse of its medicalization in terms of so-called youth gender disorders, which Sedgwick suggests are mainly targeted at boys. Instead we are faced with other kinds of questions.

Both *My Brother* and *The Women* revisit youthful sexualities. I suggest that by refusing to justify black homosexuality, these texts place the origins of black homosexuality in some relief, thus making homosexuality an immediate given. In both texts the category of the child is a category to be troubled, as the child becomes an adult who lives a life outside the boundaries or rules of normative blackness and preconceived standards of sexuality and sexual practice.

More generally in the context of black diasporic discourse, homosexuality and therefore queer identities continue to be contested terrain. Afrocentric thinkers such as Francis Cress Welsing and Molefi Asante have argued that homosexuality among black people is a learned European behavior. Asante wrote:

> Homosexuality is a deviation from Afrocentric thought because it makes the person evaluate his own physical needs above the teachings of national consciousness. An outburst of homosexuality among black men, fed by the prison breeding system, threatens to distort the relationship between friends. . . . We must demonstrate a real antagonism toward those gays who are as unconscious as other people. (57)

And further:

> The rise of homosexuality in the African-American male's psyche is real and complicated. An Afrocentric perspective recognizes its existence but homosexuality cannot be condoned or accepted as good for the national development of a strong people. . . . We can no longer allow our lives to be controlled by European decadence. . . . All brothers who are homosexuals should know that they too can become committed to the collective will. . . . The homosexual shall find the

redemptive power of Afrocentricity to be the magnet which pulls him back to his center. (57–58)

Those on the other side of the argument have sought to demonstrate that homosexuality is as African as many other cultural retentions and practices that characterize black diasporic life. I am not interested in those valences of the argument from either side. I am interested instead in the metaphor of diaspora as family and kin and what that means when we must account for living with queers *as if*. Such a claim places motherhood as central, since motherhood is essential to kinship discourses.

Homosexuality exists among people of the black diaspora, and that is what I want to probe—not its origins, but what might be a necessary ethical stance to bring to the rearing of black queer youth. I want to probe the ways in which two authors writing memoir or (auto)biography figure queer sexualities in their texts. I am interested in a diaspora ethics and discourse that can move beyond the theme of toleration of same-sex desire to a place where, to slightly rephrase Sedgwick, an erotically invested queer blackness might be possible. Als's *The Women* and Kincaid's *My Brother* opens up the possibility of an erotically invested queer blackness in very different ways, and each author makes present, following Sedgwick, a "haunting abject" of black sexuality.

Als articulates a notion of black women, especially mothers, that he calls the "Negress." He states that "the Negress has come to mean many things" (6). Among these things are selflessness, welfare and social-assistance recipient, good neighbor, godly, depressed, bearing many children, sexless, lacking in mental capacities but emotional, and a host of other qualities that both contradict and supplement the construction of the black woman as other, especially the black mother. Als is most explicit in his desire to write against the rules of normative blackness in his discussion of black female representation but also in debate with and against black women.

Als not only launches a particular critique of U.S. social constructions of black women; he also launches a critique of some black feminists' positions. In fact, Als problematically claims that black feminists, especially novelists like Toni Morrison, need and in fact reproduce the Negress as a significant feature of what he terms their angry and sympathy-seeking literature, a practice that he finds at the least troubling. And yet Als offers us something quite complex in his trope of the Negress when he states: "I have expressed my Negressity by living, fully, the prescribed life of an auntie man—what Barbadians call a faggot" (9). He continues:

> [This] is a form of kinship, given that my being an auntie man is based on greed
> for romantic love with men temperamentally not unlike the men my mother

knew—that and an unremitting public "niceness." I socialized myself as an auntie man long before I committed my first act as one. I also wore my mother's and sister's clothes when they were not home; those clothes deflected from the pressure I felt in being different from them. As a child, this difference was too much for me to take; I buried myself in their clothes, their secrets, their desires, to find myself through them. (9)

Als recognizes his Negressity from childhood; and his mother and sisters found his Negressity disturbing, to say the least. This is the point that Sedgwick sets out to make when she writes that "the wish for the dignified treatment of already-gay people" (26) is threatened by the discourses and practices of revisionist psychoanalysis and psychiatry, which treats childhood queer expressions as pathological. Als's mother and sisters operated on the assumption of queer pathology. But as Als writes poignantly about his childhood, "Being an auntie man enamored of Negressity is all I have ever known how to be. I do not know what my life *would* be, or if it would be at all, if I were any different" (9, emphasis in original). Such a sentiment is a strike against a normative and proper heterosexual blackness. Such a claim exists within and against blackness, since Als is always already gay and black.

Als presents us with the problem of how to ethically take up the relation of the queer child to its mother. A mother that is both hated and loved simultaneously. Melanie Klein's insights on child individuation can help us make sense of Als's emotions. His working through of his sexuality and his recognition of his Negressity, even when he remains ambivalent to it, are not unlike Klein's conception of reparation. Reparation can be understood in its simplest form as the relation of love, guilt, and hate that the child must hold toward its mother in order to eventually individuate. The work of reparation, then, is to redirect guilt for destruction and separation or hate felt toward the central figure of the mother to the difficult task and work of loving her again. For the work of reparation to begin, one must acknowledge that something has been destroyed or would be destroyed. And in Klein's view, the work of separation is the work of the infant.

Reparation therefore becomes the means through which guilt is reduced and displaced, making the possibility to love at the moment of separation possible and even evident. It is in its capacity to find love for the mother even in the most trying circumstances that Als's *The Women* is an homage to women of various sorts: his mother, the first Negress in his life; Dorothy Dean, a very interesting pre-Stonewall "fag hag" who organized the social calendars of some of New York's most prominent and influential white gay men; and Owen Dodson, an important figure of the Harlem Renaissance. In addition to reading Als against himself, the work is an homage to the black feminists he feels compelled to engage and critique. We are then left with the question, Is Negressity a form and expression of love?

Finally, Als's contradictory identification with the Negress and his taking on of an aspect of her identity—"romantic love with men temperamentally not unlike the men my mother knew" (9)—might be understood as positing the argument that Als is suggesting a different take on queer normativity. In this version of queerness, Negressity is not a malady in need of treatment but a state of being that requires a space for a more active acknowledgment.

Als ups the ante on readers in his discussion of his cross-generational affair with his mentor, Owen Dodson, whom he met when he was thirteen, writing: "I was nineteen the last time we allowed this intimacy to happen between us. I was nineteen when I left him forever" (144). The intimacy and mutual sharing of this cross-generational relationship raise many questions concerning how to bring kids up queer and black.

REMEMBERING HIS childhood from the place of adulthood, Als addresses the crisis language of role modeling, denying that Dodson was a role model or father figure to him. And then Als offers us something more to think about. Warren Crichlow has pointed out that much role-modeling discourse is premised upon a pathologizing of blackness and black people. It is accessing what the something more of Als is that I am attempting to define. I suggest that the something more is a profound critique of black diaspora normative claims of heterosexual kinship. However, I want to tentatively state that that something more might be merely how to make queer kids, to borrow from Alexander Doty's title, perfectly queer. Als writes: "One sister in particular (the one most like me) criticized our relationship beyond recognition. She said: 'He's turning my brother into a faggot.' I remember how I tried to avoid my sister's scorn by not speaking of Owen, and how often I saw him, how often the dust floated around our joined lips" (142). Als's refusal to situate his sexual and other desires within any frames of normativity or respectability opens up for consideration ethical concerns. His refusal to make sense of himself as anything but a Negress is crucial for thinking about the ethical imperatives of his claims and insights. And whenever ethical concerns arise, rules are at stake.

In speaking of ethical concerns, I mean to signal a complex web of concerns that speak to the context in which black queer sexualities might be conceived as belonging within the category of blackness. Michel de Certeau writes of ethics, "With ethics, social practice becomes the area in relation to which a theory of behaviors can be elaborated" (149). I am convinced of de Certeau's formulation of ethics as "a theory of behaviors," because embedded in such a formulation is a theory of relationality and relation.

Social relationality requires an ethical dispensation, that is, a behavior that recognizes our responsible relation one to another. What that looks like is always in the process of being revealed. Both Als and Kincaid open up the concern of our responsible relation to one another on the terms both of sexuality and sexual practice and of kin and community. The ethical always pushes toward a something more that is awaiting revelation in the form of social behavior and conduct but can never fully utter its end point, for there is no end point in the realm of the ethical; there is only ongoing social relationality and responsibility.

Thus, the something more of Als's account that we must contend with is this: "It is only now that I attempt to let slip past the identity they have established for me, as their younger sister, and into a narrative that, even as I write, rejects my intellection, my control, because I betrayed its central character so long ago: Owen. Back then, I did not say to my mother and sisters: I am already a faggot" (142–43). Such an account requires more than the nature/nurture debate can offer. Such an account takes us into the Foucauldian realm of care of the self and an ethics for living. Such an account requires us to think differently about childhood. I shall return to this later. But Als's account requires ethical thought. It requires that normativity in any guise be questioned or at least seriously grappled with. It requires that we take the child's utterance seriously, if only in retrospect.

Jamaica Kincaid's brother died the year *The Women* was published. Kincaid's *My Brother* comes to the issues or tensions discussed above from another place. In her impressionistic memoir of her brother, who died of HIV/AIDS, the ubiquitous evil/loving mother haunts each scene. Anyone familiar with Kincaid's fiction or nonfiction knows that mothers, and her mother in particular, always represent a certain "problem-space" within her texts (D. Scott). There is no sentimentality for her mother or for mothers in general. *My Brother* is no different in those terms, except that one might argue that the representation of the mother this time around creates a bit more space for seeing other sides of her. For example, Kincaid makes clear in the text that her mother felt that it was her duty to look after her dying son, to move him into her home from his shack in the back of her house, and to care for him every day when he was in the dilapidated hospital ward in Antigua. Yet Kincaid still faults her mother for inhibiting her children's growth. This critique of her mother is evidently in conversation with Kincaid's anxieties about her role as a mother to her own children, whom she must leave in Vermont when she takes the HIV drug AZT to her brother in Antigua; and, she tells us, she sometimes prefers a book to children. Thus childhood, like mothers, is a general and troubling problem for Kincaid.

Kincaid's brother died of HIV/AIDS in Antigua in 1996. After she made many trips to Antigua to deliver AZT to him, his health improved for a while and then faltered again. As his health improved, so did his desire for sex. In her book, Kincaid remembers that at the time of her brother's death she could not write about him, because "I could not think about him in a purposeful way" (91). Yet she gives us a memoir to help us think about his life and its broader implications in a purposeful way. It is the purposefulness of *My Brother* that I pursue in this essay.

Kincaid learned of her brother's sexuality, or rather the secret of her brother's sexuality, not in Antigua, where he lived his whole life, but while she was on a trip to Chicago promoting one of her new books after his death. On that trip Kincaid encountered a woman who remembered her from an HIV/AIDS workshop in Antigua, and it was she who revealed evidence of her brother's sexuality to Kincaid. The revelatory passage in her book orients much of what I have to say here:

> And then she said that she had been a lesbian woman living in Antigua and how deeply sad it made her to see the scorn and derision heaped on the homosexual man; homosexual men had no place to go in Antigua, she said, no place to simply meet and be with each other and not be afraid; and so she had opened up her home and made it known that every Sunday men who loved other men could come to her house in the afternoon and enjoy each other's company. My brother, she said, was a frequent visitor to her house, a safe place to be with each other; and my brother who had just died was often at her house, not as a spectator of homosexual life but as a participant in homosexual life. (161)

Up until that point Kincaid had every reason, she tells us, to believe that her brother was heterosexual. Kincaid's claim lies somewhere in what Samuel Delany might call "the margin between the claims of truth and the claims of textuality" (28). It is with sadness that she writes:

> He has died without ever understanding or knowing, or being able to let the world in which he lived know, who he was; that who he really was—he could not express fully: his fear of being laughed at, his fear of meeting with scorn of the people he knew best were overwhelming and he could not live with it all openly. (162)

Kincaid knows all too well what revealing his nonheterosexuality to everyone would have meant for her brother in Antigua. At stake were a care of self and an ethics of living conditioned by a community's inability to do more than repress and punish attractions other than opposite-sex ones. Kincaid's brother continued to pursue opposite-sex attractions even when he was forced to acknowledge his HIV/AIDS status. His own deep refusal, on some level, of the complexities of his sexual practices was part of the "problem-space" of an ethics of living *as if*. His own refusal of sexual and diseased categories also made the rules of sexuality and illness a difficult context for ethical consideration.

The question of mothering is played out in a context much larger than that of how we understand mothering. I therefore suggest that at stake are the question of kin and kinship and the larger question of family. In fact, I want to suggest that part of the problem of black diaspora Afrocentric discourse is that the discourse of family is too bound up with it. Kincaid gives us an example from the first person in Antigua to publicly acknowledge his HIV status, a man named Freeston. Freeston made his seropositive status public in an effort to perform a public service. Kincaid recalls a visit with him:

> One day I was visiting with him and we were sitting on the gallery of his mother's house, a group of older school boys passed by and they called him an auntie-man and in other ways referred to his homosexuality, using vicious language; they were a chorus of intimidation, of scorn, of ignorance. Freeston was too ill to be upset, he was quite used to it. . . . His mother came from that generation of Antiguan women (older, around my mother's age or older) who did not know of homosexuality, or any kind of sexuality. To say that he was gay or homosexual was something he said about himself; to say that he was an auntie-man was something people said about him. She understood him better when he was the person people said something about, not when he was the person who said something about himself. (147)

Kincaid makes clear the link between family, community, and the "thing that dare not speak its name"—homosexuality. The above passage demonstrates the inability of the structure of family to work without the structure of community naming. Community thus takes on a kind of mothering role, in this case the role of the evil mother, for this is not a mother that allows a healthy separation from her. She must brutalize before the separation occurs. This is not a heroic mother figure. The Kleinian bad-breast theory becomes applicable here. Community in this sense is unable to allow for a kind of erotically invested sexuality not marked as heterosexual; not even his biological mother can identify with Freeston. This inability to recognize Freeston or to recognize him except as an insult places him against the rules of blackness: his existence is outside assumed normative blackness.

Kincaid continues, nonetheless complexifying mothering: "But whatever people said about him, whatever he said about himself, it did not matter to his mother; she took care of him, he lived with her in a house with a beautiful garden full of zinnias and cosmos and some impatiens and all sorts of shrubs and with glossy and variegated leaves. She was so different from my brother's mother" (147). Although Freeston's mother is the antithesis of Kincaid's, she is still bound by community standards as she tries to make sense of her son. It is this larger question of community as mother that I finally turn to.

I want to make at least three points by way of three different theorists. In 1983 Cheryl Clarke wrote an essay titled "The Failure to Transform: Homophobia in the Black Community," in which she predicted the limitations of any black revolution in the United States because it would fail to acknowledge the complexities and diversities of black sexualities, especially lesbian and gay sexualities.

Some thirteen years later, in his essay titled "Decolonisation and Disappointment: Reading Fanon's Sexual Politics," Kobena Mercer, following Clarke, argued that sexual politics remained "the Achilles heel of black liberation" (116). What these two essays share is the theme, and emotion, of disappointment, but disappointment as the ground upon which a more hopeful politics might be desired. These essays also share a desire for liberation so that life can be lived *as if.* Embedded in both arguments is a tacit acknowledgment of family or at least kin, as well as a larger and more important discourse of community. Both essays also offer a critique of some forms of black nationalism as it morphs into the Afrocentrism of the late 1980s to mid-1990s, in which I am particularly interested here.

Reading Clarke and Mercer alongside Klein, I want to consider some political resonances of mothering in order to tease out other aspects of the Achilles heel of black diaspora desires and antagonisms. A major part of the problem with discourses of blackness in the black diaspora can only be worked out by working through the difficult and unrelenting relationship of diasporic subjects to Mother Africa. In this regard I want to suggest that until black diasporans make reparation with Mother Africa, the local contexts of mothering, not to mention myriad other relations, will remain deeply fraught. Making reparation with Mother Africa requires a healthy separation so that something of the New World black might be revealed.

Stuart Hall has identified at least two different versions of black diasporic identity that inform this condition. The possibility of such reparation is only evident when the latter of the two versions of cultural identity and diaspora that Stuart Hall identifies comes into play. Hall argues that the first version centers Africa and the enforced conditions of diaspora. In this version "Africa is the name of the missing term, the aporia, which lies at the center of our cultural identity and gives it a meaning which, until recently, it lacked." The discourse of "loss of identity" via the forced migration into slavery in the Americas opens up a discourse of healing that concerns itself with peeling away layers of oppression to arrive at the kind of core identity that is often articulated in Afrocentric thought (for example, by people like Welsing and Asante). On the other hand, a second way of thinking about identity acknowledges the intervention of history. This intervention of history can be, and is, the basis upon which a healthy separation might be achieved. Thus Hall cautions us that diaspora is also about departure and that departure does not merely signal origins, that is, Africa and having left it. Instead departure might signal "axes or vectors . . . the vectors of similarity and continuity; and the vectors of difference and rupture" ("Cultural Identity and Diaspora" 24). These vectors signal the more nuanced and complex facets of diasporic identities. Hall further states: "Diaspora identities are those which are constantly producing and reproducing themselves anew, through transformation and difference" (31).

I suggest that it is the second version of diasporic identity that allows for the making of reparation with Mother Africa. Furthermore, any return to Mother Africa for New World black peoples must simultaneously be a break with Africa as well. For many, this is to flaunt the rules of origin, to be against blackness, but I am interested in the attempt to come to terms with oneself as emblematic of what Paul Gilroy terms the "counterculture of modernity" (*Black Atlantic* 1). Such an understanding of blackness displaces conversations of origins in a certain and stable homeland in favor of thinking about origins as process and importantly embedded in the violent and traumatic making of the Americas. Here I am not suggesting that Africa is outside the modern. In fact, if we follow Valentine Mudimbe, any invocation of the term *Africa* suggests an invention of the modern. This effort to make reparation, then, is an attempt by New World blacks to work through their relation to the Americas. Working through their relation to the Americas cannot, then, be conditioned by a search for an authentic African sexuality but rather might concern itself with the "new" and recombined sexualities of the black diaspora—the second version of identity. Such an approach places Africa as one position within a narrative of the past and opens up other positions for identification as well. For example, one of those other positions might be the tragedy of HIV/AIDS as a basis for the formation of a black queer diaspora.

Constituting queer as a diaspora is problematic. As Alan Sinfield has argued, queers do not find one another because of a trauma that united them into a particular historical narrative that they might use as the basis for the making of community. Sinfield argues, and correctly so, that despite the numerous atrocities that some queers are exposed to on the occasion of coming out, these are not the kinds of trauma that make a diaspora. I think Sinfield's argument works better for Euro-American queers than it does for black diaspora queers. I have argued elsewhere that HIV/AIDS is a pandemic for which there is no outside, which means that we are all positioned in relation to it, whether or not we have sex (Walcott, "Queer Texts"). Thus, a black queer diaspora might exist as a kind of typology of desire as opposed to an empirical reality.

HIV/AIDS connects New World blacks to Africa in myriad ways, from the stereotypically racist representations of AIDS and its origins to planetary activist politics around its spread and treatment. I want to propose, therefore, that the fluidity of HIV/AIDS allows for a New World black disposition whereby identifications useful beyond the desire and insistence of homeland and/or origins discourse can produce some kind of common feeling or connectivity. In this sense New World black persons can model an identity or activate new identifications accessed cross-culturally in the Americas, where, Sylvia Wynter argues, "new forms of human life" come to be ("1492" 6); this is so even if it happens through the tragedy of the HIV/AIDS pandemic. But new forms of human life also suggest new relations of mothering and motherhood, in short, a new set of rules.

Both Hilton Als's *The Women* and Jamaica Kincaid's *My Brother* inaugurate New World black reparation, because both texts refuse the posture of representing black queer sexuality as a special effect in need of repair, especially in its youthful eruptions. Each text takes seriously the old adage "Rules are made to be broken" and breaks the rules of normativity, respectability, and assumed blackness. But even more importantly, both texts refuse to be surprised by black queerness. This is in fact the fundamental place where Sedgwick might say we can begin to live within a culture for which no explanation for queerness is necessary. But such a place is against the rules of the human as presently constituted. To offer no explanation for queerness, especially its childhood utterances, would be to live against the rules, for the rules require an explanation; to offer none is to invite questions, concerns, even violence.

I am ultimately suggesting that such a culture, *a black queer culture of as if,* is only possible when reparation is made both in terms of Mother Africa and in terms of actual black mothers both generally and locally. Both texts, I believe, attempt to make reparation and thus to enable separation and love for mothers locally. Diasporically, the general situation that requires a healthy break with Mother Africa is achieved not through the old-time black conservative tropes of hatred, shame, and denial of and for Africa, nor by Afrocentric glorification and veneration, but rather by affixing the place that Africa is called upon to play in all forms of black diaspora desires. Until that historical trauma is worked through or continually worked upon, any other discourses concerning mothering will remain troubling, indeed faulty, for diaspora black peoples; and young and other black queers will remain beyond and against the rules of the category black.

Francophone Caribbean Women Writers

Rethinking Identity, Sexuality, and Citizenship

Odile Cazenave

IN A NUMBER of recent articles, I have examined the implications of age, space, and gender for the postcolonial Francophone novel. Notably, in "Francophone Women Writers in France in the Nineties" I look at Francophone women authors and what it means to be writing a postcolonial novel within France—how Caribbean women writers in that instance have shifted their gaze, no longer necessarily directing it only toward the Antilles, and how some of the more recent narratives address the question of French Caribbeans living in the metropole and in the United States.

In "Écritures des sexualités dans le roman francophone au féminin" I analyze how Francophone women novelists write sexuality into the Francophone novel, in particular how writing of sexuality allows the Guadeloupeans Maryse Condé and Gisèle Pineau to recapture the missing genealogical link and reconstruct French Caribbean his/her/story. Finally, in "Le roman africain et antillais" I address the issue of political commitment for Francophone African and Caribbean women authors in the last fifteen years, looking at the textual strategies they may be using to rally political energy and express or resist the ways globalization affects postcolonial identities within the specific configuration of Francophone literatures and cultures.

In the present essay, I focus more specifically on the representations of sexuality and citizenship in Francophone Caribbean literature. Looking at the latest works by the Martinican Suzanne Dracius, the Guadeloupeans Gisèle Pineau and Maryse Condé, and the Haitian Marie-Célie Agnant, I address the issue of sexuality, identity, and citizenship in their narratives—how sexuality becomes a topos to express the ambiguities of a Francophone Caribbean identity; how each writer negotiates the tensions between the different possible poles of identity and their definitions of citizenship; how through sexuality they explore these different sites. I examine in particular how migration intersects with or affects the notion of identity and citizenship, how the mental or physical going back home in Condé's *Desirada* (1997) and *Histoire de la femme cannibale* (2003), in Agnant's *Le livre d'Emma* (2001), and in Pineau's *Chair Piment* (2002) pushes (or does not push) each protagonist to find new strengths within the Caribbean space.

As Carole Boyce Davies demonstrates in her introduction to *Black Women, Writing and Identity: Migrations of the Subject* (1994), the question of renegotiation of identity for the migrant protagonist is central to the narratives of black women writers. As I have shown in "Calixthe Beyala's Parisian Novels," this renegotiation operates along two axes: a geographic one (Africa/Europe) and a temporal one (yesterday/today). The success of the protagonist's transformation depends on the importance granted to one rather than the other parameter.

Black women's writing, Boyce Davies points out, must go through an initial phase of demystification of home, of the motherland and family. It is only then that the black woman writer will be able to redefine a new geography and her own individual identity. Once that stage has been reached, the writer must explore the contours of her new environment, including its new community and cultural components. The diasporic communities living in that new space must also be looked at, as its profile may have been modified.

These different concerns are at the core of several novels by French Caribbean women writers. Some, like Suzanne Dracius's *L'autre qui danse* (1989), focus on the issue of finding a place to fit in within French society, black Paris, or the Caribbean. Others focus on the dilemma of choice of space anchorage. The most recent ones add new trajectories to the initial journeys—from the island to Paris/the metropole, from the metropole to the African continent (and not necessarily restricted to Francophone countries), or from Paris/the metropole back to the Caribbean.

In the late eighties and early nineties, several French Caribbean novels addressed the issue of finding one's sense of identity by reconnecting with the home space (Warner-Vieyra, *Femmes échouées*). Dracius's *L'autre qui danse* is particularly representative of the dilemmas revolving around the issues of identity and citizenship. The novel offers a picture of the return to the island and raises the question of belonging for "Negropolitains" in either space, the Antilles or the metropole. The narration describes the mental and physical decentering of Rhevana, a young French Caribbean born in Paris who is in search of her historical and spiritual roots. After initially being attracted by the Son of Agar's community and the illusory dream of precolonial Africa,[1] she eventually follows her Martinican lover to the island, hoping to (re)connect with a Caribbean identity. Her experience soon turns into a nightmare: with no money, pregnant, beaten by her lover, unable to even feed her baby, she borrows money from her sister to fly back to Paris. While her sister illustrates successful integration into French society, Rhevana tragically fails and lets her baby and herself die. The novel illustrates the character's inability to fit in a society or a community that, without necessarily rejecting her, created both in the metropole and on the island a certain distance that proved fatal.

Through the two sisters, Dracius illustrates two possible trajectories in terms of identity and citizenship: that of playing the French card and opting for a French citizenship, as Rhevana's sister does, but without showing any strong sense of identity; and that of trying to retrace one's collective roots, first in Africa, then in the Caribbean. The novel shows that the second trajectory entails the risk of alienation, of marginalization, and eventually of rejection to the periphery by both the central society, whether in Paris or on the island.[2] Interestingly, almost twenty years later the Haitian Yannick Lahens's novel *La couleur de l'aube* (2008) plays on a similar construction of complementary/antithetical female characters. Yet, with Joyeuse and Angélique, the former working in a shop, ready to provoke life, using her body as her passport, the latter a nurse in a Port-au-Prince hospital and the image of sacrifice and submission, the accent is put primarily on the economic disarray of Haiti today. Through her two characters, Lahens aims at presenting the ordinariness, the unbearable endless struggles and sheer survival, of daily life.

Maryse Condé's *Desirada* explores the notion of cultural survival examined by Dracius, but through the lens of the migration experience.[3] Her protagonists are confronted with what seems to be their logical destiny, leaving the island for a new space. To the usual route, from the islands to Paris (or to the dream of returning to Africa), Condé adds migration from one island to the other (La Desirade to Guadeloupe), from Paris to the United States and Boston, and a back-and-forth between the United States and the Caribbean, between the United States and France. Three generations of women illustrate the complex evolution of the dynamics of migration.[4] Through these three generations, Condé illustrates the phenomenon of globalization as it translates today for Guadeloupe and its inhabitants. Ironically, in "O Brave New World" Condé declares herself fairly optimistic about the positive aspects of globalization: "Globalization does not frighten me. For me it means reaching out beyond national and linguistic borders both in actual exchanges and transatlantic influences and in the expressive imagination of diasporic black communities" (2). Likewise, talking about migrations and the redefinition today of diasporic communities, she maintains that migration is potentially enriching, and the migrant community the seat of extraordinary creativity (4). Yet, in her fictional writing Condé explores a more somber side of this phenomenon. In *Desirada*, the displacement experienced by each generation of women results in nothing but an uneasy personal identity quest. Wherever Marie-Noëlle is, once she has left the protection of her childhood, she carries her pain around. She is traumatized by her mother's indifference and lack of love, and her traumatization is reflected in her relationships with men. She is numb, feeling empty, aimless, almost sexless. Unlike *La colonie du nouveau monde*, Maryse Condé's previous novel, where religion did play an anchoring role, here neither religion nor love nor education nor professional success can prove strong enough moorings.

Some of the recurrent features in Caribbean fiction by women mentioned earlier are part of the narrative: Marie-Noëlle has been abandoned as a child by her mother and left in her grandmother's care (Reynalda is thus essentially only a surrogate maternal figure). Likewise, Marie-Noëlle leaves the island (which marks the end of her childhood innocence) to join her mother in Paris. The similarities end there, however. The often recurrent element of incestuous abuse of a teenage girl by her father, stepfather, or uncle (Agnant; Danticat; Emecheta; Warner-Vieyra, *Le quimboiseur*) is absent from the plot, or at least it is inverted in its representation: it is Marie-Noëlle who, once a woman, undertakes a journey and flies from the United States to France to try to provoke it, but her stepfather refuses this scenario. On Marie-Noëlle's part, it is less from real desire than from a desire to revenge her mother's indifference. Also unlike in previous novels, the protagonist is able to unknot the mystery of her paternal origins, but it is only to find that her father is the vicar who, back in La Desirade, facilitated her grandmother's moving to Guadeloupe. Because of her origins, she considers herself a monstrosity.

Maryse Condé's depiction of Antillean women is quite striking in its absence of a strong sense of cultural belonging. The issue of citizenship, of cultural identity, is never examined per se, but it looms in the background. The phenomenon of migration is examined in terms of uneasiness and malaise resulting from an incomplete identity; unsatisfied with the hiatus in their origins of birth, suffering deeply from lack of maternal love, three generations of women carry a feeling of alienation and aimlessness. Although new routes appear for their migrations, whether Paris or the United States (thus a new space that takes them away from the usual cycle of departure and return), the space where they live becomes inconsequential. Although new destinations are explored, they do not play a significant role in the characters' sense of identity. While being in the States enables Marie-Noëlle to understand race relations, it does not contribute to her exploration of the Caribbean identity and of herself. Nor does education play a significant role; although it brings her material security, it does not give her a higher sense of self.

While migration is central to the narrative, it is examined in terms of inner malaise rather than as displacement. The main source of this sense of unhappiness goes back to unknown origins and questions of legitimacy. Female characters show the impossibility of becoming fully themselves because of a lack of retraceable memory. Not until Marie-Noëlle is able to fill in the gap, the missing link of origins, can she truly inhabit the space she lives in. Until that moment, wandering about is her definition, her second nature.[5] The same goes for her love relationships: Marie-Noëlle drifts from man to man, essentially numb. This novel attempts to identify the roots of a deeply engrained malaise that the characters carry within themselves. For Marie-Noëlle, moving away does not resolve any quest for identity or personal malaise. The absence of personal and cultural anchoring is reflected in her relationships with men. The past and the absence of traceable genealogy make her a wanderer. As such, she appears at the far end of the spectrum of female African writers' protagonists; she is like the Cameroonian Calixthe Beyala's protagonists, who, in contrast to Caribbean women writers, welcome departure (leaving the motherland) and migration as a potential for change, for becoming somebody new, more fulfilled. To Condé, however, these three generations of women illustrate the evolution of the Caribbean people, from a secluded, easily classifiable community to a nomadic people creating a world of its own wherever it finds itself. Maybe to be a Caribbean or an African is no longer a matter of the place where one is born, the color of one's skin, and the language one speaks. In her eyes, what is important is the remapping of the diasporic community in its many extensions and choice of new destinations.

Condé does draw a fairly somber portrayal of both Caribbean youths and the island. Through Garvey, Marie-Noëlle's half-brother, though, the author does gives us a note of hope. Condé explores the aspirations of the adolescent and young Antilleans living in the metropole, who do not know the Antilles other than through their parents' eyes. Garvey is representative of a new generation: for him, Guadeloupe and Africa represent nothing concrete. He defines himself as a "Black" (the term used in France to designate first-generation Antilleans and Africans born in France and living in France) and a Frenchman.

With regard to belonging and cultural roots, Elizabeth Wilson's "Le voyage et l'espace clos" (1990) is still helpful. In her analysis of the intersections of geography, migration, and entrapment as central to women's shaping their identity, she points out that the journey becomes a conduit for self-knowledge but as such leads to destruction. If the journey remedies the stifling feeling of the island, it is not necessarily a figure of hope; rather, it becomes another metaphor for displacement and entrapment, a closed space in itself. *Desirada* takes this idea further to show that the journey becomes even secondary, that regardless of space, the character feels this inner malaise, which is only symptomatic of a larger ontological malaise.

The Caribbean voices are still haunted by a lack of official acknowledgment of their traumatic past and history, and they are still trying to find some anchor within themselves. They point to the protagonists' wandering, whether to the African continent, to the metropole, or more recently to the United States, and, conversely, their attempts to return to the island as strategies of cultural survival. Women authors have turned toward their past, exploring the genealogical missing link (the absent father-genitor) as a step toward defining their Caribbean selves. Their preoccupation with legitimacy reflects a broader scope wherein they undertake to recapture their history through the telling of women's stories. Displacement in that context is subsumed in a general malaise linked to an ontological feeling of displacement going all the way back to the traumas of slavery and the forced exile (Cazenave, "Francophone Women Writers" 138).

Furthermore, the notion of citizenship, of a Caribbean identity, remains in limbo. The absence of cultural and historical roots, of an anchor, impels Caribbean expatriates to create a substitute identity (Cazenave, "Francophone Women Writers" 138). Garvey (in *Desirada*), Rhevana (in *L'autre qui danse*), and Nicolas (in Pineau's *L'âme prêtée aux oiseaux*) are all illustrations and variations of these different attempts. But the same conclusion—that there is no communal feeling of belonging—is repeated again and again. In that respect, Adlai Murdoch's analysis, in "Negotiating the Metropole," of Gisèle Pineau's and Suzanne Dracius's takes on exile and cultural survival in their narratives is quite pertinent and fitting here, for these are all multiple variations on how the characters *negotiate* the metropole.

In *Histoire de la femme cannibale*, Maryse Condé explores the issues of both exile/immigration and memory. To do that, she places her (Guadeloupean) protagonist, Rosalie, in a non-Francophone space—Cape Town, South Africa—creating an unusual background. It is unusual in the sense that the protagonist has gone from Guadeloupe to Paris to Doussou in Senegal to New York and finally to Cape Town, a city that she does not like, that she finds gray, gloomy and desperate. Through Rosalie, Condé illustrates the new effects of a globalizing process and experience of immigration, crossing the usual language barrier, as well as the habitual Caribbean migration trajectory—the French Caribbean/Paris, a Francophone African country, and more recently the United States—as, for instance, in *Desirada*.

The book opens on Rosalie's mourning, having to cope with the brutal death and shooting of her husband, Stephen, an English white professor of English literature at the University of Cape Town. Reinventing and revisiting the use of the *mirasse* mourning tradition, which can be found in the Senegalese Mariama Ba's *Une si longue lettre (So Long a Letter)*, Condé has her character reflect and look back at Stephen's life and her life with him, trying to understand what could have caused her husband's death. Progressively, as she taps into her memories, she has to negotiate the uncomfortable feeling of not really having known him as she thought she did. She soon realizes that her image of him as a liberal, loving, generous person who helped young students was false. She eventually finds out that he led a double life. Her image of him as a great mentor is shattered; he did help his male students, but in exchange for sexual favors. In contrast to the normative heterosexual frame of Condé's narratives, same-sex relationships do enter the picture here, although not in a positive light. Rather, they are complicated by issues of power, domination, and race.[6]

As Rosalie's memories unfold, it becomes clear that she has been tossed about in life, always following Stephen, listening to his advice as if he were her mentor. She always put him first. As a result, she let her painting come second and was never convinced of her own value and talents as an artist. Now, at a new crossroads, Rosalie is forced to confront the fact that her life has always been directed by men: first, by Salama in Senegal, then by Stephen, by Ariel, the Congolese Faustin, who enters her life a few months after Stephen's death, and finally, by Manolo. Through the process of remembering (in the literal sense of putting pieces together) her life before Stephen and after him, she finally comes to the conclusion that it is time for her to nurture her own self first and to fully invest herself in painting.

Condé constructs her narrative around two parallel journeys, a physical, geographic one that took her from one culture to another, from one mode of thinking to another, and an inner journey, a trip down memory lane. The conflation of different places, times, men, and cultures enables Condé to articulate a new sense of transnational being, removed from the notion of community and the national.[7] The notion of citizenship is further diluted. Rosalie, like Condé, is first and foremost a world citizen. In that regard, *Histoire de la femme cannibale* is a very rich, complex text in which the line between narrator and author is sometimes blurred. Indeed, one feels that Condé puts a lot of herself into the story, not in the autobiographical sense but rather in terms of the views expressed at times, such as about Guadeloupe, in evoking the way the island has recently become prey to delinquency and violence, how it is losing ground compared with the surrounding islands, like Saint-Martin or Saint-Barthes. Her analysis seems almost a prolepsis of the situation and conjuncture in Guadeloupe and the French Caribbean in late 2008 and early 2009. The Guadeloupean writer and member of the Cultural Council of Guadeloupe, Ernest Pépin, has been most vocal in that respect. In "Quelle Guadeloupe voulons-nous?" Pépin advocates for the "droit à l'excellence" (the right to excellence) along the lines of President Obama's thinking, hence for a redefinition of the social, political, economic, and cultural function of the island. He argues for a more responsible relationship to France, one that would bring to an end the "infantilisation" of Guadeloupe and the French Caribbean in general.

Condé also gives us an incisive cultural analysis of New York and post-apartheid Cape Town. She also gives us an insightful picture of academic life, whether in America, in England, or on the African continent, all of which are familiar territories to her. In the end, the different conflations of memories and space contribute to a complex rendering of what modern uprooting, displacement, and nomadism have become.

By contrast, Gisèle Pineau's works show a much more positive take on both the journey and the resulting crafting of an identity and notion of belonging. *L'âme prêtée aux oiseaux* (1998), for instance, has a female protagonist who finds anchorage within herself. If Sybille detached herself from Guadeloupe when she moved to Paris, as a young pregnant woman, she understands her adolescent son's need to look for his father and his roots back on the island. While he is exploring Guadeloupe, she travels to the United States with Lila, an old Frenchwoman and her longtime friend. Through this trip and her encounter with an African American man, Sybille is finally able to reconcile herself with the island. Unlike Condé's protagonist in *Desirada,* for whom traveling to the United States does not bring peace of mind, Sybille finds love, peace within herself, and a sense of being firmly anchored. In all of Pineau's texts, speaking and writing function as healers. Being able to speak out helps the protagonists resolve their inner trauma or anxieties.[8] Unlike in other Caribbean women's works, in Pineau's works narration brings a sense of relief and appeasement, offering a hopeful note to the readers.[9]

Pineau's *Chair Piment* strikes a different chord. Written in a much bleaker tone, with two-thirds of the narrative steeped in utter discouragement, its geographic setting is the reverse trajectory: first anchored in the Hexagon, then shifting back to Guadeloupe. In *Chair Piment,* migration is no longer at the heart of the narrative; rather, the writing of sexuality becomes the central element. In contrast to the writing of sexuality in African women writers' novels, for instance, Ken Bugul's *Riwan ou le chemin de sable* (1994), Tanella Boni's *Les baigneurs du lac rose* (1995), or Veronique Tadjo's *Champs de bataille et d'amour* (1998), the writing of sexuality in Francophone Caribbean women writer's novels is strikingly steeped in violence. Love and sexuality are under the sign of suffering. As I point out in "Écritures des sexualité dans le roman francophone au féminin," love is essentially absent from the text. While Pineau's portrayal of sexuality is according to the social heterosexual norms, she does depart from the conventional frame of steady relationships.

Through her repeated sexual intercourse with men whom she picks up haphazardly on the street and whom she will never see again, Mina, the protagonist, tries to forget haunting memories of her childhood, specifically the death of her sister, who perished in a fire. Haunted by the memory of her sister, she sees her all the time, everywhere, including when she is making love. She "consommait du sexe, le sexe dressé des hommes" (consumed sex, the male sex erected), to forget, to annihilate memory. The love scenes, if at times erotic, are mostly violent and emphasize a total disjunction between love and sex/uality. To have sexual intercourse is to revisit, again and again, her initial trauma (of her sister's death, of losing her parents, of growing up, raised by an aunt in Paris, estranged both from the island and from herself) and the resulting insurmountable suffering: "Ils entraient en elle, gratis, frottaient sa chair, goûtaient sa peau. Fallait quelle soit prise. Possédée. Traversée, sans parole par des sexes d'hommes" (17; They were penetrating her, for free, they felt her flesh. She had to be tamed. Possessed. Transpierced, without a word, by men's sex).

Unlike for Rhevana in *L'autre qui danse*, for Mina, to go back to Guadeloupe helps her confront her ghosts, reconnect with her roots, and find peace within herself. The outer journey parallels an inner journey. Eventually, Mina's initial journey through men and each sexual penetration can come to conclusion. By agreeing to see one of her male sexual partners again, by going to Guadeloupe and seeing him there, she is able to find peace and resolve the mystery behind the fire and her sister's death.

Some of the violence and language used in *Chair Piment* to describe sexual intercourse is evocative of a vocabulary that can be found in narratives about slavery and slave trafficking, about power and domination. In some ways it reminds us of Jean Rhys's *Wide Sargasso Sea* or Beryl Gilroy's *Steadman and Joanna*. Both novelists found a way to rewrite colonial domination in the Caribbean and defy the master narrative by subverting the text through literary cannibalism.[10] The constant violence present in the narratives, associated with sexual abuses, rape, and incest, can be read as a long metaphor for the initial violence forced onto Caribbean women. Through a writing of a violent sexuality, and of generations of women unhappy, unsatisfied, or abused, the Caribbean women novelists are reconstructing colonial history. The traumatic memory of their bodies is the memory of history and colonial violence portrayed through relationships between men and women, where man is always absent. The writing of the body and, more recently, of sexuality recaptures ancestral memory and Caribbean history. This is something that Marie Abraham and Gisèle Pineau explore in *Femmes des Antilles: Traces et voix: 150 ans après l'abolition de l'esclavage*. Clearly, the different testimonies raise the issue of difficult male-female relationships in Antillean society today and how they can be traced back to the trauma of slavery, in which men and women were deprecated in the eye of the other gender and violence ruled all relationships.

The Haitian Marie-Célie Agnant's *Le livre d'Emma* is another probing example of a Francophone Caribbean narrative in which sexuality and memory converge to delineate Caribbean identities and how they relate to the concept of citizenship. Much like her previous *La dot de Sarah* (1995) and *Le silence comme le sang* (1997), *Le livre d'Emma* represents a long struggle with memories and the long-term effects of speaking out.

Some of the usual recurrent features revolving around the theme of madness are present here: the protagonist is institutionalized after an episode of hysteria and suspected of homicide for the killing of her baby daughter. Marie-Célie Agnant introduces some innovative elements though. In particular she introduces the character of a Haitian interpreter, Flora. Flora is meant to translate for the Canadian psychiatrist both the linguistic and cultural contents of Emma's words after she has been institutionalized and charged for homicide of her baby child. Through her therapy the doctor is supposed to assess Emma's responsibility in her daughter's death. Through the characters Emma and Flora, the author reflects both on the role and the limits of translation or interpretation not only of words but also of a culture. Beyond that initial crafting of storytelling, Agnant tells us another story, that of the Haitian diaspora and its sometimes ambivalent ties to the island and Haitian history. For the translator herself, a process of counter-mirroring unfolds. Through her and her relationship with Emma's former companion and the father of the baby, Agnant explores the effect of cultural similarities and dissemblance between the two women of Haitian origin.[11] The narrative shows how in each case the man is unable to fill an incommensurable void felt by the female characters.

Like Maryse Condé, through Emma's story's unfolding/spilling into Flora's, Agnant highlights the similarities between mothers and daughters, from one generation to the next, with the same sense of inevitability, suffering, and doom for women. In her painting of women's suffering, Agnant reconstructs the history of the Middle Passage, of the slave boats, going all the way back, from the plantations to today. The central question of the narrative becomes how to deal with the trauma of the past. How can the page be turned so that women and men can think constructively of the present and the future? In her textual construction of familial history through generations of women, Marie-Célie Agnant beautifully captures Haitian history. In her painting of women's suffering, she joins Edwidge Danticat (*Breath, Eyes, Memory*, 1994) and the Dominican Nellie Rosario (*Song of the Water Saints*, 2002) in writing of the past and present Caribbean cultures.

Maryse Condé, Gisèle Pineau, Edwidge Danticat, and Marie-Célie Agnant, demonstrate that regardless of the space the protagonist lives in (the Caribbean, Paris, Boston, New York, or Montreal), her inner malaise remains inescapable, and she is portrayed as a wanderer, incapable of love or of enjoying a fulfilling sexuality. Edwidge Danticat's *Breath, Eyes, Memory* illustrates that point, showing that from one generation to the next the same trauma and dislike for oneself, for one's body, is carried out; in turn, Marie-Célie

Agnant's *Le livre d'Emma* focuses on the burden of collective memory, how the original trauma of the Middle Passage has been perpetuated from generation to generation. Emma's inner malaise is only metaphoric of the initial trauma and rejection of motherhood and mother's love, mothers rejecting their children because of the child's origin, as the result of rape or sexploitation. The dissertation committee's rejection of her work on slave boats is the ultimate straw that pushes her onto the path of madness. It is also symbolic of some of the disappearing of Haitian and Caribbean official history.

As I show in "Écritures des sexualités," the recurrence of violence in Caribbean narratives depicting sexuality, amorous relationships, and intercourse is a long metaphor for the initial rape perpetrated on Caribbean women. With their insistence on depicting sexual violence, women writers articulate the relationship between history, colonial violence, and the uneasy rapport between men and women in modern society: "Elles démontrent le poids de l'Histoire et de la violence coloniale dans les rapports entre hommes et femmes, dans la quasi-absence de l'homme, géniteur en passant. L'écriture de la sexualité prend le relai du corps-langage pour se faire inscription de la mémoire et bilan de la société antillaise" (63). Ultimately, these different Caribbean novels converge toward the same idea: characters are often burdened by their past, unable to look freely to the future. Through the personal stories of female protagonists, Caribbean women writers have tried to recapture a collective past, to reconstruct the traumatic effects of slavery on its people, both men and women, to build a new Antillean his/her/story. Fiction plays a crucial role in that regard. At school, Antillean children in the metropole learn French history just as the rest of the children there do. In the French history program, very little appears on slavery and colonization, on colonialism and decolonization.

In this context, folktales and storytelling become an essential channel for children and youths to learn about their heritage.[12] Conversely, as the philosopher Etienne Balibar has shown, in *We, the People of Europe?* (2004), education (schooling) is crucial in shaping citizens and the concept of citizenship in modern society; the definition of citizenship is problematic in the French Caribbean, where the individual and the collective, the local and the global, do not share the same values. The absence of an anchor impels Caribbean expatriates to create a substitute identity. Recent works such as *Desirada* demonstrate that there is not much of a sense of solidarity and even less of a sense of community among the Antilleans in Paris. The emphasis, rather, is on isolation and the absence of replenishment. Thus, the notion of the citizen as a conceptual person, as Gilles Deleuze and Félix Guattari have articulated in *Quest-ce que la philosophie?* (1991), recedes to the point of disappearing, to be replaced by the persona of the migrant.

In that respect, the rendering of an unhappy difficult sexuality, of love relations that never come to full realization, goes back to issues of Francophone Antillean Caribbean identity, showing a fracture in the concept of citizenship.[13] Whether in Suzanne Dracius's *L'autre qui danse,* Maryse Condé's *Desirada* and *Histoire de la femme cannibale,* Gisèle Pineau's *L'espérance-macadam* (1995) or, more recently, *Chair Piment,* the erotic and the sensual are essentially absent from the narration. Instead, sexuality is presented as difficult and unhappy and seems to be equated with a sense of fleetingness, of vulnerability of love, and mostly with suffering. The continuous pain running through the narratives gives a sense of the extent of the suffering caused by a situation, a context of discontinuity and fragmentation with regard to citizenship.

The metaphor is especially telling in the context of increasing discontentment in the French Caribbean islands with regard to their status as DOMs, or *départements d'outre-mer* (overseas departments), a remnant phrasing that is still part of the colonial terminology. As Adlai Murdoch most tellingly demonstrates, the departmentalization of the French Caribbean has caused the islands to suffer a continuing conundrum between "home" and "away," between finding their own position and location vis-à-vis the notions of nation and citizenship ("Introduction"; see also Trouillot, "Les pays pauvres").

IN CONTRAST to Francophone Caribbean male writers, who have been articulating their reclaiming of Caribbean identity through language mainly by championing the concept of Creolité and making Francophone French visible and acknowledged,[14] women writers have not been much engaged in that direction. True, with *La grande drive des esprits* (1993) Gisèle Pineau proved that although she was born in the metropole and spent most of her childhood outside the French Caribbean, she possessed every single nuance of Creole language and the Caribbean cultural strata; in other words, she was truly a Caribbean writer. But while all her novels, and Maryse Condé's as well, are peppered with Creole words, the crafting of a Francophone Caribbean discourse does not lie primarily, for women writers at least, in the Creole language. Rather, it lies in the polyphonic construction of voices of men and women through several generations. Thus, Francophone Caribbean women writers are engaged in crafting regional discourses, with their narratives converging around a number of similar points, that is, by directing their gaze at the past, through generations of women. The similarities of situations between mothers and daughters participate in the construction of a familial history and, beyond that, of the history of a society and a culture. Through their take on migration and sexuality, Francophone Caribbean women writers address issues of identity, of belonging, and ultimately of what remains a fragmented, incomplete citizenship.

Notes

1. On the notion of a mythical Africa and a distorted understanding of authenticity, see Lionnet.

2. In her recent collection of short stories, *Rue Monte au ciel* (2003), Suzanne Dracius gives us a much different portrayal of Caribbean (Martinican) women. Each of the nine short stories corresponds to a woman, each confronting in her very own way a threat, a danger, an issue. Together, these nine portrayals enable the reader to reconstruct and piece together a history of Martinique covering the last three hundred years. Witty and humorous, the nine stories suggest that these women are better equipped to address issues of racism, sexism, or homophobia in Martinique society today.

3. The following draws on Cazenave "Francophone Women Writers" and "Le roman africain et antillais."

4. The three generations of women are Marie-Noëlle; Reynalda, her mother; Antonine, also called Nina, Reynalda's mother and the grandmother of Marie-Noëlle; and Ranélise, Marie-Noëlle's substitute mother until her preadolescence (Reynalda leaves for France soon after her daughter's birth).

5. Interestingly, Condé has distanced herself both from home and from France, choosing the United States as her space of writing (and living). In "Finalement, on va arriver à simplement dire: Je suis ce que je suis," an interview with Catherine Dana, Condé stresses that for her France has never worked as a space of writing, that she always felt reduced to *une voix d'ailleurs* (a voice from somewhere else), somehow objectified if not exotified. For that matter, Guadeloupe did not work either, as Condé shocked her Caribbean fellows and did not fit the Guadeloupean definition. As the title of the interview suggests, it took her years, in fact, to be able to write, speak, and be as she wanted.

6. Condé's most recent novel, *Les belles ténébreuses* (2008), expands further on the same issues of power, domination, and race, showing similar ambiguities.

7. Along the same line, see Michael Dash, "Disappearing Island," in which he addresses the privileging of global interaction and the transcending of ethnocentric models of nation, race, and identity today.

8. In one of Pineau's most recent novels, *Chair Piment*, the inability to speak out is central to the protagonist's suffering.

9. Some of Pineau's more recent works belong to youth literature and address the questions of identity, belonging, and citizenship for the young generation, especially for those who were born in Paris/the Hexagon and have only a remote idea of and connection to their roots and their island of origin. In *Caraïbes sur Seine* (1999) Pineau expresses the dilemma for an entire family when faced with the decision of whether to stay in Guadeloupe or try their luck in the metropole, with the choice between life in the Parisian suburbs and life at home (home being the island). The narrative explores each character's reaction and how each processes his or her decision. Age and gender are key in that regard: unlike the father, who opts for returning to Guadeloupe only a month after their arrival in Paris, the mother decides to stick to their decision, to stay and find work; as for the children, they try to make new

friends. *C'est la règle* (2002) explores further the issue of biculturalism, of bridges to allow the Caribbean and French cultures to meet, but also issues of racism, introducing one additional element, that of divorce and children confronting their mothers' new partners. Both narratives bring a sense of validation of a multicultural identity for the characters staying in the Hexagon. It is an identity that embraces both French and Caribbean cultural roots without necessarily experiencing a sense of fragmentation.

10. Similarly, Condé's *La migration des coeurs* can be read as literary reappropriation of Emily Bronte's canonical work, *Wuthering Heights*. For an in-depth analysis of literary cannibalism in Francophone texts, see Reynolds, "Almost the same, but not quite."

11. Similar strategies can be found in Warner-Vieyra's *Quimboiseur* and *Juletane* or Maryse Condé's *Pays mêlé*, where the authors use either the recurrent feature of a diary written by the protagonist or the role of double mirror or countermirror played by a social worker or a therapist.

12. Pineau's *L'exil selon Julia* highlights the benefits of the grandmother's presence in the Hexagon, how Man Ya's wisdom enables the narrator to feel connected with her cultural heritage and gives a sense of fulfillment. In contrast, Suzanne Dracius's *L'autre qui danse* shows the devastating effects for Rhevana of an absence of cultural and historical roots.

13. It would be interesting to compare the Francophone Caribbean novel with the Indian Ocean novel and ask the following questions: to what extent does insularity play a key factor vis-à-vis the notion of citizenship? and to what extent do expatriates (from the diaspora of Francophone Caribbeans or from the Indian Ocean) reinforce or dilute the notion of citizenship?

14. On Creolité and the necessity of having Francophone literature acknowledged just as French literature is, see Bernabé, Chamoiseau, and Confiant.

Indian Nationalism and Female Sexuality

A Trinidadian Tale

Tejaswini Niranjana

This business about the women is the weakest and the irremediable part of the evil. . . . These women are not necessarily wives. Men and women are huddled together during the voyage. The marriage is a farce. A mere declaration by man or woman made upon landing before the Protector of Immigrants that they are husband and wife constitutes a valid marriage. Naturally enough, divorce is common. The rest must be left to the imagination of the reader.

—M. K. Gandhi, "Indentured Labour"

THE OTHERNESS of the Indian, or sometimes "Eastern," female body is a common enough trope in Orientalisms of various kinds and has been the focus of much postcolonial feminist theoretical intervention in recent years. A more central preoccupation among feminists in India in the last decade or two has been to understand the gendered nature of our (non-Western) modernity and its specific concern with maintaining Indianness or cultural authenticity in the midst of social transformation. Attention has been drawn to the reformulation of patriarchal authority at different moments in the history of anti-imperialist struggle and to the recomposition of "Indian women" through the contests between colonizer and colonized. This process is commonly viewed as part of an Indian history that unfolds in India. My task here is to show that the *constitutive outside* of what we in India see today as normative Indian femininity (Butler, *Bodies That Matter* 3) is the figure of the indentured woman laborer who was part of the subaltern Indian migration to the Caribbean (Niranjana).

The aim of this essay, then, is to investigate a conjuncture of modernity, Indianness, and woman that is radically different from our own in India, in the hope that it will de-familiarize our formation as well as throw some new light on the elements that led to its consolidation. I attempt to alter the lens through which we have been accustomed to viewing or framing the

emergence of that discursive subject, the modern Indian woman. In analyzing the formation of "woman" in India, we often use, almost as if by
default, the implicit comparisons with Western or metropolitan situations. I
want to ask whether our frameworks might look different when the points
of reference include other nonmetropolitan contexts, in particular those that
are historically imbricated with our own, even if in ways that are obscured
by later developments.

My investigation proceeds through an analysis of the early twentieth-
century campaign against indentureship in the tropical colonies by nationalists in India. I have chosen this moment for its foregrounding of the question
of female sexuality, an issue that is increasingly being seen as central to the
formation of gendered citizenship and to dominant narratives of nationhood. Historically, the moment is also one of "Indian" political assertion
as well as of the availability of new possibilities for "Indian" women. I put
the term *Indian* in quotation marks to signal its double use: marking on the
one hand a (future) nationality in South Asia and on the other an "ethnic"
category in the Caribbean. Much of the writing in the media, whether in
Trinidad or in India, tends to blur the difference between the two usages, a
blurring that could well serve to make Indo-Trinidadians invisible both in
India and in Trinidad, marking them simultaneously as not Indian enough
in the first location and not Trinidadian enough in the second.

The formation of the Indian National Congress in 1885 signaled the beginning of a new phase of organization in the movement against British
rule in India. Accommodating a wide spectrum of ideological strands and
reconciling a host of conflicting interests, the Congress party was able—in
the space of the next few decades—to provide focus and direction to the
anticolonial struggle, culminating in the final transfer of political power
in 1947. Among the many successful initiatives of the nationalists was the
early twentieth-century campaign against indentureship, one that contributed in significant measure to building up a moral case against colonialism.
However, in the late nineteenth century indenture did not yet figure as a
significant anticolonial issue. On the contrary, as B. R. Nanda points out,
in 1893 the leading nationalist, M. G. Ranade, actually wrote an article
entitled "Indian Foreign Emigration," in which he argued that emigration
afforded some "relief" to the growing population of India and that the expansion of the British Empire could be seen as a "direct gain" to the masses
of this country.[1]

Eventually, however, owing in significant measure to the efforts of an Indian
involved in agitations in South Africa, Mohandas Karamchand Gandhi, a
figure who was to rise to great prominence in the nationalist struggle, indentured emigration became an important issue for Indian nationalism.[2]
Born in India and educated as a barrister in England, Gandhi had gone to

South Africa in 1893 to work as a lawyer for a prominent Indian business family and ended up staying there for nearly twenty-one years (Eriksen; Fischer; Rolland). Although the early agitations initiated by Gandhi did not involve indentured workers in Natal, many of them came to participate in satyagraha, Gandhi's passive-resistance campaign against the various legal restrictions imposed on Indians in South Africa. Closer interaction with the indentured increased Gandhi's awareness of their specific problems, which he tried to bring to the attention of nationalists in India. Satyagraha, stretching from 1906 to 1914, was for Gandhi a direct ancestor of the anti-indenture agitation. When Gandhi began the satyagraha campaign in South Africa, in Bombay the Imperial Indian Citizenship Association, a group who expressed explicit concern for Indian immigrants, was founded.

Since the 1890s, Gandhi had attempted to enlist the help of the Congress leaders, and Gokhale in particular was supportive of his endeavors. In 1894 Gandhi had drafted the first petition protesting against the indenture system. After constitutional reforms in 1909, a Legislative Council, which included elected Indians among its members, was formed, dominated by the Congress. As a member of the Legislative Council, Gokhale in 1910 put forward a successful resolution to stop the recruitment of indentured labor for Natal. In spite of his failing health, Gokhale not only visited South Africa at Gandhi's invitation but "attended to the South African business night and day." "Eventually all India was deeply stirred, and the South African question became the burning topic of the day" (Gandhi, *Satyagraha in South Africa* 354, 428). The focus of Gandhi and his European Indophile colleagues (C. F. Andrews, William Pearson, Henry Polak) was indentured hardship in Fiji and South Africa, and while Indian indentureship in the West Indies seldom got special mention in this narrative, it was often subsumed within it.

Indentured Women in the West Indies

The nationalist description of the situation of indentured women drew from missionary accounts, Government of India and colonial administrators' reports, and firsthand accounts of sympathetic Europeans such as C. F. Andrews, who wrote about Fiji. The central concern of all these writers seemed to be the "immorality" caused by the disparate sex ratio of the immigrant laborers. There was also more than a suggestion that the inconstancy of Indian women could be traced to the social composition of the female migrants.

Women evangelicals of the Canadian Presbyterian Church, which began proselytizing among the Indians in Trinidad in 1868, interacted closely with the indentured women and recorded their impressions of what they saw as barbaric "Indian customs" and the reprehensible behavior of the women in particular:

There are no zenanas in Trinidad. Our women immigrants are not recruited from the class that in India are shut up in zenanas. In Trinidad they find themselves of added importance through the small proportion of their sex. They have great freedom of intercourse and much evil example around them. Sad to say they often shew themselves to be as degraded as they are ignorant. On the other hand many are beautiful and lovable, faithful to their husbands and devoted to their children. This, however, is by no means the rule. (Morton 185)

While the planters did not want a permanent community of laborers at first, preferring young male workers who would return to India at the end of their indenture period and make way for a new batch, colonial officials recommended that a certain proportion of women to men be maintained in order to avoid what they saw as social complications. For a variety of reasons, however, recruiters were often unable to obtain a sufficient number of women.

The Trinidadian feminist historian Rhoda Reddock addresses the implications of this problem in her important early work on women under indentureship. Reddock is of the opinion that modern historians do not pay sufficient attention to the disparate sex ratio, although it was a crucial point of contention during the entire period of indenture. In 1884, Government of India Act 21 authorized the resumption of emigration to the West Indies after a long break, laying down as one of its conditions that at least 12 percent of the emigrants be female, a legal proportion that, says Reddock, was rarely enforced. She points to how in a period of twenty-plus years, between 1857 and 1879, the recommended ratio of women to men changed about six times, "ranging from one woman to every three men in 1857 to one to two in 1868 and one to four in 1878–79." Reddock is of the view that these changes in the proportion of women to men were a reflection of the contradictions in recruiting "the right kind of women" (*Women, Labour* 27–29). She concurs with other historians that as early as 1851 there was a recognition of the need for women as a "stabilizing factor on" the male laborers and that by the late nineteenth century planters were convinced that they needed a stable workforce that would not return to India and were therefore willing to create the conditions for the reproduction of Indian families in Trinidad. This need for domestic units coincided, as we shall see, with the Presbyterian initiatives regarding education for Indian women and the range of housewifely skills they were expected to acquire. Among the efforts to increase the number of women emigrants was the 1890s reduction of the indenture period for women, from five years to three, and the promise to recruiting agents of an increased commission for women, sometimes 40 percent higher than that for men. Emigrants were also encouraged to take female children, preferably between the ages of ten and fourteen (29).

As the historian K. O. Laurence suggests, one of the reasons for the lack of women was that few wives emigrated, since their husbands preferred to leave them behind in the protection of their joint family rather than take them to a strange country, especially since the indenture period was presumed to be a short one (Laurence 119). The Government of India tried to set the proportion of women to men at 50:100, but there was opposition to that on various counts, including the argument that this would result, according to a former emigration commissioner, in the recruiting of "bad women" who would "do more harm than good" (123). The concern that the small number of women might lead to immorality seemed to go hand in hand with the idea that these women were in any case innately depraved to begin with and that the real solution was to obtain sufficient numbers of virtuous wives to offset the other kinds of women, who seemed most likely to want to emigrate.

If we look at the number of married women among the female emigrants, it becomes obvious that they were often in a minority. Here are some random figures for Indian female immigrants registered as married upon arrival in Trinidad from 1882 to 1900, taken from G. I. M. Tikasingh's compilation from the General Registers of Immigrants and the Register of Indian Marriage. In 1882, for example, the total number of female immigrants was 662, among whom 133, or about 20 percent, were married. In 1890, out of a total of 713, 291, or 40.8 percent, were married; in 1891, out of 1,091, 470, or 43 percent (the highest figure in the period under consideration), were married; and in 1898, out of a total of 371, 59, or 15.9 percent (the lowest figure), immigrated to Trinidad already married (Tikasingh 262). In 1900, at the beginning of the new century, out of a total of 188 female immigrants, 46, or 24.4 percent, were married. The rest of the women, from 57 percent (1891) to nearly 84 percent (1898), were single, being unmarried, widowed, or deserted. Even as late as 1915, two years before the abolition of indenture, when emigration of families was being encouraged, Commissioners McNeill and Chimman Lal found that a third of the women went to Trinidad as wives, the remainder being mostly widows and runaway wives and a small percentage of prostitutes. Also among them were women deserted by their husbands and some unmarried pregnant women (Reddock, *Women, Labour* 30).

The planters' demand was not just for more females but for the "right kind of women," who would be not only productive laborers on the estates but also faithful wives to the male workers. In response to this demand, the recruiters pointed out that a better class of women could not be induced to emigrate and that in any case they would be no good as field laborers.

As an emigration agent in Calcutta put it in 1915: "In considering this matter it must be borne in mind that genuine field laborers such as the planters require can be obtained only from among the lowest castes, i.e. from among the non-moral class of the population. A more moral type is found higher in the social scale, but such women would be useless in the fields" (Chancellor to Carnarvon, 1917, CO 571:5, WI 27680, qtd. in Reddock, *Women, Labour* 30). Recruiters also warned that if more women were demanded, they would be sending "non-effective" ones or "objectionable characters" (Laurence 124). As Basdeo Mangru points out in the case of British Guiana, Trinidad's neighbor, "Criticisms regarding the type of women imported had not been wanting. Immigration officials and others often referred to their 'loose and depraved character' and condemned the Emigration Agents for shipping 'the sweepings of the Bazaars' of Calcutta and other large Indian cities" (Longden to Carnarvon, 20 October 1875, CO 384:106, qtd. in Mangru 223–24).

Evidence from another destination of indentured emigrants, the Dutch colony of Surinam, suggests the diversity of occupations of the women who decided to migrate. An emigration agent for Suriname wrote in 1877–78 about the recruits gathered in the depot prior to departure: "Their number was considerably augmented by a batch of dancing girls and women of similar description with their male attendants. These people laughed at the idea of labouring as agriculturalists" (Emmer 192). Other descriptions of female migrants to the same colony indicate close similarities with the British West Indies. The Protector of Emigrants, writing in 1880, was of the opinion that "the class of women willing to emigrate consists principally of young widows and married or single women who have already gone astray and are therefore not only most anxious to avoid their homes and to conceal their antecedents, but are also at the same time unlikely to be received back into their families" (194).

Oral histories of early twentieth-century Trinidad provide the story of Maharani, a young Brahmin widow who ran away to Trinidad, fearing ill-treatment in her in-laws' house:

MAHARANI

I married
    me husband dead

. . . .

milk boiling
    dem go want de milk to eat
an ah cat coming to drink
    an ah hit im an de milk fall down
I say dem go beat me
    because I getting too much lix [beatings]
I say dem go beat me

well I run
   I no tell nobody I leaving
      only me modder-in-law.
         (Mahabir 79)

Given the disparity between wages for male and female laborers, young women like Maharani often found it difficult to manage on the small amounts they earned. To avoid their becoming indebted to grocers and traders, in 1879 the agent-general ordered that rations be given to all first-year immigrants, to be deducted from their wages (in some estates the rations were given free of charge). However, as Judith Weller points out, "The immigrants, especially women, frequently embarked on the second year of their apprenticeship saddled with a considerable debt for the first year's rations. The newly-arrived immigrant was the 'fag' and given the hardest work to perform" (Weller 63). There were skilled, "male" tasks (millwork, forking, truck loading) and less-skilled, "female" tasks (such as weeding, manuring, supplying, and cane cutting), which were also the lowest paid. Even women who did heavy male tasks, such as truck loading, were paid the same as other women. In 1870 and 1875, a fixed minimum wage of 25¢ per day was set for men; for women it was always less. An investigator in 1891 wrote about one estate where women earned from 10¢ to 25¢ per day and men earned from 25¢ to 40¢; on another estate, males earned from 50¢ to 70¢ per day, and all women earned 25¢. In 1913, when the two last commissioners, McNeill and Lal, visited Trinidad, women were indentured for three years technically and earned from half to two-thirds as much as males, that is, from half a crown to three shillings weekly (Reddock, *Women, Labour* 36–38). Low wages drove women to increased dependency on their male partners, although they were sometimes able to negotiate the terms of this dependency.

Maharani the Brahmin widow, for example, did not particularly want a partner but was pressured to acquire one:

an e carry me go
   e carry me he room
I no want nobody
   I say
I stop alone
   but she fadder say
I like you
   but I say
me nuh like you
[but he takes her all the same].
         (Mahabir 84–85)

Missionary Travails, Marriage, and Morals

The Canadian Presbyterian missionaries who went to Trinidad to work with the indentured Indian laborers were the first to build schools for them. Access to Western-style education was accompanied by exposure to Christianity, to which the missionaries often found the Indians quite resistant. A Girls' Training Home was established in 1890, "for the protection and training of Indian girls." Christian girls aged twelve and up were admitted, to receive instruction that would prepare them to be good wives for "our helpers" (Christian teachers). Apart from Hindi, English, arithmetic, and Bible classes, the girls were taught "washing, ironing, starching, scrubbing, gardening, sewing, and all the housewifely arts" (Morton 348–49). While some of them turned out to be apt pupils, other Indian women presented a puzzle to the Canadians, as the following comments show: "The women, as a rule, are quite as wicked as the men and more ignorant and prejudiced; thus their influence for good or evil is very great" (Morton 186). Sarah Morton wrote that

> the loose notions and prevailing practices in respect of marriage here are quite shocking to a new-comer. I said to an East Indian woman whom I knew to be the widow of a Brahman, "You have no relations in Trinidad, I believe." "No, Madame," she replied, "only myself and two children; when the last [immigrant] ship came in I took a papa. I will keep him as long as he treats me well. If he does not treat me well I shall send him off at once; that's the right way, is it not?" This will be to some a new view of women's rights. (342)

> It should be added that in some Indian nationalities women are treated with much greater consideration than by others, and that in more than one Sanskrit drama, read and sung every day by the priests among the people, and reverenced by all Hindoos, beautiful and touching love stories are related with pictures of unspotted purity and supreme devotion in married life. (347)

The rapidity with which Indian women formed new relationships in Trinidad was a matter for comment by contemporary writers as well as latter-day historians. Early twentieth-century visitors to the West Indies, such as the British novelist Charles Kingsley, tended to see women's behavior as stemming from practices such as child marriage, which Kingsley called "a very serious evil" but attributed to customs brought from India: "The girls are practically sold by their fathers. . . . Then comes a scandal; and one which is often ended swiftly enough by the cutlass" (Kingsley 192). Kingsley talked of child brides, although many of the examples in the missionary writings are of older women, who seemed to have constructed for themselves spaces of negotiation to offset their lack of privilege in the wage system of the plantation.

As Tikasingh remarks, the most common type of union was the "keeper union," "whose stability depended primarily upon the satisfaction of the female partner." He cites the case of a woman named Mungaree, who had an arrangement with one Namoomarlala on Orange Field Estate. He gave her $150 in clothes and silver, and she lived with him for eight years. She then went to live with another man, Nageeroo, "with the understanding that she could return to her former keeper at any time"; subsequently, at the time of the court case mentioned here, she was living with yet another man, a shopkeeper. "As soon as females were ill-treated by their 'papa,' . . . they were quite ready to break the existing union and form another" (*Mungaree v. Nageeroo,* 13 July 1878, qtd. in Tikasingh 270).

Speaking about British Guiana, Basdeo Mangru points out that the "paucity of women made polyandry almost an acknowledged system. Very often an Indian woman was found to have two husbands and to be unfaithful to both" (Mangru 227, citing *Daily Argosy,* 23 March and 24 April 1913). That this kind of relationship was also common in Trinidad is borne out by the experiences of Sarah Morton and other missionaries. Mangru cites official correspondence that expressed concern about the "loose domestic relations" among the indentured laborers: "It is not uncommon for a woman of this class to leave the man with whom she has cohabited for another, and then for a third, perhaps for a fourth, and sometimes to return to one of those she had previously deserted; and this she does in most cases with impunity" (Mangru 227, citing Scott to Kimberley, 15 August 1870, CO 111:376). As K. O. Laurence puts it, "Women sought to maximize their bargaining power and shifted their allegiance to the male who presented the best offer with great facility." He quotes the research of B. L. Moore on British Guiana, giving the 1887 example of a woman at Bush Lot who was "married with Hindu rites to three different men in a single year" (239). He also points out that "in Guiana polyandry with two or three, sometimes even four men became fairly common. Similar situations were also known in Trinidad, though probably not widespread. Keeper unions however were very common there" (236).

The Anti-Slavery Society proposed banning the recruitment of single women to avoid what they saw as inevitable immorality, but it was pointed out that to circumvent this rule recruits would pretend to be married to each other at the time of emigration. In any case, some opponents of indentureship believed, as Gandhi did, that marriages between recruits were often fictitious. The point is not whether the marriages were false or real, or whether single women were entirely responsible for "immoral relations," but how critics and commentators chose to define a situation clearly related to the displacement of men and women to a diasporic condition where new opportunities presented themselves to people married as well as unmarried. Colonial officials persisted in seeing the "notoriously lax morals" of the indentured as resulting from the significant proportion of "sexually permissive women" on the estates, where they claimed the general "level of sexual morality" was lower than in a typical Indian village (Laurence 126).

Wife Murders

The prevalence of "wife murders" by indentured Indians in Trinidad and British Guiana in the nineteenth century was attributed to the inconstancy of the women. According to David V. Trotman, between 1872 and 1880, 27 percent of all murders in Trinidad were committed by East Indian immigrants; between 1881 and 1889, 60 percent; and between 1890 and 1898, 70 percent ("Women and Crime," *Caribbean Freedom* 252). Tikasingh says that between 1872 and 1900, eighty-seven Indian women were murdered in Trinidad, 65 (74.7%) of which were wives (Tikasingh 272). The majority of the murderers were men, and those killed were women who were either wives, concubines, or fiancées. Although there have been quite a few court cases involving men who killed child brides whose fathers had promised them to several men for a hefty bride price each time, many of the cases have involved men who murdered their wives for having taken up with another man. It was also not uncommon for Indian women to form relationships with overseers and white estate managers, as depicted, for example, in A. R. F. Webber's 1917 novel *Those That Be in Bondage*. Trotman contends that the women received very little sympathy despite their difficulty in resisting the advances of their employers, most officials choosing to blame "the very loose character of the majority of coolie women, and the temptations to which men in the positions of managers and overseers are subjected" (Longden to Kimberley, 21 August 1873, CO 295:269, qtd. in Trotman, "Women and Crime," *Caribbean Freedom* 253).

"Wife murders," D. W. D. Comins wrote in 1891, "form the foulest blot on our whole immigration system" (31; see also Minutes of the Legislative Council, 21 October 1890, qtd. in Tikasingh 272). A variety of explanations were offered for this phenomenon, ranging from the cultural (wife murder as proof of the moral depravity of heathens, as resulting from "Asiatic idiosyncrasies" or from the "constitutional jealousy of Orientals") to the materialistic (Indian men outraged at having the woman they had paid for become the wife of another man), the psychological (envy, jealousy, rage, and revenge), and the demographic (the disparity between the numbers of men and women). Whatever they saw as the causes of wife murder, the only possible remedy for the problem, according to some colonial officials, was the introduction of larger numbers of females (Tikasingh 272).

Other colonial officials, however, refused to accept the idea that the shortage of women recruits was at the root of the trouble, "suggesting that it was a question of quality rather than numbers: that the women were of such 'low class' that the men regarded them as chattels and treated them as such. Much was ascribed to 'Asiatic ideas' of the low value of female life" (Laurence 239). Prison authorities in Trinidad were of the view that "so long as there shall be in the Colony a large body of Asiatics who live as a race distinct from the rest of the labouring classes, keeping their own style of dress and observing their own peculiar traditions, it is useless to expect that the mere risk of death upon the scaffold will prevent their holding in Trinidad the same views with regard to their womankind that exist in the country from which they come" (Council Papers 47, Prison Report for 1885, 618, qtd. in Weller 66).

Charles Kingsley seems to concur: "Wife-murder is but too common among these Hindoos, and they cannot be made to see that it is wrong. 'I kill my own wife. Why not? I kill no other man's wife,' was said by as pretty, gentle, graceful a lad of two-and-twenty as one need see. . . . There is murder of wives, or quasi-wives now and then, among the baser sort of Coolies—murder because a poor girl will not give her ill-earned gains to the ruffian who considers her his property" (192). There is perhaps an additional hint here that the woman's "ill-earned gains" may be money obtained from another man than her husband.

Oral histories confirm the prevalence of wife murder, as in Fazal's testimony in Mahabir's *The Still Cry:*

> if e run way nex man daughter
>> e go beat e arse too
> if you have to run way wid man wife
>> leave one time
> dat man go kill e wife
>> kill two a dem. (56)

Much of the information about the nature of the relationships that led to wife murder comes from anecdotal sources. It was not easy to obtain statistical data about wife murder, since, as Judith Weller suggests, most of the time the crime was recorded as murder only when a conviction was obtained, and very often there was not enough evidence to convict the murderer (66). It is perfectly reasonable to imagine, then, that the incidence of wife murder was even higher than the records indicate. Early punishments for those caught enticing women away from their husbands included flogging, shaving, transfer of guilty parties to other estates, fines, and imprisonment, but these did not bring down the number of wife murders.

The eventual solution to the problem was sought in legislation about marriage, not just in punishment upon the scaffold. There seemed to be agreement on this score between the colonial authorities and the immigrant men. Witness this petition from Indian immigrants, signed by 274 Indians and witnessed by Canadian missionaries, Reverends Morton, Grant, and Christie, seeking enactment of an ordinance for registration of Indian marriages. The purpose of the registration was to enable "any person" to "prosecute an unfaithful spouse and their partner in guilt either in the Magistrates' Court, the Complaint Court or the Supreme Court, according as damages are laid at £10, at £25 or upwards, with provision for imprisonment if the damages be not paid, for the imprisonment of the wife if she refused to return to her husband, and also for the continued prosecution of the parties if the offence be persisted in" (Minutes of the Legislative Council, 28 January 1881, qtd. in Weller 74).

Interestingly, the petitioners did not demand divorce, but "the preservation of their households." Ordinance No. 6, of 1881, was passed to make the necessary provisions for the marriage and divorce of Indian immigrants. This applied only to Hindus and Muslims among the immigrants, since Christians were already covered by the existing laws of the colony (Weller 69). Tikasingh, however, speaks of the problems connected with registration under the Immigrants' Marriage and Divorce Ordinances, Nos. 6 (1881) and 23 (1891), suggesting that the difficulty was in part owing to the framing of the ordinances. "For example, the marriage ordinance of 1881 was really concerned mainly with the prevention of wife-murders rather than with the recognition of Indian marriages" (266). He goes on to say that "the act of registration itself was subject to numerous difficulties such as the age of the bride, *the lack of accurate information concerning the former marital status of either party,* and the refusal or neglect of either party to apply for registration of the marriage" (266, emphasis added).

Other kinds of solutions were sought too. In 1879, for instance, the acting governor of Trinidad, William Young, demanded measures to improve the "moral status of the Coolie woman." Only by recognizing their traits of character, among which he included thrift and industry, and initiating measures to develop them, Young contended, could "civilization and morality" be substantially improved among the Indian population. He maintained that Indian women were not strong enough for strenuous plantation labor but could exert a "civilizing and humanizing influence" if they devoted themselves to domestic duties (Young, qtd. in Mangru 224–25). This impulse coincided with that of the Canadian missionaries who in 1869 started the first schools for Indians, where there were distinctly different curricula for boys and girls, those for girls focusing primarily on the production of housewives.[3] Just a couple of years before Young's statement, the planters had passed a resolution asking for the indenture-free importation of Indian widows and "betrothed women" who had lost their intended husbands. This proposal had been suggested by the emigration agent at Calcutta, who commended the "pure and blameless lives" of these women; other colonial officials agreed that bringing in a higher class of females would ameliorate what they thought was the cause of the problem of wife murder: the immorality of immigrant women. This new scheme of emigration did not find support among recruiters in India, however, and eventually had to be dropped (Mangru 224–25).

Increasingly, the shameless Indian woman was represented as a matter of grave concern not just to colonial officials but also to Indian men, as we see from a 1916 letter written by Mohammed Orfy, who wrote numerous letters to the secretary of state for the colonies, the Indian government, and other authorities "on behalf of destitute Indian men of Trinidad": "Another most disgraceful concern, which is most prevalent, and a perforating plague, is the high percentage of immoral lives led by the female section of our community. They are enticed, seduced and frightened into becoming concubines, and paramours to satisfy the greed and lust of the male section of quite a different race to theirs." Having mentioned the susceptibility of the women to seduction, Orfy goes on to say that "they have absolutely no knowledge whatever of the value of being in virginhood and become most shameless and a perfect menace to the Indian gentry" (CO 571/4, WI 22518, qtd. in Reddock, *Women, Labour* 44).

Between Sarah Morton's comment about the Brahmin widow who took a new "papa" and the reasoning of educated East Indian men as exemplified by Mohammed Orfy, the difference might not be that the first stresses the wilfulness of the Indian woman, while the second is inclined to emphasize her susceptibility to "enticement," as did the colonial authorities who framed the marriage laws. Both Orfy and the colonial authorities were in agreement on the lax morals of the Indian woman immigrant. We might see the two—an emerging East Indian middle class in Trinidad and the colonial rulers—as complicit in the reconstitution of patriarchal structures that had become visible by the early twentieth century. However, it might not be accurate to assert, as Reddock appears to do, that "Indian tradition" simply comes to the fore once indentureship ends.

Let us briefly examine two kinds of approaches to the culture of Indians in Trinidad. The pioneering work of Morton Klass in the 1950s typifies one kind, in which classical anthropological paradigms prevail and indenture is seen as a temporary disruption in well-established patterns of living. In fact, Klass contended that village life among Hindu East Indians in Trinidad was

a faithful reproduction of village life in northern India, whence most of the indentured laborers came. The stress here is on cultural persistence and survival,
since culture is framed as that which continues through time and includes characteristics of people, for example, the supposed docility and submissiveness of
Indian women (a prevalent stereotype even today among Afro-Trinidadians
and other Creoles). The work of Rhoda Reddock typifies another approach,
one that employs a consciously historical paradigm and in Reddock's case
provides us with a nuanced understanding of women's lives under indenture. The emphasis, however, is on the twentieth-century reconstitution of
the Hindu and "Indian" family, with all its patriarchal features, including
proscriptions for women. The suggestion here is that "tradition" won out
in the end and was able to subjugate women, so that their options today
are not very different from those of women in India who have not shared
their history. The stories about immoral Indian women result, in Reddock's
analysis, in the construction of a new patriarchy and in the closure of the
question of women's agency, or "freedom denied." The implicit argument
here concerns East Indian women in the present and Reddock's perception
that like women in India, they do not live lives that are "free."

It is interesting that although historians and anthropologists are able to
document changes in areas such as caste, religion, and customs, they seem
to insist that with regard to women there were no changes at all or that if
they did occur, they were eventually reversed. Generally, they make a series
of culturalist assumptions according to which "Indians," no matter where
they are, continue to manifest certain behavioral patterns. Against both
these approaches, I would argue that the displacement caused by indenture
made for irreversible transformations, and the discursive deployment of the
East Indian woman in the anti-indentureship campaign, for example, is an
indicator of some of these changes.

Abolishing Indenture

In 1896 Gandhi, who was still living in South Africa at the time, had a
meeting with the nationalist leader Gopal Krishna Gokhale to try and interest him in the cause of overseas Indians. In 1901 Gandhi again spent some
time with Gokhale, who was to become one of his earliest admirers and
supporters in India. At Gandhi's urging, in February 1910 Gokhale guided
a resolution through the Imperial Legislative Council, of which he was a
member, calling for a complete ban on the recruitment of indentured labor.
In 1911 a ban was imposed on recruitment for Natal, and in 1917 the ban
was extended to all overseas colonies, but not before Gandhi and a host of
other nationalists had mounted a large-scale campaign against indenture.

As the historian Hugh Tinker points out, the campaign was, in fact,
Gandhi's first big political intervention in India. He gave anti-indenture

speeches all over the country, wrote about the topic at length in newspapers, and was able to get an Anti-Indenture Resolution passed at the Lucknow Congress in December 1916. By 1915 the indenture issue had become "the central question of Indian politics." Even as emigration itself declined for a variety of reasons, there was widespread nationalist protest, with meetings organized in Hyderabad Sind and Karachi (then in northwestern India), Allahabad (in the central region), Madras (in the south), and parts of Bengal (eastern India) (Tinker 334–47). The agitators called for an end to a system that they said was a "moral stigma" for the country. As Rhoda Reddock reiterates, issues of low wages or poor working conditions were far less important than "women's moral condition" in the campaign to abolish indentureship (*Women, Labour* 45). The historical significance of the anti-indenture campaign lies, Tinker suggests, in the fact that "this was the first major Indo-British political and social issue to be decided in dependent India, and not in metropolitan Britain" (288).

An examination of the nationalist discourse on indenture would reveal the crucial place occupied in it by the question of women's sexuality, helping us to understand why it was believed to be something unspeakable and why, paradoxically, it needed to be spoken about so interminably. Given this campaign's centrality to nationalist thought, it would be interesting to see how women were represented in the criticism of indentureship. I take as my point of departure some aspects of Partha Chatterjee's well-known argument about the nationalist resolution of the women's question. Chatterjee has tried to account for the relative insignificance of the "women's question" in the late nineteenth century by suggesting that nationalism was able to "resolve" the question by this time in accordance with its attempt to make "modernity consistent with the nationalist project" (*Nation and Its Fragments* 121).

In constructing a new woman—the middle-class, upper-caste *bhadramahila* (Bengali for "bourgeois lady")—nationalism in India was able to produce and enforce distinctions between the material might of the colonizer and the spiritual superiority of the colonized. Chatterjee suggests that the distinctions were embodied in new oppositions between public and private, the "world" (*bhaire*) and the "home" (*ghare*). In the former realm the Indian man acquired English education and took on the manners and dress of the British, while in the latter realm the Indian woman took on new markers of ethnicity and new responsibilities for maintaining the sanctity of the home, which was now additionally seen as a refuge from the world where the colonizer held sway, a point also made by Sumanta Banerjee in his study of nineteenth-century popular culture and the emergence of the *bhadralok*, or respectable classes (76). Although both Chatterjee and Banerjee write about Bengal, there are many parallels in relation to women and nationalism in other areas of India directly ruled by the British. The new woman envisaged by nationalism was "modern" but not heedlessly Westernized. Nor was she like the uneducated, vulgar, and coarse lower-caste/class working woman (Chatterjee 127). The lower-caste woman would be a central figure in the labor migrations of the nineteenth century.

The processes of differentiating the upper-caste woman from the lower-caste woman unfolded in a variety of spheres and were often based on seemingly "natural" categories. A comment in a Brahmo Samaj newspaper, *Tattwabodhini Patrika,* in 1880 opposed a proposal to educate respectable Bengali women so that they would become self-reliant, saying that "they did not have to be self-reliant since they were being looked after by their menfolk, and then added: 'Only among the women of the lower classes in this country, we come across some sort of self-reliance'" (qtd. in Banerjee 56). Banerjee's argument is that throughout the eighteenth century, lower-caste groups in Bengal rose in the social hierarchy, in the process distancing themselves from their poor and/or rural kinfolk and becoming a new middle class through access to an English education. "The stratification was ideologically buttressed by the *bhadralok* concept of *itarjan* and *chhotolok*—the pejorative terms used to describe the lower orders and evoke the picture of a lifestyle that was to be scrupulously avoided by the educated and privileged Bengalis" (71–72).

Among the features of a lifestyle to be avoided by the educated bhadralok was the close interaction between middle-class women and the wandering female artistes from the lower castes, who were a source of entertainment and education for those confined to the inner space of the courtyard. There was a concerted attempt by the bhadralok in the late nineteenth century, for example, to eliminate from the *andarmahal,* or women's quarters, the *panchalis,* or folk songs described as "filthy" and "polluting" by missionaries. This description was also echoed by Indians such as Shib Chunder Bose, in a book titled *The Hindoos As They Are:* "The Panchali (with female actresses only) which is given for the amusement of the females . . . is sometimes much too obscene and immoral to be tolerated in a zenana having any pretension to gentility. . . . Much is yet to be done to develop among the females a taste for purer amusements, better adapted to a healthy state of society" (qtd. in Banerjee 172). By the end of the nineteenth century, panchalis had ceased to be performed. We may speculate whether the de-skilling of large numbers of performers resulted in some of them joining the indentured migration to the Caribbean and elsewhere, as shown by the report on the dancing girls and their troupe waiting to embark for Surinam.

That the making of the bhadramahila involved a new domestication is evident from the effort to dissuade women from attending public recitals of epics, or *kathakata.* It was feared that descriptions of the erotic affairs of the gods, as in the *Krishna-leela,* for example, would be a bad influence on respectable women. According to a commentator in the Bengali journal *Somprakash* in 1863,

> Since it [*kathakata*] has become a source of so much evil, it is not advisable for bhadraloks to encourage it. Those who allow their ladies to go to kathakata performances should be careful. . . . If, during kathakata performances, women stay home and are provided with opportunities to listen to good instructions, discussions on good books and to train themselves in artistic occupations, their religious sense will improve and their souls will become pure and they will be suited to domestic work. (Qtd. in Banerjee 171)

The genealogy of the domestic woman has been traced in contexts other than Bengal, as the nationalists attempted to fashion a purified civilizational essence in the face of missionary and colonialist criticism. As Susie Tharu and K. Lalita argue,

> In India . . . the middle-class woman's propriety was also to be vindicated under the glare of the harsh spotlight focused right through the nineteenth century on what was described as the moral degeneration of the Indians. Bureaucrats, missionaries, journalists and western commentators of various kinds filed sensational reports about Indian culture and made authoritative analyses of Indian character, which was invariably represented as irrational, deceitful and sexually perverse. The ultimate thrust of these descriptions was usually quite clear: the situation in India was so appalling that it called out for intervention by rational and ethical rulers [such as the British]. ("Empire, Nation" 208)

Tharu and Lalita wrote this in the context of the controversy about reprinting *Radhika Santwanam* (Appeasing Radhika), by the eighteenth-century Telugu poetess Muddupalani, a *ganika* (courtesan) at the royal court of Thanjavur. In 1911 another learned woman in the tradition of Muddupalani, Bangalore Nagaratnamma, reprinted her predecessor's poem, only to be charged with obscenity. The poem describes the relationship between Radha and Krishna and the nature of their intimacy and was considered a fine literary work in its time. Copies of the book were seized and their sale forbidden. In an 1887 edition of the poem by the linguist Venkatanarasu, an associate of the lexicographer C. P. Brown, the verses considered sexually explicit and obscene had been removed. Initiatives led by the nationalist upper caste, such as the construction of the good Indian woman, sometimes found unlikely allies, such as the non-Brahmin Self-Respect movement, which in the 1920s provided support to the anti-nautch campaign, also setting up as normative "the virtuous domestic woman" (Tharu and Lalita, *Women Writing in India* 13). The anti-nautch campaign, which reached its peak in 1911, was initiated by Western-educated reformers in the early 1890s who wrote about the degradation of women and the threat posed to the purity of family life by devadasis, temple and court artists, often derogatorily referred to as "nautch girls." The bill prohibiting dedication of women in temples was finally passed in 1947 (12–13).

Another figure evolved to complete the picture of virtuous womanhood was that of the upper-caste widow. The historian Tanika Sarkar contends that the Hindu widow emerged as a significant figure in nineteenth-century Bengal because her "purity," chosen consciously by her, "becomes at once a sign of difference and of superiority, a Hindu claim to power" (41). Women's monogamy, then, made possible the existence of the Hindu nation. As a contemporary writer, Srinibas Basu, put it, "This so-called subjection of our woman produces this sacred jewel of chastity which still glows radiantly throughout the civilised world despite centuries of political subjection" (*Hindur Achar Vyavahar,* qtd. in Sarkar 41). Sarkar argues that the ascetic widow was seen as gaining moral and spiritual energy through her "voluntary abdication of all earthly pleasures," thus ensuring "a reservoir of spirituality in each home and for the Hindu order as a whole" (42).

Although in the nineteenth century and later various forms of widow remarriage and cohabitation were prevalent, ascetic widowhood and sometimes sati (immolation with the husband's corpse) came to be seen as the norm in nationalist discourse. This would serve to illuminate Sarah Morton's annoyance and bewilderment at the behavior of her prospective Indian converts in late nineteenth-century Trinidad, who seemed so far removed from ascetic upper-caste norms.

The period when indentured emigration to the other colonies began, the 1830s, was also the period of the initial formation, via the social-reform movements, of nationalist discourse in India. Since the nationalists believed that official modernity would be produced through the project of the future nation, there was no room for formations of modernity other than those involving middle-class, upper-caste Indians. The problem with indentured laborers, both men and women, was that their geographic displacement and the new context they came to inhabit was enabling them also to become "modern." The transformations in the lives of the indentured caused by displacement, the plantation system, the disparate sex ratio, racial politics, and so on, had to be made invisible by nationalist discourse in order for the indentured to be claimed as authentically Indian. This was accomplished, I suggest, by erasing the difference between the agricultural laborer in Bihar and the one in Trinidad ("Chinitat," as the indentured called it) or in other parts of the subaltern diaspora and imaging these latter in particular as victimized, pathetic, lost, and helpless. Even when the changes in the emigrant were acknowledged, they were criticized as "artificial" and "superficial," loss rather than gain. Gandhi writes that the laborer came back to India "a broken vessel," robbed of "national self-respect" ("Speech on Indentured Labour" 133). Any economic gain he might have obtained could not be set off "against the moral degradation it involves" ("Indentured Labour" 249).

The indentured woman in particular could not be accommodated in the nationalist discourse, again except as a victim of colonialism. By 1910 or so, when the campaign against indenture was gathering momentum, nationalism had already produced the models of domesticity, motherhood, and companionate marriage that would make the Indian woman a citizen of the new India. The question of what constituted the modernity of the Indian woman had been put forward as an *Indian* question, to be resolved *in India*. What, then, of the Indian women who were "becoming modern," but elsewhere? For nationalism, theirs would have to be considered an illegitimate modernity, because it had not passed through, been formed by, the story of the nation-in-the-making. By the late nineteenth century the route to modernity—and emancipation—for the Indian woman in India was a well-established one: education, cultivation of household arts, refinement of skills, regulation of one's emotions. The class-caste provenance of this project, and of the new woman, needs no further iteration here.

What sort of ideological project, then, did nationalism envisage for the indentured woman laborer who was shaping her own relationship with the "West" in a distant land? Reform was not practicable. Disavowal of this figure would not have been possible while the system of indenture still existed. The only solution, therefore, was to strive for the abolition of indenture. The manifest immorality and depravity of the indentured woman would not only bring down the system but also serve to reveal more clearly the contrasting image of the virtuous and chaste Indian woman at home. As Gandhi asserted, "Women, who in India would never touch wine, are sometimes found lying dead-drunk on the roads" ("Indenture or Slavery?" 147). The point is not that women never drank in India and started doing so in Trinidad or British Guiana but that for Gandhi and others this functioned as a mark of degraded Westernization and "artificial modernity." The nationalist reconstitution of Indian tradition, I suggest, was still incomplete when the new phase of the nationalist struggle, marked by the anti-indenture campaign, was inaugurated.

Although according to Chatterjee the nationalists had "resolved" the women's question without making it a matter for political agitation, with the anti-indenture campaign there seems to have been a renewed focus on women. At the end of the first decade of the twentieth century a *political* campaign was undertaken—mobilizing against the colonial rulers "a wider public than any previous protest" (Kelly 48)—to dismantle a system that was said to be turning Indian women into prostitutes.[4] As Gandhi wrote,

"The system brings India's womanhood to utter ruin, destroys all sense of modesty. That in defence of which millions in this country have laid down their lives in the past is lost under it" ("Speech at Surat" 349). The nationalist discourse on indentured female sexuality, however, veered time and again from denouncing the women as reprobate and immoral to seeing them as having been brought to this state by colonialism.[5]

The Indian nationalists were joined by the European critics of indenture, led by C. F. Andrews, Gandhi's associate, who had worked with him in South Africa and had been mobilized by him to prepare a report on Indians in Fiji. As the anthropologist John Kelly puts it, Andrews and others "portrayed indenture . . . as a degenerating force and blamed it for the moral condition of the 'helots of Empire.' But they accepted the claim that the 'coolies' were degraded, and they agreed especially about what we might call the 'harlots of Empire'" (33–34). Gandhi's focus on the alleged sexual availability of women can also be read as a strategic move to counter the colonial administrative reports that defined, as Susan Bayly puts it, "the dependent status of unclean menial groups . . . in terms of the sexual availability of their womenfolk" (196). If indenture were ended, and the conditions for chastity for women thus provided, they would cease to be available, for instance, to their white employers in the colonies; thus, nationalism could refuse menial status for Indians in relation to the colonizer.

The nationalist campaign to end indenture was supported by a series of developments in Trinidad. By 1870, voices were being raised in the Creole press against importing Indian laborers. There was public criticism of the size of the subsidy for immigration, especially by cocoa interests (who used free labor, compared with sugarcane planters, who used indentured labor) and the professional colored and black middle class. The Creole middle class also sought to diminish the influence of the planters during the campaign for constitutional reform in the mid-1880s. Creoles who feared the influx of Indians into the political system they hoped to capture found new reasons to attack the system of immigration (Laurence 432–34). After the Hosay riots of 1884, when Moharram processionists in Trinidad were killed by the colonial police, the interest of the Indian press in the conditions of indentured laborers began to grow. The Anti-Slavery Society, in England, which had long criticized indenture, renewed its attacks after the 1884 riots (Laurence 448–54).

After immigration to Natal and some other countries was prohibited, Gokhale moved in the Legislative Council on March 4, 1912, that indentured emigration be wholly prohibited. He spoke eloquently of the misery of the immigrants, of the "immorality" resulting from the disparate sex ratio, and of the blow to national self-respect. The agitation to end indenture was fueled by the publication of reports from Fiji. An Anti-Indentured

Emigration League was formed in 1914. As Laurence writes, "Centred in Calcutta, it organized public lectures and the distribution of pamphlets against emigration and tried to discourage recruits on their way to Calcutta from continuing their journey. Soon it also began to operate in the United Provinces" (465). Leaflets were distributed in towns and villages, recruiters were molested, and relatives were brought to Calcutta to secure the release of recruits from the depot.

In 1915 Gokhale died, but Gandhi had returned from South Africa by then to provide leadership to the agitation. On March 20, 1916, Pandit Madan Mohan Malaviya's motion was discussed in the Legislative Council. He listed all the evils of the immigration system, drawing extensively on the situation in Fiji, and spoke of indenture as "a horrifying record of shame and crime," demanding that "the system . . . be abolished root and branch." In February 1917 Malaviya sought permission to introduce a bill for immediate abolition, which was disallowed. Not being able to obtain a clear assurance from the government about ending indenture, Gandhi toured the country and addressed public meetings, demanding that the abolition be announced before the end of July (Gandhi, "Abolition of Indentured Emigration"). Large demonstrations were held in Madras and Bombay. The viceroy, Charles Hardinge, was "pelted with telegrams," and his wife received many "asking her whether she approves of Indian women being converted into harlots and imploring her to help." Attempts were made to mobilize the opinion of Indian women. An appeal by Andrews to Indian women was printed in several languages and widely distributed in the United Provinces (Laurence 477–78).

As the final phase of the campaign against indenture gained momentum, among the delegations that met with Viceroy Hardinge to press for action were several organized by Indian women's associations. At the meeting between Colonial Office and India Office representatives on May 9, 1917, James Meston, representing India in the War Cabinet, stated that "the women of India" felt "deeply on the question [of indenture]." Satyendra Sinha, the other India representative, declared that "there was an intensely strong feeling of concern," including on the part of "ladies who lived in purdah, but read the news" (Tinker 350–52). In spite of Englishmen such as Alfred Lyall, governor of the North Western Provinces, and G. A. Grierson, who reported on emigration from Bengal and recommended it for its benefits to women, saying that it gave a chance for a new life to "abandoned and unfaithful wives" (Tinker 267–68), Viceroy Hardinge was unwilling to continue supporting a system whose "discussion arouses more bitterness than any other outstanding question." Hardinge was convinced that Indian politicians firmly believed that it "brands their whole race . . . with the stigma of helotry" and condemned Indian women to prostitution (340–41).

By mid-1917 the end of indenture was certain. Historians tend to see it as an issue that brought a new focus to nationalist politics in India and gave it a wider base. I would argue that it was not simply that. We need to reframe the indenture question so that it can be seen as marking the consolidation of the early national-modern, a putting into place of new (nationalist) moralities, new ways of relating between women and men, appropriate "Indian" modes of sociosexual behavior, the parameters for the state's regulation of reproduction as well as sexuality, and the delineation of the virtues that would ensure for Indian women citizenship in the future nation. It should be obvious that the historical formation of these virtues, for example, and the contemporaneity of their description were obscured by the nationalist presentation of them as the essential, and "traditional," qualities of Indian women.

While it is evident that the emigrant female was an important figure invoked by Indian nationalism in India, the centrality of this figure to "East Indian nationalism" in Trinidad has not yet been systematically elaborated.[6] With regard to the indentured woman too, the immediate contrasting image for the colonialist was the African woman, the ex-slave, the urban *jamette* of Carnival, whose sexuality was othered, and sought to be regulated, by the European ruling class (Rohlehr, ch. 1). The jamette was seen as vulgar, promiscuous, loud, and disruptive, and the removal of this figure from Carnival and related activities became part of the project of creating a new urban middle class in Trinidad in the early twentieth century. Charles Kingsley, visiting Trinidad in 1909, sketched his impressions of African and Indian women. Describing the "average negro women of Port of Spain, especially the younger," he called attention to "their masculine figures, their ungainly gestures, their loud and sudden laughter, even when walking alone, and their general coarseness, shocks, and must shock." In contrast to the "the superabundant animal vigour and the perfect independence of the younger [African] women" is the picture of a young Indian woman "hung all over with bangles, in a white muslin petticoat . . . and green gauze veil; a clever, smiling, delicate little woman, who is quite aware of the brightness of her own eyes" (72).

Much of the elite's anxiety surrounding the jamette or even the rural Creole woman seemed to hinge on the fact of her being seen as independent, in both sexual and economic terms. The East Indian woman in postslavery society, then, brought in to compensate colonial planters for the loss of captive labor, had to be imaged as completely different from the African woman. For this, "Indian tradition" was invoked by different groups, and indentured women's failure to conform to the virtuous ideal of Indian culture was deplored. In post-indenture society the need to differentiate between the

African and the Indian woman would take on a new kind of urgency, both for the emerging Indo-Trinidadian middle class and for the dominant Creole imaginary. One important mode of differentiation would have to do with denying the obvious similarities between women of all races in Trinidad and emphasizing instead the similarities between indentured women and women in India. However, as I have tried to argue, the indentured woman was a figure that the nationalist construction of Indian womanhood had to disavow precisely in order to ensure its own coherence. If one set of reasons for the disavowal arose from the non-upper-caste provenance of the indentured woman, another set had to do with her incorporation into Creole modernity. But clearly, what placed indentured Indians outside the normative frameworks that were being assembled in India was not one set of reasons rather than another but the combination of both sets.

Thinking about Trinidad might be interesting to those of us investigating the processes by which contemporary feminism in India comes to rest on the historical disavowal of lower-caste/class women even as it claims to speak for them. The Trinidad example shows that for Indians in India this also involves a disavowal of other forms of modernity that have not passed through the anticolonial struggle or participated in its inevitable outcome. As Mrinalini Sinha contends, "The nationalist construct of the modern Indian woman also created the climate both for women's reforms and for women's entry, under male patronage, to the male-dominated public sphere." Sinha describes the early initiatives of Indian feminists as being linked to the "unprecedented mobilization of middle-class women" in the nationalist movement, manifested, for example, in the all-India women's organizations of the early twentieth century (483), many of which would have petitioned the viceroy in support of the campaign to abolish indenture. While nationalism provided the language and the spaces in which the middle-class woman could become modern, it also made her a representative, one who spoke for all other Indian women, who became, as Sinha puts it, "the transmitter of the fruits of modernization" (494). The indentured woman in the subaltern diaspora could never be seen in India as this kind of figure, given her caste/class characteristics and the tangentiality of her modernity to the project of the future nation. It is not just the notion of the female in India today, therefore, that rests on a disavowal of the indentured woman, but also the notion of the feminist, who has crucially been implicated in the project of nationalism even as she tried to formulate a critique of it.

In this essay I have tried to suggest that the present-day critical interventions in relation to the formation of the Indian national-modern might be strengthened by an examination of its illegitimate and disavowed double, "Indian" modernity in the Caribbean. It is hoped that this exercise will also yield unexpected benefits for those intervening in issues of modernity and gender in Trinidad, affording especially for feminists a different purchase on the production of normative femininities and their complicity with discourses of racial difference.

Notes

1. Ranade's article was published in October 1893 in the *Sarvajanik Sabha Quarterly Journal,* edited by Gokhale. See Nanda, bk. 4, ch. 37.

2. At the Calcutta meeting of the Congress, Gandhi had Gokhale's assurance that a resolution on South Africa would be passed, and when his name was called, Gandhi read the resolution. As Gandhi wrote about that moment, "Someone had printed and distributed amongst the delegates copies of a poem he had written in praise of foreign emigration. I read the poem and referred to the grievances of the settlers in South Africa." Since all resolutions passed unanimously, Gandhi's too was passed, which did not mean that delegates had read and understood it. "And yet the very fact that it was passed by the Congress was enough to delight my heart," wrote Gandhi. "The knowledge that the *imprimatur* of the Congress meant that of the whole country was enough to delight anyone" (Gandhi, *My Experiments with Truth* 341).

3. According to Reddock, in 1891 only 6.2 percent of the female Indians were officially "housewives" rather than estate workers. The later years of indenture saw women's withdrawal into the domestic economy. Depressed wages for Indian laborers were accompanied by permission to produce cane and food crops on a piece of land that would be looked after by the wife and children. Women who worked for the family thus received no wages, although they were involved in "cane farming, market gardening, rice production and animal husbandry" (*Women, Labour* 39).

4. Note that after the end of indenture, the women's question in India became a social issue, to be resolved through legislation, not political mobilization.

5. John Kelly, for instance, points out that in the case of Fiji the critics of indenture stressed the sexual abuse of Indian women (30).

6. Recent unpublished work by Rhoda Reddock and Patricia Mohammed makes interesting beginnings in this direction.

Caribbean Migrations

Negotiating Borders

Evelyn O'Callaghan

Why do they go?
They do not know.

. . . .

What do they hope for
what find there
these New World mariners
　　　　—Edward Brathwaite, *The Arrivants*

IN HER STUDY *What Women Lose,* María Cristina Rodríguez
unpacks literary accounts of migration—what Alison Donnell calls the
condition of "elsewhereness" ("What It Means to Stay")—by Caribbean
women writers. However, it is increasingly tricky to distinguish between
Caribbean and migrant or diasporic Caribbean writers, since contemporary writers from the region tend to spend extended periods of time "elsewhere" (Europe or North America) as temporary, permanent, or "strategic"
migrants. But returning to Rodríguez's title, it is necessary to clarify that
she also speaks to what Caribbean women are seen to *gain* "elsewhere,"
mainly in the British and North American cities where they have made a
space for themselves. I want to make a connection between constructions of
home and "elsewhere" for Caribbean women and permissible sexual subjectivities in and between both sites. Specifically, this essay suggests that
women's narratives frame the West Indian home space as a place where
traditional gender roles are rigidly upheld and transgressive female sexualities are punished, via rejection by the national body and/or violence against
the woman's body. By contrast, the texts construct metropolitan centers as
offering options for the "freeing up" of alternative sexual subjectivities. But
if the fictions indict the heteronormative patriarchal structures of Caribbean
nation-states, do they also imply that women who claim a certain kind of
sexual freedom must explicitly or implicitly qualify their Caribbean citizenship? Put simplistically, do the writers depict Caribbean women as forced
to choose between exploring unorthodox or non-normative sexualities and

gender norms "elsewhere" and settling for a repressed, cowed existence "here"? More insidiously, can migration deliver this liberation, or does Caribbean culture continue to police females in exile, even if the sanctions are different in the diasporic location?

Moving between sociological and literary sources, Rodríguez records the marked shift from predominantly *male* migrations in the first half of the twentieth century to migrations including large numbers of Caribbean women traveling alone to cities to take up service-sector jobs in North America or Europe since the 1960s. Both women and men "go to cities for economic reasons," but the women also go "to free themselves" from the "family stronghold of island culture" in which they are configured as subordinates (15). Rodríguez concludes from the textual evidence that "Caribbean women always migrate to acquire some degree of independence" (12). And such independence involves leaving behind "negative gender assumptions: a woman's 'place' in island society as sex object, a faithful, passive and subservient wife, or the sacrificing mother of baby boys" (12). She cites Carole Boyce Davies and Olivia Espín in support of the claim "that even if the loss experienced by these women can never be compensated, there are decisive advantages in living outside the homeland" (14).

I set up these claims in Rodríguez's study rather baldly in order to open up some questions. For example, in the realm of gender and sexual relations, *what* advantages accrue to Caribbean women from living outside the homeland? What do the narratives suggest that Caribbean women *gain* by migrating, given that they lose a great deal (connections, relationships, cultural certainties) and face inevitable encounters with racism, suspicion, and marginalization, as well as the loneliness of dislocation, rupture, and "elsewhereness"? For one thing, they escape abuse. Rodríguez argues that the losses and hardships of migrant women are balanced against some aspects of what it means to be female in the Caribbean: "kinship abuse, gender oppression, sexual repression, violence . . . . The women . . . recall repressive and controlling fathers and mothers, abusing husbands . . . and gender fixity" (19–20).

Donnette Francis supports this claim. She describes "third wave" Caribbean women's writing as finally addressing the "unspeakability" of intimate violence in women's lives. Such writing is "transnational," the work of women such as Edwidge Danticat, Patricia Powell, Elizabeth Nunez, Oonya Kempadoo, and Shani Mootoo, all of whom have lived and/or written for extensive periods outside the Caribbean. Caribbean women's writing in the 1980s and 1990s, she notes, interrogated Caribbean female socialization and its "restrictive social scripts" concerning sexual behavior ("Uncovered Stories" 68). For example, Jamaica Kincaid's *Annie John* (1983) challenges and ultimately destabilizes middle-class codes of female respectability privileged by the nuclear family, school, and community, leading Annie to seek a home *outside* the Caribbean, where class-inflected gender roles might be less rigidly enforced. And the "third wave" of textual production (from the late 1990s on) more forcibly foregrounds the clash between Caribbean women's sexual choices and their "sense of belonging to the national community" (70), so that the migrant context is envisaged as more empowering.

Danticat's *Breath, Eyes, Memory* (1994), for instance, is a painful text in which the narrative exposes a nation-state that normalizes violence against women and de-romanticizes cultural mythology that condones (by concealing) sexual abuse as "appropriate punishment for a subordinate who has misbehaved" (Francis, "Uncovered Stories" 70–72). Bad girls and women are brutalized by male agents of state power and, more insidiously, by women in the "testing" ritual, in which girls' vaginas are manually checked by mothers or mother figures to determine that the hymen remains intact. In a culturally sanctioned yet perverse scenario, Danticat's rape victim violates her own daughter in an effort to police the girl's chastity. Powell's *The Pagoda* (1998) and Nunez's *Bruised Hibiscus* (2000) are other examples of "third wave" writing, nasty stories of damage done to women's minds and bodies by sexual violence in the name of moral righteousness. What surfaces in this writing is a current of rage and disgust at Caribbean societies for their failure to offer equal rights and protection to women, children, and others marginalized for sexual difference. Francis considers such literature crucial interventions into the "hushed up" stories of Caribbean sexual subordination and abuse, challenging "dominant sexual ideologies" in the region (78).

How do Caribbean women *now* read and respond to "dominant sexual ideologies"? For instance, in the twenty-first-century Caribbean, how do my (predominantly female) undergraduate students respond to these textual border clashes? What gender and sexual subjectivities do they see as permissible "here" and what can only be tolerated "elsewhere"? I have been teaching Caribbean women's writing at the University of the West Indies (UWI) since the early 1980s, and increasingly, I have been puzzled by the reactions of the women in my classes, who may range from eighteen-year-olds fresh from high school to working women in their mid-thirties. Many are mothers (often single); most are fashionably (often skimpily) dressed and apparently comfortable with their sexuality. Yet even though they apparently buy into the celebration (and sometimes commodification?) of women's bodies in Caribbean popular culture, female sexuality tends to remain a difficult, even taboo subject for them when it comes to literary discourse, so that I have been astounded at their conservative and judgmental responses to narratives dealing frankly with this subject.

Case 1: A visiting Fulbright doctoral student sitting in on a seminar was shocked by the unsympathetic reaction of female Caribbean classmates to Sam Selvon's construction in *The Lonely Londoners* of white women as "flesh . . . skin. . . . thing." After all, they argued, the white female characters were promiscuous, had no business sleeping with the immigrant men, and deserved the humiliating treatment they received. The "poor black men" were only doing to these women what had, in some sense, been done to them by English society.

Case 2: Discussing a brutal rape scene in Leone Ross's *All the Blood Is Red,* women students deplored the assault yet endorsed a female character in the novel who blames the victim: "She should have watched out for herself some more. It was a matter of self-preservation. Men would always be tempted" (186).

Case 3: The reactions of women students to depictions of gay or lesbian sexual desire, such as the lesbian relationship in Alice Walker's *The Color Purple* or homoeroticism in Kincaid's *Lucy,* were disgustedly visceral: "Yuck!" And the notion that children could not only be fascinated by sex but also take sensual pleasure from their own bodies—as in Kempadoo's *Buxton Spice*—drew vehement objections from several young mothers, who said that children "don't have no business with that!"

I am attempting, then, to measure these anecdotal accounts of responses to Caribbean women's fiction against the writing itself, which, as I have previously suggested ("Compulsory Heterosexuality"), exposes national cultures as invested in denying and repressing female sexuality, shrouding it in secrecy and shame. When women act on their desire, it is configured as acquiescence to male pressure and inevitably devalues the woman as "damaged goods." Worse, several texts point to the reinforcement of this ideology by Caribbean mothers, godmothers, sisters, aunties, grannies, and neighbors. So much for an idealized community of women passing on cultural values and postcolonial resistance; instead, the fictions evoke the matriarchs as (often brutal) enforcers of patriarchal sexual morality. Young women who do not observe the rules deserve their fate, for, as Jeanette's mother reiterates throughout Ross's narrative, "who can't hear must feel." *Buxton Spice* openly depicts young Guyanese girls exploring their bodies and reveling in sensual pleasure, albeit within the learned (heterosexual, hierarchical, gender-specific) paradigm of "Husbands and Wives." But once this experimentation graduates into the real thing—as in Judy's clandestine interludes with a young (black) man—the women of the tribe close in with repressive violence. It is swift and brutal, administered by the mother as directed by the (law of the) father: "Emelda, you deal wid dat" (164). Her way of dealing with her daughter is to beat a confession out of her, concluding with a violation of the girl's body commensurate with rape:

> "How long now you openin yuh legs fuh he?"
> "No Mammie . . . aagh . . ."

Emelda slapped her loud. . . .

"Yuh can't hide nuthing from me. You. Yuh lying little whoa. I always suspect you. *Blight.*" She got the panty off one foot, Judy not resisting. Pushed open her legs. "Agnes, look!" (167–68)

Kempadoo's description is, as my students say, "raw." Other writers depict older women as slightly more circumspect in monitoring girls' chastity and respectability, but the violence differs only in that it is not physical. Annie John's mother spits out the label "slut" at her daughter simply for being seen publicly conversing with a group of schoolboys (102). Similarly, the mother in Ross's text invokes a socially sanctioned Caribbean construct of female desire as "nastiness" to be rigorously repressed and denied. Shame at her own sexual past as an *"ol' whore"* (239) motivates her to run with her daughters from such temptation in the Caribbean, where men *"will promise you dem liver an' dem kidney if dem ah go get de crotches"* (72). But tormented by *"de sinful part of me [that] did like de work"* (137), she weighs all women, including her own daughters, on the same unforgiving scales of "nasty" and "good."

Girls and women who are found wanting, who fail to learn their "proper" gendered place, or who disrespect husbands and fathers meet with similar judgment in Powell's *Me Dying Trial.* Gwennie tries for years to conceal the sordid reality of her marriage—"how Walter beat and abuse her, how him take her money and keep other woman with her, how life hard and miserable with the man" (13). Yet she accepts her victimization out of guilt for a past love affair: "She have a feeling this was her punishment from God because of what she do with Luthor, and so she just lie down on the floor, and hide her head and her face from his blows . . . and listen to him curse" (19). Through the rhetoric of judgment and punishment, these narratives implicate fundamentalist Christianity in women's acceptance of their own degradation. Gwennie's brutalization haunts her even in exile, and sex cannot be de-linked from shame (117). As with Ross's mother, the Bible is invoked to condemn assertive (ergo unchaste) women and to censor "unnaturalness" and deviant sexualities: "According to Pastor Longmore those things wrong. One Sunday in church, him mention how all those men who go to one another for love and affection had better change them ways, for God just going to shut the doors of heaven in them face" (96). Indicting the wilful blindness of Caribbean communities to violence against women and children, Powell parallels the plight of gay men in a fiercely homophobic society with the suffering of beaten women in what appears a misogynistic culture.

Mootoo's *Cereus Blooms at Night* pushes the boundaries further. Jane Bryce observes that Mootoo, like Kempadoo, is concerned with sexuality and violence, transgression and retribution (72), an observation that applies equally to the other writers discussed. At the novel's dark heart is Chandin, an Indo-Caribbean laborer converted and adopted by a white Presbyterian missionary family, with whom he lives as a second-class "son." His "unnatural" love for his white "sister," Lavinia, is, of course, forbidden, and he marries one of his own kind. But his wife, Sarah, and his "sister" fall in love—another taboo alliance—and once discovered the women can only escape Chandin's murderous rage by emigrating, leaving behind Sarah's two daughters. In revenge for this betrayal, Chandin repeatedly rapes his elder daughter until the ruin of her life leads her to end his, a secret that emerges, along with others, only at the end of the tale. As in *Me Dying Trial,* the collusion of the community in male abuse of powerless women and children is exposed in the devastatingly polite euphemism of the father's having "mistaken Mala for his wife." Does the parallel suggest that the daughter is enduring what a wife *normally* endures? Must she pay for the fact that after all, Mala's mother "had mistaken another woman for her husband" (109). Does it make respectable people less uncomfortable with child abuse and incest to invoke the normative relations of marriage? The silencing of such perversion, the inability or failure to name it, and the equation of the unnatural sexual behavior of the father with the same-sex desire of the mother underscore the deeply conservative nature of Caribbean sexual morality, its intolerant and repressive attitudes toward inappropriate desire and sexual difference. This brings me to my final observation.

For Bryce, Mootoo's challenging of categories of gender and sexual orientation makes a space for the silenced stories of gays, lesbians, and transgender West Indians. Donnell tellingly observes that while "freedom struggles and rights movements have been the foundation of postcolonial studies from its very beginnings," the "campaign for gay rights" has not been part of the postcolonial agenda ("Spectacle of Deviance" 1). Significantly, it is writers like Mootoo, who have *left,* who are safe in North America or Europe, that dare to treat of such issues in their work. Several of Mootoo's characters evade biological categorization and ambiguously "perform" gender, in Judith Butler's sense of the term; but in the Caribbean this ambiguity must be hidden. *Cereus,* then, bravely attempts to de-familiarize what Bryce terms "the rules of gender and identity which blight the lives of those they bind" (73). And the authority consistently cited for these "rules of gender and identity" is the fundamentalist Christian rhetoric of sin and retribution, co-opted—as in Powell's and Ross's texts—to punish perceived sexual transgression on the part of women and "deviants," who are constituted as second-class or noncitizens of the nation.

Back to my students for a moment. For some years the extracurricular activities participated in by the majority—and the majority are women—are organized around the Inter Varsity Christian Fellowship, with its variety of spin-off associations and clubs: prayer groups, Campus Crusade for Christ, faith fellowships, and church services. I would venture to say that this is the case on all three UWI campuses, as well as at the associated tertiary-level institutions in the Eastern Caribbean where UWI programs are offered. West Indian nation-states pride themselves on being "Christian," Bible-reading, churchgoing, and morally conservative—bordering on prudish—when it comes to female sexuality. "Ask most Caribbean women if religion is an oppressive force to them or anyone else," observes Tomiko Ballantyne-Nisbett, a self-styled "open-minded" North American college student of Trinidadian origin, "and they will laugh in your face and quote you a psalm" (1). Caribbean women rarely achieve positions of public leadership, and "if you ask a Caribbean woman about this, chances are she will say that the man is the head of the household and should rule over her. And she will quote Scripture to support it too. And she will say that she is free, and the truth is that the Church or Temple or Mosque or Kingdom Hall is the one place that her husband will let her attend without complaint" (2). Admittedly, West Indian women complain "that domestic violence, incest, and rape continue to spoil the lives of many women and children. They know that they are paid less than men for doing the same jobs," but "they are reluctant to concede . . . the significant role that religion plays in maintaining the status quo" (3–4). This insight comes from a young woman who knows, but has achieved critical distance from, her home culture.

Another "outsider," the Australian Annette Daley, observes that studies of Caribbean women's writing rarely focus on the representation of religion, suggesting a taboo that needs to be addressed. If the critics are reticent, I would argue that the *fictions* of Caribbean women writers interrogate the power of institutional Christianity in reinforcing heteronormative patriarchy, the denigration of the body in general and female sexuality in particular. Ross's *All the Blood Is Red,* for example, illustrates the dead hand of doctrinaire moralizing that travels from Jamaica to London, still fulminating in the language of sin versus righteousness: *"Me bring dem up in de ways of de Lord . . . warn dem how life hard an' man nasty . . . warn dem mustn't fornicate"* (239, emphasis in original).

In the public sphere, investment in a biblically authorized notion of the "moral fabric of society" privileges a specific model of gender hierarchy and heterosexual normality. Yet as Mootoo demonstrates, heterosexuality has a pathological side. This is confirmed by countless court reports cited in the media. "Spurned lover jailed for 10 years" records the sentencing of a twenty-seven-year-old man in Trinidad who had strangled his common-law wife after she told him he could not satisfy her. "Crushed by His Love" cites the testimony of the Barbadian accused who had dropped a large boulder onto his victim, "crushing the left side of her face into her brain":

"I lose my control but I ain't kill she for purpose," he quietly told lawmen. "The Lord knows I love she," he said.

"Explain," the lawman across from him said, pencil poised above his notebook.

"I get frighten after she say she gine tell that I screw she so I drop the rock 'pon she face," Clarke volunteered. (Evanson 16A)

Does the diaspora space as configured in Caribbean migrant women's fiction offer some refuge from this kind of pathology? As I have noted ("Settling into 'Unhomeliness'"), Mootoo's *Out on Main Street* is enlightening in its contrast of attitudes toward same-sex desire in the West Indies and in Canada. In "Lemon Scent" a suspicious Trinidadian husband warns his wife about her close friendship with another woman: "'You know, she might be one of those types who likes only women.' . . . With his lips almost against hers he whispers, 'If I ever find out that you two have slept together I will kill you both'" (28). By contrast, in the title story, "Out on Main Street," lesbian Caribbean women in Canada are unabashed about their sexuality, displaying it in ways that would disturb the "moral fabric of society" at home.

Migration for Gwennie in Powell's *Me Dying Trial* provides asylum from her abusive marriage, and she guards her new independence, refusing to move in with her lover: "I live with husband too long. When them own everything in the house, them think them can own you too. Them boss-boss you around as them have a mind. I want a different life. I didn't come all the way to Foreign to put up with that same damn foolishness" (114). Caribbean migrant women in the text are free to choose independence, even to embrace alternative lifestyles (Gwennie's daughter experiments with lesbianism). Ross's text too depicts young West Indian migrant women in London as far more open about their sexual needs and acting on them in ways that would be condemned at home. Like Kincaid's Lucy, Ross's Jeanette refuses the oppressive moral regime imported by her immigrant mother. Jeanette acts on her desires, "using every single flick of hip and eyelash, every brain cell, every bit of punani power" to attract male partners (15).

Yet how free *are* they? Gwennie may opt for independence from traditional gender roles for herself, but her son's homosexuality is "nastiness" to her, as it is to the moral majority at home. And this revulsion is a sobering reminder that even in diasporic spaces an internalized "Christian" patriarchal morality still haunts women, still taints certain kinds of desire as sinful and shameful. Even in "elsewhere," Rodríguez reminds us, generations of older Caribbean women continue to socialize their daughters to be obedient, respectful and respectable, god-fearing and above all (at least in public) to close their legs to men (173). And for all her defiant sexual assertiveness, Jeanette experiences the same kind of sexual violation in the diaspora that her mother faced—and fled from—in the Caribbean. At the core of Ross's text is Jeanette's traumatic discovery that her mother not only passively watched her daughter being beaten and raped but consistently refuses to condemn the crime. Mavis is proud that she managed to *"come out of de whorin' business"* (174); for her, female sexuality is a degraded, shameful indulgence: *"Spread-leg business ah nastiness. . . . What it good fah, eh? Some likkle sweetness an' de man dem do dem t'ing, an' baby probably come an' den you haffi deal wid dat"* (45). Therefore any woman, her own daughter included, who *chooses* "nastiness" deserves to be reviled and punished. The attitudinal difference between the two generations of West Indian women is reflected in their very naming of the incident. "Me see you a sex de man," says the mother. "You watched him *rape* me?" the daughter asks incredulously. The mother turns her back, "stolid in the knowledge that she had a bad daughter, and she was a good woman" (89). Ross's novel interrogates this still pervasive binary, good woman/bad woman, and implicitly critiques the Caribbean sociocultural context that maintains it, even beyond regional boundaries.

It is worth reiterating that the violence, the abuse, and the subordination that women seek to escape when they migrate has at its core a flawed concept of Caribbean masculinity. Faith Smith links male violence against women with male violence against gays, hostility toward "women in the company of other women [i.e., "unmanned" women] . . . even more so, male-male sex puts ('real') men at risk" (Preface vi). Why? Because such alien, "godless" practices threaten not just the "moral fabric of society" but also "the image of the virile, straight, Caribbean man" and thus cannot be authentically Caribbean; hence the public denunciation of homosexuality in particular as an infection from "elsewhere" (vi). The threat is real, obsessively rehearsed in letters to the local press. "Take the high road on moral values," by Angelo Lascelles, castigates homosexuality and prostitution because "these two acts, which are based on no morals whatsoever and which by *The Bible* are deemed as fornication, would be basically giving these two classes of people license to parade up and down our streets displaying what they do in their spare time." Such folly sends the wrong message to future generations. "If God made man for man, he would not have made Adam and Eve. And if God made women to exploit themselves . . . he would not have instituted marriage." The logic is that in marriage it is *men* who do the exploiting of women, so that's all right. Women and men whose sexuality does not conform to the moral norm of the patriarchal model are feared, hated, and targeted for discrimination, if not violence, here in their Caribbean homes.

Stuart Hall argues that "black masculinities" are too often "the very masculinities that are oppressive to women, that claim visibility for their hardness only at the expense of the vulnerability of black women and the feminization of gay black men" ("What is this 'Black'" 473). This "hardness" is interrogated by such different commentators as Edward Seaga, a former prime minister of Jamaica, and the gay Jamaican scholar Thomas Glave. "Male power" in Jamaica, argues Seaga, "rests in the ability to demand respect, particularly from their peers and women," and is aggressively and often violently extracted from subordinates (2). Glave challenges the "Jamaican climate of prevailing virulent homophobia, sexism, and ongoing psychological, social, and physical violence aimed at lesbian, gay, bisexual and transgendered people" (*Words to Our Now* 240), usually by men. Caribbean "men in crisis"? A much-abused rallying cry used to blame women for "marginalizing" men. Caribbean masculinity in crisis? Definitely. It would be interesting to compare representations of masculinity in fictions dealing with diasporic spaces, for perhaps "elsewhere" might offer Caribbean men too a space to perform their gender differently and with less hurt to others.

To a great extent, it is this insecure Caribbean masculinity that insists on forcing a rigid moral template on sexed bodies. And the impact of global capitalism on non-Western states leads to prevailing economic conditions that further undermine traditional Caribbean indices of male identity. Un- or underemployed, lacking the financial status and social status that guarantee respect, how can men assert their "rightful" place? Perhaps by demanding respect from subordinates and demonizing any who challenge "the image of the virile, straight, Caribbean man." Perhaps the link between the Caribbean fear of "unmanned" women and unmanly gay men, on the one hand, and the increasing invocation of scriptural authority to police an unquestioningly heterosexual and patriarchal moral fabric, on the other, suggests a wish for a return to the perceived safety of a familiar hierarchy in which men were men, women were women, and everyone knew his or her place.

A flyer on a campus notice board at UWI is indicative of this call for clarification as to what constitutes authentic Caribbean sexual citizenship:

"Protect human rights . . . embrace tolerance." But what about the right to publicly disagree with and openly denounce deviant behavior and spurious beliefs?

Project PROBE Ministries
Presents
Understanding the New Tolerance

A panel discussion taking a critical look at what is undoubtedly one of the most complex philosophical issues to challenge the Judeo-Christian ethic upon which our society was largely built.

- Are all lifestyles, beliefs, values, and truth claims equal?
- Is truth relative?
- Can one accept others without approving of their behaviour, beliefs and values?

The panelists include a pastor of the Church of the Nazarene, a political scientist, an executive of Street Gospel Ministries, and a lawyer.

What to do with the "new tolerance"? Do not tolerate it in the Caribbean! The downside of this reaction is the insidious promotion of an increasingly restrictive society, increasing intolerance of difference, and increasing calls for policing transgressive sexual behaviors. Why do Caribbean women choose "elsewhere" over home? In the fictions I have mentioned, the quest for safe spaces in which to explore alternative models of sexual citizenship without enforced subjugation to an unquestionable moral code suggests that these women's physical and literary migrations will continue for some time to come.

Note

An earlier version of this essay was first presented at the conference "Caribbean Migrations: Negotiating Borders," Ryerson University, Toronto, 18–22 July 2005.

Reflections on She Web

Susan Dayal

In 2000 I was invited to contribute images of my artwork to *Small Axe,* then published by the University of the West Indies Press in Kingston, Jamaica, for a special issue entitled "Genders and Sexualities." I was excited about being included, and I looked forward to seeing the result of this kind of collaboration.

My artwork in the period 1989–99 dealt with women's attitudes toward their bodies and their images as women. I cannot neatly categorize this work, but these pieces consist of wearable sculptures, or costumes, accompanied by self-portrait photos in which I am wearing and performing the costumes. The process of making the costumes and taking the photos with a self-timer provided an opportunity for self-reflection and self-exploration. These costumes and photos are meant to give the viewer some insight into the private struggles that women face when dealing with body-related issues. I endeavored to weave parody, playfulness, humor, and seriousness into these images. The costumes represent some of the stereotypes into which we as women either fall or are forced. The photos document our negotiation with these roles, revealing how we sometimes resent them and sometimes embrace them.

In some of the photos I am nude beneath my handmade costume. This was an aesthetic as well as a conceptual consideration but not a social consideration. Many people were shocked, titillated, or somewhat offended by the nudity, which prevented them from seeing the work for what it is. In fact, the UWI Press felt obliged to censor me and did not want to print the issue.

Four of my images were intended to be featured in this issue of *Small Axe.* The cover image was one from the series *Miss Universe as a Pin-Up.* The press was offended by the prosthetic breasts made of clay. In the end, the image did appear on the cover, but with text over the nipples.

The other three images were from the series *She Web.* These were black-and-white images in which I am nude, wearing, posing in, and sometimes

Portrait of Susan Dayal performing *Miss Universe as a Pin-Up*, a costume consisting of a crown made of wire, human hair, and butterfly hairclips and a dress made from black cord with prosthetic breasts made of terracotta. (*Miss Universe as a Pin-Up* © 1999 Susan Dayal, photo © 2010 Noritoshi Hirakawa/Artists Rights Society (ARS), New York. All images courtesy Susan Dayal)

Self-portrait of Susan Dayal performing *She Web,* a corset made of 18-gauge galvanized wire. (*She Web* © 1999 Susan Dayal, photo © 2010 Susan Dayal)

wrestling with the costume *She Web,* which is a wire corset. The images of *She Web* were meant to appear in a foldout, but although the foldout was printed, it was not inserted into the issue.

My personal feelings of discomfort and rage about being sexualized from a young age were the impetus for this body of work. Looking back on it now, I realize that by initiating the whole process—making the costumes, photographing myself wearing them, and then showing the work to the

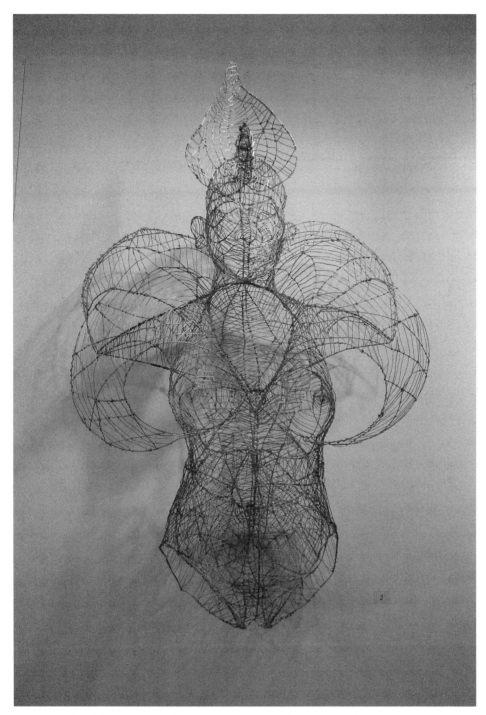

Torso with head, headpiece, and costume, no arms and no legs, made of
18-gauge galvanized wire and 26-gauge sheet aluminum. (*Third Eye Flowering 4*
© 2007 Susan Dayal, photo © 2010 Susan Dayal)

public—I forced myself to deal with these issues. The controversy surrounding the *Small Axe* issue contributed to and marked the conclusion of that chapter of my artwork.

For the 2005 piece entitled *These cages cannot hold us,* I went back to the starting point, to *She Structures,* the piece that inspired *She Web. She Structures* is a series of five wire torsos depicting women of varying ages. With *She Structures,* I was responding to the rape and abuse of women in Trinidad. The torsos were meant to serve as protection from violation; they are densely woven, the nipples are accentuated with copper wire, and the genitals are represented by a codpiece of serrated sheet copper.

Cages was a series of ten wire torsos, all built over my body. The wire was more loosely woven than in *She Structures,* subtly describing the nipples and without genitals. Some of the wire was rusting. As I was making *Cages,* my thoughts were of something more positive: *Cages* represented the deterioration of the sexist institutions that try to imprison women.

Soon after I exhibited *Cages,* I cut up the torsos and started to layer them and rework them. The five torsos that emerged from that process were even denser than the *She Structures.* I took them further by putting heads on them and building outward beyond the torso to create elaborate headpieces and collars. Ornate wire flowers sprung from their foreheads, the third-eye chakra. I called this series *Third Eye Flowering.*

Photography was not a feature in *She Structures, Cages,* or *Third Eye Flowering.* My physical connection to these pieces is suggested in the shape of the torsos. They describe the body that they were formed around, but unlike the costumes, are not wearable. Instead they are wired closed.

The torsos represent the words that cannot sufficiently describe the complexity of women. *She Structures* is about self-protection, self-reliance, and fighting back.

Cages asks us to gently slip through the wires, never again to be defined or constrained by our biological functions and the shape of our bodies. *Third Eye Flowering* celebrates and embraces the power of our femaleness, while also inviting us to expand beyond the boundary of the body, to blossom outward and regard ourselves not just as female but as human.

Desiring Subjects and Modernity

Threatening Sexual (Mis)Behavior

Homosexuality in the Penal Code Debates in Trinidad and Tobago, 1986

Yasmin Tambiah

SEXUAL BEHAVIORS and their organization have been subjected to serious contestation since the 1980s in legal terrains of states in the global south. Scholars of challenges faced by postcolonial societies have demonstrated how definitions of the reproductive and sexual roles of (especially female) citizens in "state" texts, such as constitutions and other law codes, have had important implications for the self-representation of a postcolonial state. Nationalist leaders concerned with the development of postcolonial states have negotiated between, on the one hand, embracing a secular, scientific model for modernization that draws on post-Enlightenment schemes of reasoning and knowledge and, on the other hand, recalling or re/inventing cultural and religious traditions from an inevitably glorious, autonomous, precolonial past. This tension between "modernity" and "tradition" appears to have remained at the core of epistemological and moral dilemmas being negotiated by postcolonial states in the global south.

As would be familiar to the reader, anticolonial, nationalist movements have charged women with "bearing" the nation, physically and symbolically. Central to this mandate are women's conformity to particular constructions of the family and their compliance with prescriptions that reify female sexual containment through virginity, compulsory heterosexuality, marriage, and motherhood. "Woman" is often inscribed as a natural, predetermined category requiring protection, whether by individual men, families, communities, or the state (see, e.g., Kapur, *Erotic Justice;* and Parker et al.). In each of these contexts the law has been implicated. Definitions of sexuality and sexual actors and the companion constructions of morality and respectability, whether within or outside the law, have undergirded both colonial projects and anticolonial movements.[1]

Anxieties about sex and sexual behaviors are easily stoked. Sometimes sexual behavior itself may be the primary issue under debate. At other times, sexuality serves as a site of strategic displacement for restrictions on the freedom of expression.[2] Couched in concerns for morality and public order, and through these implicating the law in the constructions of normative and deviant behaviors, such anxieties continue to intrude on, and be informed by, more recent economic, political, and social developments at the local and the global level.

Thus law, intimately linked with the processes of governance and the ordering of society, has been, and increasingly in new ways, a site of discursive contest regarding sexuality. The Foucauldian nexus between knowledge and power can be referenced at several sites in the making of law (see Foucault, *History*). In particular, criminal law and its interpretations are implicated in the permissions and denials of sexual behavior; the constructions of legitimate and illegitimate sexualities, in which sexual behavior meshes with morality; and the frequent gendered differentiations (among other differences) that underpin such binaries. In turn, laws themselves are often premised on notions of sexuality that lawmakers (rightly or wrongly) presume reflect national or public values. Such values tend to be conceptualized as static, ahistorical, undifferentiated markers of a (homogenized) national culture, anchored in a male-centered viewpoint.

It is in such a field of contest that this essay is located. Specifically, I examine the discursive construction of homosexuality and the homosexual (male and female) in the parliamentary debates surrounding the creation of the Sexual Offences Act in Trinidad and Tobago in 1986, in which the "moral" location of Trinidad and Tobago vis-à-vis the metropolitan centers of the North Atlantic was also a concern. This examination links with the problem of how to articulate cultural and epistemological autonomy from a postcolonial location while at the same time drawing upon the scheme of knowledge and reason universalized by the colonial power (Chatterjee, *Nationalist Thought* 11). It is done with the recognition that articulating such autonomy is attempted in a context in which law seeks to be a hegemonic discourse par excellence, continuously recalling colonial domination in its invocations and enactments. I engage with, and elaborate on, the pioneering work of M. Jacqui Alexander regarding the discursive construction of sexual-(im)moral citizens in this parliamentary legislation of sexuality, drawing on legal texts, parliamentary debates, newspapers, and interviews.[3]

Legislating Sex and Sexual Offences in Trinidad and Tobago

The genesis of the Sexual Offences Bill in Trinidad and Tobago in the early 1980s is rooted in a historical period that witnessed a high level of sexual violence against women, accompanied by a growing feminist consciousness around this violence and its implications, both locally and internationally. Trinbagonian women's-rights advocates have suggested that the increase in the levels of misogynistic violence may be linked with economic changes such as the oil boom in the 1970s and the growing economic hardship and increasing men's unemployment at its end (Gopaul et al. 38–39; T. Johnson 127; Mohammed, "Reflections" 40). While women were more likely to be employed in clerical and service-oriented jobs, men dominated the fields of production, transport, and construction (Reddock, "Social Mobility" 210–233). In most occupations, women earned much less than men, reflecting the sexual division of labor and related remuneration (R. Clarke 5), both of which would have a direct impact on the level of material autonomy a woman might enjoy, which in turn would affect her capacity to make informed choices elsewhere in her life, including her sexual choices.

The Earliest Draft

Work on the Sexual Offences Bill was initiated in the late 1970s by Trinidad and Tobago's Law Reform Commission. In making recommendations, the commission appears to have taken cognizance of issues relating to violence against women, the vulnerable locations of youth, children, and others in positions of dependency, as well as existing laws affecting sexually stigmatized persons such as homosexual men. The commission drew upon legal reforms in other states of the British Commonwealth, such as the United Kingdom, Australia, and Canada, to develop the new legislation for Trinidad and Tobago.[4] Among other issues, it considered criminalizing sexual assault in marriage (marital rape) and modifying the statute on buggery so that consenting adults would no longer be penalized (Trinidad and Tobago, "Commentary" 1, 4, 6).

As a former law commissioner remarked, the commissioners relied on Canadian and British precedents because they believed that the social values in Trinidad and Tobago had become more liberal (private interview, July 1998). This view is supported by a report from the National Commission on the Status of Women indicating that the legal status of women had advanced significantly by the mid-1970s. Consequently, there were few discriminatory legal provisions on the basis of sex, and work to remove even these was under way throughout the 1980s (Mohammed, "Reflections" 36–37). Therefore, the principle of equality between men and women in law does not appear to have been in question. At the same time, to quote Alexander, the process of the Sexual Offences Bill represented "the first time that the coercive arm of the postcolonial state had confronted the legacy of its colonial trauma," specifically in the regulation of sexuality ("Redrafting Morality" 135). The commission, which was multiracial in composition and made up entirely of lawyers, appears to have been guided by the need to find the best examples of legislative reform within the British Commonwealth, thus yielding reforms rooted in the shared heritage of British law. Simultaneously, I would suggest, the main systems drawn on were the advanced capitalist states in the British Commonwealth—the United Kingdom, Canada, and Australia—which, while multiethnic and multiracial, also had white-majority governments. Legal developments in these states were perceived as guided by contemporary, liberal values such as gender equality and women's autonomy, as evident in the proposed legislation regarding marital rape (drawn mainly from Canada), and notions of privacy, as in the suggestion that consensual homosexual acts between adults in private be decriminalized (as in the United Kingdom). It appears that in drawing on these states, the commissioners did not comprehend Trinidad and Tobago as anything other than a society functioning within a broadly "Western" scheme of values regarding equality and privacy, now imagined to be approaching those of the global north, albeit with different ethnoracial communities in contests for political and economic power.

At a pragmatic level, a second former law commissioner observed that, given the proximity of Trinbagonian law to British law, and the highest court of law for Trinidad and Tobago still being the British Privy Council, local acceptance of legal reforms was generally easier to obtain if those reforms had a British precedent rather than purely local roots (private interview, November 2001). Such assumptions by the commissioners regarding values and strategies probably accounted for their surprise when several of their key recommendations for change were rejected, first by the Ministry of Legal Affairs and later in Parliament (private interview, July 1998). I would argue that this pitted the lawmakers who conceptualized the reforms (the law commissioners) against the lawmakers whose business it was to concretize them through legislative enactment and implementation (the members of Parliament), although uniformity in each camp cannot be regarded as a given.

The 1984 draft of the Sexual Offences Bill was significantly modified in areas such as marital rape and homosexuality by the time the bill came before Parliament for the second reading in 1986. The 1984 draft is therefore important as the articulation of the Law Commission that would have had the least interference from the Ministry of Legal Affairs or other parliamentarians. The "Explanatory Note" of the 1984 draft asserted that the Sexual Offences Bill's main purpose was "to codify the law on sexual offences and to bring the law more in accord with modern day thinking in Trinidad and Tobago" (Trinidad and Tobago, "Bill," 1984, 1). This again suggests the belief among the law commissioners that social values in Trinidad and Tobago had altered sufficiently in the late 1970s and early 1980s to merit changes in these laws, the clauses criminalizing marital rape and permitting acts of "serious indecency" and buggery between consenting adults being cases in point. This also suggests the assumption, at least on the part of the commissioners, that the changed values included, on the one hand, recognition of rights such as that of a woman to her bodily integrity and her capacity and right to negotiate sex within marriage and, on the other hand, at least tolerance for consensual acts such as oral sex and anal intercourse in both heterosexual and homosexual contexts. I would argue that this also suggests an equation of modernity with the capacity for such recognitions and acceptances.

Some notions of equality and rights were tempered, however, as in the instances relating to married women. While drawing on Canadian legislation for its formulation, and declaring that it regarded wives as equal, not inferior, to unmarried women, the proposed Trinbagonian law differed from the Canadian law in not constructing the husband-rapist as equal to any other rapist. Instead of "marital rape," such an offence would be called "sexual assault," because "the position of the husband is peculiar to that of other men" ("Bill," 1984, 4), suggesting that at least some commissioners were uncomfortable with equating a husband with any other man on the question of rape. Thus, even while the proposed law recognized that "a wife must not be placed in an inferior position as regards other women" ("Commentary" 4), it cast heterosexual marriage as a privileged site for both sex and procreation given that there is no indication that a male partner in a common-law arrangement, for example, would have a similar special status.

The "Commentary" accompanying the 1984 draft drew attention to the key challenge posed to Trinbagonian lawmakers: "to decide what conduct is generally thought to be morally wrong and what conduct should be subject to the criminal law. The question is, 'To what extent should the criminal law reflect the fact that certain kinds of sexual conduct are commonly thought to be morally wrong or an outrage to public standards of decency?'" (1). Essentially, then, they had to ask what the relationship was between criminal law and morality. The "Commentary" pointed out that a similar conundrum had faced the Wolfenden Committee in the United Kingdom, which had convened in 1957 to address legislation pertaining to homosexual offences and prostitution. Citing the following excerpt from the Wolfenden Report regarding the function of criminal law, the "Commentary" indicates that these conclusions are contained in the approach attempted by the Sexual Offences Bill: "to preserve public order and decency, to protect the citizen from what is offensive or injurious, and to provide sufficient safeguards against exploitation and corruption of others, particularly those who are specifically vulnerable because they are young, weak in body or mind, inexperienced or in a state of special physical, official or economic dependence. . . . It is not, in our view, to intervene in the private lives of citizens, or to seek to enforce any particular pattern of behavior" ("Commentary" 1; Wolfendon Report, par. 13).

The law commissioners' decision to link the reasoning behind the bill with that informing the mandate of the Wolfenden Report places this particular example of postcolonial lawmaking squarely in the bind observed by Partha Chatterjee: how to articulate postcolonial autonomy while at the same time drawing on the scheme of knowledge and reason universalized by the colonial power (*Nationalist Thought* 11). In the case of Trinidad and Tobago, this was especially potent given that the country's highest court of appeal is the British Privy Council. The treatment of Clause 4 in the 1984 draft of the Sexual Offences Bill suggests that some of the commissioners sought to extricate themselves from this bind by calling marital rape "sexual assault," thereby asserting "Trinbagonian-ness" by granting marriage a privileged place in sexual arrangements and a reduced sentence for the husband-rapist. The treatment of women with the legal status of "wives" as equal to all other women in the context of vulnerability to rape was traded for the assertion of an aspect of national uniqueness whose universal validity within Trinidad and Tobago itself was presumed and tentative. As their protests against the compromise of the marital-rape clause in 1986 demonstrated, female members of the Trinbagonian polity were under no illusion regarding sexual violence by husbands; their protests question the assumption of universal validity.

The minister of legal affairs later asserted similar sentiments in Parliament. Although the proposed legislation was influenced by experiences elsewhere in the British Commonwealth, the standards of morality would have a unique cast: "What has been paramount in our minds is the consideration of our moral standards as obtained in our beloved Republic of Trinidad and Tobago. We hold firm to the view that what is good for England or Canada or Australia is not necessarily good for Trinidad and Tobago." He added, "We feel we have to bring our laws relating to sexual offences into the twentieth and twenty-first century" ("Verbatim notes," MG/pjc, 21/2/86, 2:10–2:20 p.m., 1). On the one hand, then, what worked elsewhere, specifically in the advanced capitalist, white-dominated states, was not necessarily acceptable at home; on the other hand, some standard was required by which the premodernity or modernity of national laws could be measured. But what would constitute such a standard?

As the citation from the Wolfenden Report suggests, central to the entire scheme was the assumed content of the term *morality*. Having no discernible separate definition in the context under scrutiny, one is led to assume that morality, and therefore its negation or lack, was linked with sexual behavior. Jacqui Alexander concludes that "*morality* has become a euphemism for *sex*. To be moral is to be asexual, hetero(sexual), or sexual in ways that presumably carry the weight of the 'natural'" ("Redrafting Morality" 133). Additionally, the values accorded to (sexual) morality and immorality emerged in relation to the preservation of public order and decency. Sex acts in private, between consenting adults, whether or not they were married, were (allegedly) not the concern of criminal law (Trinidad and Tobago, "Bill," 1984, 1).

The Bill, 1985

In the 1985 version of the bill, which was accessible to the public, some noteworthy modifications were made compared with the 1984 draft. Among others, Clause 4, covering sexual assault of a wife by her husband, had an additional subclause that barred proceedings except with the consent of the director of public prosecutions (Trinidad and Tobago, *Bill*, 1985, 9). While the clause on serious indecency remained unaltered, presumably accommodating all consenting adults irrespective of marital status or gender combinations in sexual activity, the clause on buggery was recriminalized for everyone, regardless of marital status or sexual orientation (12–13). What could have provoked such a reversal on the latter?

Rhoda Reddock, a feminist academic long active in the women's movement, wondered whether the public forum convened in 1985 by the group Working Women to examine the 1984 draft and formulate a public response had inadvertently contributed to the re-criminalizing of buggery (private interview, June 1998). This public forum was probably the first inkling the Trinbagonian public had of the impending legislation, because although the public had been invited to comment on the bill, it had proved difficult to obtain copies (private interview, June 1998; T. Johnson 129). While several in the women's movement welcomed the positive changes the bill heralded, especially for girls and women, as well as for stigmatized sexual practices and communities premised on these, including the decriminalizing of consensual male homosexual sex, wider public approval for certain aspects of the reforms was not forthcoming. Many Trinbagonians continued to regard homosexuality as not only repugnant and deviant but also sinful from a religious viewpoint.[5] Tina Johnson pointed out that the first publicizing of the bill, in the mid-1980s, coincided with the initial panic regarding HIV/AIDS in the country, with HIV regarded as a "homosexual disease" (129). Stigmatized as homosexual men already were, and given the popular elision between buggery and homosexuality, it would have required little additional justification for the Ministry of Legal Affairs to disregard the Law Commission's recommendation to decriminalize consensual anal intercourse.

In the published version of the Sexual Offences Bill, released a week after the first day of the debate in 1986, the provision covering marital sexual assault within an existing marriage had been deleted, while it remained applicable in instances where the spouses were separated under a decree nisi or by judicial separation (Trinidad and Tobago, *Bill*, 1986, Clause 4). The criminalization of buggery persisted, but the bill reinscribed permissible acts of serious indecency as the exclusive right of consenting heterosexuals, whether married or not (Clause 15). By the same move, it criminalized forms of sex between men other than anal intercourse (already covered under the buggery clause) and, for the first time, sex between women as well.

The Second Reading of the Bill, 1986

The second reading of the Sexual Offences Bill took place in the House of Representatives from February 21 to March 5, 1986, and in the Senate on November 4. It signaled also the beginning of a sustained public debate in the media that engaged lawyers, academics, clergy, newspaper columnists, and newspaper readers. In discussing the parliamentary debate on the second reading and its fallout, I shall also engage more closely with some of Jacqui Alexander's analyses and insights, bearing in mind that Alexander did not have access to the parliamentary transcripts and relied primarily on newspaper reports and the different versions of the Bill (see Alexander, "Redrafting Morality" 136).

In her essay "Redrafting Morality," Alexander traces discursively the production of morality in a legal text—the Sexual Offences Bill—in which morality or its lack comes to be equated with the "naturalness" or "unnaturalness" of a sexual act. She assesses how legislators established sexual activity as the basis for different hierarchical relationships between various categories of persons. Essential to this exercise, as well as to the production of morality, was the construction of categories of illicit sex—sex between men, sex between women, prostitution, sex between adults and youth—in order to establish the arena of licit sex articulated as normative (hetero)sexuality idealized in marriage and procreation. In the text of the bill, women become the terrain upon which ideas about sexuality, gendered behavior, constructions of family, and consequently a citizen's worth are contested and negotiated. But in the debates around the text, women actively engaged with certain of its terms, refusing to be simply the objects of privileged discourse. Alexander is particularly concerned to demonstrate how homosexuality and lesbianism become exceptionally qualified to be designated as unnatural, therefore immoral and criminal: male homosexuality continued to be criminalized, while lesbian sex, because of its newness, was specially targeted. While most of her central theses are confirmed in the themes I explore below, there are some significant differences, most notably on the place accorded to same-sex activity, whether between men or between women, in the delineation of normative sexuality in the course of the debates.

In presenting the bill, the minister of legal affairs argued that the crux of the bill was the question, "To what extent must the criminal law deal with sexual conduct—conduct involving morality and indeed public standards of decency." He recognized that there would be diverse opinions on this question, and he concluded that a national consensus had to be sought on what standards the law should protect, cautioning that the criminal law should not try "to make everything you consider to be immoral or wrong something that is punishable by the criminal law. We know for example in the field of literature that what today is forbidden reading, tomorrow is a best seller" ("Verbatim notes," HC/as, 21/2/86, 2:00–2:10 p.m., 1–2).

As in the 1984 draft, in the minister's statement morality and public standards of decency are explicitly connected with sexual conduct, but there is also the caution against criminalizing certain behavior simply on the grounds that it is disagreeable. Simultaneously there is a recognition of the diversities of value systems, as well as an assertion of the need to serve national interests by establishing a consensus, presumably out of such diversities, on what constitutes morality within the context of the bill. There is, however, a contradictory core. By invoking a literary example, the minister appears to recognize the dynamic, therefore changing, nature of social values, but at the same time he seems to presume that whatever constitutes (sexual) immorality, not simply the idea of immorality itself, would be universal and timeless within Trinbagonian society. This is best exemplified by the ongoing characteristic of unnaturalness accorded to buggery and thus to homosexuality. The question he poses becomes, then, not whether notions of what constitutes sexual immorality will change with time, but whether (allegedly) timeless notions of what constitutes sexual immorality will at all times be criminalized.

The minister declared that the bill was also propelled by a need to protect citizens from the offensive and injurious and to provide safeguards against sexual exploitation not only of females, as had hitherto been the case, but of males as well ("Verbatim notes," HC/as, 21/2/86, 2:00–2:10 p.m., 3). Protection figured prominently on two accounts: for (adult) citizens, protection from what constituted the offensive; and for youth, protection from both sexual exploitation and their own sexual curiosity. The suggestion inhering here is that lawmakers, especially parliamentarians, were best positioned to determine the nature of such protections. The implications of such protection are especially apparent in regard to women of all ages. For, while asserting the need to "uphold the dignity of the female sex," such protection also suggests that female dignity be linked to women's compliance with certain social constructs of respectable femininity. That is, for girls and women, exercising sexual autonomy, which would take them outside the sexual-moral categories approved by lawmakers, would preclude the possibility of protection by the state if such girls and women found themselves in situations of risk. The nature of the anxieties underlying the debate emerge more fully when we reckon that for women dignity, respectability, and autonomy all hinge upon the constructions and deployments of permissible and impermissible sex set within the extremely powerful discourse of law. As we shall see, the location of women in relation to marriage and the availability or denial of female sexual autonomy are also linked to the construction of the "homosexual."

Homosexual Behaviors and Persons

The content of consensus on standards of (sexual) morality appears to have already been presumed by the minister of legal affairs prior to the debate. He seemed reasonably sure that male homosexual behavior,[6] including buggery, would not be decriminalized by his fellow parliamentarians, recommendations to the contrary by the Law Reform Commission and the Bar Council of Trinidad and Tobago notwithstanding. Equating buggery with homosexuality ("Verbatim notes," MG/pjc, 21/2/86, 2:10–2:20 p.m., 1), a slippage with thought-provoking implications, since the 1985 bill had criminalized it for all, regardless of sexual orientation or marital status, he argued that anal intercourse, like bestiality, was an activity to which humans were "not naturally given" and that legislation to discourage it was connected with the need to maintain certain standards of public decency ("Verbatim notes," CLJ/sh, 4/11/86, 3:15–3:25 p.m., 2).[7] As has become evident above, the natural in the realm of sexual activity was coded as (almost) any sex that occurred between a single man and a single woman, whether within or outside marriage, while all other combinations of sex partners occupied the unnatural space, as did their sexual activity. Buggery, even between a man and a woman, became the exception for parliamentarians: not only was it unnatural and equated with homosexual sex but it defined an essential state of being homosexual. How one had sex defined one's personality and being; sex acts were equal to a persona. It was acceptable to retain the (British) spirit of the Wolfenden Report when it came to marking the "unnatural."

The criminalization of buggery across all sex-partner combinations and sexual orientations also underscores the point that parliamentarians had defined exclusive categories of what constituted the natural and the unnatural in sexual behavior. At the same time, one is compelled to inquire whether the prior, essentialized connection of buggery with homosexual sex made heterosexuals who engaged in it more like homosexuals, thereby threatening to undermine the exclusive binary of natural and unnatural sexual behaviors—hence the need to criminalize buggery so totally as to preempt this possibility.

The continued criminalization of homosexual sex and homosexuals found support among some women members of Parliament as well. An MP who had vigorously protested the removal of Clause 4 from the Sexual Offences Bill ("Verbatim notes," CN/gf, 21/2/86, 4:00–4:10 p.m., 2–3) crafted the male homosexual as a direct physiological threat to the heterosexual conjugal union when she remarked that a married man who had sex with a homosexual man could return home and infect his chaste wife with HIV/AIDS ("Verbatim notes," LR/gf, 21/2/86, 5:40–5:50 p.m., 1). For this MP, the conjugal union needed to be premised on sexual respect between spouses, but the sexual protection of the moral wife necessitated ensuring that extramarital sex by the husband, if it occurred, took place with a partner who was not of a category as contaminating and as stigmatized as a man who had sex with other men. The man who had sex with a woman and also with another man was not deemed bisexual or marked by any term other than *homosexual*. The implication was that it was the unmarried, habitual homosexual who was thrice marked—as engaging in unnatural sex; as a carrier of a lethal, sexually transmitted infection such as HIV; and as a detonator who, through anally penetrating a "heterosexual" male, exploded infection into (marital) heterosexuality, with a debilitating and terminal disease that heterosexuality/heterosexuals could otherwise rarely acquire.[8] The male homosexual thus facilitated the *physical* disintegration of the (hetero) sexual/moral/marital society.

Throughout the debate, it was male homosexuality that was explicitly scripted as the overt threat to institutionalized heterosexuality. Sex between women was barely discussed, and when it was, it was not with the same notion of danger. To the MP who made an issue of it in Parliament, lesbian sex was invoked as a means by which older women could "corrupt" young girls. He thus scripted lesbian sex not only as unnatural but also as predatory and premised on intergenerational sex—a performance, I would argue, that emulated a heterosexual script in which older men seduced young girls, toying thereby with the stereotype of the "manly" lesbian. In such a context, then, a female subject who demonstrated a capacity for sexual agency outside heterosexuality could be accorded recognition *only* as simultaneously unnatural and criminal.

The reluctance of the minister of legal affairs to make an especially big issue of criminalizing sex between women, when compared with his reactions to male homosexuality, also supports the position that it was not perceived to be as threatening to institutionalized heterosexuality as sex between men. I would further posit that this was because the reference point for sex meriting discussion, whether natural or unnatural, heterosexual or homosexual, was penetration by the penis: which orifice a penis made contact with determined whether or not it was sex worth discoursing on in the realm of law. For instance, not only does penetration by the penis establish whether or not rape has taken place (Trinidad and Tobago, *Bill*, 1986, Clause 24; *Sexual Offences Act 1986*, sec. 25) but whether a married man has been penetrated by another man establishes whether he is an explicit threat to a wife and to marriage itself.

Thus, Jacqui Alexander's compelling theses have certain shortcomings, of which I offer two. First, the argument that the possibility that sex between men might be decriminalized was as responsible as was Clause 4 for the public furor that resulted in the innovation of a select committee of the entire Parliament for private readings of the Bill (Alexander, "Redrafting Morality" 136) is not borne out in the parliamentary transcripts that were available for public review. Buggery was recriminalized for all persons beginning with the bill of 1985, and there is no indication that issues on sex between men also informed the decision to hold closed sessions of Parliament. Because of the emerging national fear of an HIV/AIDS epidemic and the scripting of AIDS as a "gay disease," there was no parliamentary support for liberalization.

Second, while Alexander's argument that marital heterosexuality and its procreative promise were elevated by the simultaneous criminalizing of sexual practices that were posited as "other" (such as prostitution, pleasure-premised nonmarital heterosexual sex, and same-sex sexual activity) is sustained, her point that legislators felt prompted "to ensnare and to specifically control lesbian sex" ("Redrafting Morality" 136, 138–39) is not supportable either in the accessible parliamentary transcripts or in the contours of changes in the 1985 and 1986 bills. Rather, as Rhoda Reddock observed and as I would conclude from my research, it appears more likely that the obsession with "equality," as in men and women being equally culpable for sexual offences and moral transgressions, that so vividly marked the hostility of male parliamentarians and the male public to Clause 4 ("Verbatim notes," EE/ct, 21/2/86, 4:10–4:20 p.m., 3, and Cl3/cmi, 21/2/86, 4:20–4:30 p.m., 1) prompted the gender-neutral language criminalizing serious indecency in all instances except that of heterosexual sex. As Reddock cautioned, the deployment of the "equality" principle in the Sexual Offences Bill, in which equality was equated with equal culpability, is a salutary warning about the use to which equality arguments may be put (private interview, June 1998).

The fate of homosexual sex, whether between men or between women, was determined by a process through which the moral worth of a post-colonial nation was measured in terms of its sexual rectitude. This process was established not only through the discursive centering of marital, procreative sexuality, which simultaneously marginalized all other sexual activity and compelled much of it into the realm of criminality, but also through the suggestion that the correct measure of sexual rectitude determined the nation's uniqueness and distance from the (sexually degenerate/deviant) metropolitan centers of imperialism. This struggle was sharpened by the ambiguities surrounding the political and cultural "location" of Trinidad and Tobago. One parliamentarian suggested that religiosity could serve as a bulwark against the country's being "subjected to western influence" and the moral/sexual degeneracy of (Western) civilization ("Verbatim notes," JS/cmi, 5/3/86, 4:10–4:20 p.m., 1–2). But where would that "locate" Trinidad and Tobago? If the country continued to be imagined as "western," what kind of West was the referent? How could it define itself differently if the conceptual tools for articulating values continued to work with colonial frames, especially persistent in the context of criminal law?

Trinidad and Tobago is a multiracial, multiethnic society with a postindependence history of ethnoracial groups competing for political and economic power (Meighoo). In such a scenario, could there be traditions in common that would constitute Trinbagonian representations to be set against the global north? The struggle to imagine an autonomous location, culturally and epistemologically, is complicated by such contests. Like the issue of marital rape, anxieties shared by parliamentarians from different ethnoracial locations about according legitimacy to same-sex relations probably helped, especially in an election year (1986), to displace ethnoracial tensions in formal Trinbagonian politics onto potentially uppity women and potentially recoupable sexual deviants and tentatively and temporarily to cement ethnoracial fissures by suppressing the possibility of (multi-ethnoracial) sexual insurgency.

Notes

An earlier version of this essay appeared in the *Caribbean Review of Gender Studies* 3 (October 2009) under the title "Creating (Im)moral Citizens: Gender, Sexuality and Lawmaking in Trinidad and Tobago, 1986." My gratitude to CRGS for permissions. The essay draws selectively from my study "Defining the Female 'Body Politic': Women, Sexuality and the State," which compares the impact of sexual-offences legislation on women and sexually marginalized persons in Sri Lanka and Trinidad and Tobago. The study was supported by a postdoctoral research fellowship from SEPHIS (South-South Exchange Program for Research on the History of Development) that covered 1997–98 and 2000–2002. A copy of the original study is deposited with SEPHIS; the manuscript is currently being revised for publication. At the time of holding the fellowship, I was a senior research fellow at the International Centre for Ethnic Studies in Colombo, Sri Lanka. My deepest appreciation to SEPHIS, to the regional office of the Caribbean Association for Feminist Research and Action (CAFRA), to all who agreed to be interviewed, and to friends whose critical feedback, support, and examples of scholarship have enriched my thinking on this project, especially Ratna Kapur and Tracy Robinson. My gratitude as well to Parvani Pinnewala, and thanks to the editor of this volume and the editorial team at the University of Virginia Press.

1. For an overview of the Caribbean under colonialism, see Kempadoo, *Sexing*, ch. 2.

2. For India as an example, see Kapur, *Erotic Justice*, 51–94.

3. See Alexander, "Redrafting Morality," 133–152. Alexander revisits these issues in *Pedagogies*, 180ff.

4. Trinidad and Tobago, "Verbatim notes," MG/pjc, 21/2/86, 2:10–2:20 p.m., 1. Since parliamentary proceedings, usually published as *Hansard Parliamentary Debates,* were unavailable for the debate on the Sexual Offences Bill in 1986, I worked from the transcripts made available by the Parliamentary Library, Port of Spain, in 1998 and 2001. The notations refer to identification markings preceding each 10-minute segment on the transcript pages. Verbatim notes are identified by the uppercase initials of the parliamentary reporter and, after a slash, the lowercase initials of the typist, followed by the date, time block of reporting, and page number. I have changed the order of the date to day/month/year.

5. For a Roman Catholic view, see Pantin.

6. I avoid referring to male homosexuals as "gay men" because in the Trinbagonian debates the term *homosexual* was contextually linked with legal conventions.

7. This part of the articulation was made before the Senate.

8. Recall that this was 1986, when information about multiple means for transmitting HIV/AIDS was still emerging through medico-scientific research and only recently had begun to receive wide publicity.

Sexual Awakenings and the Malignant Fictions of Masculinity in Alfonso Cuarón's *Y tu mamá también*

M. S. Worrell

IN "The Truth of Fiction" Chinua Achebe contends that the human desire and capacity for fiction can emancipate us from orthodox ideological enslavement and recalcitrant literal-mindedness (141, 151). Although Achebe articulates the epistemological and ethical merits of the art of fiction, he contends that the gulf between *being* and *knowing* necessitates the construction of fictions, some of which demand one's total and unconditional fidelity (141). Achebe considers the human capacity for fiction an existential requirement for dealing with the apparent obscurity toward which human experience tends. This does not mean that all of our fictions, however appealing, are useful or desirable. In our own narrative, our fervent desire to establish ownership of our existence, our self-projections tend to mask silent and invisible fictions that insulate our perspective from any "reality" we would rather not own as a sensible account of our psychic history. In other words, psychic security is maintained by categorically dismissing some existential possibilities as inimical to psychic viability. For instance, given the constraints of patriarchal masculinity, heteronormativity must be adopted as a guarantee of authenticity. Authentic self-identity becomes a recognition of the inviolability of the standards of heteronormativity, which must be maintained via a wilful forgetfulness of its malignancy,[1] that is, of its impotence for facilitating authentic or transformative self-discovery. Patriarchal masculinity must disguise its prejudicial and superstitious repulsion of *transgression* as a rejection of heretical imposition on its conventions. This constitutional rejection informs foundational fictive imaginings about valid self-stewardship and stultifies that stewardship.

In Alfonso Cuarón's *Y tu mamá también,* viewers see how malignant fictions are used to insulate the fragile masculinity of two teenagers as they mature into young adults. The film offers a documentary-esque exposé on the process of their emergence into adult masculinity. Presented as an odyssey film, it is the story of two naive, sex-obsessed teenage Mexican boys, Julio (Gael García Bernal) and Tenoch (Diego Luna), who take an older woman, Luisa (Maribel Verdú), the Spanish wife of Tenoch's cousin, on a quest for a mythical beach paradise, where they plan on having sex with her. Through the physical journey, a triangular trajectory from Mexico City toward the Caribbean coast of Veracruz to the Pacific coast of Oaxaca and back to Mexico City, and a psychic odyssey for Julio and Tenoch, the viewer witnesses how malignant fictions gain mythical status through the negotiation and maintenance of masculine self-identity under patriarchy. Julio and Tenoch struggle to become *macho* men via a nihilistic and moralistic indifference qua contempt for others. They denigrate the honor of government officials; display a privileged insensitivity to the plight of the *campesinos,* who are subject to brutalization and exploitation (including by Julio and Tenoch); flout parental authority; and openly deride models of their own and future mendacious masculinity as evidenced by their rejection of Tenoch's cousin Jano's (Juan Carlos Remolina) fraternal advice.

My contention is that Julio and Tenoch's struggle for validation demonstrates that artifice is essential for the maintenance of masculine self-identity under patriarchal masculinity. They boast of their absolute autonomy regarding the foundational values of their self-identities. As expressed in the dictates of their Charolastra Manifesto,[2] their bravado is the pretext, the fiction of independence that macho masculinity must declare. This psychic swagger highlights the insecurity of patriarchal masculine identity. Drawing insights from Foucault's and Nietzsche's remarks on the corrosiveness of conventional norms for self-affirmation and self-validation, this essay analyzes how the film frames the boys' emergence into adult masculinity. Specifically, this essay examines how the underlying homoeroticism and explicit homomagnetism express various internal conflicts that the codes of machismo delegitimize as valid constitutive psychic elements.

As evidenced in Julio and Tenoch's delusory venture for sexual conquest, macho men must reject any homosexual encounter as fundamentally psychically debilitating. The boys' desire for sexual adventure cannot transcend stereotypical conceptions of masculinity. Any homoerotic breach of the bounds of masculinity must be invalidated as a viable existential option no matter how orgiastic or transformative the experience may be. The malignant fiction, which they must regard as proven fact, is that sexual submissiveness is irremediably emasculating. Although the boys present themselves as sexual provocateurs, their failure—as sexual adventurers—to expand the bounds of masculine validation reveals their honor to be a malignant fiction inhibiting sexual awakening. Luisa, the third element of their triangular adventure, usurps their role by becoming the sexual *provocatrice* who simultaneously initiates the boys in a detour from traditional masculine sexual roles and defies the patriarchal apparatus that binds them.

In the Mexican sexual system, human beings are subjected to a logic according to which meaning is conferred on the sexual aim of sexual practices as opposed to the actual object chosen.[3] According to Tomás Almaguer, in Mexican culture the sexual landscape is organized around a configuration of gender/sex/power that equates activity and passivity with particular sexual roles (257). Sexual participants, then, are defined by the roles they play in sexual acts. One's gender is secondary to the act one wants to perform with the person toward whom sexual activity is directed (257). Honor/shame and status/stigma become the coordinates for organs and roles deemed "active" in contrast to body passages and roles deemed "passive," resulting in a patriarchal cultural equation of passivity and submission with shame and stigmatization (Lancaster 123). Consequently, elements of power/dominance are constitutive of the cultural meaning of sexual engagement and practices. Thus, Julio and Tenoch, given their allegiance to stereotypical conceptions of masculinity in sexual encounters, must be "givers" as opposed to "receivers." Slippage into the latter category would constitute feminization.

As Marvin Goldwert suggests (utilizing insights derived from Octavio Paz), the gender-coded equation of honor and shame with masculinity and femininity, respectively, is founded in the archival myths relating to the Spanish conquest of Mexico in the sixteenth century (162). The colonial drama of Mexico's founding in which the Spanish *conquistadores* serve as the active, masculine intruders who raped the passive, feminine Indian civilization (after laying anchor in the Caribbean waters of the Yucatán Peninsula) becomes the underlying drama of the hermeneutics and signification of the Mexican sexual system. La Malinche's betrayal is the figurative representation of the fascination, violation, and seduction of the Indian women by the Spanish conquistadores: the passive yielding before the active/dominant personality, namely Cortés (Paz 86).[4] This leaves a veritable phylogenetic residue whereby Mexican men attempt to affirm what is in effect (as effect) their insecure masculinity—the Mexican being the shameful offspring of a violation, according to Paz—through the symbolic conquest of women. Therefore, Cortés and La Malinche cannot be easily expunged from the Mexican sociocultural imagination and sensibilities given the manner in which this conquest/violation trope resurfaces in the ensemble of sexual meanings and categories that form the Mexican sexual system.

The valorization of hypermasculinity underlies the extent to which the cultural myths retain their anthropological force as the bedrock upon which the psychic structuring of *los hijos de la chingada* (the sons of the violated mother) rests, La Malinche's betrayal being the cultural archive (Almaguer

259; Paz 79–80). For Mexican males, this expresses itself as a fundamental disdain for whatever is feminine, and it is displayed through a general resentment toward women. Thus "Mexican men often find a tenuous assurance of their masculinity and virility in aggressive manliness and through a rigid gender role socialization that ruthlessly represses their own femininity" (Almaguer 259–60). On the other hand, the adoration of the virgin and consequently of women as mothers makes for a binary perception of women: *la chingada* (the whore) and *la madre* (the mother). It should be noted that Luisa is childless (although her potential motherhood is highlighted at the end of her voyage) and thus fits into the role of la chingada. As a facilitator for Julio and Tenoch's homoeroticism, she is a traitor to the Mexican sexual paradigm's status quo. She is also a betrayer of her betraying husband, the two-faced Jano, so she defies/betrays patriarchy in at least two ways.[5]

In the film, the boys' journey away from the city symbolically represents the power of Mexican cultural myths in their maturation to adult masculinity. The boys' choice of "sexy space" is intriguing. They decide that it is better to secret Luisa away from the city, the capital, to the uncultivated landscape leading to the Caribbean shore. The Caribbean is thus framed as a conduit for sexual release and psychic empowerment. If they (truly) intend to be sexual explorers, why do they not examine the transgressive sexual possibilities their hometown, that is, *la ciudad,* allows? Their friend Saba (Andrés Almeida) is already doing so by partaking in group sex.[6] Another character, Danilo (who is only an abstract reference in the film), discloses his homosexuality to the rest of their Charolastra society, a disclosure generally evaded. In the "sexy city," however, the boys find their sexual strategies frustrated now that their girlfriends have deserted them for the Old World. Moreover, the city is congested with power eruptions (and exclusions): leftist protesters (including Julio's sister), parties for elite officials and their coterie of corrupt government associates (like Tenoch's father) and opportunistic champagne intellectuals (like Tenoch's cousin Jano), and the sometimes fatal economic struggles of migrant workers. Their venture to an imagined Caribbean paradise—a space marked by a certain fluidity of borders—seems a desperate apprenticeship for future sexual and political games in la ciudad.

As Almaguer's work indicates, because of the compulsory code of masculinity, men must demonstrate their autonomy and sexual potency in order to establish their masculine identity. Consider the scene in which the boys first meet Luisa. They physically pin her up against the railing, essentially cordoning her off while the Mexican cowboys in the bullring below ceremonially twirl their lassos. It is Tenoch, the middle-class *patron*, who takes the lead in "trapping" her, while Julio remains behind as a good squire to prevent any "escape." In appearance—dressed in an alluring light cream dress and wrap—she is the ceremonial sacrifice for their achievement of manhood, while Tenoch's father is heard over the microphone thanking the guests for their attendance at this "humble celebration." She remembers Tenoch as a distressed child worrying about the loss of his Thundercat doll (a North American toy derived from a television cartoon serial). She deftly bends away from him and "escapes" when she "accepts" their beach invitation on behalf of herself and her husband. The lads' blindness to her existence as subject in turn blinds them to the extent to which she, by virtue of her subjectivity, repeats Cortés's original seduction of the Aztecs. They are immediately fascinated by and with her, an apparent interloper in this Mexican celebration, though as it turns out, she, like Hernán Cortés before her, becomes very much at home due to the natives' attraction to her.

In another scene, the boys are shown at Tenoch's father's country club. They lie on separate springboards, alone, in a masturbation race. As with their underwater plunges, the goal is to be the victor. These events are the emergent foreplay of the homoerotic undercurrents of their friendship, as exemplified by their scoptophilic survey of each other's penises after one of their underwater races.[7] Alone in the hot, steamy environment of the showers they need not fear disclosure of their homoerotic skylarking. Responding to Tenoch's mockery of his penis, Julio challenges him to excite it, to bring it to life, "to blow it up, faggot"; Tenoch runs away from Julio's lower-class, bullish onrush. This avoidance and rejection is climaxed when Tenoch is the first to have sex with Luisa. However, their clumsy sexual forays with her amplify their insecurity and pretentious erotic expertise. Each fails to have a sustained encounter. Like their masturbatory competition, it is merely a race, a sexual rush of self-absorbed, abbreviated, masculine jerking. It is no wonder then that when Julio disrupts Tenoch's triumph by informing him that he has cuckolded him with Ana (Ana López Mercado), it turns out to be a devastating psychic coitus interruptus, one that has more lasting reverberations than their pathetic ruttings with Luisa. By taking the honor of "conquering" (fucking) Luisa first, Tenoch shames Julio in their race to masculinity. Julio *must* counter by denigrating Tenoch. He, the "peasant," informs Tenoch that he has "fucked" the sexual prize of the "preppie." Julio is then forced to make amends on his knees before his more privileged patron. (Given that Julio's surname is Zapata, the name of the hero of the southern site of the Mexican Revolution, his supplication before Tenoch in order to secure forgiveness is devastating.) Later he is told that Tenoch has triumphed over him again through secret trysts with Cecilia (María Aura).

Whether these confessions are true is never confirmed for the audience; nonetheless, they unmask the boys' strong friendship, revealing the bitter class conflict in their association. As Cuarón remarks, "Ultimately, that is their biggest conflict. Their two characters are very similar, they are essentially the same. What keeps them separate is the social conditioning more than their upbringing. When they start finding out their identity, that they are so similar, they get so scared that they have to seek shelter in some mask. The tragedy at the end is that the mask is the social conditioning they were trying to escape from the beginning" (Cuarón, "Sexual Awakenings" 28). The boys can no more escape the customary mores they denounce than they can establish an entirely new locus, as evidenced by their need for directions to the mythical—though real—place Boca del Cielo (Heaven's Mouth). Their lack of navigational skills is evinced by their spatial confusion. When they leave Mexico City, they drive through the state of Puebla toward Veracruz—significantly the most important port in colonial Mexico, a veritable contact zone facing the Caribbean—but in a sudden change of direction, mirroring the imminent change in their friendship, they turn south to the Oaxacan shore.

Luisa is implicitly aware of the political game imbuing the boys' friendship and tries to make amends by having sex with Julio, thereby shaming Tenoch. Tenoch, unable either to stop her or to bear this transgression, removes himself from the scene. In seducing both boys and intending thereby to repair their friendship, Luisa continues her colonizing, repeating Cortés's previous plunder; she partly intends to use them to assuage her own hurts. (Her surname, Cortés, symbolically accounts for the victory she achieves over Julio and Tenoch and its consequent devastation.) The boys, unaware of this, continue to reveal, to "open" themselves before her, venting their repressed conflicts and thereby shaming themselves. Their ultimate shame is disclosing their insecurity before the alluring power of femininity, thus accelerating their emasculation. The further the boys travel toward the Caribbean, the stronger Luisa's symbolic exploitation of them becomes (a dramatic recurrence of the original Spanish plunder of the now hybristic offspring and the Caribbean). The literal penetration into the gritty countryside and life draw the boys further away from the comfort zone of their psychic and sexual mendacity. Like Betsabé, the 1983 Chrysler Le Baron station wagon, their ancient road ship, their fictional phallic projections must break down on this journey. Amidst various contrasting realities of hardship and survival, arid barrenness and tropical beauty, the lads' fictionalizations are continually disempowering. Luisa becomes more alive in spite of the dread that consumes her; the boys grow more deadened, as their masks and screens become transparent and permeable.

Julio's and Tenoch's embellished personal mythologies only intensify the truths not offered in their avowals, that is, the ones not disclosed by them discursively. These lie in their homoerotic and homo-magnetic sexual competitiveness and sexual deceit. Thus, the boys can *chingar* (fuck), but they cannot be *chingados* (fucked) by others (Alonso and Koreck 9–10). As machos, as Charolastras, they cannot relinquish their honor as *the* sexual pursuers, the sexual conquistadores, and the virile, maverick adventurers plundering territories and bodies (Alonso and Koreck 10; Paz 76–80). This only indicates how normative mechanisms of machismo effect their impotent existentiality. As postcolonials, they do not want to shame themselves before Luisa Cortés, their female Spanish trophy, herself an ironic symbolic incarnation of the original Spanish conqueror. Nonetheless, they show by their actions that they are prisoners, not liberators; blunderers, not conquerors. Their "triumphant" sexual declarations mask their failure to escape their own mediocrity and that of social climbers/flunkies such as Jano, who hanker after the paradigmatic trappings of societal validation.

In contrast, Luisa's willingness to be more fluid in her interactions as the journey progresses—in spite of her silence about her terminal condition—indicates her emancipation from external markers of self-validation. Illustrative of her dominance, as the feminine force over the self-avowed superior young machos, she declares their cherished Charolastra code a farce. She sets express terms regarding her sexual availability and discredits their claims of sexual mastery: "Your Manifesto is bullshit. Typical men! Fighting like dogs and marking their territory! . . . Who cares who you two screwed, when you come that fast! Play with babies and you'll end up washing diapers!"[8] Luisa does not affirm their maturity; she announces that they—like "typical men"—are stuck in a prolonged adolescence. Not only does she prove her*self* their master but they willingly crown her so, relinquishing any claim to authority, especially over her. "We admit we are assholes. We will do whatever you want. You'll be the boss." When the *boys* are reduced to begging her to continue the journey with them, it signals the formal conclusion of their escapade. They turn away from the perceived wantonness and promiscuity of the Caribbean coast and travel south to the barren, untamed Pacific shores of Oaxaca.

In the boys' last gasp with Luisa, she completes their sexual journey (and sadly, their psychic journey as well), not by being the prize but by being the facilitator for the eruption of their implicit homoeroticism. She literally dances the boys to each other, lowering the erotic barrier between them. This is also the boys' ultimate submission and therefore ultimate transgression of the masculine code they have championed and are to honor as machos. This unsettling realization is only achieved in its aftermath. Awakening to find themselves fully naked to each other, they repel each other. Tenoch's vomiting is not the result of late-night drunken partying, but of a psychic and erotic denudement that must be repressed as untruth. Sexual and psychological responsiveness to each other is not the sort of adventure that can be validated or embraced by the dictates of the hierarchical norms governing sexual relations for males; it would only flout such dictates and as such imperil their masculinity (Butler, *Gender Trouble*).

Their turning away from Caribbean waters to enact their roles as explorers of the southern coast and their subsequent return to the city trace a return to their appropriate places within the juridical regime of masculinity. Whereas before, their adolescent bluster was the effect of epistemic naiveté about the force of the hierarchical norms that govern masculinity, their transgression enlightens them to the necessity of masking and illusion for achieving accreditation as men. Their final rejection of either coast, Caribbean or Pacific—the beginning of the final leg of the journey—needs no more than formal narration. Although they (may) meet and exchange contact details, they will never again engage as friends. Their physical repulsion after their orgiastic encounter was the psychic rejection of the compatibility of any express homoerotic reciprocity with masculinity and their emerging middle-class roles. Their movement away from Puebla and Veracruz—the physical/geographic departure from the Caribbean—is transmuted as a psychic rejection of the sort of self-exploration that the Caribbean might have offered. Instead, their physical/sexual turning away from each other after the ménage à trois is a psychic affirmation of the embedded sexual and gender categories of Mexican society; hence the quick and necessary return to Mexico City.

Although their Caribbean trek brought the boys close to the shores of multiple subjectivities as a geographic and symbolic locus of global interplay and exchange, it turns out to be the space of error, for the true Boca del Cielo is to be found elsewhere. The Caribbean, as a space marked by multiple ventures of conquest, languages, ethnicities, migrations, *mestizaje* or *métissage*, and hybridity, becomes revolting because of its indeterminacy and because it has become the impetus for their transgression. For them, the evidence of their transgression does not result in doubt about their identity; it constitutes a repulsion, a turning away. In fact, their naiveté insulates them from any doubt about their identity and their homoerotic attraction. This transgression cannot count as *evidence* that their macho pretensions are in jeopardy. There is neither a psychic nor a cognitive challenge that the boys must confront and resolve. Their sexual frenzy, though unexpected, only serves to entrench them within already established social and sexual parameters.

Cuarón declares that it is not the sex that is the cause of the friendship's termination. Luisa is merely a conduit for a variety of interpersonal dramas between the boys that can be attributable to class conflict (Cuarón, "Sexual Awakenings" 28). Throughout the film, however, the class conflict between the boys is continually sexualized. The boys' induced homosexual experience results in a decision that rejects the encounter as contributing to "the truth" of their psyches and sexuality. Their literal turning away from each other is thus apropos. The boys' encounter does not become an opportunity for redefining their perspective on their *selves;* it does not turn into a reassessment of their subjectivity as maturing machos. They suppress the experience as a fleeting, insubstantial transgression. Their response is a silence—a repression, a burial. They quickly focus on returning *inland* to Mexico City, a journey needing no narration or commentary.

The boys derive no personal truth from the potentially psychically liberating situation that their encounter elicits. They leave the normative preconceptions of heterosexuality intact. For them, their emerging identity is a stable political, descriptive category, an inevitable unfolding from a nascent given (Butler, *Gender Trouble*). As a result, they fail to realize the extent to which they are continually accepting and appropriating a number of compulsory truths as participants *within* the discourse of Mexican heteronormative gender expectations. They also fail to appreciate how their homosexual encounter could generate productive psychic turmoil (Prado 129–31). Their rejection of both the Caribbean and Oaxacan coasts—soon subject to exploitation for resort pleasures—and their return to Mexico City indicate that no progressive experiential insight is drawn from their encounter; it does not result in any productive cognitive dissonance that might condition transcendent psychic reflection.

The automatic rejection of their homosexual encounter turns out to be the generative realization of their gender expectations within compulsory heteronormative masculinity. For them, the "coherent" projections of masculinity are not fiction (Butler, *Gender Trouble* 172); they are their deliverance from their unruly attempts to flout its attendant truths. Their encounter is a false retreat from the gender stabilization ahead. In fact, their fast return to Mexico City after their diverse explorations is a flight, a desperate natal return to the coherent expectations of adult Mexican masculinity. They return with their psychic projections intact, apparently untroubled by any serious intellectual turmoil about them.

Were the boys willing to be baffled by their experience, they might find that its discontinuity with their preferred self-conception allowed for liberatory and transformative self-projections (Foucault, "Truth and Power" 131–33; MacIntyre; Prado 128–30). However, the viewer finds their subjectivities crippled by the power relations of their machismo. In refusing to interrogate the conventional rules undergirding their psychic projections, Julio and Tenoch succumb to psychologically debilitating gender roles and affirm a static truth about gender identity. Luisa suggests that the boys learn to be more elastic in their conceptions of them*selves*, that is, that they relinquish the fictions that must constitute the masculine, or "macho," persona. In this encounter, the feminine emerges as the dominant personality, not because it obliterates or attempts to subjugate the *selves* it encounters but because it is willing to relinquish so as to transform itself. Although Foucault may have repudiated the naturalism of underlying truths, Julio and Tenoch's silence about their encounter grants their transgression an essence, a veritable determinacy, a hidden reality, a suppression, which can only effect their continued conventional gender performance as a mask (Foucault, "Truth and Power" 118).

Our final viewing of Julio and Tenoch must be a sombre one. We find them, now young adult men, engaged in staid middle-class pursuits, wary of adventurous sexual exploration since it would entail a hybridist transgression of the masculine codes they must now embody. Where, then, is the final bit of wisdom Luisa tried to impart? "Life is like the surf, so give yourself away like the waves," she had said. This particular "giving," this unfettered freedom, is irreducibly feminine, submissive. It is the edict of a repulsive complex: *una chingada pero una conquistadora*. Luisa is a model the boys cannot emulate, precisely because, under the terms of patriarchy, she is a "fiction." She, the feminine, has made them the objects of her subjectivity. This does not present a liberating perspectival shift or enable them to "create dangerously" or to "live dangerously" and so transform their psychic identities beyond patriarchal conventions (Camus; Nietzsche, no. 283). The personal truth she offers *cannot* be their story, though it is indeed so. She has forced them to disclose themselves, to surrender, replicating the humiliation of the indigenous Mother, La Malinche. What she reveals is a disabling horror. It is better to hide, to mask, and to run away from this truth.

Their voyage of exploration concludes in a return to the colonial structures of Mexico City, under which lie buried the foundations of Tenochtitlán, the core of the Aztec civilization. Despite the protestations of their adolescent Charolastra Manifesto, they must submerge a truth that they cannot will into reality, like their fictional—but actual—Boca del Cielo. The homoerotic undercurrents of their incessant sexual competitiveness and friendship reveal the extent to which Tenoch and Julio are lost in the tide of masculinity and mendacious machismo: two stifled narratives imperiled by malignant fictions.

Notes

1. There are other forms of malignancy implicit in the categories of patriarchy, for example, its compulsory misogyny. This denigration of the feminine and feminization is crucial to the maintenance of patriarchal masculinity and contributes to the rejection of homoerotic possibilities for self-identity (see Butler, *Gender Trouble*).

2. The Charolastra Manifesto comprises the following precepts: "(1) There is no greater honour than being a Charolastra. (2) Do whatever you feel like. (3) Pop beats poetry. (4) Get high at least once a day. (5) You shall not screw a fellow Charolastra's girlfriend. (6) Whoever roots for Team America is a faggot. (7)

Whacking off rules. (8) Never marry a virgin. (9) Whoever roots for Team America is a faggot. [The boys emphasize the importance of this precept by reasserting it.] (10) Truth is cool but unattainable." To this Julio adds that "the truth is really amazing but you can never reach it. (11) The asshole who breaks any of the previous rules loses his title of Charolastra." Cuarón, *Y tu mamá también*. All quotations from the movie are taken from the English subtitles.

3. In this regard the erotic hierarchies of the Mexican sexual system share some parallels with the categories of sexual life and the conceptualization of sexual desire found in classical Athenian society (see Halperin).

4. La Malinche, also known as Doña Marina, was a concubine given to Cortés by a Tabascan chief. Because of her remarkable linguistic talents, she became Cortés's constant companion, facilitating his successful interaction with and conquest of the various tribes in Mexico (McHenry; Parkes). *Malinche* is a pejorative colloquial term that denotes a Mexican who imitates the language and customs of foreigners (McHenry 18).

5. Jano, a serial philanderer, has continually humiliated Luisa.

6. It should be noted that Saba's "transgressive" sexual activity nonetheless supports the patriarchal convention that men are to exploit women for sexual pleasure.

7. We also learn later in the film that the boys have precise comparative measurements of their penises, further evidencing not only their competition with each other but also the prominence of homoeroticism in their relationship.

8. Luisa establishes her own manifesto, with the following principles: "(1) I won't screw either of you. You can screw each other if you like. (2) I'm going to sunbathe naked and I don't want you sniffing around like dogs. (3) I pick the music. (4) The moment I ask, please shut your mouths. (5) You cook. (6) No stories about your poor girlfriends. (7) If I ask, stay 10 yards away from me. Or, better 100. (8) Obviously, you do all of the manual labor. (9) You may not speak of things you do not agree on. Even better just keep your mouths shut! (10) You're not allowed to contradict me. Much less push me!"

Living and Loving

Emancipating the Caribbean Queer Citizen in Shani Mootoo's *Cereus Blooms at Night*

Alison Donnell

PUBLISHED IN 1998, Shani Mootoo's *Cereus Blooms at Night* intertexts both with Caribbean literary works and with the political and ethical debates relating to the regulation of Caribbean sexualities in disturbing and yet productive ways. The text issues a roll call to some of the most sensitive issues around sexuality in the Caribbean—same-sex loving, transgender identities, incest, and rape—many of which remain almost silent within literary critical discourses. I seek here to explore the ways in which this novel not only raises interesting and troubling questions about how sexual identities come into being and the attitudes toward sexual orientation that resonate for the Caribbean region but also imagines a new ontology of desire that redrafts the ethical limits and boundaries of Caribbean subjectivity by extending the grounds of the possible beyond the politics of the present. In the present historical moment, when the issue of representing and governing lived sexualities in the Caribbean region so urgently demands our attention, my aim is to read *Cereus* as a piece of literature that can bring us to an understanding of the conditions of being, specifically in relation to sexual agency, in such a way as to increase the possibility of positively reshaping those conditions.

Cereus Blooms at Night is told by Tyler, a nurse in the almshouse in Paradise, a town on the fictional Caribbean island of Lantanacamara, who is given the task of nursing an old lady who is as socially marginal and stigmatized as he is. This old lady, Mala Ramachandin, is discovered in the overgrown ruins of her childhood house and taken to the almshouse as a frail, emaciated but physically restrained body—an accused murderer and a town myth in bodily form. As Tyler devotes himself to Mala's care, she begins to eat and make noises, and along with him, we become intimate with her sensual world and eventually her past.

But the narrative structure ensures that we hear the story of her father, Chandin Ramachandin, before we hear Mala's, this time from Tyler's grandmother and in response to his question, "Nana, can your Pappy be your

Pappy and your Grandpappy at the same time?" From Nana we discover the sad and belittling life of Mala's father. Chandin had been taken from his East Indian parents by a white missionary family, the Thoroughlys, on the promise of a home, an education away from the cane fields, and a career with the church. Chandin embraces this as an opportunity to escape his designated identity, but despite his willingness and aptitude to transform himself into a "mimic man," he is never accommodated within the family. His awareness of himself as an outsider in terms of race is most painfully experienced when his romantic intentions toward Reverend Thoroughly's daughter Lavinia are cruelly dismissed by the reverend and he is rejected by Lavinia as well—later revealed as motivated by sexual, rather than racial, preference. Chandin instead marries Sarah, an Indian girl educated within the mission, as he "wanted nothing more than to collapse in the security of a woman, a woman from his background and Sarah was the most likely possibility," and they have two daughters, Mala and Asha (Mootoo, *Cereus* 45). However, when Lavinia returns from Canada, having broken her engagement to a promising suitor, she becomes increasingly attached to the Ramchandin family, much to Chandin's delight and excitement until he eventually realizes that Lavinia and his wife Sarah are lovers. Chandin ruins their plans to escape the island with the girls, and the two sisters are left behind with their distraught and destructive father.

Because of the way the narrative is constructed, as we discover that the aged Mala is accused of having killed her father, so too we discover that after her mother's desertion, her father had, as the narrative expresses it, "mistaken Mala for his wife" and had been sexually and physically abusing her for years, if not decades.[1] As the narrative of Mala's life emerges, we come to realize that she has taken on the roles of "wife and mother" to a disturbing degree, mainly in order to protect her sister, Asha, whose escape she plans but whose sisterhood she craves. With Asha and her mother both gone, Mala is heartened by the return of Ambrose, her childhood friend who had gone to the "Shivering Northern Wetlands" to study. Mala and Ambrose begin a romance that is both tender and loving, although this is not how the respectable citizens of the village perceive it:

> Ambrose E. Mohanty returned from study abroad to become the most eligible young man in Paradise, a foreign-educated fop with the airs and speech of a Shivering Northern Wetlandsman lord. It seemed a waste to the townspeople that such a catch would be so preoccupied with *a woman whose father had obviously mistaken her for his wife, and whose mother had obviously mistaken another woman for her husband.* (109, emphasis added)

Nevertheless, the relationship blossoms, and eventually they make love in a scene of great emotional charge for us as readers, knowing of Mala's other sexual trials and the high price to be paid if they are discovered. This is indeed what happens, and after a violent scuffle Ambrose leaves the house and Mala to her father's rage. Ambrose is in shock, not just at the events of the present but at the terrible realization of the nature of Mala's life with her father, which dawns in a moment of anguish from which it takes him decades to recover. Mala's multiple rape and attack by her father is related in disturbingly graphic and physical prose. Attacking back, Mala drags her father's body down into the basement room. So traumatized is she by Ambrose's desertion (when he does return, she is too transformed to recognize him) and her father's attack that she disassociates from her adult self, caring for herself as the Poh Poh of her girlhood. She also begins to withdraw, not only from society, which had already withdrawn from her, but also from language—the basic link to the social world—embedding herself more deeply and securely in a natural world populated by insects, animals, and plants and dominated by often bizarre and painful rituals that are difficult to analyze from a point within the rational.

> In the phase just before Mala stopped using words, lexically shaped thoughts would sprawl across her mind, fractured here and there. The cracks would be filled with images. Soon the inverse happened. . . . Eventually Mala all but rid herself of words. . . . Mala's companions were the garden's birds, insects, snails and reptiles. She and they and the abundant foliage gossiped among themselves. (126–27)

It is the discovery of Mala by Otoh, Ambrose's child, on one of his monthly "food runs" decades later that brings us back to the beginning of the story and Mala's transportation, in restraints, to the almshouse at Paradise. Although Ambrose has married and had a child, Ambrosia (who later transforms into Otoh), he copes with his abandonment of Mala by sleeping, waking only to assemble food parcels for her. Although the circle is in a sense complete, for the liberation of Mala and her story and the liberation of Tyler and Otoh are intimately entwined, this is not the end of the story.

As Tyler tells us at the beginning of the narrative, "I and the eye of the scandal happened upon Paradise on the same day" (5). Tyler is the only male nurse on the island, and his presence anchors an explicit intertextuality to Michelle Cliff's *No Telephone to Heaven* and Harry/Harriet, a homosexual transsexual who lives as a woman and works as a nurse. However, it is not only Tyler's choice of profession that casts doubts on his masculinity. Tyler, although not openly transvestite, is "the figure that disrupts" in his unsettling of the binary categories of male and female.[2] He is labeled a pansy and taunted because of the clothes he wears and the sexuality they imply. But as the alliance between Mala and Tyler grows stronger, based on a recognition of their "shared queerness" (53), both grow in confidence. While Tyler nurses Mala, she begins to tend to his broken identity. She steals a nurse's uniform from the washing line and presents it to him both as a gift and as a call to be himself, the self that she can perceive but that is not openly stated: "But she had stolen a dress for me. No one had ever done anything like that before. She knows what I am, was all I could think. She knows my nature" (76).

When Ambrose and Otoh begin to visit Mala in the almshouse—a process of reparation for all—they help Tyler to piece together her life and join in the narration of her story, but there is another kind of attraction emerging between Tyler and Otoh: "On visiting days . . . I practically hover above the ground with excitement," Tyler tells us (247), and this new relationship becomes an important dimension of the novel's ethical closure. Yet, throughout his narration Tyler has struggled to come to terms with the fact that Asha left her sister, and he makes all possible efforts to contact her, thinking of Mala's sister as the last link to her recovery and his orchestration of reparation. Finally, Ambrose prompts the judge, who had taunted Mala as a child, to make amends, and he locates a dusty bundle of Asha's letters in the post office. In a clear reference to Alice Walker's novel of paternal abuse, *The Color Purple*, we learn from these letters that Asha had been searching for their mother and seeking to bring Mala to her. However, in *Cereus* the center does not hold, and neither Asha nor their mother is restored. Unlike *The Color Purple, Cereus* is not a fable, and women who love other women are "forced to lose their families, their communities, or their lives" (B. Smith 121).[3]

It might seem curious that a harrowingly lyrical and sensual novel that is ostensibly about an abused recluse, a repressed transvestite, and a masked transsexual, that is set mainly within an almshouse, a derelict house, and a house of sleep, and that is clearly autobiographically informed makes such an important intervention in relation to the acute intolerance of sexual diversity in Caribbean societies. However, that this is a narrative interested in the question of sexual identities is made very explicit. Tyler declares: "Over the years I pondered the gender and sex roles that seemed available to people, and the rules that went with them. After much reflection I have come to discern that my desire to leave the shores of Lantanacamara had much to do with wanting to study abroad, but far more with wanting to be somewhere where my 'perversion,' which I tried diligently as I could to shake, might be either invisible or of no consequence" (47).

This impossibility of reconciling the identities queer and Caribbean is spoken by Tyler in very direct terms: "How many of us, feeling unsafe and unprotected, either end up running far away from everything we know and love, or staying and simply going mad" (90). He persistently narrates his consciousness of difference and his inability to articulate his identity in his Caribbean home. His emotions are reminiscent of both Michelle Cliff's "killing ambivalence" (*Land of Look Behind* 1) and Judith Butler's "domain of abject beings, those who are not yet 'subjects,' but who form the constitutive outside to the domain of the subject" (*Bodies That Matter* 3). He never names himself sexually, and when he repeats what others call him, he sees no match between what he knows himself to be and the identities offered to him: "Nana had accepted me and my girlish ways but she was the only person who had ever truly done so. Thoughts of her suddenly lost their power. Try as I might, I was unable to stand tall. I wondered for the umpteenth time if Nana would have been able to accept and love the adult Tyler, who was neither properly man nor woman but some in-between, unnamed thing" (71).

Tyler's awareness of his identity as being in-between and unnamed does not, however, situate him within the matrix of a celebratory postcolonial identity that is hybrid, fractured and mobile, in enabling ways. Indeed, differences in sexual orientation have no place as yet on the identity map of multiple and intersecting models of difference that has epitomized theorizations of Caribbeanness and arguably of postcoloniality in its contemporary fashionings. It is important to recognize that while discussions of same-sex loving remain socially explosive in Caribbean societies, the aftershock has not really disturbed the terms on which conversations about "difference" unfold in theoretical discourses. Even though in theoretical terms there are strong persuasions toward reading in-betweenness as fashionable and difference as strengthening, creolized sexualities have no currency as yet. Tyler's is a difference that removes him from that very map; he is outside of social definition and approval, possibly even—he wonders—beyond emotional kinship. His sexuality, like that of Boy Boy in H. Nigel Thomas's *Spirits in the Dark,* "was a constant point of reference for what society would not accept" (N. Thomas 94).[4]

This issue of naming sexual selves and practices is crucial in this novel, as the lack of positive self-definitions for queer subjects means that all seemingly "other" sexual acts are flattened out onto a continuum of deviance when calibrated against heterosexual norms. The linguistic negotiation of what Chandin does *to* Mala and what Sarah does *with* Lavinia implies an equivalence between incestuous abuse and a lesbian relationship: "a woman whose father had obviously mistaken her for his wife, and whose mother had obviously mistaken another woman for her husband" (109). The repeated formulation of sexual substitution seems to present these acts as equally transgressive misrecognitions rather than to differentiate between abusive and consenting relations. It is the recognition of this crucial differentiation that I want to argue *Cereus* demands.

For Otoh, whose story of sexual reidentification is somewhat different from Tyler's, somewhere between gender transformation in Virginia Woolf's *Orlando* and Butler's discussion of gender as a performance in *Gender*

Trouble, the relationship between naming and belonging actually enables him to claim a social identity:

> By the time Ambrosia was five, her parents were embroiled in their marital problems to the exclusion of all else, including their child. They hardly noticed that their daughter was transforming herself into their son. Ambrose slept right through the month, undisturbed until the first Saturday of the next, and Elsie, hungry for a male in the house, went along with his (her) strong belief that he (she) was really and truly meant to be a boy. Elsie fully expected that he (she) would outgrow the foolishness soon enough. But the child walked and ran and dressed and talked and tumbled and all but relieved himself so much like an authentic boy that Elsie soon apparently forgot she had ever given birth to a girl. And the father, in his few waking episodes, seemed not to remember that he had once fathered one.
>
> The transformation was flawless. Hours of mind-dulling exercise streamlined Ambrosia into an angular, hard-bodied creature and tampered with the flow of whatever hormonal juices defined him. So flawless was the transformation that even the nurse and doctor who attended his birth, on seeing him later, marvelled at their carelessness in having declared him a girl. (110)

The linguistic flow from *her* to *he (she)* to *he* and the emphasis on the flawlessness of his transformation are interesting precisely because they rely on the absence of biological sexual difference as a guarantee of gender identity. Otoh's transformation epitomizes Judith Butler's argument that "gender is always a doing, though not a doing by a subject who might be said to preexist the deed. . . . There is no gender identity behind the expressions of gender; that identity is performatively constituted by the very 'expressions' that are said to be its results." Otoh's regendered self is persuasively "structured by repeated acts that seek to approximate the ideal of a substantial ground of identity" (*Gender Trouble* 25, 141). Ambrosia's ability to become Otoh betrays the fact that sexual identities are actually social contracts between individuals and their societies, contracts that can seemingly only be negotiated around heterosexual and gender-normative imperatives in the Caribbean.

As Otoh, Ambrosia takes on a new, seemingly essential and fully realized sexual identity that guarantees him the social acceptance that Tyler, who is visibly ambivalent, "not a man and never able to be a woman" (77), cannot expect.[5] It is therefore almost something of a shock, given this acceptance of Otoh and the fact that he behaves and indeed is treated by the whole community as a man, when his mother turns to him and demands:

> "She know you don't have anything between those two stick legs of yours? Don't watch me so. You think because I never say anything that I forget what you are? You are my child, child. I just want to know if she know. She know?"

"Ma!" was all Otoh, thoroughly embarrassed, could utter.

"What you ma-ing me for? You think I am stupid or what? Now the fact of the matter is that you are not the first or the only one of your kind in this place. You grow up here and you don't realize almost everybody in this place wish they could be somebody or something else?" (237–38)

Two points are interesting here. First, the fact that Otoh's mother articulates her understanding that identities in general are never natural, stable, or self-present in the context of a novel in which sexual identity is only acknowledged in those terms. Her implication that Otoh's difference or imaginative reconstruction of himself is somehow equivalent to others' is not confirmed by the novel's social world. The second point concerns the social organization of sexual behavior and identities. Otoh can identify as a man because, although he is not a man, man is a stable, socially assigned sexual identity offering an apparently essential guarantee of the natural, through which he can be accommodated. In fact, Otoh needs to identify as a man (to hide the obvious flaw of his transformation), because what he cannot be, because there is no name, no tolerance, and no place for it, is that in-between, unnamed thing that Tyler knows himself to be—a transsexual or a transvestite.

This cultural imperative toward socially sanctioned sexual identities is also confirmed through other incidents in the novel. The description of queer figures does not affirm a potential community to which Tyler and Otoh might belong, but rather the prohibitions and tensions around queer identities and the need to make strongly normative reidentifications. At one point, Otoh is propositioned by a stranger who offers him a lift:

"Who is this lucky friend you dress up nice-nice so, goin' to see? Tell me, na? Why she—is a she you going to see or is a he? Don't mind me asking, you know. Why she so lucky and not me? A nice fella like you need a friend to show you the ropes. Let me give you a ride, na?" (148)

When Otoh declines, saying that he is courting a woman, though he admits enjoying the flirtation, the man retreats to his normative identity, signaled not only by his wife but also, significantly, by his children, who figure productive sexuality:

"Oh, you courting her. You? You courting a woman! I see. Is a lady you courting, eh. Uhuh. Well, I better not keep you back, because I have to go and meet my wife to take she to matinee. And my children coming with us too. What I was asking you was to come to the pictures with my family. You understand, na." (149)

Even this casual and anonymous exchange creates a danger zone in which identities have to be brought back into socially acceptable categories. When Mr. Hector, the gardener at the almshouse, confides in Tyler about his brother, Randolph, who had been sent away because he was "funny," the stakes involved in speaking such stories are registered in Tyler's extraordinary reaction:

> "He was kind of funny. He was like you. The fellas in the village used to threaten to beat him up. People used to heckle he and mock his walk and the way he used to do his hands when he was talking."
>
> That he was brave enough to say it suddenly lifted a veil between us. Unexpectedly, I felt relief it was voiced and out in the open. I had never before known such a feeling of ordinariness. (73)

This recognition of sameness in a life lived through an acute awareness of difference is deeply comforting to Tyler, who is more clearly marked by ambivalence and difference than Otoh. But it is not a sustaining comfort, for Randolph could not stay, and he no longer occupies the same position as Tyler.

In many ways, then, this text seems to represent the way in which sexually transgressive identities need to be contained in order to preserve social citizenship. Sarah and Lavinia are exiled as soon as they come out, Tyler is isolated before he finds Otoh, and all other queers in the text are either in denial or in the United States. Accordingly, perhaps one of the most urgent questions that we need to ask of this text is whether it actually participates in this act of containment by representing a romance between an anatomically heterosexual couple at its center? The question whether Tyler and Otoh's relationship is a structure that brings difference back to sameness, the transgressive into the normative, is significant to the debate about Caribbean sexualities. Does this coupling of a man who desires men and a biological woman who has the social identity of a man enable a kind of anatomical normalization to take place that is reassuring to a homophobic society?

In order to answer this question, I want to read Otoh and Tyler's relationship alongside the history of state regulation of sexuality in Trinidad and Tobago, where Mootoo grew up. In her article "Redrafting Morality: The Postcolonial State and the Sexual Offences Bill of Trinidad and Tobago," M. Jacqui Alexander examines the consequences and effects of the legal status of sexual practices in Trinidad and Tobago. She centers her discussion on the controversy over the Sexual Offences Bill (1986), which in Clause 4 of its first draft decriminalized buggery committed in private between consenting adults. However, after great public outrage, Parliament was reconvened to redraft the bill, and not only did the resultant legislative document recriminalize homosexuality but in addition lesbian sex became punishable under a new offence called "serious indecency" if "committed on or towards a person sixteen years of age or more" (Alexander, "Redrafting Morality" 136). As Alexander points out, the government used the fact that Trinidad and Tobago had the highest incidence of AIDS within the Caribbean as its extrajudicial rationale for criminalizing homosexuality, but it also declared that the new legislation was designed to restore the moral fabric of society, and it was presumably under this rubric that lesbian sex was criminalized.

If we read *Cereus* in this context, a new possibility emerges for the coupling of Otoh and Tyler to represent a more radical and disruptive version of "erotic autonomy" than that offered by a representation of loving homosexuality.[6] Their relationship suggests a sexual continuum that destabilizes the oppositional construction of homo- and heterosexuality through which sexual identities are taken to be constituted, represented, and governed. It enacts "resistance to the normativity which demands the binary proposition, hetero/homo" (Hawley 3). Indeed, the union between Tyler and Otoh is radical precisely because it is anatomically normative but socially queer; it represents a sexuality that is neither criminalized nor legalized, a sexuality that the state has neither the will to condone nor the legal power to punish. It helps us to think about desire and sexual relations outside the discourse of the state by de-segregating ideas of the "natural" and those of sexual identity.

Other aspects of the text are similarly brought into focus alongside Alexander's discussion. She examines the way in which the 1986 legal measures made the newly defined crime of rape within marriage difficult to prosecute, and her detailed analysis of the bill and its social contexts and contestations concludes that the political aim of this legal redefinition of normative sexuality was to conflate "morality with heterosexuality" and to "[reassert] the conjugal bed" (Alexander, "Redrafting Morality" 147, 138). In *Cereus,* the conjugal bed is reasserted through a terrible and violent substitution of daughter for wife. It is a bed that represents violence, crime, corruption, and death, for it is on this bed that Chandin rapes his two daughters and on this bed that Mala deposits her father's body for his rotten remains to be discovered decades later. It seems reasonable to conclude that in concordance with Alexander's analysis, Mootoo's writing points to the damage done by imposing the centrality of so-called natural and moral relations between husband and wife as the only available paradigm for sexual relations.

The discussion of lesbian identity is not prominent in the novel but rather operates as an unspoken relation. The intimacy between Sarah and Lavinia is first observed by Mala, who has "no words to describe what she suddenly realised was their secret" (56). Outside of the social order and the social imagination, lesbian relations can only exist as unspoken secrets. However, when Chandin recognizes the intimacy between his wife and Lavinia, the two women are forced to plan for an alternative future together. No longer secret, their relationship cannot exist in Lantanacamara: "'We have no choice but to make a decision.' There was a pause and then Aunt Lavinia said, 'Don't worry. Please don't worry about that. I have known that at some time in my life I would have to face it.'" The exchange goes on to focus on the children: "They are every bit a part of our lives. I too want them with us, no less than you. We will *never* be parted from the children. I promise you that." And eventually on the promise of a life together not caught in secret snatches: "We will be able to be together within the next few days. We can sleep at night and hold each other and . . ." (*Cereus* 59). The ellipses, although suggestive of the sexual desire as well as the deep emotional bond that binds these women, repeats the refusal to give words to same-sex loving between women and can be theorized as careful omission. As Dionne Brand has argued, "In a world where black women's bodies are so sexualised, avoiding the body as sexual is a strategy" (27). And perhaps it is a strategy that is even more urgent for queers, for whom, in the eyes of the state, as Alexander states, "sex is what we do and consequently the slippage, sex is what we are" ("Not Just (Any) *Body*" 9).

In terms of nonrepresentation, it also seems strategic that Sarah's words beyond the faint "Yes yes . . . as long as the children can be with us" are not heard. Throughout, she is a backgrounded figure, but all the same, the abandonment of the children is a problem within the narrative. Sarah does not intend to abandon them, so the narrative is not challenging the assumption that it is unnatural for a mother to leave her children. Indeed, what is missing from this text is what we have perhaps come to see as the anchor theme of Caribbean women's writing: the mother-daughter relationship. Sarah is one figure who cannot be integrated. Asha is recuperated through her letters, but part of what they relate is that she does not find their mother. The lesbian still has no place.

Perhaps most crucial to my reading of *Cereus* is Alexander's proposition that through the 1986 bill the state created a broad category of "criminalized sex" in which buggery, bestiality, and serious indecency "occupy contiguous spaces in the unnatural world of the legal text" and receive equal punishment ("Redrafting Morality" 141). In her later piece she further details this consolidation of illegal and unnatural sex as she draws attention to the way in which both the Trinidadian and Bahamian Sexual Offences Acts "conflated buggery, bestiality and criminality," as well as "violent heterosexual domination, such as rape and incest, with same sex relations" ("Not Just (Any) *Body*" 8, 10). Although Alexander is more interested in the implications that this categorization has for marginalized woman (not only lesbians but women who endure rape and violence within marriage) and their agency, I wish to foreground the facts that under the 1986 bill incest carried the same penalty as male homosexual sex and there was no legal distinction between male homosexual consensual relations and male homosexual rape.[7] It is against these aspects of the bill that I read *Cereus* as making an intervention in our understanding of how sexuality is represented and managed in Caribbean societies.

It may appear anomalous that in a novel all about desire and the conventions, restraints, and channels through which it is guided and policed, the central narrative spectacle is the act of incestuous rape, an act that has nothing at all do with desire. Yet, I would argue that the effect of having the rape of a daughter by her father at the center of a narrative that is occupied by characters with diverse sexualities is precisely to break open what is commonly represented in the Caribbean as a flattened continuum of sexual deviance, running from homosexuality to incest, encompassing rape, bestiality, and other acts of nonconsensual sex. In its place *Cereus* works to realign sexual identities around issues of consent and desire on the one hand and socially sanctioned power and violence on the other.[8] Perhaps the climate of gross intolerance and prejudice toward queer sexual practices that exists in the Caribbean means that it is necessary to stage the violence of incestuous rape in order to provoke a recognition of the meaningful difference between sexual practices that are harmful and those that are expressions of reciprocated desire.

I want to read *Cereus*, therefore, as a text that historicizes the present through its discussion of sexual identity and social intolerance. The novel demonstrates the consequences of a belief system that places the queer as beyond, outside of, and other to the social subject that postcolonial Caribbean governments have obliged their citizens to become. It also offers a way of reading this intolerance as a historically implicated operation implicitly aligned to the systems of racial classification, gender socialization, and moral rectitude naturalized by colonial domination. Read in this way, Mootoo's novel, like Patricia Powell's *A Small Gathering of Bones* and Lawrence Scott's *Aelred's Sin*, testifies to the fact that the space of articulation still is not owned by those who need to make self-representation and reveals the painful and damaging consequences of the heterosexual imperatives that operate in the Caribbean. Importantly, though, it also offers us a shift in the terms on which the debates about sexual identifications are being framed and contested that will allow sexual difference to be mapped onto the identity matrix of Caribbeanness.

I do not seek to position *Cereus Blooms at Night* as a literary response to the 1986 bill; rather I seek to read it as a text located in a particular historical and political moment that opens up a new discursive space in which to rethink the demands currently placed on Caribbean subjects in terms of their sexual conduct and sexual identification.[9] It inscribes lives and loves that take themselves seriously on their own terms and yet radically destabilize all ready-made categories and names for sexual and gender relations.

Cereus Blooms at Night's discourse on sexuality may appear radical in its emancipation of the queer citizen, and yet it should not be forgotten that the politics of freedom and of justice—based on equality, mutual recognition, and mutual consent—that this novel restores is also, pointedly, the very basis of postcolonial citizenship that Caribbean nation-states have themselves championed.

Notes

This essay is a lightly revised version of my reading of *Cereus* in "Sexing the Subject."

1. One reading of Chandin's incestuous abuse of Mala might be as a displacement of the incest taboo that Reverend Thoroughly had invoked to prevent Chandin from establishing relations with Lavinia. Chandin knows it to be racial prohibition and that the real taboo that cannot be broken is miscegenation.

2. This figure is identified by Marjorie Garber in her pioneering 1993 book on cross-dressing, *Vested Interests: Cross-Dressing and Cultural Anxiety.*

3. I should acknowledge here that my work on *Cereus* strategically invests in the possibilities of a social realist reading. In fact, the novel is far more formally complex and unsettled than I am able to represent. For a reading of how "Mootoo takes a flight from certainty to subvert the categories of 'real' and 'imaginary,'" see Conde.

4. It is also important to note that in *Cereus* Sarah is also taken off the map, as there is no space on the matrix for the lesbian mother.

5. The name Otoh comes from his nickname, Otohboto, meaning "on the one hand but on the other," which seems to confirm the radical undecidability and unreliability of his gender and sexual performances within the text.

6. I am thinking here of the kind of erotic autonomy that Alexander outlines as a politics of decolonization in "Erotic Autonomy."

7. Most critical analysis of the 1986 bill has centered on the issues of rape and lesbianism. See Atluri; and Robinson, "Fictions."

8. For an astute discussion of the way in which the state co-opts the right of consent in the service of its own moral agenda, see Alexander, "Redrafting Morality," 141–42. Narmala Shewcharan's 1994 novel, *Tomorrow Is Another Day,* which connects the corruption of Guyanese party politics to male sexual misadventure, seemingly confirms this continuum of deviancy in its description of a homosexual who threatens rape and a husband who actually does rape his wife. The former is described as essentially depraved, "like animals . . . perverted and sadistic" (222), while the latter is depicted as a victim of circumstance, "the ragged, driven man who had almost become a stranger to her" (197).

9. In 1999 Amendment 2 to the Sexual Offences Bill was passed in Trinidad and Tobago. Attorney General Ramesh Maharaj argued that the existing legal framework was not adequate to protect citizens: "If ever there was a crying need for [the] legislature to act in a matter, it is for this matter." About the proposed amendment, he declared, "I make no apologies for this Bill if it is considered to be ferocious. Laws, at times, have to be ferocious because we are not living in a society of yesteryears" (Richards). The amendment made provision for men to be convicted of rape and sexual assault against their wives, although the penalties are less than for raping strangers. Incest now carries a penalty of life imprisonment, and there is a compulsion by law to report violence against children. A differentiation in the penalties

for incest and buggery was introduced, although the latter now carries a sentence of twenty-five years' imprisonment. Certain objections to the amended bill indicate that many of the problems identified in response to the 1986 act remain. Senator Dr. Eric St. Cyr argued that the bill would actually increase antagonist relations between men and women, that it was anti-men, and "that the logical consequences of the proposed legislation would be to drive men into homosexuality." The leader of opposition business in the upper house, Nafeesa Mohammed, expressed concerns over the provision for husbands to be charged with raping their wives. "And you have the other side of the coin, that in some situation if a woman is perturbed in her marriage, that her husband is involved with somebody else or there is some problem, she could easily cry rape too" (ibid.). Both the act itself and these responses clearly indicate that the politics of sexuality remains an urgent area of contestation and struggle.

Le Jeu de Qui?

Sexual Politics at Play in the French Caribbean

Vanessa Agard-Jones

IN APRIL 2007 the Paris-based gay magazine *Têtu* published an article by Martin Barzilai provocatively titled "La douleur des makoumés: Homophobie en Martinique" (The sorrow of the faggots: homophobia in Martinique).[1] The piece appears under a photograph of black male bodies, shown from the neck down, in motion, presumably dancing. They are clothed in vaguely "tribal" wear: all are bare-chested, and the man at the center of the shot wears a leopard-print armband and a leather and raffia belt, slung low. The caption identifies the photograph as a scene from Carnival, taken at a party called "Jungle Juice," where during a "moment of détente, homos are accepted" (Barzilai 112).[2] The article's spectacular title and the exoticizing photograph set the stage for an exposé, ostensibly penned to reveal the kinds of violences and exclusions that gay and lesbian Martinicans face on the island. In this essay I chart what else this scene and the article that follows reveal both about the politics of representation and the rights-based rubrics through which those representations are framed in the "conversation" between French Caribbean subjects and their metropolitan counterparts. Moving from representations to the lived experiences of the subjects being represented, I use discourse as a starting point for an interrogation of matters that are often missed in analyses of Caribbean sexual politics.

"La douleur des makoumés" was published in the context of an increasing interest within *Têtu*'s pages in the question of homophobia in the Antilles; the number of articles on the region appearing in the magazine had gone from two in 2005 to eight in 2006 and then there were fifteen interventions of varying lengths into the limited public discourse on the topic in 2007.[3] This evolution was marked by a shift on the part of the metropolitan-based editorial staff from an interest in Martinique and its "sister" island Guadeloupe as potential (gay) tourist destinations to a consideration of the role that sexuality plays both in local politics and in the everyday lives of gays and lesbians on the islands.[4] Beyond the gay press, Martinique and

Guadeloupe enter the French public sphere more regularly than other islands in the region because of the unique relationship they retain to France: since 1946, they have been *départements d'outre-mer* (DOM), politically integrated territories of that power's first colonial empire.[5] By virtue of their nonindependent political status, Martinique and Guadeloupe operate under a legal regime unique to the Caribbean vis-à-vis sexual rights. While in certain independent countries in the region homosexuality is criminalized and "homosexual acts" are punishable by law, France's legal code both affords protections and extends certain rights, such as access to the PACS (the *pacte civil de solidarité,* a form of civil union that has been available to both same- and opposite-sex couples in France since 1999), to Martinican and Guadeloupean citizens.[6]

In the same month that "La douleur des makoumés" appeared in *Têtu,* posters reading "ATTENTION! DANGER! Ségolène ROYAL veut marier les Makoumés—Nous disons NON!" (Attention! Danger! Ségolène Royal Wants [to allow] Faggots to marry—We say No!) cropped up at numerous sites across Guadeloupe's city of Point à Pitre. This was during the last rounds of France's 2007 presidential election, when the electoral race had narrowed to a contest between the conservative Nicolas Sarkozy and the progressive Ségolène Royal. Far from an isolated series of postings, the production of the signs was coordinated by local political actors who were rumored at alternate times to be members of either Sarkozy's Union pour une Mouvement Populaire (UMP) or Royal's own Parti Socialiste (PS) on the island. In Martinique, in the wake of the poster campaign local political figures argued that homosexual practices (and, moreover, ideas about gay marriage) were unacceptable to 95 percent of the Antillean population, largely because the Antilleans were said to hold "Christian" beliefs that differed from those of French metropolitans.[7] To many interpreters, the debate signaled a clear distinction between the moral codes deemed acceptable in hexagonal France (the part of the country located in Europe) and those valorized in its territories in the Caribbean. Dramatically and quite clearly, sexuality and sexual rights have emerged as a flashpoint in an ongoing political and social negotiation of the relationship between France and its dependent territories in the Caribbean.[8]

In this essay I seek to understand the modes of representation that frame lesbian and gay Antilleans as subjects of particular (European) rights and victims of certain (Caribbean) violences. Representations such as the ones circulated through *Têtu* are key sites where the metropole's authority over its noncontiguous territories is both enacted and consolidated. I attempt to document the loci of power that emerge as these discourses develop in a circuit between France's Caribbean *départements* and the metropole, paying particular attention to the questions of legitimacy and authenticity that have been mobilized in these fields. I argue that despite the best intentions of (mostly) metropolitan-based advocacy groups, these discourses unwittingly support the mapping of a developmental teleology on France's Caribbean territories, labeling them less "modern" than their hexagonal counterparts. I wonder how this framing dovetails with other French nationalist projects, particularly as they relate to the country's self-perception as an originator and defender of human rights. Because these discourses sometimes occlude the complicated, everyday experiences of queer Antilleans (both at "home" and in the diaspora), I also integrate into my analysis interview material from conversations with various interlocutors both in the Antilles and in Paris.[9] Ultimately, by examining the politics of sexuality in the French Caribbean, I attempt a simultaneous consideration of teleologies of development and the limits of liberal rights paradigms, teased out through an analysis of the politics of representation that impact queer lives in the Antilles as well as in their French metropolitan diasporas.

"La douleur des makoumés"

In bright red letters a floating text box on the second page of "La douleur des makoumés" asserts: "If you don't have a computer and you want to meet people, you risk your life."[10] This dire pronouncement sets the tone for the article, which begins with the story of Michel, a teacher and activist who was attacked in Fort de France, Martinique, in late 2006. Michel was distributing condoms on behalf of an advocacy organization at the port, which was well known as a pick-up spot for gay men (presumably those without computers), when a group descended on him with knives, leaving him in need of twenty-one stitches.[11] Seeking to account for the forty-three instances of homophobic aggression that were reported in Martinique in 2006 (in addition to what Michel suffered), *Têtu* contracted the journalist Martin Barzilai to write "La douleur des makoumés." The article points to two key features of Martinican society thought to be at the root of its homophobia.[12] The first is many Martinican citizens' adherence to forms of conservative Christianity.[13] Barzilai writes:

> The strong influence of different churches, Catholic, Protestant, or Evangelical, constitute [*sic*] a form of social pressure. It is not rare to hear readings of the most contested passages of the Bible on this question (Leviticus XVIII, 22 and XX, 13). . . . This omnipresence is also found on a local television station, KMT, that systematically ends its programs with "That God might save Martinique." It is also in the name of their religious convictions that numerous elected social-ist officials on the island have taken positions against those of their party on

gay marriage or in respect of laïcité. That's the case with Marlène Lanoix, first federal secretary of the PS, who in July 2004 called the PACS a "by-product of a decadent society." (113)

Here Barzilai activates a common frame for understanding sexual mores in the Caribbean, one rooted in the politics of respectability and deeply informed by Christian orthodoxy (P. Wilson).

As the anthropologist Deborah Thomas explains with regard to Jamaica, "Respectability . . . is a value complex emphasizing the cultivation of education, thrift, industry, self-sufficiency via land-ownership, moderate Christian living, community uplift, the constitution of family through legal [heterosexual] marriage and related gender expectations, and leadership by the educated middle classes" (D. Thomas, *Modern Blackness* 5). This vision of respectable conduct has been roundly criticized by Caribbeanist scholars, even as it has been taken seriously as a response to labeling the region and its people as hypersexual (Kempadoo, *Sexing;* Mohammed, *Rethinking;* D. Thomas, *Modern Blackness*). But beyond the usual skepticism about this approach to the nexus between religion and sexuality, the revelation that a local television station uses a tag line that references "God" in its programming would be particularly surprising for a metropolitan French audience because of the deep resonance that the political value of *laïcité,* or (public) secularism, has in that country. Further, that Marlène Lanoix, an elected official aligned with one of the more progressive of the national parties, would use even vaguely religious reasoning in her articulation of a position against gay civil unions (the PACS) would be downright shocking.

For French metropolitan audiences, the blows keep coming. In a text box on the following page of the article, in large black letters, the words "In the Bible, God says it's an abomination" appear above the smiling face of Raymond Occolier, another PS member and mayor of the Martinican commune of Vauclin. In the mini-interview that follows, Occolier calls for "the next government to consult the Martinican population, by local referendum, on the question of gay marriage," stating that "after Madame Royal announced her political program, which included gay marriage, a lot of Socialist Party members [militants] turned in their membership cards. We must stop the hemorrhaging [from the party]. I don't want to be cut off from my electorate" (114). Quite clearly, conservative Christianity and its interpretations of scripture emerge to explain the homophobia that causes Martinican "makoumés" such sorrow.

The article goes on to articulate a second rationale for this state of affairs:

Martinique must face important social problems: high rates of unemployment, notably for youth, social precariousness that is not abating, undeniable economic difficulties, and the ravages of crack. Baseball caps, baggy pants, and Nike, many young people sport the bad boy outfit of the West Coast [presumably, of the United States] and listen to ragga or dancehall. This style could be innocent if certain singers didn't call for the murder of homos. (113)

In this instance, homophobia is interpreted as the result of the diasporic cir-culation of cultural forms, themselves understood to have arisen as a result of social inequality.[14] Rather than the hagiographic framing of this circula-tion invoked by the seminal critic Paul Gilroy (*"There Ain't No Black"*), the movement of these cultural products between the United States and among the islands of the Caribbean is reframed as a threat. This echoes the kinds of arguments that have been made, particularly in Caribbean cultural analyses, about musical forms popularized since the 1980s. Almost invariably with reference to Jamaica, these works have focused on critiques of dancehall and ragga music—for their misogyny and/or their homophobia—and have inspired vociferous debate both within the academy and beyond.

Much has revolved around Buju Banton's 1991 track "Boom Bye Bye," a song wherein the dancehall don quips, "Boom bye bye inna batty bwoy 'ead . . . rudebwoy nuh promote nuh nasty man dem haffi de'd." This track's circulation, first as an underground product in Jamaican dance halls and then internationally when released on Banton's Mercury Records–produced album, led to what Tracey Skelton has referred to as "the airing of a debate about race and sexuality" (275) in certain parts of the Caribbean and its diasporas in North America and the United Kingdom, and this same debate has only recently made its way onto the Francophone circuit. With this airing, though, has come the consolidation of a type of binary critique: on the one hand, of what many (white) gay activists have referred to as the "exceptional" homophobia of "Jamaican (and by extension—Caribbean) culture," and on the other, of what Jamaican/diasporic activists have charged is another round of cultural imperialism emanating from the West, crystal-lized by the censorship of Banton's songs and boycotts of both his music and his concerts.[15]

On one front, in these debates dancehall has been elevated as a beacon of resistant artistry, positioning the Caribbean against the decadent West, and heralded as the voice of the Caribbean's margins—the poor, the youth, and the disenfranchised (Bakare-Yusuf; Cooper, *Sound Clash;* Niaah, "Making Space"). On another front, dancehall has become emblematic of a form of violent black pathology, uniquely homophobic and illustrative of the cul-tural backwardness of the region. As Faith Smith has remarked, in this era "issues of sovereignty seem to be waged more forcefully in the domain of sexuality" (Smith, "Crosses" 136) than in any other, as these debates and the ways that they have called up international human-rights standards, sanctions, and the withholding of global capital have made clear. "La douleur des makoumés" sits smack in the middle of these conversations, as Francophone artists such as Admiral T., Krys, and D. Pleen are identified in its pages as torchbearers for the translation and rearticulation of the homophobic speech found in the dancehall music of their Anglophone counterparts.[16] Studies of homosexuality and homophobias in the broader Caribbean have paid attention to these issues, as well as to the particular intersections of cultural politics and national discourse on various islands of the region (Barrow, de Bruin, and Carr; Glave, *Our Caribbean;* Kempadoo, "Centering Praxis").

Still, the discourse on *homosexualité* in the Francophone Antilles continues to be framed (by French journalists, activists, scholars, and politicians alike) as a binary opposition between Caribbeanness (associated with violence, black popular culture, and Christianity) and an implicit Frenchness (associated with rights, safety, and secularism). The solidification of this ideology inserts the Antilles into a developmental teleology that is less aligned with the tradition/modernity binary that we often see in postcolonial contexts and organized instead around a religious/secular one. Because "tradition" is arguably a less applicable conceptual frame for the Caribbean, a place that many argue has always been "modern" (Khan; Mintz; Trouillot, "Caribbean Region"), this binary gets reworked through the French political value of *laïcité,* which itself functions as an index of modernity. The political division of the private and public spheres in French thought is, as in other liberal traditions, one that places politics in the "public" category and both religion and sexuality in the "private" category.

Feminist critiques of this spurious division aside, the ideologies that reinforce this separation continue to have powerful resonance. The article in *Têtu* is but one place where the representation of the Antilles as gripped both by a conservative Christianity gone wild and by a retrograde set of (black) cultural values is juxtaposed against the properly secular (white, European, though tacitly Christian) public space of the French republican state. This discourse draws lines of radical cultural difference to ostensibly "explain" the homophobic violence that occurs in a place like Martinique, even when much the same can be found in a place like Provence.

Within this logic, remedying the problem of homophobic violence would require admission that the Antilles are places in need of "development"—secularization and Europeanization—in order to fulfill the promises of their inclusion in France's liberal-rights regime. Here "development" is tied not to neoliberal humanitarian programs like those promoted by economic-development industries elsewhere in the region but instead to ideas about the proper place for both religion and blackness in the French public sphere. While the article does not point to "development" as the explicit solution to the Antilles' purported problem with homophobia, the suggestion is that Martinique departs from hexagonal France's model due to a set of cultural values that are both behind the times and beyond the pale for a modern democratic state.

Qui Parle?

Returning to the opening gambit of "La douleur des makoumés," the preview of the article reads, "Between the declarations of hostile elected officials against homos, the sermons that keep with the same sentiment, and the local singers who call for the burning of 'faggots,' the climate in Martinique is not the most welcoming. But gays and lesbians are not ready to laissez-faire" (112). But who are the "gays and lesbians" to whom this preview refers? Who are the subjects who will not let this Bible-beating and identification with homophobic (black) popular culture continue? Are these local actors? Diasporic ones? From whom did Barzilai get his information in order to represent the issue in this way?

Beyond the conversation with the local politician Raymond Occolier, "La douleur des makoumés" reads like a who's who in the debates over queer sexualities and their place in Martinique, including quotations from the organizers of various activist and advocacy groups, entrepreneurs, and scholars based both in Paris and in Fort de France. While Barzilai is careful to present a fairly diverse set of positionings and experiences, a certain narrative about "good" and its battle against "evil" still emerges between the lines. Although this is a reductive frame, it still bears mentioning: activists, social-welfare workers, and entrepreneurs are written into the narrative as the ones fighting the good fight, and they are clearly positioned against locals with religious convictions, including public figures such as Marlène Lanoix and Raymond Occolier.

Among the "good" guys is Amvie, the organization that Michel was working for when he was attacked at the port, though no representative of the organization is quoted in the article. Patricia Louis-Marie, the director of Action Sida Martinique, the island's oldest and most established HIV/AIDS organization, is referenced as having told Barzilai that condom distribution was still blocked by many institutions on the island (including secondary schools and prisons), even though the statistics for HIV transmission were dire (Barzilai 112). Finally, Barzilai draws heavily on the analyses offered by David Auerbach Chiffrin, then secretary general of An Nou Allé, an organization founded in 2004 as both the Antilles-Guyane arm of France's nationwide network of gay and lesbian centers (Centres Gaies et Lesbiennes, or CGL) and as an activist organization for black and mixed-race LGBT people in France. While An Nou Allé has had representatives based in Martinique and Guadeloupe, the majority of the adherents to the organization—including its founder, Louis-Georges Tin, and Auerbach Chiffrin—now live in Paris.

That metropolitan-based queer subjects play such a dominant role in the debates about queerness, race, and rights in the Antilles speaks to the ways in which the power of representation gets concentrated in diasporic hands. Further, while *Têtu* can be exceedingly difficult to find among vendors in Martinique—during a recent stay on the island I could find it in only one store—in hexagonal France it is the flagship publication for the mainstream gay and lesbian demographic and as such is widely available.[17] The conversation that takes place in the magazine's pages, then, is largely a closed-circuit one, between people in the metropole rather than between the metropole and the Antilles. While remaining vigilant against a tendency to flatten and reify a North-South or diaspora-local divide, we must nonetheless question how emplacement either within the region or outside of it matters in these political fields.

Têtu is sited in a field of knowledge production and circulation that centers on international human-rights-based advocacy, and while they are not as nefarious (nor as coordinated) as what Joseph Massad calls the "Gay International," the modes of representation that are circulated through *Têtu* are not only similar to but largely derived from the discourses developed by activist groups, with the French Caribbean material being tied closely to the statements made by (mostly) metropolitan-based members of An Nou Allé.[18] Given these dynamics, the conversation increasingly inscribes a narrative whereby metropolitan queers are mobilized to "save" local (Antillean) queers from local (Antillean) people.[19]

This framing is troubling, in part because of the way it reifies and reinscribes colonial categories (the backward Caribbean versus the enlightened West) but even more so because it reflects the genuine good intentions and sincere desires of metropolitan subjects to both document and combat violence. In her article "The Tragedy of Victimization Rhetoric," the feminist legal scholar Ratna Kapur maintains that any attempt to argue with inequality starts with showing that it exists, usually by showing its victims. There is no denying that people fall victim to homophobic violence, both symbolic and physical, in Martinique (just as they do in Paris, Bordeaux, and Marseilles). Nor is there any denying that even the threat of violence, as well as of less spectacular exclusions, shores up a regime of sexualized inequality in the Antilles. But the crafting of a particularly Antillean victim subject and a particularly Antillean homophobic subject backs our political responses into a contradictory corner. When the problem is framed in this way, the possibilities for resistance get limited to calls for "development," usually through public education. This discourse often leaps over actual queer Antilleans and their experiences to privilege the interpretations of activist subjects, themselves usually based in (or from) the metropole.

Rajeswari Sunder Rajan and Zakia Pathak have argued that "discourse . . . works only by significantly excluding certain possibilities [in this case full representation of the subject]. It achieves its internal coherence by working within parameters which are ideologically fixed" (Pathak and Rajan 563). Similarly, Dorothy Ko questions the framing of the victim subject and the ways in which the binary through which it operates conceals the actual subjects of the discourse and turns them into a one-note monolith, united (and given voice) solely through their victimization.

A number of my interlocutors in Martinique and Guadeloupe have emphasized to me that they cannot be reduced to victimized subjects living in a universally homophobic place. One, a lesbian based in Fort de France who publishes anonymously on her *Blog de Moi,* wrote upon first learning about An Nou Allé's existence, "I am not going to deny everything they say, but believe me, there are ways of living one's homosexuality here. 'Constant clandestiny,' 'social outcast status'? . . . No. Well, yes and no! So sorry to be raining on parades again! It really depends on individuals and their histories and it's not worse here than it is in a small rural town. But I concede that some probably have difficult lives on the day to day."[20] Her urban, middle-class milieu makes her experience of living as a lesbian in Martinique something much less fraught than Barzilai's article might have readers believe. Equally, her experience of sexual politics as a lesbian is inscribed—though not unproblematically—in the tropes of silencing and invisibility that Makeda Silvera highlights in her now-classic essay "Man Royals and Sodomites: Some Thoughts on the Invisibility of Afro-Caribbean Lesbians." Referencing the work of An Nou Allé, other interlocutors have wondered aloud to me whose interests the negative representations that they proffer ultimately serve. They suggest that in the absence of an ongoing and serious engagement with the lives of people on the ground in the Antilles, these forms of advocacy serve to do little more than benefit the personal political and professional trajectories of the mostly diaspora-based advocates.[21]

In "La douleur des makoumés" a similar problem emerges: local people unaffiliated with either activist or advocacy organizations make only cameo appearances. Even Michel, the "victim subject" whose story opens the article, is little more than a name, an age, and an incident—in other words, a prop. Everyday queer Antilleans only appear between the lines of the argument about homophobia that Barzilai and his interlocutors build in this article, though the violent incidents that impact (but do not necessarily define) their lives are mobilized for activist purposes. Pathak and Rajan convincingly demonstrate how discourses of protection, in addition to giving "authority to speak for the silent victim . . . can [also] serve as a camouflage for power politics." This move "conceals" the power differentials between the protectors and the protected, while granting legitimacy to the protectors to speak on behalf of the protected. When this happens, an important consideration drops out of the picture: that emplacement in the metropole and emplacement in the Caribbean come to matter differently to queer subjects' understandings of safety, strategy, and the "development" necessary to rid their communities of homophobia.

Activist proponents frame the limited rights that France extends to its LGBT citizens as critically important. The right to the PACS and the ongoing fight for rights to adoption, medically assisted reproduction, and marriage all activate a narrative about LGBT identity that centers coming out, the assumption of queerness as an identity, public visibility, and political action.[22] If outness, visibility, and the spoken are taken as the measure of these rights, queer subjects in the Antilles are understood to experience them only as unrealized, particularly because so few people choose, as they term it, *s'afficher* (to wear their sexuality on their sleeve). But the narrative that rarely gets taken seriously in this formulation is one that centers on discretion. Among my gay and lesbian interlocutors in Martinique and Guadeloupe, by far the majority have chosen to live their (sexual) lives discreetly, at least when they are at home. François-Xavier, a metropolitan man who lives and works in Fort de France as the proprietor of a cyber café, tells Barzilai that he approaches his outness in Martinique in this way, "I don't hide anything, but I'm not ostentatious" (113). Similarly, many of my interlocutors have described their forms of passing to me, delineating the ways in which normalized gender presentation helps reduce questions about their sexual orientation in their everyday lives, be it at school, at work, or with their families.

Conventional interpretations of this choice would highlight its groundedness in fear—of gossip, of outing, or of violence. But I would caution against making the analytical slip of understanding discretion to be equal to either passivity or some crude form of false consciousness.[23] In an effort to take seriously the belief of some of my interlocutors that political inaction and personal discretion are preferable to the kind of action initiated by activist groups in response to homophobia, I wonder what it would mean to think about their position as both a call for an alternate understanding of the steps necessary to make their living conditions more ideal and an instantiation of what Judith Jack Halberstam has called "radical passivity." In Halberstam's hands, radical passivity describes a subject position that declines the contestatory, that either cannot or refuses to speak, and can be used conceptually to rethink both passing and passivity as active in their own way.[24] Halberstam's analysis gives us a different, perhaps more generous way of reading people's actions and offers an alternative to liberal teleologies for social change.

The complicated stories of negotiation that my interlocutors in the Antilles shared with me highlight some of the contradictions between having access to sexual rights and living under intense social pressure to "pass" as heterosexual. Even given this tangle, some still understand the political projects of a diasporic activist group like An Nou Allé to be participating in a game—one that privileges outness, visibility, and confrontational protest—that they would otherwise decline to play.

C'est le Jeu de Qui?

While sitting in the parking lot of her apartment complex in Schoelcher, a bedroom community of Fort de France, my interlocutor "Jewel," a Martinican lesbian in her thirties, insisted that I answer her questions: "Whose game are they playing? Whose game are you playing?" We had been talking for nearly an hour about the "Ségolène ROYAL veut marier les makoumés" poster campaign, Raymond Occolier's call for a referendum on gay marriage in Martinique, and An Nou Allé's advocacy on behalf of victims of homophobic violence. I had expected a conversation with her about why there were no queer women involved in local contestatory projects, but instead we were talking about whether the issues themselves were worth contesting, particularly given the way they were framed. She wanted to know whose game An Nou Allé was playing when it contributed to stories like "La douleur des makoumés," which would run, and be read, largely in the metropole. She wanted to know whose game Occolier was playing when he spouted off about calls for a referendum even though the French legal code would never allow such an initiative. She wanted to know where I stood too—whose game I was playing—as I talked to her about my desire to craft a dissertation project on sexuality and politics in the Antilles.

Surprised by her adamant tone, I stumbled. I hedged. But Jewel insisted. She approached these topics with an intensely skeptical (and expansive) eye and tried to shift our conversation away from the questions that interested me then—Had she ever been to an An Nou Allé meeting? Why didn't she consider that to be a good use of her time? Did she know the members?—to the larger politics at play. While I would later come to understand (and agree with) her skepticism, our reasons for doubting ultimately differed. Like Jewel, I was concerned that the (mostly) diasporic subjects who purported to speak "for" lesbians and gays in the Antilles were complicit in other projects, ones that demonized Martinique and labeled its queer inhabitants victims. Not only did Jewel decline to construct herself as a victim but she focused her critique on how very different Martinique was from a place like Jamaica, a place she understood to be a "real" (and spectacularly unique) site of homophobic violence in the Caribbean. Jewel confessed a deep love for her island and its Frenchness. She understood Martinique to be France, not a place in need of some sort of ideological development in order to be equal to France.

While I share Jewel's critique of observers' representing Martinique as a place in a state of developmental delay, I am equally skeptical about the kinds of complicities that are shored up by insistently framing Martinique as France. I question how all of these positionings participate in a narrative about French national pride that many of its postcolonial subjects, from the Caribbean as well as other parts of the world, have contested. I see both sides of this discourse—framing the Antilles as radically religious and Other to French secularism and downplaying island homophobia in order to claim those places to be "as French as France"—as contributing to a reductively nationalist, or if looked at through the lens of *Têtu* and An Nou Allé's advocacy, as part of a "homonationalist," project (Puar, *Terrorist Assemblages*).[25]

Furthermore, I would like to suggest that current concerns with sexuality and its relationship to religion in the Antilles are haunted by the debates happening in the Hexagon about the integration of postcolonial, often religiously marked migrants into France's political community.[26] Numerous scholars have written about the fraught relationship that France continues to have with Muslim populations, particularly Algerian or Algerian-descendant ones (Cohen; Shepard; Silverstein). French anxieties about these populations' integration into the national body have flared around the question of the headscarf and what its wearing is thought to represent about gender parity, ideas about women's sexuality, and Muslim incompatibility with the French civilizational project (Bowen; Keaton; J. Scott). This is the paradigmatic battle in the French public sphere, while questions about homophobia in its Caribbean territories represent, by comparison, mere blips on the metropolitan radar screen. For this reason, conversations about postcoloniality and modernity, particularly as they are filtered through debates about gender and sexuality, continue to refer to the perceived "Muslims versus France" crisis in the country. If queer activists are not careful, they may also contribute to the consolidation of France's congratulatory narrative about its role in the global adjudication and spread of human rights.

The congratulatory narrative goes like this: France is the home of *liberté, égalité,* and *fraternité.* French universalism guarantees rights to all people, who are seen as equal (and unmarked by any form or group membership) before the state.[27] Because of this political heritage, France is a beacon for other polities and has taken a progressive stance on forms of inequality related to race, gender, national origin, and sexuality that other states should want to emulate. Given this narrative, ideas about French exceptionalism and the relative enlightenment of other countries' governance systems are increasingly indexed by issues such as the "emancipation" of women and the treatment of queer subjects.[28] Indeed, when activists who want to contest homophobic violence in the Antilles call upon tropes of Frenchness and lean upon French rights as the solution to the problem, they may end up playing a game that ultimately disserves them.

Who Speaks? Whose Game? What Next?

Throughout this essay I have sought to understand how modes of representation impact the subjects being represented, how having the power to speak may not run parallel with having the most politically efficacious things to say, and how the problem of advocating for the end to violence against queer subjects in a postcolonial (or neocolonial) context is fraught with pitfalls. By grounding their reasoning in one line of logic, advocates for change may fall in line with homophobic projects. By grounding their reasoning in another, they may support imperialist ones. While sketching a map of the political field, as well as the seemingly intractable problems that are part of it, remains an important endeavor, where does this critique leave us? Will we ever find a way to work around having the locus of power for representation rest in the metropole? What can we do with the good intentions of those metropolitan actors? Even more importantly, what do we do with the real violences that people suffer and the rights that might, in whatever incremental way, protect them?

Even given the enormous diversity that characterizes Antillean experiences in the metropole and in the Caribbean (Beriss), there remains a complex gap between these groups' understandings of the nexus between sexuality and rights in the Antilles. As an example of one way to bridge it, the Martinican lesbian responsible for *Blog de Moi* has forged another locus of representation for queer subjects in the Antilles. In this digital age, her work points toward the opening that new forms of media might provide in shifting the metropole-weighted distribution of those who are given the platform to "speak," though the class-laden implications of this form of action remain intact. Whereas previously the only way to learn about Martinique was from analyses refracted through Paris, her blog is but one outcome of more democratized access to various public spheres.[29]

Perhaps the more difficult problem to confront, though, is the conflict between the sincerely proffered political projects of those who seek to "liberate" queer Antilleans and the local (queer) resistance to those interventions. It bears remembering that both sincerity and good intentions were at the heart of most colonizing missions, and France's *mission civilisatrice* acted as the standard-bearer. Returning to this time-worn yet still present dynamic forces us to acknowledge the limits of our political imaginations.

I offer these analyses not as an incitement to close down political projects but rather as an urging to open them up, to question them in new ways, and to reconfigure and realign them as critically as we dare. Jewel's reminder that we look to the big picture as we engage in these politics is one we might well heed, while also paying more sustained attention to the everyday experiences of the people most affected by them. As an anthropologist, I am particularly interested in the relationship among imaginaries, representations, and materiality, and I am moved by the complicated ways in which our imaginations sustain us but also work to occlude certain experiences. While some imaginaries function as necessary means by which we can dream and actualize certain futures, others turn into representations that bypass the experiences of everyday people. For the latter reason I am convinced that ethnography, that sustained engagement with people who do not necessarily have recourse to authorial or artistic authority, is of the utmost importance as we seek to understand sexual politics in the Caribbean. As we ask politically urgent questions about human rights, homophobias, the politics of respectability, and sexual "freedoms," it would behoove us to also ask questions of those who every day negotiate these politics as they go about living their lives, for in the end none of this really *is* a game.

Notes

I would like to thank all of the people who read and commented upon early drafts of this essay, foremost among them Andil Gosine, Lila Abu-Lughod, Yasmin Moll, Ram Natarajan, Faith Smith, Marie Varghese, and Anna Wilking. The arguments contained herein were productively honed additionally in conversations in the New York University Institute of French Studies doctoral student and faculty seminar. Sections of this work were presented at the 2009 conferences of the Collegium for African American Research and the Caribbean Studies Association, in Bremen and Kingston, respectively, where questions from the audience and from copanelists proved invaluable. Finally, I am grateful for the interventions of the anonymous readers for the *Caribbean Review of Gender Studies,* whose insightful comments continue to push my thinking as it relates to the larger project of which this paper forms a part.

1. *Makoumé,* sometimes spelled *makomé* or *makomè,* is a Créole colloquialism that roughly translates as "faggot" in English. In Anglophone Caribbean slang the word is most equivalent to *battybwoy.* Unless otherwise noted, all translations from Créole and French are my own.

2. *Homo* is a French slang word that is used more often than its Anglophone equivalent in everyday speech between self-identified gay subjects. For more on language and sexual identity in French, see Provencher.

3. *Antilles,* the French word for "Caribbean," is used to refer solely to Martinique and Guadeloupe or to the region on the whole in French parlance.

4. While I recognize that in Martinique, as in the rest of the world, not all people who engage in same-sex sexual activity identify themselves as gays and lesbians, for the purposes of this essay *Têtu*'s interest in sexuality in the Caribbean is clearly

tied to the subjects who assume those identity markers. For a compelling analysis of the relationship between sexual identity and those categories in Martinique, see Murray, *Opacity*.

5. The *départements d'outre-mer* number four: Martinique, Guadeloupe, Guyane (also considered, depending upon the observer, to be a part of the circum-Caribbean), and Réunion. As departments, they are technically comparable to Provence or Brittany. *DOMien(ne)s*, as their inhabitants are sometimes called, are citizens of France, eligible to vote in national elections and to participate in national political parties.

6. Ratified in France in 1999, the PACS allows any two nonrelated people, regardless of their gender, to enter into a formal relationship of "solidarity" similar to civil marriage. According to France's Institut National de la Statistique et des Études Économiques (INSEE), in 2003, 43 PACS were signed in Martinique. In 2004 there were 94, and in 2005, 124. More current statistics have not yet been released; earlier figures were: for 2000, 20; for 2001, 23; and for 2002, 79. To provide a point of comparison, in 2006 INSEE reported 1,477 marriages on the island.

7. See http://www.dailymotion.com/video/x1i17o_occobondamanjak_politics.

8. The activist Mario Kleinmoedig has analyzed a similar dynamic in Curaçao and Aruba, islands of the Dutch Caribbean. There, gay marriage functions as a pivotal issue for indexing sovereignty when questions of political in/dependence are being debated (personal communication, 2009).

9. I use *queer* as a convenient shorthand here, fully cognizant of the fact that there is no equivalent term in French, nor is it the way in which my interlocutors define either themselves or their sexual practices. My interlocutors in Paris have been fairly evenly divided between lesbians and gay men, while my interviewees in Martinique and Guadeloupe are more often lesbian and/or bisexual-identified women, save for self-defined activists with whom I have interacted in Martinique, all of whom are gay men.

10. The "you" being interpellated in this message is somewhat ambiguous: it is both the (presumably white, metropolitan) *Têtu* reader and the gay Antillean person, indexing a kind of community between those readers and the article's subjects. I thank Ram Natarajan for helping me clarify this point.

11. I use Michel's real first name, as the article does, but do not include his last name, which follows *Têtu*'s convention, though I met with and interviewed him in July 2008 and May 2009. A note: the article misidentifies the advocacy organization's (Amvie's) work as being directed only toward HIV-positive people, but its charter includes advocacy for LGBT people and sex workers (Fred Cronard, director, personal communication, July 2008).

12. There is a limited effort at the end of the article to articulate a more nuanced third "explanation" for Martinican homophobia. Toward this effort Barzilai quotes Stéphanie Mulot, an anthropologist whose thesis research was on sexuality and matrifocality in Guadeloupe: "Antillean identity is constructed on the basis of the individual having to respect the rules of the community. Identity must be collective and not individual" (Barzilai 114). Rather than blaming Christianity or popular culture, she points to the smallness of the islands and the community ethos that springs, in part, from propinquity. Parsing these explanations allows us to begin to examine the function of homophobia(s) in particular contexts.

13. The generalized anxiety about conservative Christianity may also reflect the shifting demographics within Christian adherence in the French Caribbean. While the majority of the citizens of the islands have traditionally been Roman Catholic,

evangelical Protestant churches have been making significant headway within these populations.

14. In keeping with a typically French reluctance to articulate the racial markers of these forms, Barzilai never calls them "black," even though that is the implicit marking.

15. The response of J-FLAG, the Jamaica Forum for Lesbians, All-Sexuals and Gays, to the 2009 Boycott Jamaica campaign illustrates the ways in which local queer subjects have sought to develop and disseminate their own critique of both lines of argumentation.

16. A wave of critics have sought to make a more complicated intervention into this debate, acknowledging that in cases like these the stakes are high and therefore the imperative for nuance is great. Rather than forcing a choice between "colonial and sexual politics" (T. Chin), certain critics have been moved to develop an intersectional blending of the two, both in this controversy and beyond (R. Ferguson, *Aberrations;* Gopinath; Johnson and Henderson; Muñoz). Sara Salih, in a 2007 essay on the Banton controversy, struggled to come to a less reductive reading of the dissonant registers at which it was (and continues to be) racialized, sexualized, nationalized, and gendered. In an attempt to stake out her own position she asks, "What does it mean to be postcolonially queer, or/and queerly postcolonial, particularly in a context where the self-styled 'local' values of the post-colony are pitted against what are regarded as the permissive sexual mores of the west?" (Salih, "Our people" 1). As just one possible research agenda to which future scholarship might attend, I would like to suggest an ethnographic analysis mindful of Salih's questions that examines the relationship between popular culture and the forms of violence—both corporeal and symbolic—that shore up heteronormativity. Locating antigay ideologies and their continued relevance in authorizing discourses—be they religious, biological, or merely "popular"—may be an important way to evaluate the construction of both sexual and racial normativity, claims to authenticity, and their attendant formulations of the abnormal. Looking to "the multiple spaces where these contestations occur—the church, the dancehall, the street—and the increased visibility of lesbian and gay organizing in the Caribbean" (Alexander, "Danger and Desire" 160) is one of the tasks to which social analysts might set themselves, particularly as they work to disrupt the spurious binary that positions the "queer-friendly, progressive West" against its "retrograde, homophobic" counterpart in the Caribbean.

17. The magazine may be something akin to what the *Advocate* represents in the United States.

18. Since the publication of Barzilai's article, An Nou Allé's role has been increasingly fulfilled by TjenbéRèd, a splinter group based more self-consciously in the metropole, which began its work in May 2007. Frequently, TjenbéRèd's interventions and public statements are picked up by *Têtu* reporters and used as the basis for their stories. See http://www.tjenbered.com. It is fairly clear that the organization's positions have been influenced by the work of Peter Tatchell, a London-based self-proclaimed human-rights activist who has taken up controversial, universalist positions on a variety of LGBT issues. Jasbir Puar offers an insightful and important critique of his oeuvre, highlighting its investment in notions of Western supremacy (Puar, *Terrorist Assemblages*). See also the critique put forward in the hotly contested essay by Jin Haritaworn, Tamsila Tauqir, and Esra Erdem, "Gay Imperialism: Gender and Sexuality Discourse in the 'war on terror,'" in Kuntsman and Miyake. After significant pressure from Tatchell (and a threat that he would sue for defamation),

the press published an apology in August 2009 that is widely viewed as a Tatchell-penned stopgap measure. See http://www.rawnervebooks.co.uk/outofplace.html.

19. Here I am echoing the postcolonial theorist Gayatri Spivak's classic critique of representation and the victim subject in her 1988 essay "Can the Subaltern Speak? Speculations on Widow Sacrifice."

20. I thank Alice Backer for this translation.

21. While no one to whom I spoke questioned the advocates' sincerity, the gap between these actors suggested that the advocates' intentions themselves emerge as a result of the development teleology at work.

22. For important critiques of these teleologies of gay identity and the political projects of which they form a part, see, for example, Decena; Gopinath; Manalansan, "Speaking in Transit"; Muñoz; and Wekker, *Politics of Passion*.

23. As Neville Hoad has argued insightfully, "The claim to rights on the basis of homosexuality has been a fraught business in the modern West. A universalizing faith in the liberatory potential of such politicization of sexual minority identities repeats the failures and fantasies of modernization theory without taking into account its devastating riposte: underdevelopment theory."

24. I am aware, here, that even this formulation of passivity insists upon an agentive subject, itself usually formulated as the measure of the full exercise of a rights-bearing subject's humanity. Halberstam's intervention with the notion of radical passivity is meant, in part, to circumvent the privileging of acting/action as the only proper way to deal with power relations. Rather than engage the active/passive binary much further here, I would like to suggest that the passivity I describe may be diagnostic of the forms of power at play in the Antilles, as well as in other communities where most queer subjects understand sexual discretion to be the best option for their public lives. I thank Yasmin Moll for stimulating my thinking on this point.

25. Puar defines homonationalism as "a form of sexual exceptionalism—the emergence of national homosexuality . . . [that] operates as a regulatory script not only of normative gayness, queerness, or homosexuality, but also of the racial and national norms that reinforce these sexual subjects" (Puar, *Terrorist Assemblages* 2).

26. This is also a trend in Europe more broadly, as countries from the Netherlands to Denmark to Spain participate in a nearly continentwide conversation about the relationship between Muslim migrants, "security," and the neoliberal political order.

27. France has a peculiarly romantic, self-congratulatory narrative about its relationship with rights talk, given the nation's central place in the genealogy of those frameworks. The Declaration of the Rights of Man and the Citizen (1789) was a founding document of the modern French state, initially composed by the Marquis de Lafayette during the French Revolution, and is widely cited as a forerunner to documents like the Universal Declaration of Human Rights.

28. When French Secretary of State for Human Rights Rama Yade announced in 2008 that France would bring a resolution to the United Nations calling on all member states to decriminalize homosexuality, it was with the framing that this was a fitting call coming from France, the home of human rights. Playing on the idea of France as both originator and arbiter of a morally superior set of human-rights standards, Yade has consistently referenced the more than ninety countries in the world where homosexual acts are penalized and the five or six (Islamic) states where a conviction on charges of homosexual practice carries the death penalty.

29. A number of anthropologists of culture and media have made important interventions on this front, documenting the development of indigenous "media worlds" and their interactions with global communications networks. On these topics, see Ginsburg, Abu-Lughod, and Larkin. I thank an anonymous reviewer for the reminder that the Internet, like the diasporic music circuit, harbors both revolutionary and reactionary potentialities. I acknowledge that while functioning as a site for the proliferation of previously unheard voices, it can also function as a site for the development of antigay political positions.

Reimagining Pasts and Futures

Our Imagined Lives

Tracy Robinson

A PRESSING demand of Caribbean feminism now, I believe, and I am speaking particularly to the English-speaking Caribbean, is to mark out as we see them the shapes of women's imagined lives. If the contemporary Caribbean is, as I have suggested elsewhere (see "Fictions"), mired by fictions of women's citizenship, then in addition to, and not at the expense of, the labor Caribbean feminists already engage in, part of feminism's ongoing and collective project is to piece together with the *force of imagination* rich descriptions of our aspirations for women, including ourselves.

I am speaking of full lives, with all their complexity and tentativeness, not identical ones or perfect ones. Ones that contemplate the macrocircumstances or relations of gender and more, and ones that take us beyond women's relation to the state. Included would not just be our need for the basic resources for health, physical sustenance, and shelter, for decent work and freedom from violation. Also included would be our interest in emotional well-being and development, community and connection to others and separateness too at times, leisure and play, spiritual bonds and space, and the capacity to exercise our imagination and to reason (see Nussbaum, "Humanities").

I am urging that an elaboration of the idea *our imagined lives* become more overtly rooted within Caribbean feminist praxis, not as segregated work within feminism, either in terms of who does it—resisting an instinct to say that this is labor for academics or those who work on sexuality, for instance—or in terms of how it is done, that is, not independently of our other work. I view this as a cooperative, dynamic, and iterative venture that all of us participate in all the time. To illustrate, I see it as a complement to recent feminist initiatives around reproductive health and rights,[1] now decades of evolving antiviolence activism,[2] feminist efforts to strengthen women's political participation,[3] and a generation of Caribbean feminist efforts to reveal and respond to the gendered face of domestic and international economic policies and globalization, including an early groundbreaking gender critique of structural adjustment policies in the Caribbean (see Reddock, "Women's Organizations and Movements") and a more contemporary evaluation of trade policies (see Caribbean Gender and Trade Network). *Our imagined lives* is therefore not a programmatic intervention; it is more in the nature of an auxiliary methodology that consciously proceeds from a sympathetic reading of feminism and feminist work.

I have made a point of describing the feminist project of *our imagined lives* as being about *women's* imagined lives. I hold to that, with some nuance to come later. I defend its woman-centeredness in a very particular way here: that the identification of feminists with the "woman question" has been crucial for the "self-definition and ability to act" (Lloyd 68) of many women, including me. I quite deliberately refuse the description of Caribbean feminists as *other* women, both the ungenerous view of feminism as irredeemably alienated from women and thus irrelevant and the more charitable view that feminism is fundamentally altruistic (work for others). Feminists represent women's concerns, but equally our lives represent women's ways of living, in all their intricacy (Robinson, "Gender, Feminism" 621). This is not the usual defense of feminism, nor need it be the only one, but it might nevertheless be valuable to think that a virtue of feminism is that it has shaped many of us profoundly in the ongoing process of becoming who we are.

This essay is based on regard for feminism and my debt to it for helping to construct my "imaginary domain," as Drucilla Cornell refers to that space "for the renewal of the imagination and the concomitant re-imagining of who one is and who one seeks to become" (*Imaginary Domain* 5).[4] In that vein, mine is, as might be suspected, a sanguine view of feminism's place in Caribbean futures. I have argued elsewhere that citizenship is a valuable theoretical tool for analyzing women's subordination and a potentially powerful political device for transforming women's lives, and I urged that both become more firmly part of Caribbean feminist practice (Robinson, "Beyond the Bill" 232). What I have not yet said, in this way at least, is that I believe that the ways feminists live—our use of feminism to "contest and re-imagine ourselves" (Cornell in Cornell and hooks 263), our claiming of the political as "subjects-in-progress" (Lloyd)—can be crucial in enabling citizenship and ensuring that anybody can be a citizen (see Alexander, "Not Just (Any) *Body*").

By invoking Caribbean feminism as the basis of a community I wish to belong to, I am of course also reifying Caribbean feminism. I recognize this effect and do not wish to diminish the fluidity and diversity within Caribbean feminism or the contestability about what it is. Not all women's organizations, including those explicitly concerned with the emancipation of women, would describe themselves as feminist. Alternatively, many women describe themselves as *becoming* feminist over the course of woman-centered work. The political work feminists choose is also undertaken by the state and by intergovernmental and nongovernmental agencies that do not claim feminism. Conversely, self-defined feminists work through their feminist ideals not just in discrete feminist institutions but in diverse professional contexts. These are overlapping streams of ideas, communities, and work, with the regional, diasporic, and international also flowing into one another. I do not intend to resolve this absence of fixedness with an all-encompassing definition of Caribbean feminist. As a core, I nevertheless recognize a group of women (and some men) for whom the Caribbean is a serious concern and who have claimed the name *feminist* as an entitlement "to focus on all the strategic issues facing women in our societies; issues which span the range of social, economic, political, cultural, political and sexual" (Baksh-Soodeen and Reddock ii).

Curiosity

As a legal feminist, I have been necessarily taken with the accomplishments of the Caribbean campaign addressing violence against women (VAW), which began in the 1980s, for they are mostly laws or associated with the law, and despite their limitations, they far exceed the accomplishments of any other feminist lawmaking initiative in the region.[5] Once more, VAW is where I begin (see, e.g., Robinson, "Fictions"), and it informs my case for *our imagined lives*. Recent evaluations of the VAW campaign recognize the progress made in securing for victims of violence greater access to justice and services; at the same time, they point out that the initiatives to end the violence warrant far more resources and commitment than are being applied. The provision of services for victims and perpetrators is still very modest (see ECLAC/UNIFEM), there are generally very few protection orders granted through the courts (see Lazarus-Black, "Law"), and there is a clear need for further law reform (see Robinson, "Changing Conceptions").

An assemblage of governmental, nongovernmental, and intergovernmental actors and individuals, not all of whom would describe themselves or their work as feminist, have been key players in the Caribbean VAW campaign, pursing research, guiding law and policy development, and providing services and training. Additionally, gender-based violence is but one of a wide range of endeavors that Caribbean feminists are involved in. Even so, there is a powerful association between anti-VAW activism and Caribbean feminism. We have said this in every decade since the eighties—that the VAW campaign has been one of Caribbean feminism's greatest preoccupations and most likely represents its largest legacy (see Mohammed, "Reflections" 33; Reddock, "Men as Gendered Beings" 93; and Robinson,

"Fictions" 2). Violence against women, we are told, has "emerged as the *single* issue capable of uniting [Caribbean] women" (Reddock, "Men as Gendered Beings" 93, emphasis added), and it is also viewed as the issue *about* women most able to coalesce collective empathy and rage, even if this is momentary and despite the glaring silence at other times.

In the midst of what at times appears to be a uniquely shared concern and the bursts of universal outrage, the character and, many believe, the measure (although this is hard to assess) of danger to women obdurately persists, and an end to the violence is maddeningly elusive. There are brief, repeated moments of intense public engagement, when it seems as if everyone in the nation is distressed about and disturbed by the pained bodies of women and girls who make the headlines (see Robinson, "Changing Conceptions"): "Woman Torched" on J'ouvert by a male relative who accuses her of dancing with a man (Alonzo), "Sexually abused girl murdered" by a male relative who buries her body in a pit latrine (Heereral). The nation is "rocked," communities are "in shock." Politicians visit families, attend funerals, offer assistance (see Williams). Pastors sermonize, pundits editorialize. All become interpreters of the suffering.

These periods of public outrage are by no means the entire landscape of public affect to violence against women; much of women's suffering through violence goes unmentioned and is normalized, but these moments of heightened concern might be more defining than we have imagined. We become voyeurs of a sort, captivated by a flattened idea of womanness, that of a woman/girl overcome by her suffering, eviscerated and determined by it, a woman/girl who is nothing but the pain. We are intrigued by her lifeless body, her "thingly" quality. We want to know who discovered "it"—the body—and how. Was it a group of children playing in the pasture, or a man on his way to work? Was it rotting? Was it lying face down in a pool of blood? (see, e.g., Renne; and N. Thomas). And we want to see it, so crowds gather at the scene of discovery.

This kind of female suffering is at once spectacular and noteworthy and ordinary. The bodies of the silent and silenced girls and women become fungible; their suffering is made generic and co-opted to symbolize injustice in general (Hartman, *Scenes of Subjection* 21; Robinson, "Beyond the Bill" 244–45). Soon we lose sight of the women and girls and their specific experiences. Saidiya Hartman describes this as the "double-edge" of empathy, its "precariousness." In her provocative work on slavery, Hartman concludes that the witness often "must supplant the black captive in order to give expression to black suffering, and as a consequence, the dilemma—the denial of black sentience and the obscurity of suffering—is not attenuated but instantiated" (*Scenes of Subjection* 19). Likewise, the interpreters of violence against women assume righteousness and goodness by taking over the violated and translating the violence against her into something that represents their own interests and qualms, displacing the suffering and making it more opaque.

In part, then, my worry is that the universal concern about horrific incidents of violence against women, the force of imagination exerted here—which is sometimes read as part of the exceptionalism of violence against women—produces and often reproduces a very meager description of women's diversity and possibilities. The idea of woman is made and remade in these moments through the spectacle (see Hartman, *Scenes of Subjection*), and the meaning of woman becomes mostly, essentially, her capacity for subjection and powerlessness.

I have a related uneasiness about the distinction of violence against women as the "one issue capable of uniting women of all classes, races and ethnic groups" (Reddock, "Women's Organizations in the Caribbean" 12). I am reluctant to take this direction, because I am acutely aware that it might be read as an argument that feminists in the region should do less VAW work or that this work is less urgent and critical than feminists have argued, both of which I emphatically reject. So it is with a measure of reservation that I suggest that the engagingness and naturalness of anti-VAW activism as woman-centered work can be precarious too. There is now a taken-for-granted-ness about Caribbean feminism and VAW work, a kind of obviousness and inevitability about why we do it, that it is ours to do and that we will always do it. My worry is that the axiomatic compels as it dulls. Its shortcut to righteousness is what enchants us, and we are all less curious in virtuous moments.

The idea that violence against women escaped the vagaries of difference, that there is some singular sense of womanness that made violence, more than anything else, readily comprehended by all kinds of women, should itself cause some hesitation. In our certitude, we spare little irony for the ways in which as feminists we are producing our own conceptions of womanness through our politics, not simply representing already established interests of women (Lloyd 68–69). These conceptions become overdefined by women's assumed commonality, a propensity for violation by men. We focus on a "limited slice of the individual," and victimhood sometimes becomes for us the "primary source of identity" (Minow 1433).

One effect of this is that we see relations of power—and more profoundly human relations, including those of affinity and closeness—as firmly heterosexed. Put differently, we notice power most when men do it to women, just as we notice intimacy most when men do it to women, or, more generously, when both men and women participate in it. More than this, when we as feminists also reduce women to the experience and risk of violence, we sometimes fail to articulate feminism's aspirations for women beyond the cessation of the violence. As an ethical response to the condition of women, Caribbean feminism has been at its most persuasive in theorizing that condition and in articulating precisely what it is about that condition that feminism seeks to save women from—poverty, violence, disease, bigotry, and so on. Despite this, in my view, the efficacy of Caribbean feminism is being thwarted by the opacity of what we want to save women *to*, however modest, partial, unsettled, and diverse our sense of the futures feminism can contribute to bring into being.

Our imagined lives is an argument for intensifying our curiosity. With an engaged curiosity we can choose to make much, politically, of what we think our commonalities are (and I believe we must where violence and many other issues are concerned). At the same time we can recognize their instability and openness to contestation as part of the arena for feminist politics (Lloyd 66), sites where we can, among other things, disrupt empathy's disembodiment of women. Talking in terms of *our imagined lives*, I suggest, is one way of maintaining the intensity of our commitment to ending harm to women and also providing rich descriptions of women—our experiences, cares, identities, and lives.

Contention

The story of Caribbean feminism is in good measure a contest over meaning. The rise of gender has become as much the nemesis of Caribbean feminist politics as it is its progeny. Terms such as *gender, equality,* and *justice* are open to reinterpretation by persons besides feminists. There are now a multitude of postfeminist renderings of gender, ideas and concepts that gained new meaning "in feminist politics" and "have become, or are fast becoming, something else" (Antrobus 25).

One dimension of this I call "gender somethings" (Robinson, "Gender, Feminism" 612), and I attribute these largely to the professionalization and internationalization of gender (see Andaiye, "The Angle You Look From" 15; and Lazarus-Black, "(Heterosexual) Regendering" 1002). Gender somethings are goals related to gender that have gained wide bureaucratic currency because they are signifiers of progress and development and provide opportunities for political rectitude, especially in the international context. They have a bureaucratic buzz. Feminist actors are decreasingly driving their invocation; in fact, often they are nowhere to be seen, such as when constitutional change to remove gender-discriminatory constitutional provisions in the Bahamas was put to a referendum vote in 2002. Gender somethings are, however, idiosyncratic in that they are articulated with strong official support yet are quite amorphous and vague (see Robinson, "Gender, Feminism" 612–17). They are unwieldy; they multiply, overlap, and replace earlier ones—gender analysis was the old something, gender mainstreaming is the new. Depending on the discipline, gender equality and gender equity are the same or different somethings. Their meanings get confounded, but their production signals gender getting larger. The emphasis of gender somethings is always on "doing gender" instrumentally, because gender matters, usually to some development goal. Gender becomes an end in itself.

The defining edge of some gender somethings is what they are *not;* notoriously, sex does not include sexual orientation as an antidiscrimination principle (see Robinson "Gender, Feminism" 617–20; and Trinidad and Tobago, "Equal Opportunities Act," sec. 3). Alternatively, gender serves as a contrast to, a self-conscious distancing from, woman-centered things (Robinson "Gender, Feminism" 612). Caribbean feminists have fiercely resisted this last move. For at least a decade and a half, Caribbean feminists have ardently countered allegations that feminist goals having to do with women and girls have been achieved and that the primary gender question of the day is the marginalization of boys and men.[6] In defense of the continuity of woman-centered work, and in response to what is often a virulent antifeminist backlash, regional feminists have provided elegant analyses of the contemporary situation, indicating the contradictions that belie claims of equality:[7] while improvements in the material relations of gender have benefited some women, their improved situation has been marred by continued hostile ideological relations of gender (V. Barriteau, "Conclusion"); high levels of female participation in the formal labor force have not shifted male dominance of political and economic decision making or the primary burden for unwaged work in the home from women (Andaiye, "Smoke and Mirrors"); female-headed households often signal not so much power as propensity to poverty; women have higher levels of participation in secondary- and tertiary-level education in the Caribbean, but this has not guaranteed them the expected economic, political, or social development (Bailey); and so on.

In some ways, this kind of response (which I also routinely give), though powerful, is oblique. Although it plainly demonstrates that the meaning of feminist ideals like gender justice and gender equality are deeply contested, extraordinarily, the feminist rejoinder often avoids the very question at stake in public imagination by failing to offer affirmative notions of what feminists mean by gender equality or gender justice.[8] Caribbean feminism has provided very credible theories of exclusion, saying what equality *is not* and why the present conditions *do not* amount to the realization of feminist aspirations. Less and less do we say what our larger, one hopes multitude, visions are for the communities and society within which those assessments are secured. Gender equality and justice as abstract standards have been naturalized as self-evident feminist ideals that need little explanation, compendious descriptions of feminism's projected end results that now have the imprimatur of international conventions, national constitutions, and governmental, nongovernmental, and intergovernmental organizations.

We frequently present gender politics at the front lines in stark oppositional terms, with "sophisticated" feminist analyses of gender—the "striking . . . consistency with which [feminists] point to contradictions in the contemporary situation" (Massiah xiii) in the name of gender equality—on one side and "pedestrian" civic understandings that "bleach" gender of its "feminist roots" (V. Barriteau, "Confronting Power" 60) on the other. While I share the anxiety about public conversations about gender that seem intent on "keep[ing] 'man' as the subject of intellectual inquiry" (V. Barriteau, "Confronting Power" 74), I am increasingly uneasy about this schism. I am not sure that we want to invest too heavily in this idea that as feminists we all agree, even though I recognize the political benefits of cohesion. Nor do I think that feminists should be unwilling to consider that public and intellectual discourse that we assess is not well intentioned or benign could nevertheless be instructive.

In the persistent discussions in the Caribbean about "male marginalization," "female ascendancy," and the description of parenting, child care, and support as a gender battleground, to mention a few, I certainly hear reasonable questions about what feminism wants for women that pick at our cohesive responses about equality. What precisely makes high female participation in secondary- and tertiary-level education inconclusive of women's equality but makes low female political participation highly significant of inequality? When and how do numbers matter to our ideas of equality? Is our sense as feminists that numbers are important influenced by our understanding of equality as "a question of the distribution of power" (MacKinnon 40)? How do we figure the relationship between gender, agency, and equality? Do we from time to time reproduce images of men, especially black men, as superagents—autonomous, sexualized, fully formed beings—choosing even marginal roles (E. Barriteau, "Requiem"), while women emerge for us, especially through gender and development discourse, as desexualized, completely determined by the circumstances of gender and its relations of power? What is our take on the old debates about sameness and difference and the many challenges that arise from the persistent sexual division of labor and the realm of "female familial responsibility"? In our struggle for equality, are we most interested in, for instance, an ethic of care, in which women's caring labor is properly counted and compensated (see Andaiye, "Smoke and Mirrors"), or are we looking forward to that burden of care being shared by men and women? (see UNIFEM).

We are being entreated, even through some of what we might consider crude public discourse, to unpack our broad commitment to gender equality and justice and tackle our differences regarding the meaning of equality and gender justice. My proposal is even more open-ended: I think we should allow ourselves to engage in discussions about our hopes for women's futures using whatever linguistic and conceptual devices we choose, and not necessarily be bound to common concepts like equality or justice. This presupposes that we do not rely on or necessarily agree on the same words and concepts to express our commitment to women's freedom. To my mind, rich descriptions of women's promise make our shades of difference the grist of feminist interrogation, encourage us to revisit and refine our thinking, and will help us to produce the "healthy crop of ideas and practices to emerge with a new generation" that Patricia Mohammed speaks optimistically of ("Future of Feminism" 116).

Imagination

These very particular descriptions of women's promise or our aspirations for women underpin *our imagined lives* as a feminist methodology. It should become a process feminists engage in all the time in our organizations, as we develop policies and programs in our varied communities, in our scholarship, pedagogy, and consciousness raising, as we meet women and men whom we intend to serve and in relation to whom we intend to conduct research, and in our ongoing conversations with one another.

As method, *our imagined lives* is a very loose structure held together largely by an insistence on detail. There should be sufficient specificity in the images produced of women's promise that women materialize in them. We should see the shapes of lives, including our own, through these rich descriptions—the kind of detail I acknowledge will invariably invite debate and disagreement among Caribbean feminists. In other words, *our imagined lives* contemplates that we hear in one another's contributions a tangible embodied analysis that we feel competent, more often than not, to respond to with words and ideas we already own, both sophisticated and pedestrian words.

There is always the risk that the kind of fleshing out I am encouraging might imply that there is one way, or a right way, to be a woman; or that it might produce static images that confine rather than enable; or that it might suggest that there is a singular, clear outcome that we can anticipate and will all agree on. I acknowledge that risk, but more abstract goals in the Caribbean have become, if anything, homogenized into gender somethings—fuzzy everywhere with very few venturing in to pick apart and refine understandings of them. Internal contestation is masked or never makes it to the surface. The threat of rigidity that detail could produce can be resisted if detail becomes the fulcrum for debate by producing materialized images within reach outside rarefied circles and serves as a common denominator of expression that encourages varied and open-ended exploration of the diverse ways we can live.

Importantly, these rich descriptions of women's promise should be constructed with the force of imagination. What I am after is what Drucilla Cornell speaks of as "the space of the 'as if' in which we imagine who we might be if we made ourselves our own end and claimed ourselves as our own person" (*At the Heart of Freedom* 8). Cornell thinks of this mostly as an individual venture, while I am convinced that these spaces are usefully also developed by groups and in communities. The imagination can be incited by reflection on the lived realities of women, the kind of feminist knowledge that has always fueled woman-centered work in the Caribbean. However, this might not be the starting point, even less so the end point, for everyone. Our desires are often more than the inverse of what we think is undesirable; they may be differently oriented or arise distinct from a conceptualization of wrongs about the present.

What we know about the present is valuable and, at the same time, already a constrained field. Notoriously, traditional research about women in the Caribbean has often neglected consideration of the extent of women's "hedonic lives" (see R. West). Even in the feminist literature of the English-speaking Caribbean, Kamala Kempadoo warns, "sexual desires, agency and identity . . . have barely been broached" (*Sexing* 25). Likewise, in the more than half-century that the Caribbean has been a well-trod anthropological field, the vibrant intellectual tradition of family studies in the Caribbean has rarely even hinted that all intimacy and family life might not be heterosexed. There are some things, especially about our interior selves and about ways of living and being sexed that are available to us, that we only know could or might be so because they have been imagined, especially by the literary and artistic genres.

One demand of *our imagined lives* is that the lives we imagine must include our own, so that our own destiny, desires, and communities as feminists are alive within the larger images we debate and help construct. This project is not about "social mothering," being the good woman, who "has no needs, never speaks about herself, and never expresses anger except on another's behalf," "works tirelessly for the welfare of others," and "is passively heterosexual, or if necessary, asexual" (Ford-Smith 247). Insisting that the self/ves be part of the subject of feminist exploration is yet another means of tackling the persistent concerns about hierarchies based on class, race, sexuality, and nation (among others) among women. It also reinforces expectations of accountability and internal critique for Caribbean feminism. Admittedly the process of internal reflection is fraught and sometimes seems like too much, too perilous given what a life of politics has already cost many feminists and the further exaction from the fierce gender politics of the present. The force of imagination, the space of the "as if," might at moments better hold together and attend to our vulnerability for the purpose of collective reflection.

Gender as a Suggestion

A feminist political agenda that takes seriously *our imagined lives* can legitimately be woman-centered for the reasons I offered earlier, but never just that. It must also adopt an expansive method that I now frame as treating gender *as a suggestion*. It is not dissimilar to the focus of other feminists on the intersections of gender and other axes of power, marginalization, and differentiation—race, class, gender, geography. By treating gender as a suggestion I mean treating gender as less an end in itself, a rejoinder to the rise of gender somethings, and reclaiming gender's analytical gravitas as suggestive of multifaceted agendas for social justice that are premised on the diverse and often shifting ways in which we imagine ourselves and our communities, and in which we and our communities are imagined. In this essay, which is a provocation of sorts, my goal has been to talk about women, but women are also symbols of this "mobile subjectivity," as Kathy Ferguson (154) describes these unstable, multiple identities we all have.

Caribbean feminism is rather unnerved by the specter of "mobile subjectivity," or at least often speechless in its face, that is, in the face of women who "trouble fixed boundaries," "are ambiguous, messy and multiple, unstable but persevering . . . ironic, attentive to the manyness of things," and "are politically difficult in their refusal to stick consistently to one stable identity claim" (K. Ferguson 154).[9] This troublesome energy could become a source of vibrancy within Caribbean feminism if we think of gender as a suggestion. In this view, the dissipation of what many regional feminists thought of as a movement need not produce the utter despondency we often hear of if we can nurture coalitions and plural and imbricated agendas contemplating what Jacqui Alexander calls, at the end of her essay "Not Just (Any) *Body* Can Be a Citizen," "a collectively imagined future that takes account of [the] dismemberments, fractures, migrations, exiles and displacements that have been part of [the] processes of domination" in the Caribbean (22).

Notes

I am grateful to Michelle Rowley, Donette Francis, and Roberta Clarke for their helpful comments.

1. The initiatives of Advocates for Safe Parenthood: Improving Reproductive Equity (ASPIRE) in Trinidad and Tobago and St. Lucia to reduce the incidence of unsafe abortions and promote respect for sexual and reproductive equity and the

work of Development Alternatives with Women for a New Era (DAWN) to advance sexual and reproductive freedoms through research, education, and dialogue, for instance.

2. This activism includes not just initiatives on domestic and sexual violence (see ECLAC/UNIFEM) like the wide-scale regional police training on domestic violence recently undertaken by the Caribbean Association of Feminists for Research and Action (CAFRA) but also the activities of organizations like Red Thread in Guyana and the Women's Institute for Alternative Development (WINAD) in Trinidad and Tobago drawing attention to the gender of racialized, political, and small-arms violence (see Trotz).

3. I am thinking especially of the kind of feminist activism led, significantly, by the Directorate of Gender Affairs, which contributed to the election in 2004 of the first woman to the House of Representatives of Antigua and Barbuda, Dr. Jacqui Quinn-Leandro.

4. My approach is naturally susceptible to criticism that it is too respectful. Assuming nothing, making everything contestable or arguable, is a legitimate form of critique, but I think that assuming the virtue of some things and an admiring stance offers us access to ways of comprehending life that cannot be simply rejected as out of hand.

5. In the space of a decade, almost every Caribbean country enacted domestic-violence legislation, including the Antigua and Barbuda Domestic Violence (Summary Proceedings) Act, 1999; the Bahamas Domestic Violence Act, 2007; the Bahamas Sexual Offence and Domestic Violence Act, 1991, ch. 99; the Barbados Domestic Violence (Protection Orders) Act, 1992, ch. 130A; the Belize Domestic Violence Act, 2007; the Bermuda Domestic Violence (Protection Orders) Act, 1997; the British Virgin Islands Domestic Violence (Summary Proceedings) Act, 1992; the Cayman Islands Summary Jurisdiction (Domestic Violence) Law, 1992; the Dominica Protection Against Domestic Violence Act, 2001; the Grenada Domestic Violence Act, 2001; the Guyana Domestic Violence Act, 1996; the Jamaica Domestic Violence Act, 1995; the Montserrat Family (Protection Against Domestic Violence) Act, 1998; the St. Christopher-Nevis Domestic Violence Act, 2000; the St. Lucia Domestic Violence (Summary Proceedings) Act, 1995; the St. Vincent and the Grenadines Domestic Violence (Summary Proceedings) Act, 1995; the Trinidad and Tobago Domestic Violence Act, 1999 (repealing the Domestic Violence Act of 1991), ch. 45:56; and the Turks and Caicos Domestic Proceedings Ordinance, 1985, ch. 89.

Initiatives to reform laws relating to sexual violence have been more modest, including the Antigua and Barbuda Sexual Offences Act, 1995; the Bahamas Sexual Offences and Domestic Violence Act, 1991; the Barbados Sexual Offences Act, 1992, ch. 154; the Belize Criminal Code (Amendment) Act, 1999; the Dominica Sexual Offences Act, 1998; the Jamaica Sexual Offences Act, 2009; the Trinidad and Tobago Sexual Offences Act, 1986; and the Amendment Act, 2000, ch. 11:28.

There has been even less reform in relation to sexual harassment: the Bahamas Sexual Offences and Domestic Violence Act, 1991; the Belize Protection Against Sexual Harassment Act, 1996; the British Virgin Islands Anti-discrimination Act, 2001; the Guyana Prevention of Discrimination Act, 1997; and the St. Lucia Equality of Opportunity and Treatment in Employment and Occupation Act, 2000, St. Lucia Criminal Code, 2004.

6. E. Barriteau, in "Requiem," offers the strongest broad theoretical responses to the male marginalization thesis, while others, such as Aviston Downes, in "Gender

and Elementary Teaching Service," have tackled the thesis in specific contexts, such as education.

7. The best representation of this kind of analysis is found in Tang Nain and Bailey, an edited collection of essays commissioned by the Caribbean Community (CARICOM) and the United Nations Development Fund for Women (UNIFEM).

8. The principal shortcoming of the fine collection of essays in Tang Nain and Bailey's *Gender Equality in the Caribbean: Reality or Illusion* is that despite its title, the collection fails to consider what gender equality means to the contributors or to establish some understanding of the concept, including important differences, among them. V. Barriteau, "Confronting Power" 68, offers a clarification of the term *gender justice* in another edited collection. Among other things, she defines a "commitment to gender justice" as "working to end hierarchies embedded in the current gender ideologies that construct and maintain particular configurations of gender identities and the often punitive roles that flow from these for women and men."

9. Andaiye—her disenchantment with Caribbean feminism, her decisions to participate in activities in its name or not, her multifarious political passions, her pugnacity, persistence, and variousness—is perhaps the best illustration of this, though not the only one (see Andaiye, "Counting Women's Caring Work").

New Citizens, New Sexualities

Nineteenth-Century *Jamettes*

Rosamond S. King

THE ABOLITION of chattel slavery caused upheaval everywhere
and every time it happened, literally creating new citizens out of people
previously categorized as property. This was certainly the case in Trinidad
when emancipation became official in 1834. By the late nineteenth century
the transformation of Trinidadian colonial society was well under way, with
the transition from Spanish to British colonial powers, the arrival of Indian
and Chinese indentured workers to take over plantation labor, and the rise
of the black Creole *jamette* class.[1] Not surprisingly, the new black citizens
in this colony inhabited citizenship in new ways and created new behaviors
and social practices. Black Creole Trinidadians' citizenship was necessarily
different, both literally and materially, from their own previous status on
the island and from the European minority's citizenship. Jamettes in particular were known for wreaking havoc upon Victorian morals, particularly
with their sexualized Carnival performances and with the many street protests led by jamette women.

Indeed, the social and economic transition of emancipation, combined
with mass black migration away from plantations to cities, encouraged the
possibility for and the expectation of the creation of new social and political
identities and practices that were exemplified by jamettes. The term *jamette*
itself is unique to Trinidad and other eastern Caribbean Creole languages
and derives from the French *diamètre*, originally referring to those considered below the "diameter" of respectable society.[2] Jamettes were poor
black Creoles who worked in marginal or illegal sectors such as prostitution and gambling. The available archive of information about them largely
comprises articles and editorials from colonial newspapers and colonial
laws that attempted to restrict their behavior, especially women's behavior
in general and transvestism in particular. As I detail in this essay, because
jamettes dominated both emerging social protests and sexualized Carnival
performances, we can and should link these behaviors to the creation of new
citizenship and, in part, new sexualities.

Migrating from rural to urban areas was a typical way for many Creoles to distance themselves from the work they had done as slaves. But in Port of Spain and San Fernando, Trinidad's two main cities, the poor had few options. Most worked as domestics or manual laborers, and many were unemployed. The implicit promises of emancipation—primarily upward economic mobility and control of one's body, labor, and relationships—remained largely broken or unfulfilled. "Freedom" consisted of inadequate and limited employment and education and was further restricted by the laws and ordinances passed to control black bodies and behavior.

Not able to fully inhabit their new "citizenship," limited though it was, and with insufficient legitimate jobs available, frustrated but enterprising poor black Creoles discovered and created underground industries below society's respectable "diameter." In the late nineteenth century, jamettes became notorious for behavior that scandalized whites. Their modes of work and play offended the upper classes—as did their protests of government laws and policies.

Although during slavery black Trinidadians were not permitted more than token participation in Carnival, shortly after emancipation in 1834 the urban Creole poor began to dominate the festival, in part because of their increased presence in the urban areas around which Carnival activities were centered. Participation in Carnival was, in effect, a tangible benefit of their new citizenship, one that was often used to mock and sometimes to scare the elite.

Since its beginnings as a festival for the French planter class, Trinidadian Carnival has provided both a time and a space in which social, racial, and sexual taboos were allowed to be exposed and broken. Carnival occurs in the days just before Lent begins, and its costumes, characters, music, and dances often express irony and social or political commentary as well as pleasure (see Cowley; and Hill). As black Creoles and jamettes in particular participated in the festival more, they changed its tone to include "ridicule and derision" of Europeans (Pearse 21). Significantly, Carnival existed then and still exists in the *public* sphere, in which performance and display are privileged over restraint or modesty.[3] For jamettes, Carnival became an opportunity for men and women whose work was often hidden—in the dark, inside, or "underground"—to appear in public and in daylight, reminding others of their presence, "getting on bad" and shocking the middle class and elites. Indeed, the importance, especially for recent ex-slaves, of playing "mas,"[4] of taking over public space and choosing the manner of displaying one's body, should not be underestimated.

Although Europeans often dressed in blackface during Carnival and at least occasionally gender cross-dressed (Pearse 15), when blacks followed suit there was an uproar in colonial society. The Carnival historian Errol

Hill describes upper-class opposition to the transformation of Carnival as follows: "With the kind of campaign waged in the press, the hysterical letters to the editor by outraged residents—most of them newly arrived from Britain—and the deterioration of the festival into what came to be known as the *jamet* carnival, it was only a matter of time before steps were taken to suppress the masquerade" (20). What, specifically, offended those in power? Histories of and documents relating to nineteenth-century Carnival describe transvestism and masking as the behaviors most objected to in the press and most prosecuted in the courts. The fact that such performances continued—and were often tolerated—indicates that there was pleasure both in performing and in viewing the supposedly lewd and obscene masquerades. Nevertheless, no matter how ineffective, these attempts at restricting performance did affect jamette Carnival participants, because certain forms of revelry became acts for which one could be fined or imprisoned.

Newly classified citizens' performances of three transvestite characters popular among the jamette class—the Dame Lorraine, the pisse-en-lit, and the cross-dressed woman—can be linked to the creation and exhibition of new sexualities.

The Dame Lorraine Mas

Although individuals from a number of social and economic backgrounds originally participated in it, the Dame Lorraine mas exemplified the explicit sexuality that Victorian Trinidadian colonials abhorred, desired, and overwhelmingly associated with blacks as a whole, but especially with jamettes. The performance first appeared in Trinidad in the 1880s as a "bawdy folk play" in two parts with a detailed script that included specific dialogue and particular music (Hill 40; Cowley 137). The first act was played "straight," with participants wearing "eighteenth-century costumes of the French aristocracy" entering and dancing while the slave or servant characters looked on (Hill 40). The second act was complete parody, as physically and comically disfigured characters with names such as M'sieur Gros Coco, M'sieur Gros Boudin, and Mlle Jolle Rouge emphasized their namesake body parts during their comically incorrect and lewd attempts at dancing. Throughout, a Maître L'Ecole instructed the raggedly dressed performers to dance "properly." Significantly, in the second act all participants were masked, and among the characters "inversion of the sexes was a common practice" (Hill 40).

There are several reasons to conclude that Dame Lorraine players meant to ridicule Europeans. As Hill writes, "Mockery of their masters' dancing eccentricities had been . . . a common form of private entertainment among estate slaves" for a long time (40). This mockery was formalized into the Dame Lorraine play. During the second act, the Maître "kept up the appearance that everything was quite proper and aboveboard; any obvious looseness, improper or incorrect dancing on the part of his pupils, was promptly punished *by the application of his whip*" (41, emphasis added). The use of a whip and the word *maître* (master) allude, of course, to slavery and slave owners. Finally, another reason that it is probable that Dame Lorraine was meant to ridicule European culture is that the first act, which mimicked more than it mocked, was the first part of the masquerade to disappear.

The end of Dame Lorraine marked the beginning of Jouvay,[5] with audiences and still-masked performers going out into the streets (Hill 40). Thus the name Dame Lorraine became associated not only with the folk play but also with its characters cavorting, unchoreographed, with other Jouvay and Carnival revelers. Since English was fast replacing French Creole as Trinidad's lingua franca, fewer people could understand the play's dialogue, and that aspect of Dame Lorraine largely disappeared. Furthermore, Carnival has never been conducive to large-group, minutely choreographed performances, which explains why the second act and the play itself eventually disappeared, though the costumes remained. It is less clear why cross-dressed female characters faded away, but today *Dame Lorraine* refers mostly to a man in woman's clothes, "dressed as a fashionable lady with large bosoms and posterior" (Mendes 176). Dame Lorraine is accepted as a traditional character in Trinidadian Carnival, although it is not often addressed in scholarly or popular discussions of the festival.

The Pisse-en-lit Mas

Several nineteenth-century newspapers described the pisse-en-lit—literally, "piss in bed"—as one of the most vulgar Carnival masquerades being performed. It was a band made up exclusively of "masked men dressed as women. They wore long nightgowns, often transparent, and decorated with ribbons and lace. Others wore very little except menstruation cloths liberally stained with 'blood'" (Crowley 46–47). Sometimes the nightgown itself was stained with fake blood, or the man wore a stick protruding between his legs, or the cloth carried was soaked in urine (hence the mas's other name, *stinker*) (Crowley 46). An 1884 commentator in the *Port of Spain Gazette* stated that "there are some costumes—the *pisse-en-lit* for example—which are so very indecent they should not be tolerated" (qtd. in Cowley 99). More than fifty years later, in 1944, a *Guardian* writer commented, "Pissenlit, a disgusting and foul-smelling practice is now practically stamped out" (qtd. in Crowley 46). Its complete disappearance is a direct result of the attacks on it. Aside from sometimes literally stinking, the former revealed black men's bodies, complete, at times, with an exaggerated penis, an exaggerated physical representation of black masculinity that was then very much feared.

Indeed, although *all* transvestism in Trinidadian Carnival was outlawed in 1895, the pisse-en-lit was probably more objectionable to Europeans than other masquerades, such as the Dame Lorraine. Unlike early stagings of the Dame Lorraine play, which were held in areas where few whites would enter, the pisse-en-lit was performed in the streets. And while Dame Lorraine performances also included exaggerated genitalia, such displays were part of costumes that covered the entire body. A black man dressed completely as a woman with huge breasts and buttocks was surely less frightening than an almost naked black man wearing a shift stained with blood. Even if the blood was fake and meant to imply menstruation, it also implied violence, and the poui stick between the performer's legs could easily both signify and *become* a weapon.

Under any circumstances black Creole men's "near nudity" was frightening and threatening because it embodied the stereotype of black men's predatory sexuality by emphasizing the body and subsequently black masculinity and black male sexuality itself. As M. Jacqui Alexander writes, "Black male sexuality was to be feared as the hypersexualized stalker," and almost naked black men playing pisse-en-lit literally flaunted and shook this fear in front of Europeans ("Not Just (Any) *Body*" 12). While it was (and is) acceptable to believe in this stereotype, it was not acceptable to display an embodiment of it. Even—and perhaps especially—during Carnival it was important to restrain the perceived threat of black masculinity and black sexuality, to quell the possibility that Carnival could become riot. Thus, while the Dame Lorraine mas is hardly mentioned in the nineteenth-century press, the pisse-en-lit was frequently attacked.

Jamette Women's Transvestite Mas

Compared with their treatment of other masquerades, nineteenth-century newspaper reports, editorials, and letters singled out jamette women for particular disdain. The following were typical complaints: "The musicians were attended by a multitude of drunken people of both sexes, *the women being of the lowest class*" (1846); and "all the rabble of Port of Spain [were present during a riot]," among whom were "a large number of loose women including the vilest of their class" (1849) (qtd. in Cowley 41, 44, emphasis added). When the "misconduct" or "obscenity" of which these women were guilty was named, it was often transvestism.

One of the instances of explicit reference to women's gender cross-dressing and its prevalence is found in an 1849 article. "As for the number of girls masked in men's clothing, *we cannot say how many hundred* are flaunting their want of shame" (qtd. in Cowley 73, emphasis added). An 1877 description of a group of jamette women's Carnival costumes reads:

The women of this "band" are also to appear, uniformly accoutred, namely, in short trowsers *a l'homme*, to the knee, wearing a short red jacket ending at the waist-band, over a chemise, round which on the stomach there is to be a narrow *tablier* or apron. Their top-gear is a sailor-hat covered with white, circled by a blue ribbond. . . . Each woman is to carry a wooden hatchet (painted to resemble iron). (Cowley 79)

In addition to the jamettes' racial and gender cross-dressing, two aspects of this masquerade are especially notable. The first is that the women were wearing *short* men's trousers. Typical clothes for women of any class in the nineteenth century included a dress or skirt that swept the ground. Within such a context, in which women's revealing an ankle could be considered erotic, showing an entire calf was both scandalous and provocative. The second significant detail is that the women carried weapons, perhaps intended to represent both aggression and defense.

In any society the body is conceived of as metonymic, made to stand for "an entire repertoire of human and social arrangements" and for "the condensation of subjectivities in the individual" (Spillers 66; S. Hall, "Who Needs 'Identity'?" 11). Jamette women's double cross-dressing threatened the colonial social hierarchy because it was an attempt not only to change the outward symbolism of their bodies but also to briefly superimpose the representation and meaning of the white male body and its socially granted subjectivity and power over their own lack of power—while also shocking the elite with the titillating and/or horrifying revelation of their own black women's bodies. These women took the inch of freedom that was offered to them as new citizens and attempted to stretch it into a mile.

While transvestism was perhaps the offense most cited in laws and media, these poor black women were also engaged in other transgressive behavior. The jamettes' Carnival performances did not change the material conditions in which they lived, nor did they alter the existing hierarchies of power and economics or of race and gender. But their Carnival behavior was all the more threatening because of the additional willingness of many poor urban Black Creole women to instigate direct political action and violence against colonial power.

Carnival celebrations took place primarily in Port of Spain and San Fernando, and, from about 1839, "females dominated" these urban areas (Trotman, "Women and Crime," *Caribbean Quarterly* 60). David V. Trotman, in his study of women in nineteenth-century Trinidad, summarizes the population of non-European women of the time as "predominantly Creole . . . young and unmarried; urban; and marginally employed" (61). This group of poor Creole women, with perhaps little investment in the society on whose edge they lived and certainly with little to lose, often shocked elite sensibilities and violated morals as well as laws by participating in violent protests and extramarital relationships, as well as by their Carnival behavior. The charges most often brought against black Creole women at this time were "indecent behaviour, riotous and disorderly conduct, and obscene and profane language" (71). These charges correspond both to Carnival performances and to activities outside of the annual festival.

Indeed, the same women who were labeled as jamettes were also prominent in nineteenth-century political action in Trinidad. Barred from formal political participation, the most marginalized urban blacks, the poor, the un- or under-employed, the jamettes—and especially jamette women—took to the streets. Poor black Creole women were at the forefront of demonstrations against various policies and insults. As Trotman notes, women "were highly visible participants in the violence of the late nineteenth century and a shocked elite commented frequently on their behaviour" (68). For example, they protested the bans on particular aspects of Carnival and the restriction of water in public baths (Reddock, *Women, Labour* 100–101). In 1873 one journalist wrote, "The police reported that it was women who encouraged men to riot during a massive demonstration marking the departure of the Chief Justice Gorrie, a hero of the lower classes" (qtd. in Trotman, "Women and Crime," *Caribbean Quarterly* 68). In many cases, "women taunted men for their lack of aggression" (68). The following description of women protesting as they complied with the 1869 Contagious Diseases Ordinance and "voluntarily" submitted to medical exams (required of any woman *accused* of prostitution and thus in practice any poor black Creole woman) is probably representative of their actions: "Without political power, unorganized and mostly illiterate, they used the only tools available to them, shouting and screaming" their objections to specific and general oppression (71). As jamette women exercised their new citizenship as social and political actors, their behavior and sexuality were both criminalized and demonized by the English upper class.

Social protest was also an element of jamette transvestism. Women jamettes cross-dressing as European men during Carnival were not only parodying their pomposity and their self-important mannerisms but also impersonating their power. If class, status, and power (to vote, to sit on juries, to rule others) were correlates of race and gender in nineteenth-century colonial Trinidad, and both of these became things one could mock and "put on," then theoretically, at least, the correlating hierarchies might begin to waver. In their racial and gender transvestism, jamette women appeared in a guise of power that, if unchecked, could lead to civil unrest confined neither to Carnival week nor to black women.

These assertions of subjectivity by Caribbean poor women and men insist on their individual choice of self-representation within their new status as citizens, and therefore also create the possibility of choosing alternative human and social arrangements—including new sexualities.

New Sexualities

We know that jamettes and other poor black Creoles were engaged in a range of sexual activity disapproved of by the colonial elite. These behaviors included extramarital sex and childbearing, nonmonogamous relationships, non-nuclear family structures, and prostitution. Such activity certainly existed before emancipation and sometimes was actually encouraged during slavery. Nevertheless, when these practices were engaged in after slavery by new black citizens, they acquired a more significant weight, because they were practiced by *free* citizens. Europeans acknowledge this weight in their own historical accounts, which reflect the vitriol directed against jamette "immorality."

Certainly, *new sexualities* is a problematic term, because none of the behaviors described above are, strictly speaking, *new*. However, in the specific context of the nineteenth-century, postemancipation Caribbean, the combination of such behaviors and their *public exhibition*, along with the fact that these were engaged in by new black Creole citizens, means that we *can* call them new sexualities.

Jamette masquerades embodied, embraced, and performed the stereotype of black bodies as "unruly sexuality, untamed and wild" (Alexander, "Not Just (Any) *Body*" 12). The implications of these performances were profound: the simultaneous possibilities of black women and men economically profiting from their own bodies and, through the ridiculing of Europeans, disrupting the gendered and raced social, political, and economic hierarchy of Trinidad.

The transvestism of all three Carnival characters discussed here—the Dame Lorraine, the pisse-en-lit, and the transvestite woman—was considered transgressive. But with the pisse-en-lit and the women's mas, the *revealed* body, the possibility of disorder, of sexual and social deviance, was an additional problem. For white Creoles, the revealed black man's body pointed to the threat of physical and sexual violence. Similarly, the revealed black woman's body pointed to unsanctioned sexual behaviors and relationships.

Significantly, jamettes were engaged in performances of *false identities*, impersonation, meant to parody and entertain but not to deceive. Jamette women and men were not actually trying to pass as European men and women. Rather, their dress and very *inability* to pass were meant to provide pleasure for themselves and other Carnival revelers, while also mocking the European elite.

In fact, jamettes were rejecting a colonial, racial, and patriarchal structure to which they had no access, except at the lowest levels. Unlike the colored middle class, jamettes and other poor, often unskilled, black Creoles had little chance of ever significantly raising their social or economic status. So, with the limited amount of freedom and citizenship available to them, they chose their sexual partners, family structures, and modes of self-preservation. Faced with unemployment, they exploited *European* "immorality" and earned money through an underground economy. And then during Carnival jamettes, explicitly labeled as a despised underclass, flaunted their blackness and their sexuality, while mocking Europeans.

An article from the *Trinidad Chronicle* in 1877 declares ironic and sarcastic befuddlement at why carnival participants enjoyed "the *privilege* of appearing in the streets in worse than common clothes and of being well stared-at, of playing what antics they choose, under mask and of bawling dull refrains, discord and folly, by the hour" (qtd. in Cowley 82, emphasis added). The author of the article was more accurate than he probably realized. Carnival was the one time during the year that the poor were allowed the *privilege* of entertaining themselves as they *chose*, even if their desires included parodying the elite, impersonating European power, espousing non-hegemonic values, and parading the new sexualities they practiced throughout the year.

In recent years there has been much public discussion about Caribbean sexual conservatism and homophobia, but analysis of jamette performances reveals that these convictions have a long history. As Alexander writes, "Whereas in Europe these [moralizing] processes were indigenous to the formation of the middle class, in the Caribbean it [*sic*] was imported through imperialism" ("Not Just (Any) *Body*" 12). Europeans and white Creoles maligned jamettes because their sexualities did not adhere to strict Victorian morals, in part because Europeans in the Caribbean were themselves suspected of "loose morals" by those on the Continent. Similarly, contemporary Caribbean mores should in part be attributed to a desire to display conformity to a heterosexual, nuclear family "norm" as part of a regional desire to participate in—and to be seen as participating in—middle-class "Western" values. In the nineteenth century, Europeans and white Creoles condemned those they deemed to be outside of respectable society; in the twenty-first century, much of the Caribbean middle class is making similar judgments. While this knowledge does not excuse discrimination, oppression, or violence, such a history is no small matter for a people who have been historically and continuously stereotyped as embodying and exhibiting excessive sexuality and aberrant genders.

In jamettes' new sexualities and other transgressive behavior we can see both the limits and the possibilities of black Creole Trinidadian new citizenship in the nineteenth century. The new sexualities implied by jamette Carnival performances, combined with overt social protest, marked significant opposition and threat to the heterosexual patriarchal colonial order, even while black Creoles were largely ruled by this order. A close examination of jamette behavior and responses to it reveals the history of linking sexuality and citizenship both to support and to challenge social, racial, and economic hierarchies.

Notes

1. Throughout this essay, *Creole* refers to individuals of whatever race born in the Caribbean. For a detailed analysis of this complex term, see F. Smith, *Creole Recitations;* and C. Allen. It has been proposed that in the mid- to late nineteenth century jamettes "almost amounted to a class" themselves (Pearse 31).

2. In current usage *jamette* means "slut."

3. This public was often differentiated, however, by class, race, neighborhood, and band, a practice that continues to some degree today.

4. *Mas* is short for *masquerade.*

5. Jouvay, also *J'ouvert,* from *jour ouvert* (opening, first day), is the late night before Carnival Tuesday; it is traditionally when revelers perform "old mas" and "dirty mas," which can include wearing old costumes, smearing the body with mud, or wearing "vulgar" costumes, including transvestism.

Macocotte

An Exploration of Same-Sex Friendship in Selected Caribbean Novels

Antonia MacDonald-Smythe

There was a girl from school I used to kiss, but we were best friends and only using each other for practice.

Jamaica Kincaid, *Lucy*

IN ST. LUCIA, Martinique, and Dominica the intense friendship shared by young adolescent girls is typically described as a *macocotte* relationship.[1] This relationship is characterized by exclusivity, devotion, and intense emotional passion. Best friends, secrets-sharing and inseparable, the young girls demonstrate the intensity of their affection through constant hugging and kissing. Although there is no English translation for this Kwéyòl (French Creole) word, the macocotte practice also exists in other Caribbean countries.[2] In all instances this bonding space is defined by expressions of pleasurable intimacy, the sensuality of frequent bodily contact, the tenderness of devotedness, and the "rightness" and the joy that one girl feels in the company of another. While the participants in this relationship may feel pleasure that later in life will be associated with sexual pleasure, for adolescents it is not defined as such, given that their sexuality is in a nascent, or what developmental psychologists refer to as plastic, stage. Moreover, while these same-sex friendships between preadolescent girls may involve genital contact, this contact is not typically viewed by the participants or their community as lesbian. The young girls are interested in boys—even while they are mindful that adults may view such interest as inappropriate for their age—and anticipate future heterosexual relationships.

Defined by an erotic energy that helps sustain and nurture the young girl, the macocotte relationship can facilitate the psychosexual maturation of the adolescent girl. This close female friendship affords her a confidante with whom to share her experience of sexual maturation. Issues such as menstruation and masturbation are processed through this relationship as the young girl articulates, explores, and comes to understand her changing body, her sexuality, and the appropriate gender behavior and social roles attendant to those changes. Anticipating the traumas associated with growing up and therefore forsaking the ways of childhood, the adolescent female is comforted by the laughter, the resilience, and the fellowship that characterize life within this space. Through the sharing of experiences, the young girl creates a sororal group within which she learns how to grow into a woman. And it is within this circle that the young girl safely experiences and acts on the early stirrings of libidinal desire. Tacitly condoned but never publicly discussed, the macocotte relationship becomes the testing ground for the affectionate behavior and sexual responsiveness that will become advantageous to the young woman in her future, and presumably heterosexual, relationships. Thus, there is an absence of social disapproval of the "practicing" that goes on, because it is viewed as natural to this safe and separate haven, an activity that helps the young girl negotiate the incremental transfer of attachment from macocotte to adult romantic partner.

The psychologist Marilyn Frye advocates separatism as crucial to the building of female friendships and the dismantling of the male-serving prejudices that women may harbor against each other. However, separatism, while it denies others access to and control over the magic of the female world of love and supportive rituals, also prevents women from learning about the power that men wield and the ways in which women need to empower themselves within the patriarchal systems that Frye references. By contrast, the macocotte relationship does not generate a separatism that isolates the young girl from the outside patriarchal world; rather, it allows her controlled access to that world. Social approval allows the macocotte relationship to be absorbed into a wider female kinship circle, thus becoming part of the social milieu in which the developing Eastern Caribbean early adolescent female also learns the value of sisterhood with other women. The macocotte friendship, in offering emotional bonding, knowledge sharing, and support, provides the adolescent girl with a support system that will later help her survive in the public realm—a realm where patriarchal hegemonies are entrenched.

The social and environmental conditions under which macocotte friendships take place do not have a significant impact on adult sexual orientation.[3] Young girls who have in preadolescence formed intense macocotte relationships may, in adulthood, continue their macocotte relationships in a modified form while they are involved in heterosexual relationships. The devotion remains, and the intimacy is no longer physical but manifests itself in soul-baring. Often the macocotte of one's youth becomes the *macommère* of one's adult life,[4] the best friend who still serves as confidante, with whom one can confide adult tribulations as they relate to life and to men, facilitating what Helen Pyne Timothy refers to as "the relations of caring and sharing between Caribbean women."[5] Accepted as an important aspect of women's relations with one another, these relationships form sustainable communities that imitate the kinship networks so vital to preslavery African society, networks that were lost in the experience of diaspora. Not only do these relationships help the female develop an erotic consciousness but the sharing that is at their core gives her the fortitude to survive adversity—the very characteristics that have contributed to the now iconoclastic representations of the Caribbean woman as a triumphant figure of survival.

Accordingly, within Afro-Caribbean contexts, even while the macocotte relationship provides support systems for women and aids in the creation of female libidinal subjectivity, it operates within a heterosexual paradigm. Girls share their dreams of finding good men, of marrying, of raising a family. At the same time they are reminded that relationships with boys are dangerous liaisons for which they are as yet unprepared. While they are warned of the dangers associated with boys—loss of virginity, early and/ or unplanned pregnancy—they learn that sexual relations with boys are part of their future. Nor does the macocotte relationship challenge patriarchy. Instead, it creates structures of socialization that reinforce the status quo. Nowhere are masculinist paradigms of economic power and authority threatened. For while the macocotte relationship is a site for the production of sexual knowledge, and even as adults acknowledge that the affection shared by the young girls may sometimes be sexual, there is a tacit understanding that this sexual behavior is merely for "practice" and that young girls will have normal heterosexual relationships as adults. Indeed, the affection that develops in the macocotte relationship is seen as a trait that will serve the female well in her heterosexual future.

Typically, studies on the development of homosexual identity development read preadolescent same-sex attraction, same-sex experimentation, and lack of interest in the opposite sex as part of the process of self-labeling as lesbian or gay. While no such formal studies exist in Caribbean psychology, this essay explores the ways in which the macocotte relationship might be included as part of the genealogy of a Caribbean sexual identity so that conversations on female sexuality in the Caribbean context can be discursively nuanced. Leila Rupp makes a stirring case for an interrogation of the concept of sexuality within transnational contexts and suggests that "assumptions about the meanings of desire, acts and relationships by using terms such as 'same-sex' sexuality may inadvertently lump together phenomena that are quite different" (287). In establishing that part of the sexual experimentation that comes with puberty involves sexual activity between females, either because of the closeness and emotional intensity of the friendship or because of curiosity, I am interpreting these forms of adolescent sexual activity as manifestations of sexual awakening rather than solely as indicators of homosexual desire. Upon arriving at sexual consciousness, one may well become lesbian, but at this stage sexuality is still plastic, and sexual orientation unfixed.[6]

While there may well be other vocabularies for talking about this form of female friendship,[7] I deliberately locate my exploration of Caribbean female friendships within the indigenous vernacular of macocotte friendship because it is a vernacular that gives prominence to the culture that shapes our bodies, our desire, and our sexuality. In her now classic article "Compulsory Heterosexuality and Lesbian Existence," Adrienne Rich suggested that a useful way of understanding female sexual development was through the conceptualization of a "lesbian continuum," one that recognizes passionate yet platonic same-sex friendships at one end and explicitly sexual female friendships at the other. Both forms of friendship are, however, inscribed as "lesbian." While there is merit in Rich's sexual categorization, I find such a way of looking at sexuality a little disarming insofar as "lesbian" is set up as the main referent and automatically becomes a descriptor for women who, while they partake of the sexual behavior Rich describes in her continuum, may not identify themselves as lesbian.[8] In reducing intimacies between women to the somewhat static category "lesbian," Rich's lesbian continuum is potentially prejudicial to a discussion of variant Afro-Caribbean female sexualities. Hence, I would like to suggest that what may obtain in Caribbean interventions on female sexuality is the evocation not so much of a continuum but of a spectrum of passionate relationships, one that, like a rainbow, has variations, latitude, and seeming boundarylessness and, because of its complexities, allows females to locate themselves in ways that are appropriate to their life experiences. Implicit to this is the notion that female sexuality is fluid, capable of changing over time, and that this plasticity is both situational and social.

In arguing that the social constructedness and the cultural specificity of macocotte interactions render inadequate the label "lesbian," which is so commonly deployed in discussions of same-sex friendships in Western societies, I am mindful of Jay and Glasgow's warning that "gendered experience is simply not the same for lesbians as for non-lesbians. Women's experience of gendered culture and gendered texts is filtered by sexual preference and sexual behaviour" (5). My articulation of a macocotte aesthetic is ultimately a product of my own Eastern Caribbean locatedness, a manifestation of a heterosexual citizenry that is specifically "small-island" and Kwéyòl-influenced, one that is inevitably gendered and undeniably insistent on a multivariant Caribbean cultural reality. Moreover, it is by privileging the exploration of these activities within their sociocultural contexts, rather than the imported psychosexual perspectives popularized by Freud's libidinal theory and supported by Western feminisms, that we can come to understand Caribbean culture's impact on gender and sex roles.

There are, of course, important caveats. One is the conceptual difference between the macocotte relationship and what Audre Lorde, in describing same-sex activities among Carriacou women, calls "zami" relationships: while macocotte activity partakes of what Lorde has described as "zami" behavior, that is, "the Carriacou name to represent women who work together as friends and as lovers" (*Zami* 255), macocotte friendships need to be separated from the theoretical and political agenda to which Lorde deploys *zami*. For in the instance of her book *Zami* Lorde is exploring her own psychosexual journey to acceptance of her lesbian sexuality and accordingly uses *zami* to speak to the particular configurations that emerge from the intersection of her race, class, gender, and sexual orientation.[9] Significantly, whereas Lorde has defined *zami* solely as "lesbian," on the Kwéyòl-speaking islands of St. Lucia, Martinique, Dominica, Guadeloupe, and Haiti the noun *zami* also means "close friend," a derivation of the French word *amie*. The phrase *making zami* relates to lesbian activity. Here it is the verb *making* that indicates, and qualifies, the nature of the friendship. It is important to establish this difference because on islands such as Trinidad, Grenada, and Carriacou, where French Creole was once spoken, *zami* has lost those nuances and is now used primarily as a noun meaning "lesbian." While in many ways the macocotte relationship captures the multiplicity of meaning embedded in the original word *zami,* the fact that conventional usage now limits *zami* to "lesbian" makes it an inadequate term for describing the sometimes sexual intimacy between young women engaged in macocotte friendships.

These variations in social perceptions and interpretations of same-sex friendships confirm that in the Caribbean the quality and context of female friendships are as yet undertheorized criteria for tracking the development of libidinal subjectivity. This lack of theorizing may be in reaction to the historical construction of Afro-Caribbean female sexuality within the cultural and social frameworks of postslavery societies. To speak to female sexuality was inevitably to direct the inquiring gaze to black women's bodies. Read by colonial masters as naturally licentious and given to the display of animal passions, the enslaved African woman, in resisting these representations of promiscuity, did not readily exercise libidinal desire (Beckles and Shepherd). Moreover, the conditions of her enslavement did not allow the slave woman the time or space to act on her desires, for often she was forced into satisfying the desires of others, whether they were masters, overseers, or fellow slaves (Higman). Sexual activity was often more transactional than recreational, and where it was procreative, the sex act did not occur within the African-derived context of maintaining family lineage, since slave laws forbade marital unions between slaves. With emancipation, the ex-slave woman became a participant in the circulating Victorian discourse of sexual virtue and morality, wherein, according to Mary Poovey, the good woman was constructed as "the sexless, moralized angel" and the sexual woman as an "aggressive carnal magdalen" (11).[10] Accordingly, sexuality was not seen as a proper topic of discussion, public or private. Anxious to escape images of her hypersexualization, the Afro-Caribbean woman became part of discursive alliances that established her as loyal to middle-class morality, respectability, and asexuality.

Correspondingly, in dismantling the received notions of the Caribbean as a space of "sun, sea and sex" to which the tourist brochure continually invites the speculative and eroticized gaze, academic conversations on sexuality did not occupy any place in Caribbean discourse. Indeed, Caribbean social historians have yet to see this subject as suitable for study, and so it remains an underresearched area of critical inquiry that, where it exists, constitutes part of quantitative surveys that relate sexuality to social problems—sex work, sexually transmitted diseases, and reproduction. Discourses in sexuality often reference texts from a variety of genres—fiction, medical treatises, sex manuals, boudoir memoirs, annotated erotic prints, philosophy, and legal cases—to substantiate their theses. In the instance of Caribbean studies, such data are not readily available. However, although the sociological and anthropological documentation of Caribbean female sexuality is scanty, and information often anecdotal, the literary text confirms that within a Caribbean sociocultural context there are many examples of the ways in which female libidinal subjectivity is produced and managed through macocotte relationships.

Jeffrey Weeks argues that "there cannot be an all-embracing history of sexuality. There can only be local histories, contextual meanings, specific analyses" (6). If, therefore, a discussion of sexuality is accompanied by many narratives, it is important that the stories offered by Caribbeanists take into account our specific cultural contexts. Evelyn O'Callaghan offers one such local narrative in her exploration of representations of sexuality in Caribbean literature. She argues that "female sexuality in the works of West Indian women prose writers is either shrouded in secrecy and shame, or a matter of casual and unfeeling acquiescence to male pressure" ("Compulsory Heterosexuality" 297). Remarking on the absence of what she refers to as a "joyful eroticism," O'Callaghan goes on to explore the ways in which sexuality, when it is explicitly presented in the writings of Caribbean women writers, is connected to mother-child nurturing or the lack thereof. Moreover, according to O'Callaghan, within this paradigm same-sex relations become "an eroticized evocation of a paradisal unity with the mother's female body" (309). Like O'Callaghan, I recognize that where Caribbean literature has dealt with the issue of sexual identity development, it has done so within the context of the mother-daughter relationship. My intervention also concedes that in the novels of many Caribbean women writers, sexuality is linked to the desire for a lost maternal imaginary. However, where O'Callaghan reads the erotics of homosexuality as the reaction to that loss, I offer an alternative rendition. In assembling the social relations and cultural practices attendant to macocotte relationships, I am suggesting that in Caribbean society these same-sex female friendships among adolescent girls become a site for the erotic, a site that needs to be established as different from the ones occupied by homosexual desire, and that these same-sex relationships develop naturally out of, rather than compensating for, the mother-daughter imaginary.

Be they from Jamaica, Guyana, or Antigua, Caribbean women writers engage with macocotte erotics as I have defined them. The Guyanese novelist Oonya Kempadoo and the Antiguan Jamaica Kincaid present same-sex friendships as integral to the shaping of libidinal subjectivity and the coming of age of young female protagonists. Michelle Cliff, in *Abeng,* also explores the nature and function of same-sex friendship, albeit without the same level of emphasis as Kempadoo and Kincaid.

In *Buxton Spice,* Oonya Kempadoo narrates the sexual awakening of Lula, a young, mixed-raced Guyanese girl, within the context of a politically unstable society in which young girls find succor and comfort in same-sex friendships. In exploring the adolescent maturation process, Kempadoo enters Lula's consciousness and highlights the contradictions, the confusion, and the naiveté that constitute the privatized space wherein early negotiations of gender and sexuality occur, a psychosocial space from which adults are frequently and deliberately barred. Lula and her confidantes Judy and Rachel d'Abreo help one another fill in the spaces about sexuality that their mothers are reluctant to talk about. Lula's attachment to Judy and Rachel provides her with companionship, security, affection, and intimacy and becomes a learning space for heterosexual identity development.

In this delineation of an almost sororal community, Kempadoo is careful to relate Lula's sexual awakening as part of a shared process, one through which young girls naturally progress, singly or in the company of same-sex friends. In their incessant curiosity about sex, Lula and her macocottes find avenues for sating this interest. Permitted unrestricted and unsupervised play with the D'Abreo sisters, Lula explores with her friends what it means to experience sexual interest—"feeling things changing right here in ourselves. New sex parts growing, hot things running through your body" (137)—and because of that interest engages in same-sex sexual activity. It is through this experimentation that Lula learns and practices sexual intimacy.

Where Kempadoo is explicit in her focus on adolescent sexuality, Kincaid encodes her exploration of the sexual within the erotics of a mother-daughter relationship. In *Annie John* she details the trauma of a young Antiguan girl's emotional separation from her mother and the passionate compensatory friendship she develops with a schoolmate, Gweneth Joseph: "We'd set off for school side by side, our feet in step, not touching but feeling as if we were joined at the shoulder, hip, and ankle, not to mention heart" (48). Annie speaks of her attachment to Gwen in the passionate and excessive language that Eastern Caribbean girls typically use to describe their macocottes: "My own special happiness was, of course, with Gwen. . . . I would . . . kiss her on the neck, sending her into a fit of shivers, as if someone had exposed her to a cold draft when she had a fever. Sometimes when she spoke to me, so overcome with feeling would I be that I was no longer able to hear what she said, I could only make out her mouth as it moved up and down" (50–51).

Similarly, in *Abeng* Michelle Cliff explores the friendship that Clare Savage, the middle-class, mixed-raced protagonist, forms with a village girl, Zoe, so as to foreground the impact that people and place have in the shaping of libidinal subjectivity. In this novel, the macocotte relationship is between socially unequal young girls, and this inequality eventually causes its demise. Cliff presents the two young girls spending carefree days roaming the village woods, playing games adapted from movies they have seen, or teasing village boys. Clare and Zoe share their curiosity and anxiety about the grown-up world around them and find safety in each other. "Lying besides Zoe on the rock, she felt warm. Safe. Secluded. She felt that this was something she had wanted all along" (126). Significantly, it is when this intimate interlude between the two girls is intruded on by judgmental jeers of village boys that the differences in race and class highlight the inequality between the two girls and, accordingly, the impossibility of a macocotte relationship. Clare, in her assertions of middle-class near-white superiority, sacrifices this relationship when she shoots at the boys and instead kills her grandmother's bull. Through this act of rupture Clare marks herself as a near-white girl accustomed to privilege, daughter of the *massa*, who cannot, therefore, have Zoe, daughter of a peasant woman, as a friend. While in *Annie John* and *Buxton Spice* parents feared their daughters' interaction with boys, here it is Clare's acting like a boy that brings her censure. Isolated by her actions, she is banished to live with two embittered old women, a reminder to her of the cost of transgression. In a grim parody of macocotte and macommère friendships, these women do not offer Clare a supportive female community within which she can be rehabilitated. To compensate for the loss of her macocotte relationship with Zoe, Clare claims herself as her own best friend and in this new self-reliance celebrates her menarcheal moment as one in which she is birthing her adult self, significantly a self who is both friendless and outside of community.

The reticence that often defines conversations on Caribbean sexuality is made manifest in the language that some Caribbean women writers deploy to describe sexual activity. In *Annie John,* Kincaid heavily lacquers her presentation of adolescent desire and sex play with descriptors that evoke, without ever making explicit, the erotic power of what Lisa Moore describes as "something more tender than friendship." Where Kincaid uses an incantatory prose that, in its incessant repetitiousness, distracts readers from manifestations of Annie John's early, hesitant stirrings of sexual interest, Kempadoo's language has a disarming frankness that may alienate. *Buxton Spice* explores adolescent desire with an earthy directness that eschews tenderness. Indeed, Kempadoo opens her story with an anecdote about the young girls' fascination with the sometimes exposed genitals of the vagrant Uncle Joe and their persistent efforts to stir him into visible tumescence. Locating her pubertal protagonist as a sexual subject, Kempadoo boldly violates Caribbean literary conventions that had used imagery to mask the erotic and the sexual. Her directness reminds us that the tumultuous world into which Lula is about to enter is hardly a romantic one.

While in all three novels masturbation is presented as part of the young girl's exploration of a new sexuality, the authors address the issue in markedly different ways. Kincaid briefly skirts the issue of the adolescent girl as a desiring or masturbating subject.[11] In *Annie John,* when the protagonist awakes one night after what can be described as a symbolic wet dream, she recounts to the reader her sitting across her father's naked legs and sensuously moving her legs back and forth against his. In a novel that has so thoroughly examined the gamut of feelings populating the adolescent consciousness, all the reader is privy to here is Annie's comment that she experienced "a funny feeling" that she "liked and was frightened of at the same time" (113). In contrast, Cliff and Kempadoo are explicit in their representation of the libidinal adolescent. Both portray masturbation as the indicator of budding sexual interest and sexual desire, the natural development of the adolescent protagonist's sexual response.

In the novels of these two writers there is, however, a sense of an implicit cultural resistance to this form of self-pleasuring. Accordingly, masturbation is presented as an act shrouded in secrecy, an activity that, while never exposed, may be socially frowned upon.[12] In *Abeng*, this autoeroticism is presented as part of Clare's developing sexual awareness, as "something that would change her for good" (107): "When she took off her school blouse in the evenings . . . she stroked her nipples and found them tender but also wanting of her strokes. The stroking, back and forth and up and down made her pussy warm. She would raise an arm and run the other hand . . . across her breast and into and through the lips of her vagina, where her fingers settled and gently rubbed" (106). Significantly, Clare's curiosity about her changing, desiring body occurs within a context of furtive self-pleasuring. While typically the macocotte is the one with whom the adolescent girl would share the experience of masturbating, "Clare did not mention to her friend the sweet and deep feeling when she did these thing" (107), for she believes that Zoe, because of the space and privacy constraints of her class position—living in a one-room house with her mother and siblings—cannot experience or explore libidinal desire. Clare, then, has no one with whom to share the experience of coming to know and love her developing body and is unable to publicly testify to or valorize adolescent sexual pleasure.

In *Buxton Spice,* Kempadoo also depicts the initiation into sexual pleasure, sexual expression, and sexual experimentation in a safe and private setting. Whereas in *Abeng* Clare's masturbatory activities reinforce her solitude, Kempadoo's Lula enters into masturbation as a fantasy outlet for the powerful desire she feels for Iggy D'Abreo, Judy's older brother, the fear and excitement she experiences when he pins her in a corner and presses himself to her, and her attempt to name, and through naming manage, this commingling of emotions. "I scared stiff or excited, must be what the word *fri-gid* means—frozen, your heart beating up inside and legs quivering, all freeze-up" (39). The violent orgasmic pleasure Lula experiences first when Iggy touches her in secret and then later when she touches herself leads her to perceive her sexuality as something dangerous, something powerful and explosive, something to be enacted in secret, contained within the privacy of the bathroom:

> I pushed my hips up to the base of the tap, legs splayed up against the wall, hands gripping the taphead. Had been the gentle drumming of that soft but solid stream of water that made me want that same feeling on my inflamed Tip. I shifted my hips slightly and the clear tube of water fell directly on it. Arched my back a little to get the stream on the part that felt best. The flowing must not stop. Hammering on the top of the Tip while the bomb in me was growing, making me heart faster, muscles tighter. Bomb getting bigger . . . the Tip going to blow off. Oh me Lawd. (107)

The pleasure of her "bombing" and the magnitude of her response to those feelings cause Lula to fear discovery, and ironically it is the intensity of that fear that impels her to further self-pleasuring. Sociologists such as Thomas Laqueur have seen masturbation as being "predicated on solitude, fantasy, the free play of imagination, the capacity to dwell within the self" (303), but in *Buxton Spice* it is not solitude that drives Lula to self-pleasuring. In a space crowded by family and where privacy is hard to come by, self-pleasuring is a secret act from which even the macocotte friends, with whom she has shared everything else, are excluded. The fantasies of Iggy and other sexual activities that she has witnessed, which impel her masturbation, become indicators of the insufficiency of her macocotte relationship and, in signaling her transfer of affection to an adult male romantic figure, forecast her later attraction to Mikey and to Raphael.

It is these heterosexual fantasies that are responsible for the same-sex genital play in which Lula later engages. Genital contact between young adolescent girls is presented in *Buxton Spice* with a directness that some reviewers have labeled vulgar.[13] Exploring what is still unchartered ground in Caribbean literature, Kempadoo presents this form of sex play as a manifestation of sexuality that is different from the heterosocial referents that might potentially corrupt and destroy it. While the examples of adult sexuality are often "lewd and crude," the intimacy Lula observes between her parents, although not physical, provides her with an example of tender heterosexual behavior, which her play activities with her friends replicates. In their "husband and wife games" Lula comes home from work, demands her evening meal, and then, replete, makes love to her "wife" Rachel. Placing a battery into her panties to imitate a penis, Lula then attempts to insert the tip of the battery into Rachel's naked body. Significantly, Kempadoo narrates this version of coition as fraught with laughter and gentleness. The care with which Lula uses the battery so as not to hurt Rachel contrasts significantly with the violence Lula exhibits later in the novel when she plays at making the female Barbie doll mate with the male Barbie doll, Ken (100).

That heterosexual sex is growingly linked to violence, betrayal, infidelity, and heartbreak becomes part of the socialization Lula receives, not from her parents, but from the other inhabitants of her community, Tamarind Grove. Tamarind Grove seems to abound with sexually active and available women who deliberately flaunt their availability and cash in on their sexual power. Lula is fascinated by the promiscuous Bullet, who commandeers appreciative gazes as she walks down the village streets: "Everybody from my brother to Uncle Joe couldn't help watching her or calling out to her" (76–77). She listens to the violent sounds of people having sex, vicariously becoming voyeuse to private acts that are being staged publicly and without shame. From these women, Lula learns that the sexually active woman wields significant power; she eagerly explores the source and nature of that power with her young friends and comes to a fuller understanding of the pleasure of that power in her masturbatory acts. At the same time, she becomes aware that this kind of vibrant sexuality is class bound. Good, middle-class girls such as her sisters and the older D'Abreo girls are more contained in their sexuality, and it is only through marriage that their libidinal desires will be manifested. Girls like Bullet, while they draw more attention and openly manifest the pleasures of sex, endure lives fraught with scandal and violence. They have no steady partners and therefore no fixed source of financial support. Ultimately, and inevitable to coming of age, Lula and her macocottes will have to decide which group of women to identify with.

In *Annie John,* the sexually active woman is seen by the adolescent girl as a death figure, and with great melodrama the young Annie describes her reactions to her parents' lovemaking. In spite of her disclaimer that she has no interest in, or understanding of, what her parents do together in bed, her observations are detailed enough to suggest awareness and censure: "But her hand! It was white and bony, as if it had been dead and had been left out in the elements. . . . If I were to forget everything else in the world, I could never forget her hand as it looked then. I could also make out that the sounds I had heard were her kissing my father's ears and his mouth and his face" (31). The macabre character of this depiction stands in opposition to the lyricism with which Annie describes the sweet kisses she receives from her playmates. She sees her father as a rival for her mother's affection, and the sex act becomes the materialization of that competition.

In *Abeng*, Clare is not privy to narratives of heterosexual tenderness and desire, for the uneasy relationship between her parents does not offer her any signposts to the erotic. The mother's black body continues to be inaccessible to both the daughter and the husband. Kitty sees her father, Boy Savage, as aligned to a group that historically had appropriated the naked black body into its economy of desire. Accordingly, he, like Clare, is denied emotional access. The grandmother who shares the responsibility of nurturing Clare has herself suppressed her sexual life in compensatory community-service activity. In her retreat to a space that protects her from the hurt of her husband's infidelity, Miss Mattie does not offer an example of a thriving libidinal subjectivity. Thus, Clare is denied what Audre Lorde defines as "an assertion of the life force of women, of that creative energy empowered, the knowledge and uses of which we are now reclaiming in our history, our dancing, our loving, our work, our lives" (*Sister/Outsider* 55). The protagonist in *Abeng* comes of age, then, in a space that is unmarked by definitive examples of what constitutes female sexuality.

Macocotte relationships, in rechanneling sexual impulses into same-sex friendship, defer heterosexual encounters and the threat of early pregnancies. Similarly, in the worlds of *Annie John* and *Buxton Spice* virginity has a high premium. Girls are discouraged from interacting with boys, and when they choose to do so, they are accused by their mothers of being whores and sluts. While friendships between females are not monitored, interest in boys is. Annie John's mother does not exercise any degree of strictness with regard to Annie's friendship with Gwen. The girls are part of a largely unsupervised group whose activities range from singing vulgar songs to displaying their underwear, exhibiting various parts of their bodies, and lying with their naked bosoms exposed to moonlight in order to hasten the growth of their breasts to a desirable size. Nor is the public demonstration of Annie's intense fondness for Gwen socially frowned upon. In comparison, "loud behavior," that is, behavior viewed as unladylike or not suited to girls, receives social disapprobation. Talking to boys becomes the epitome of loud behavior, and the mother's reaction when she sees a boy talking to an unresponsive Annie is both dramatic and condemnatory. "The word 'slut' (in patois) was repeated over and over, until suddenly I felt as if I were drowning in a well but instead of the well being filled with water it was filled with the word 'slut' and it was pouring through my eyes, my ears, my nostrils, my mouth" (102).

The reaction to interaction between adolescent boys and girls is equally harsh in *Buxton Spice*. The genital play of these early-adolescent girls, while it is an expression of sexual desire, takes place uninterrupted, because adults do not fear that interactions with other girls will compromise their daughters' virginity. Kempadoo uses Mrs. D'Abreo, mother to Rachel and Judy, as an example of the maternal perception that sexual awakening, typically represented as heterosexuality, presages a young woman's imminent social and economic ruin. Mrs. D'Abreo, mother of fourteen, is no stranger to sex but manages her sexuality as a commodity that has exchange value on the marriage market. It has secured her a husband who is an able provider. She perceives women like Bullet as examples of the unmanaged sexuality that can bring social and economic ruin. These women are what she fears her daughter could become if left unpoliced.

Embedded in Mrs. D'Abreo's interest in securing good marriages for her daughters are the maternal recognition that the newly libidinal female subject experiences a monstrous sexual desire and the conviction that this fearful sexuality must be bridled until marriage. In managing the sexuality of her daughter Judy, who when she chooses to have a relationship with the non-Portuguese Andre accordingly falls outside of maternal approval, Mrs. D'Abreo is as brutal and as intrusive as any police activities in the novel. When she catches Judy outside one night during curfew, she accuses her of sexual dalliance with Andre, and in a scene reminiscent of the testing in Danticat's *Breath, Eyes, Memory*, she proceeds to publicly confirm that Judy has been sexually active:

> "I goin see what you was doing!" she started pulling up Judy skirt, tugging at her panty.
>
> "Yuh can't hide nothing from me. *You*. Yuh lying little *whoa*. I always suspect you. *Blight!*" she got the panty off one foot, Judy not resisting. Pushed open her legs. "Agnes, look" . . . Emelda pushed her head closer, fixing her glasses. "*Red!* Why you crease red? *Red!*" (182)

This scene functions as the inversion of the girls' earlier sex-play scene; panties are removed, exposing the young girl to humiliation and public censure, female genitalia labeled as a site of shame. Sexual engagement reduces the female subject to whore. Lula, who is herself on the verge of transferring her attachments from her young female friends to the attractive Raphael, learns from Judy's humiliation that the cost of heterosexual alliance is induced trauma: Judy is now made to endure public censure similar to Bullet's earlier shame.

At the end of all three novels the macocotte relationship is dissolved. In these narratives, this form of friendship ultimately fails to offer the psychic sustenance that characterizes real-life macocotte friendships. For in spite of the erotic energy that initially characterizes the relationship, the young female protagonists, unlike their real-life counterparts, do not use it to construct a female community that will help them to deal with the exigencies of patriarchy as it manifests itself in the domestic world inhabited by their mothers. Nor do these young girls use these friendships as learning spaces that will enable them to form future adult romantic relationships. It may well be that in the world of these novels, Annie John, Clare Savage, and Lula are unable to sustain the erotic power of same-sex friendships because they have no evidence of the ability of such friendships to survive adolescence.

Consequential to this failure of adolescent same-sex friendship is isolation—the antithesis of what defines the *macocotte* relationship. In *Abeng*, the menstruating Clare is presented as entering into a developmental stage with very few signposts to mark out that journey, mourning the loss of her friendship with Zoe and the community implicit in that friendship. Similarly, at the end of *Annie John* the churchyard trysts give way to isolation and the devolution of Annie's macocotte friendship with Gwen. In the process of this disconnection, Annie experiences a loss of voice and of self, leaving her ambivalently desiring separation from her female friends and paradoxically yearning for the passionate connection she once shared with them. In *Buxton Spice*, Lula is presented as a lonely figure, unsure of how to step into an uncertain future, separated from the young friends who initially shared this journey to adulthood.

In these literary texts, the women writers use same-sex friendships between young girls to highlight the absence of such friendships in the adult lives of their female protagonists and to talk about the ways in which mothers fail to make use of the larger kinship networks available to them, either living primarily for and through their children or putting men first. The female adolescent protagonist, therefore, has no example of the mother as a female friend or as a woman who valorizes female friendships. Nor is she offered positive images of the mother as a sexual being. Accordingly, by the mother's example, the child becomes socialized into putting either her man or her children first. Tamed into servitude to patriarchy, the erotic energy that is so much a part of libidinal subjectivity dissipates, to resurface in her relationship with her children.

In conclusion, I have used the macocotte practice as it obtains in many Caribbean societies (and as it is depicted, although not named as such, in

Caribbean novels) to argue that while the Caribbean female forms a variety of emotional attachments during her lifetime, those formed during early adolescence are crucial to the formation of her sexual identity. Located safely within the bounds of social sanction, the macocotte relationship provides the space for female sexual desire to be produced and distributed throughout Afro-Caribbean society. Using the concept of macocotte to theorize Caribbean adolescent libidinal subjectivity, I highlight the ways in which cultural practices can become part of the transformational discourses that we apply to Caribbean literature. I hope that my attempt to ground the complexities of adolescent sexual behavior within specific social and cultural contexts may produce another reading of the social history of Afro-Caribbean sexuality, gender, and culture, one that reinforces the importance of indigenous epistemologies. Ultimately, it is by privileging the understanding of activities such as macocotte friendships within their sociocultural contexts that we can understand the ways in which Caribbean cultural practices impact on gender and sex roles. This, in turn, can allow us alternative vocabularies for describing same-sex activity.

Notes

1. In French, *cocotte* is a diminutive variant of *coq*. This familiar form is used both as a term of endearment and to refer to a young girl. *Ma* translates as "my," hence *macocotte* means "my darling." Such terms of endearment acquire both positive and negative sexual associations. In terms of *cocotte*'s Caribbean application, Pierre de Vaissière, writing about Saint Domingue society between 1629 and 1789, speaks of a *cocotte* as a confidante: "Presque chaque jeune créole a . . . une jeune négresse dont elle fait sa cocote. La cocote est la confidente des toutes les pensées de sa maîtresse (et cette confiance est quelquefois réciproque), confidente surtout de ses amours" (314–15; Nearly every young white Creole owns a .. . young negresse whom she makes her *cocotte*. The *cocotte* is the confidante of all the thoughts of her mistress and this confiding is sometimes reciprocal, the confiding above all of her loves). I establish here, based on observations of general usage, that the word *macocotte* is also used to describe female homosociability. The concept of the macocotte bears some resemblance to that of the *mattee* in Guyana and Dutch Guyana as explained by Richard Allsopp. These relationships may sometimes include same-sex intimacy.

2. In this essay, I use the literary text to support my thesis. However, my research has been supported by Caribbean informants who assure me that this homosocial practice, while not generally spoken about, exists in Haiti, Jamaica, and Trinidad and Tobago.

3. Lisa Diamond, a prominent developmental psychologist, has conducted detailed research on same-sex friendships among adolescent girls. Her research indicates that there was no correlation between adolescent same-sex friendship and sexual identification as lesbian (sexual minority) later in life. In her essay "Passionate Friendships among Adolescent Sexual-Minority Women," Diamond provides data from adult respondents who indicated that while they could not explain the reason

for their intense friendships, they knew from a process of continued soul-searching that these friendships were not sites of subverted sexual interest.

4. Within the Caribbean, the term appears as not only *macommère* but also *macomère, macumeh, makoumè,* and *makòmè.* Literally translated, *macommère* means "my co-mother." Typically, the macommère is the godmother of one's child, a woman who, by virtue of the longevity and depth of her friendship, has rights and privileges relating to your child. Richard Allsopp, in his definition of *macommère,* asserts that the term usually describes men who take an inordinate interest in "women" affairs—who act like women or who are often part of a woman's circle of confidants.

5. Timothy defends her choice of *MaComère* as the title for the journal of the Association of Caribbean Women Writers and Scholars. She claims that her spelling variant foregrounds the relations of caring and sharing between Caribbean women.

6. The notion of sexual fluidity is crucial to an understanding of female sexuality and sexual orientation. For example, the social psychologist Roy Baumeister, in his study "Gender Differences in Erotic Plasticity," presents considerable evidence showing that factors such as education, religion, and acculturation have a significant impact on aspects of female sexuality.

7. In Lesotho, same-sex female relations are sanctioned as part of the cultural coming-of-age process. In Lesothan society the term *mummy-baby relationship* describes a same-sex relationship between an older and a younger girl. Typically these relationships flourish between Basotho schoolgirls. As Judith Gay argues in her study "Mummies and Babies," they emerged out of a history of initiation whereby an older girl was selected to assist the young initiate through adolescence and to educate her in the sexual and cultural practices attending the coming-of-age process. "Mummies" provide guidance on managing heterosexual relationships, information on matters related to sex, and strategies for negotiating sexual desire within those relationships. The "mummy" views this relationship as a romance and accordingly engages the "baby" in the erotic activity that normally defines romances. Courtship and seduction rituals emerge naturally. These relationships are not restrained or punished, nor are they defined as lesbian. In a society in which virginity is prized yet female sexual responsiveness is expected, the mummy-baby relationship allows the young girl to acquire sexual expertise and sexual self-identification without compromising her virginity. Significantly, while there is genital intimacy between these adolescent girls, this intimacy is not perceived as sexual, because in that society the sexual is culturally defined as connected to penile penetration. "Mummy-baby" relationships in no way imperil heterosexual relations. Instead, female bonds, perceived to be integral to social continuity, are strengthened by these support networks.

8. By way of reinforcing the point that the cultural practices of one society may seem sexual to another, the activities that attend the enlargement of one's labia minora are useful. While the "Hottentot apron" has been looked upon with great derision by Westerners, anthropologists assert that among the Basotha enlarged labia minora are considered to endow the woman with considerable erotic power. Reputed to enhance sexual pleasure during heterosexual coitus, elongated labia minora are accordingly highly regarded. Thus, young Basotho girls spend considerable time manually lengthening each other's labia minora. Social anthropologists have cited their research subjects as indicating that cunnilingual practices among the "mummies" and "babies" are often directed at this lengthening activity.

9. Audre Lorde has popularized the word *zami* to mean "lesbian of color."

10. See Mary Poovey's monumental study *Uneven Developments* for an extended discussion of this issue.

11. The coded coyness with which this stirring of sensuality is depicted contrasts with Kincaid's more explicit representation of the libidinal Xuela in *The Autobiography of My Mother.*

12. Given that Judaic and Christian theology view masturbation as a sin—what the Vatican in 1992 described as an "intrinsically seriously disorderly act"—it is likely that masturbation would have been condemned in a Caribbean society interpellated by Christian values along with Anglo Victorian puritanism.

13. Jacqueline Brice-Finch, in her review of *Buxton Spice,* is not as generous in her assessment of Kempadoo's first novel, which she labels as a "rude, crude book [that] focuses on the prurient tastes of Guyanese society." While she concedes that Kempadoo's interest is in adolescent sexuality, Brice-Finch sees this exploration as unrelated to a weak plot and accordingly gratuitous.

What Is a *Uma*?

Women Performing Gender and Sexuality in Paramaribo, Suriname

Omise'eke Natasha Tinsley

> For people of color have always theorized. . . . And I am inclined to say that our theorizing (and I intentionally use the verb rather than the noun) is often in narrative forms, in the stories we create, in riddles and in proverbs, in the play with language, since dynamic rather than fixed ideas seem more to our liking. How else have we managed to survive with such spiritedness the assaults on our bodies, social institutions, countries, our very humanities?
>
> —Barbara Christian, "The Race for Theory"

"So yu tel, mi tel, so tel di huol a wi fain out se a di wan stuori wi a tel: Uman stori. Di siem ting uova and uova. Bot it no iizi fi get op tel piil yu bizniz na!" writes Carolyn Cooper in her description of the work of the Jamaican theater collective Sistren (*Noises* 91). Published in her 1993 monograph *Noises in the Blood,* this innovative Jamaican-language essay proclaimed Creole to be not only a subject that academics might theorize about but also a medium in which to write theory. Like the women of Sistren, Creole speaks knowledge to power here. That a prominent North American academic press published this linguistic experiment attests to the serious attention afforded Creoleness by the 1990s. Jean Bernabé, Patrick Chamoiseau, and Raphaël Confiant's seminal *Eloge de la créolité: In Praise of Creoleness,* which first appeared in 1989, as well as numerous anthologies in Kreyòl and nation language, demanded that regional and international intelligentsia listen to Creole as "the initial means of communication of our deep self, of our collective unconscious, of our popular genius, this language [that] remains the river of our alluvial Creoleness" (Bernabé, Chamoiseau, and Confiant 43). And as Cooper's essay demonstrates, the sounds of this Creole river could be powerfully poetic and powerfully political.

Cooper, Bernabé et al., and other Caribbean writers repeatedly reference storytelling and religion as "saying something" about indigenous ways of knowing. Yet they systematically pass over other distinctively Creole lexical pools that might also be read as vehicles of subordinated knowledge. If theories of Creoleness, like the testimony of Sistren, begin to seem like the "siem ting uova and uova," this is perhaps because over and over the same vocabularies are foregrounded, while others are overlooked. Following the lead of other Caribbean theorists, these authors theorize race and ethnicity in the region by highlighting uniquely Afro-Creole patterns of lexicon, phonology, and imagery. Yet little note has been made of the absence of gender within Creole languages' noun and pronoun structures and what this reveals about the culturally specific grammars of gender and sexuality in the Caribbean. Even less attention has been paid to the richness of Creole vocabulary that expresses same-sex desire. *Zanmi, madivine, kambrada, man royal, tortillera, wicca, mati wroko*—Caribbean languages have many ways of speaking of women who love women. Like other vocabularies unique to regional languages, these words speak to an intentional indigenous epistemology of sexuality. This Creole also theorizes, also acts as the "the initial means of communication of our deep self, of our collective unconscious, of our popular genius."

In Suriname, working-class Creole women who love women say they engage in *mati wroko*, literally, the "work" (*wroko*) of "friends" (*mati*).[1] In this essay I propose to read the performance poetry produced by Surinamese mati at the beginning of the twentieth century as an active theorizing of Creole women's sexuality, one that predates academic discussions of both *Créolité* and queerness by a century. Linguistically and conceptually, these texts are in Sranan, Surinamese Creole. Sung at parties and in town squares, they deployed Creole poetics and Caribbean metaphoric systems to theorize gender and sexuality through performance long before Judith Butler introduced gender performativity to the North American academy.[2] Like Sistren, mati make serious (and playful) business of telling their stories in a public setting. Through the rhythms of repeating and shifting constellations of Sranan vocabulary and imagery—*matiworking* landscape, bodies, and language itself—these Surinamese working-class women voice Creole conceptual frameworks for engaging women's sexuality in West Indian landscapes.

The Scene: *Dyari* and *Mati*

This story begins in Paramaribo, Suriname, in 1900 and in the *dyari*. Dyari, or yards, were the circular, backgrounded, movement-filled black women's spaces behind city streets where, after emancipation, small houses were grouped together around communal outdoor areas. In that time and place, dyari typically included several female-headed households where mothers lived with biological and adopted children. In order to survive extreme poverty, yards worked around an environmental ethic that looked to safeguard communal resources and so protect the welfare of households. You could tell that a yard with a flowering tree growing alongside herbs and flowers at its center was a fortunate one. This was because the ecology of the communal garden and the survival of dyari families were understood as interlocking propositions and collective responsibilities. If everyone made sure that the tree was fed, then you knew that everyone made sure that all the human inhabitants were fed. The concern was not about what remained inside or outside, since these barriers were permeable. Rather, the concern was *whether* and *how* what was in the yard grew something meaningful and useful to the dyari.[3]

With this tree in view, inhabitants and neighbors gathered to cook, gossip, fight, tell stories, sing, and hold religious ceremonies. Also with this tree in view, many dyari women engaged in the sexual and social praxis *mati wroko* (mati work). Creolized from the Dutch *maatje*, or "mate," the noun *mati* refers without distinction to female friends and lovers. *Mi mati* is like *my girl* or *my partner* in African American English, maybe "my friend" or maybe "my lover." Creole speakers say that women do mati work, talking about sexuality not as identity but as praxis and performance, something constantly constructed and reconstructed through daily actions, much like the yard's central tree. This performative construction of sexuality was not abstract theorizing; it was a communal way of knowing, built into the Creole language itself.

Oral history and colonial chronicles trace these traditions to the Middle Passage, where captive African women created erotic bonds with other women in the sex-segregated holds.[4] In so doing, they resisted the commodification of their bodies by *feeling for* their co-occupants on these ships. *Mati* also means "mate," as in *shipmate*, she who survived the Middle Passage with me. Once arrived in the New World, women in some parts of the Caribbean, particularly communities of freed slaves or maroons, continued relationships with mati in female friendship and/or kinship networks. Here women not only shared food, stories, and child rearing but also—with the same social acceptance accorded to male-female relationships—called on sexuality as a resource to share with other women. The anthropologist Gloria Wekker considers mati to be involved in a *dual sexual system* (*Ik ben een gouden munt* 165–66). In working-class Creole communities, both female and male relationships garner material resources for female participants, who gain access to shared income and property by forging kinship networks. But same-sex relationships serve the additional purpose of shoring up emotional resources, as female partners ensure companionship, moral support, and help with household management that men are not always expected to provide. *Mati* also means "mate" as in *helpmate*.

In addition to "working" sexuality as a daily praxis, mati also engaged in ritual community performances that publicized and naturalized their desires.

These included the lavish birthday parties that lovers threw for each other, featuring songs, dances, and staged flights; and the weekly performances that I discuss here, the *lobisingi* (Herskovits and Herskovits 31). *Lobisingi* literally translates as "love songs," but they are not what they seem at first glance. These musical compositions in fact acted as a form of social criticism that women leveled against mati who violated communally established codes of behavior between lovers. Song as public critique is common practice in African diaspora communities and surfaces in the context of women's sexual relationships elsewhere in the Caribbean. But Suriname's lobisingi have a unique history that dates from slavery. Lobisingi evolved from *Du*, outlawed theatrical societies comprising both men and women, slaves and free people of color, who composed and executed dances, songs, and musical comedies as social commentary. Before emancipation, competing factions of the plantocracy hired these societies to perform satirical sketches aimed at rival families. While initially elite women paid black women to act in these sketches, when the plantocracy's economic fortunes declined, so did their interest in staging such costly spectacles. By the turn of the century, Creole women had appropriated the discarded form for their own use. Instead of singing planters' grievances, they began to sing grievances against their mati.

These performances took place on Sunday afternoons between four and seven, often in a lot bordering the Suriname River, which the trader Abraham de Vries rented for three guilders during hours when no ships were docking. Situated at a literal crossroads, the songs performed on the Suriname River were, according to the Dutch musicologist Th. A. C. Comvalius, "an intermediary genre [*overgangsvorm*] of the Negro song . . . which, in form, lies between African and European songs" (355, my translation). Cited as African elements are the songs' three-line verses, performance by women, composition in Creole, and heavy use of imagistic language; and as European elements, the accompanying instruments (clarinet, flute, snare drums, tambourine), the reuse of popular Dutch melodies, and the predominance of anapestic and iambic meters. The performance began with the gathering of a mostly female crowd, who at the best-funded affairs were first offered food and drink and then walked to Saramacca Street in a musical procession. Assembled there, the organizer and fellow performers traditionally opened with a *langasingi*, an often improvised, lyric song composed of three-line verses telling the story of what the lover had done wrong. But after 1900 the langasingi began to be omitted because, as original compositions, they might bring slander charges if Paramaribo police arrived on the scene. Many lobisingi, then, were made up entirely of *kot'singi*, shorter, more fixed texts whose words the lead singer would alter slightly between choruses to speak to the wronged lover's situation. These songs were performed as call-and-response; the chorus always remained the same and ended with a series of dance steps, during which dancers lifted their skirts in back and shouted "Ha! Ha!"

The Flowers: *Roos* and *Stanfaste*

One of the oldest and most popular kot'singi proudly shames neglectful lovers by proclaiming singers' "flowerness." This song has been transcribed by several folklorists and anthropologists who note the imagistic richness of the genre, but I reproduce it here in the form noted by Gloria Wekker in her generous communication with me about her fieldwork:

> Fa yu kan taki mi no moy? (x 3)
> Na tu bromtji meki mi.
> Rosekunop na mi mama,
> Stanfaste na mi papa.
> Fa yu kan taki mi no moy, no moy?
> Na tu bromtji meki mi.
> (How can you say I'm not pretty? [x 3]
> It's two flowers that made me.
> Rosebud is my mama,
> *Stanfaste* is my papa.
> How can you say I'm not pretty, not pretty?
> It's two flowers that made me.)[5]

This song is rhythmed by two words that echo each other and are used to explain each other: *mi* and *bromtji*, speaker and "flower." The word *bromtji* draws immediate attention by its position in the middle of the song's first trochaic line; its appearance directly after the metrically free, thrice stated first line; and its inclusion in a string of alliterations in [m]. This meter and alliteration link *bromtji* rhythmically and phonetically as well as semantically to the stressed *mi* ending the line. The strong relationship between woman and flower is inscribed not only in the meaning of the song's words, then, but in their form. But what does it mean for this mi, this Caribbean woman, to tell her lover that she is made from two flowers: the quintessentially European rose and the tropical *stanfaste* (*gomphrena globosa*)?

This song sings something about what it means to answer the classic feminist question "what is a woman?" in a Creole context, in an Afro-Caribbean grammar of gender, where that question becomes, as my title asks, "what is a *uma*?" This kot'singi sings, first, that to be a Surinamese *uma* is to perform womanhood at an intersection of Euro- and Afro-Caribbean gender ideals. Introduced to colonial gardens for different purposes, the rose and the stanfaste image different models of womanhood being negotiated in the dyari. The rose, many varieties of which were imported to Europe from North

Africa and China during the Renaissance, became, in turn, one of the flowers most frequently transplanted to the Americas. Cultured roses were the European flower par excellence, valued for their visibly cool, pale, antitropical nature. Drawing on this history, mati's metaphoric language uses *roos* to refer to a pretty young woman possessing physical qualities—decorative beauty, paleness, and softness of skin—that they understand to be valuable in the dominant, Euro-Surinamese gender ideology. Many dyari inhabitants were domestic workers who saw roses in vases inside homes they cleaned and who worked under the supervision of white women whose "roseness" gave them access to the most privileged woman's work in colonial Suriname, that of elite wife. But when mati sing of mama-roses in this rented river lot, working-class women sing that they have the right to claim roseness for themselves too, that they are also born of beauty, desirability, softness—simply, that black is beautiful. This "indoors" model of femininity, meant to stay locked out of their reach, stays metrically, phonetically, and semantically linked to the woman speaker and to another flower, the stanfaste.

The stanfaste was imported directly from Southeast Asia, not to imitate European landscapes, but to flush out the borders of exotic gardens with multicolored blossoms in brilliant purples, pinks, blues, oranges, and yellows. It was especially valued for the heads of the flowers, which, if dried early, could be displayed for years. Chosen not only for its physical properties but for associations tied to its name (staying together, not falling apart), here *stanfaste* represents an Afro-Surinamese gender ideology and is a vehicle for qualities that Creole women value in themselves. These flowers' deeper colors and sturdy textures suggest physical qualities prized in the resource-sharing economy of the working class—dark skin, endurance, vitality. In dyari, the ideal model of womanhood is the *dyadya uma*, or "upright woman," who is, as Wekker writes, "a woman who knows how to take care of business, is a psychological and economical broker; she has a network that importantly includes female relatives, but also her lovers, male and female; she has command of spiritual and cultural knowledge" ("Of Mimic Men and Unruly Women" 188). Flora and women are alike in the dyari because neither can be exclusively possessed; like the central tree, both are engaged as living forces to interact with horizontally—at eye level—and responsibly.

The insufficiency of ruling-class models of botany and sexuality to explain Creole landscapes and Creole womanhood appears as a theme in a number of sayings and lobisingi, imaged as the weakness of the rose without the support of the stanfaste. "Roos e flaw a de fadon," remarks one kot'singi, "ma stanfaste dat e tan sidon" (Wekker, *Ik ben een gouden munt* 62; The rose is weak, it falls down, but stanfaste stays upright). In singing that she is part rose, part stanfaste, a mati recognizes that in a plural society not only are women made rather than born but their gendered as well as their racial identities are produced through negotiation among flowers, among models of womanhood. The mati singer publicly proclaims that difference resides not only *between* identities, between women and men or between white and black women; it is also *internal* to Creole womanhood, which is a hybrid, crossover form between rose and stanfaste that upsets and reorders both European and tropical ideals of flowers and women.

The Women: *Mama* and *Papa*

But the hybridity of *uma*hood becomes even more complex here. Women are flowers in this song, *roos* and *stanfaste*; and flowers are differently gendered, both *mama* and *papa*. *Mama* and *papa* are not only nouns that suggest female-male differentiation; they are sometimes used as suffixes to create gender markings in Sranan, which, like other Creoles, does not other-wise gender nouns and pronouns. The metaphor of *roos* and *stanfaste* as mother and father may refer to the fact that, "man" and "woman" roles exist in these relationships. "Ti toe soema di mattie, dan na wan di pree foe man" (When two people mati, then one plays the man), explains the mati worker Jet. The man is the partner who approaches the woman to express sexual interest; helps with the woman's rent, food, and clothing, if possible; has a right to keep other mati, while the woman must have only one female lover or risk anger or lobisingi; and lies on top during sex or tells the woman to. All of this is understood as robustly healthy sex play, and, as Wekker reports, mati consider it "natural" for there to be a man and a woman in mati relationships (*Ik ben een gouden munt* 163).

How, then, does this add to an answer to the question "what is a *uma*?" Are mati indeed still women, or—as the lesbian theorist Monique Wittig has suggested (49)—in playing between mama and papa do they move be-yond this category? In fact, the performers resolutely understand themselves and the other people in attendance to be women. "Mattie diesie na wan sanie foe sosso oema-soema" (This mati is something only for women), a Creole named Wilhelmina told a researcher (qtd. in Van Lier 48). Papa or mama, whatever their relationship role, mati are, as Wilhelmina states, always women. Not moving "beyond" gender at all, the mixed-gender statement "*Roos* is my mama/*Stanfaste* is my papa" instead suggests an-other layer in the internal differentiation of Creole womanhood. Creole women understand themselves as negotiating not only between rose and stanfaste, Euro- and Afro-Surinamese gender ideals, but also between mama and papa, feminine and masculine instantiations of their always plural "selves." That *stanfaste* could be at once a woman and a man is not contra-dictory in Creole gender ideology. *Uma* becomes, in mati's language, a term more internally complex than *woman/vrouw* in colonial discourses: *roos* and *stanfaste,* "woman" and "man" in mati relationships, all fall under this umbrella term.

Let me explain this further by looking at what we might call the Sranan construction of the self, that is, how language itself helps demonstrate the working of this internal differentiation in Creole grammars of "identity." European languages in the Caribbean have one first-person singular pronoun that a speaker uses to refer to her- or himself: *I, ik, je, yo.* This reflects European conceptions of the self as individual, discrete, and independent. But in Surinamese Creole a variety of words and phrases can be used. These include *mi kra* (my protective spirit), *mi yeye* (my soul), *mi dyodyo* (my ancestors), *mi geest* (my mind), and *mi skin* (my body): "mi skin e tek'i" (my body takes her), a woman says when she is attracted to another woman (qtd. in Wekker, "Girl, It's Boobies" 47). Far from a purely poetic conceit, this multiplication of first-person referents mirrors a Creole conception of self as a compound subject comprising many instantiations. These include not only the individual's body and mind, which change continually over the course of a lifetime, but spiritual components (sometimes called *Winti,* literally "winds," or figuratively, protective spirits) inherited from ancestors or acquired during spiritual practice. That is, the self is not only individual but collective, not only independent but interdependent, not only present but past and future. Men affiliated with female Winti have feminine energies, and women affiliated with male spirits have masculine energy. As Wekker notes, mati workers are often thought to be protected by a strong masculine spirit who would be jealous if his child maintained a sexual relationship with another male; her spirit (not she), then, is attracted to women ("What's Identity" 133).

Yet no element of the Creole self is dominant. The Winti may take some lovers, the skin others, the yeye yet others. Feminine energies may "speak" one week, masculine energies the next. The mutability of gender is reflected in the choice of *na* as verb in the lobisingi's metaphors: "Rosekunop na mi mama, stanfaste na mi papa." This particle corresponds only roughly to the English word *is. Na* is a copula that speaks of the subject entering into a relationship with another term rather than manifesting a fundamental property of being. Understood is that such relationships are both unstable—that umaness does not have an unalterable link to roseness—and multiple—that different lobisingers can be like, follow, desire different combinations of rose, stanfaste, mama, papa, yeye, dyodyo and still take (a speaking) part in mati work and play. The gendered self that "is" an identity for Euro-Caribbeans, then, may act as a non-identity—as a malleable performance—for Afro-Caribbeans. At the lobisingi "I" am/*na* skin and yeye, stanfaste and roos, man and woman, colonized and resistant. The self speaks as a complexly layered proposition.

It seems less accurate, then, to say that these are not women than to argue that the Sranan *uma* no longer signifies the same "thing" that *woman* or *vrouw* does in imperial gender ideologies. Like lobisingi themselves, *uma* becomes a Creole *overgangsvorm,* or crossover form, that takes a Euro-Surinamese song and dance of gender and reperforms it to speak Afro-Surinamese understandings of plural, hybrid selves. These songs drum an example of how Caribbean women theorize on their feet, singing and dancing creative, public reappropriations of flowers and constructs that were meant to stock the colonial garden but grow defiantly *moy* in Paramaribo's dyari. To imagine that rose and stanfaste are guaranteed to produce a beautiful child means, certainly, that in their sexual relationships mati act like no kind of flower or woman recorded by European botany and biology. Lobisingi, elements of the cultural knowledge the dyadya uma use to evaluate the world, turn these discourses on their heads—and I mean this somewhat literally, since at some performances mati bear flowers for their lovers on their heads.

"Tu bromtji meki mi"—the singer makes her self-identifications through a floral metaphor that naturalizes relationships between hybrid mama-papa, rose-stanfaste subjects rather than pathologizing Creole women's complex geographies of racialized gender. Here, two women can create economic and kinship ties that refuse to reproduce the patriarchal colonial order yet birth a beautiful Surinamese landscape and womanhood. When singers matiwork these flowers in Sunday songs, their geographies and rhythms evoke shouts, laughter, and skirt-lifting dancing from the audience. What makes the scene worthy of applause is the spectacle, yes; but it is also the knowledge it conveys, that *roos* can be/*na* many entities, slipping between self and other, pasts and present, garden and yard, what I could be and will be.

"In city gardens grow no roses as we know them./So the people took the name and bestowed it/generic, on all flowers, called them roses" writes the Jamaican poet Lorna Goodison (15). And as we come to the end of this short song, in its few lines we have navigated a garden of stanfaste and roses as the global north never knew them, growing intertwined, multicolored, beautiful, twisted, and resistant, revealing parts of women's stories, while concealing other parts. Navigating this imaginary and real geography, we open onto a Creole epistemology of gender and sexuality, not an epistemology of the closet but an *epistemology of the garden.* Here, nonheteronormative sexualities and complex gender (non)identities are not segregated from the everyday life of the dyari and the city, not shadowed by anxieties of being kept inside or outside. Instead, this song directs listeners to an intersection of inside and outside, rose and stanfaste, an interface between race, class, culture, and sexuality that in postcolonial societies makes gender as much a site of hybridization as of race. Not obsessed with secrecy yet not pretending to reveal transparent truths, the epistemology of the garden is rather about porousness, inclusiveness, incorporating and braiding together strands of all that may be powerful women's self-construction—as the dyari itself does. In order to theorize Creoleness we do not have to sidestep gender and sexuality, the garden contends, and in order to speak of Creole gender and sexuality we do not need to import Northern queer theory. A rose is not always just a rose, these lobisingi insist, and the closet is not always the place to find same-sex desire; and it behooves international scholars to listen to what and where else they might be.

Notes

1. In Suriname, *Creole* is an ethnic designation referring to Afro-Surinamese descendants of the enslaved (as opposed to maroons). I use it in this sense when I refer to "Creole" women.

2. I am referring here, of course, to Butler's watershed formulation of gender performativity in *Gender Trouble*.

3. For a description of yard and tree, see Stephen.

4. On this history, see Price and Price; and Wekker, *Ik ben een gouden munt*.

5. This text is quoted in Herskovits and Herskovits 29 and in Voorhoeve and Lichtveld 48. This version comes from a personal communication from Gloria Wekker, August 2001.

Colonial Girl

And What Would It Be Like

Michelle Cliff

I

And what would it be like
The terrain of my girlhood

[with you]   There is no map

Ok.
Mangoes
then the sweet liquidity of star apple
custard apple
sweetsop
cut with sharp tamarind
washed down with coconut water
ginep   slippery
papaya
where restless baby-ghosts vent their furies

all devoured
against trade winds
                Will I eternally return to the Trade?

Then—
there's more
by which I mean
hibiscus, jasmine, night-blooming   and otherwise
by which I mean
the more ancient
pre-Columbian   pre-Contact
growth

Edenic underbrush
unyielding   thick as a woman's thatch
like the [girls' school legend] un-drawered tennis mistress
who
or whom
we slid beneath
to glimpse the bright, thick ginger
womanly—
God, we wanted to be women, never knowing what that meant.
—patch
thatch so thick you'd never guess she was British
[our prejudice]

And banana leaves
wide as a girl's waist—sometimes
and as long as a girl's feathered legs
which exude the juice of the fruit
without a taste of the fruit
dependable as any aunt

down a falls once owned by an aunt
we flowed
on the impossible green
into the equally impossible blue
lit by the height of an impossible light
taking our half-naked selves
down the sweet
into the salt
water
and women
women
and water
my grandmother's river
my distant aunt's falls
no one else was allowed in
other children   [that didn't feel right]
revolutionaries are made, not born.

II

Bougainvillea
grows
[according to the botanist]

in showy profusion—
but scentless—
disappoints

III

Under the high-leggéd mahogany bed
caciques at each corner   like apostles
or caryatids
the tail of a scorpion is set to strike
transparent   dangerous
I know its poison.

IV

All feels wild from this distance.

V

One time at Cable Hut
I fell into a sinkhole
down and down and down
but came back up
suddenly
One time I had my period and swam way out
past the coral reef
and wondered if a shark would be drawn to me
as the warm salt drew the blood out   and the sea roared
One time I speared a lobster clean   underwater at Lime Key
One time I brushed beside the flimsy nightdress
of a jellyfish   and have a mark on my thigh to prove it
One time I dodged an alligator in a swamp by the Carib's edge
my mouth gorged on a hundred oysters   their grit becoming
pearl against my teeth
One time I played with a cousin's cock underwater—
he taught me to shoot coconuts between the eyes so they
rained around us on the sand   it was the least I could do
Those were the dangerous days
There was nothing to stop us   it seemed

VI

There is no map
only the most raggéd path back   to
my love   so much so
she ended up in the bush

at a school where such things were
taken very seriously   severely
                    and
I was left   missing her   never ceasing
                    and
she was watched   for signs
                    and
I was left   alone   missing her   never ceasing
                    and
she was not allowed to write   at least she never did
                    and
I walked the length and breadth of the playing fields
                              I have never felt so lost
not like that
                    and
I wanted to be dead   that's all
                                   finally
the headmistress and head girl found me
in the stacks
                    weeping
                                   violently
against spines of biology
                    running into history
I can see myself in the lapsed documentary of memory
                              curled up against books, shelves
salting the sea island cotton of my blouse
                    wanted to lose my
self   water tearing down my face, school badge
with cross & crown   & Latin motto
                    my parents were summoned
the word was not spoken
                              I was told to forget everything
I would never see her again   I would never see her again
          except with my mind's eye   and to this day
golden
                    they rifled my hiding place
ransacked my words   read me aloud   on the
verandah
                    under the impossible sun
my father   uttering
"When you're twenty we'll laugh about this."
                    that I remember

they took me, on the advice of the doctor who delivered
me,
                    to Doctor's Cave
which is a beach, not Prospero's vault,
                        for weeks
I swam
            like Caliban
her feathered legs opening under water   salt rushing into me
                    I was exhausted, they said
excitable

I wanted to be a wild colonial girl
And for a time, I was.

Bibliography

Abdur-Rahman, Aliyyah. "'The Strangest Freaks of Despotism': Queer Sexuality in Antebellum African American Slave Narratives." *African American Review* 40, no. 2 (2006): 223–37.

Abraham, Marie, and Gisèle Pineau. *Femmes des Antilles: Traces et voix; 150 ans après l'abolition de l'esclavage.* Paris: Stock, 1998.

Abrams, Elliot. "The Shiprider Solution: Policing the Caribbean." *National Interest* 43 (Spring 1996): 86–92.

Abramschmitt, Céline. "Is Barbados Ready for Same-Sex Marriage? Analysis of Legal and Social Constructs." http:sta.uwi.edu/conferences/salises/documents/Abramschmitt%20C.pdf (accessed 1 September 2009).

Achebe, Chinua. "The Truth of Fiction." In *Hopes and Impediments: Selected Essays,* 138–53. New York: Doubleday, 1989.

Agnant, Marie-Célie. *Le livre d'Emma.* Montreal: Editions du Remue-Ménage, 2001.

Aidoo, Ama Ata. *The Dilemma of a Ghost and Anowa.* 1970. Burnt Mill, Harlow, UK: Longman, 1985.

Alexander, M. Jacqui. "Danger and Desire: Crossings Are Never Undertaken All at Once or Once and for All." *Small Axe,* no. 24 (2007): 154–66.

———. "Erotic Autonomy as a Politics of Decolonization." In *Feminist Genealogies, Colonial Legacies, Democratic Futures,* ed. M. Jacqui Alexander and Chandra Talpade Mohanty, 63–100. New York: Routledge, 1997.

———. "Not Just (Any) *Body* Can Be a Citizen: The Politics of Law, Sexuality, and Postcoloniality in Trinidad and Tobago and the Bahamas." *Feminist Review* 48 (Autumn 1994): 5–23.

———. *Pedagogies of Crossing: Meditations on Feminism, Sexual Politics, Memory, and the Sacred.* Durham, NC: Duke University Press, 2005.

———. "Redrafting Morality: The Postcolonial State and the Sexual Offences Bill of Trinidad and Tobago." In Mohanty, Russo, and Torres, *Third World Women and the Politics of Feminism,* 133–52.

Allen, Carolyn. "Creole Then and Now: The Problem of Definition." *Caribbean Quarterly* 44, nos. 1–2 (1998): 33–49.

Allen, Jafari Sinclaire. *¡Venceremos? Sexuality, Gender, and Black Self-Making in Cuba.* Durham, NC: Duke University Press, forthcoming.

Alleyne, Peter. "Bag Ruling the Charts with 'In De Tail.'" *Weekend Nation* (Bridgetown, Barbados), 25 April 1997, 26.

Allsopp, Richard. *Dictionary of Caribbean English Usage*. Oxford: Oxford University Press, 1996.

Almaguer, Tomás. "Chicano Men: A Cartography of Homosexual Identity and Behavior." In *The Lesbian and Gay Studies Reader*, ed. Henry Abelove, Michèle Aina Barale, and David M. Halperin, 255–73. New York: Routledge, 1993.

Alonso, Ana Maria, and Maria Teresa Koreck. "Silences: 'Hispanics,' AIDS, and Sexual Practices." In *The Lesbian and Gay Studies Reader*, ed. Henry Abelove, Michèle Aina Barale, and David M. Halperin, 110–26. New York: Routledge, 1993.

Alonzo, Robert. "Murder, Mayhem Mar J'Ouvert—Woman Torched." *Trinidad Guardian*, 8 February 2005. http:www.guardian.co.tt/archives/2005-02-08/news7.html.

Als, Hilton. *The Women*. New York: Farrar, Straus & Giroux, 1996.

Altman, Dennis. "Global Gaze / Global Gays." *GLQ: A Journal of Lesbian and Gay Studies* 3, no. 4 (1997): 417–36.

Anarfi, John K. "Ghanaian Women and Prostitution in Cote D'Ivoire." In Kempadoo and Doezema, *Global Sex Workers*, 104–13.

Andaiye. "'The Angle You Look From Determines What You See': Toward a Critique of Feminist Politics in the Caribbean." In *The Lucille Mathurin Mair Lecture 2002*. Kingston, Jamaica: University Printers, 2002.

———. "Counting Women's Caring Work: An Interview with Andaiye." By David Scott. *Small Axe*, no. 15 (2004): 123–217.

———. "Smoke and Mirrors: The Illusion of CARICOM Women's Growing Economic Empowerment, Post-Beijing." In Tang Nain and Bailey, *Gender Equality in the Caribbean*, 73–107.

Antrobus, Peggy. "The Rise and Fall of Feminist Politics in the Caribbean Women's Movement 1975–1995." In *The Lucille Mathurin Mair Lecture 2000*. Kingston, Jamaica: University Printers, 2000.

Appadurai, Arjun. *Modernity at Large: Cultural Dimensions of Globalization*. Minneapolis: University of Minnesota Press, 1996.

Arnold, A. James. "The Erotics of Colonialism in Contemporary French West Indian Literary Culture." *Annals of Scholarship* 12, nos. 1–2 (1997): 173–86.

———. "The Erotics of Colonialism in Contemporary French West Indian Literature." *New West Indian Guide / Nieuwe West-Indische Gids* 68, nos. 1–2 (1994): 5–22.

Arondekar, Anjali. *For the Record: On Sexuality and the Colonial Archive in India*. Durham, NC: Duke University Press, 2009.

Asante, M. K. *Afrocentricity*. Trenton, NJ: Africa World Press, 1988.

Ashcroft, Bill. *The Empire Writes Back: Theory and Practice in Post-Colonial Literatures*. London: Routledge, 2002.

Atluri, Tara L. "When the Closet is a Region. Homophobia, Heterosexism and Nationalism in the Commonwealth Caribbean." Working Paper Series (Cave Hill) 5, Centre for Gender and Development Studies, University of the West Indies, 2001.

Bailey, Barbara. "The Search for Gender Equity and Empowerment of Caribbean Women: The Role of Education." In Tang Nain and Bailey, *Gender Equality in the Caribbean*, 108–45.

Bailey, Barbara, and Elsa Leo-Rhynie, eds. *Gender in the 21st Century: Caribbean Perspectives, Visions and Possibilities*. Kingston, Jamaica: Ian Randle, 2004.

Bakare-Yusuf, Bibi. "Fabricating Identities: Survival and the Imagination in Jamaican Dancehall Culture." *Fashion Theory: The Journal of Dress, Body & Culture* 10, no. 4 (2006): 461–83.

Baksh-Soodeen, Rawwidda, and Rhoda Reddock. Preface to *Creation Fire: CAFRA Anthology of Caribbean Women's Poetry*, ed. Ramabai Espinet, ii–iii. Toronto: Sister Vision, 1990.

Balderston, Daniel, and Donna J. Guy, eds. *Sex and Sexuality in Latin America*. New York: New York University Press, 1997.

Balibar, Etienne. *We, the People of Europe? Reflections on Transnational Citizenship*. Princeton, NJ: Princeton University Press, 2004.

Ballantyne-Nisbett, Tomiko. "Lost in Paradise: A Look at the Oppressiveness of Religion through the Experience of Caribbean women." In *Freethought Today*, November 2001. http:www.ffrf.org.fttoday/2001/nov01/nisbett.html (accessed 27 June 2005).

Banerjee, Sumanta. *The Parlour and the Streets: Elite and Popular Culture in Nineteenth Century Calcutta*. Calcutta: Seagull Books, 1989.

Barbados Gays and Lesbians Against Discrimination. http:bglad2000.tripod.com/articles.html (accessed 15 August 2009).

Barriteau, Eudine, ed. *Confronting Power, Theorizing Gender: Interdisciplinary Perspectives in the Caribbean*. Kingston, Jamaica: University of the West Indies Press, 2003.

———. "Requiem for the Male Marginalization Thesis in the Caribbean: Death of a Non-Theory." In E. Barriteau, *Confronting Power, Theorizing Gender*, 324–55.

Barriteau, Violet Eudine. "Conclusion: Beyond a Backlash—The Frontal Assault on Containing Caribbean Women in the Decade of the 1990s." In Tang Nain and Bailey, *Gender Equality in the Caribbean*, 201–32.

———. "Confronting Power and Politics: A Feminist Theorizing of Gender in Commonwealth Caribbean Societies." *Meridians: Feminism, Race, Transnationalism* 3 (2003): 57–92.

Barrow, Christine, ed. *Caribbean Portraits: Essays on Gender Ideologies and Identities*. Kingston, Jamaica: Ian Randle, 1998.

Barrow, Christine, Marjan de Bruin, and Robert Carr, eds. *Sexuality, Social Exclusion, and Human Rights: Vulnerability in the Caribbean Context of HIV*. Kingston, Jamaica: Ian Randle, 2009.

Barzilai, Martin. "La douleur des makoumés: Homophobie en Martinique." *Têtu* 121 (April 2007): 112–15.

Basch, Linda G., Nina Glick Schiller, and Christina Szanton Blanc. *Nations Unbound: Transnational Projects, Postcolonial Predicaments, and Deterritorialized Nation States*. Gordon & Breach Science, 1994.

Baumeister, Roy. "Gender Difference in Erotic Plasticity: The Female Sex Drive as Socially Flexible and Responsive." *Psychological Bulletin* 126 (2000): 347–74.

Bayly, Susan. *Caste, Society and Politics in India from the 18th Century to the Modern Age.* Cambridge: Cambridge University Press, 1999.

Beckles, Hilary. "Capitalism, Slavery, and Caribbean Modernity." *Callaloo* 20, no. 4 (1997): 777–89.

Beckles, Hilary, and Verene Shepherd. *Engendering History: Caribbean Women in Historical Perspective.* Kingston, Jamaica: Ian Randle, 1995.

Beenie Man. *That's Right.* Diwali Greensleeves Rhythm Album 27. Isleworth, Middlesex, UK: Greensleeves Records, 2002.

Belton, Don, ed. *Speak My Name: Black Men on Masculinity and the American Dream.* Boston: Beacon, 1995.

Benítez-Rojo, Antonio. *The Repeating Island: The Caribbean and the Postmodern Perspective.* Durham, NC: Duke University Press, 1996.

Bennet, James. "Clinton Has Knee Surgery to Repair Tendon After Fall." *New York Times,* 15 March 1997. http://www.nytimes.com/1997/03/15/us/clinton-has-knee-surgery-to-repair-tendon-after-fall.html?pagewanted=all (accessed 19 July 2010).

Bergmann, Emilie L., and Paul Julian Smith, eds. *¿Entiendes? Queer Readings, Hispanic Writings.* Durham, NC: Duke University Press, 1995.

Beriss, David. *Black Skins, French Voices: Caribbean Ethnicity and Activism in Urban France.* Boulder, CO: Westview, 2004.

Berlant, Lauren. *The Queen of America Goes to Washington City: Essays on Sex and Citizenship.* Durham, NC: Duke University Press, 1997.

Bernabé, Jean, Patrick Chamoiseau, and Rafael Confiant. *Eloge de la créolité: In Praise of Creoleness; Edition bilingue français/anglais.* Trans. M. B. Taleb-Khyar. Paris: Gallimard, 1993.

Best, Robert. "Punishing Sinners for Their Sins." *Daily Nation* (Bridgetown, Barbados), 11 March 1997, 6.

Bhabba, Homi K. *Nation and Narration.* London: Routledge, 1990.

"The 'Billing's' Over." *Daily Nation* (Bridgetown, Barbados), 16 April 1997, 11A.

"Bill Wreaking Havoc." *Private-eye,* 10 April 1997, 9.

Binnie, Jon. *The Globalization of Sexuality.* London: Sage, 2004.

Black, Stephanie, dir. *Life and Debt.* New Yorker Video, 2003.

Blaine, Betty Ann. "Jamaica the worst case on earth." *Jamaica Observer,* 2 May 2006.

Bolland, Nigel. "Creolization and Creole Societies: A Cultural Nationalist View." In *Intellectuals in the Twentieth-Century Caribbean,* ed. Alistair Hennessy, 1:50–79. London: Macmillan Caribbean, 1992.

Bowen, John R. *Why the French Don't Like Headscarves: Islam, the State, and Public Space.* Princeton, NJ: Princeton University Press, 2008.

Boyce Davies, Carole. *Black Women, Writing and Identity: Migrations of the Subject.* London: Routledge, 1994.

Brand, Dionne. *Bread Out of Stone: Recollections, Sex, Recognitions, Race, Dreaming, Politics.* Toronto: Coach House, 1994.

Brathwaite, Edward. *The Arrivants: A New World Trilogy.* Oxford: Oxford University Press, 1981.

Brathwaite, Kamau. "Caliban, Ariel and Unprospero in the Conflict of Creolization: A Study of the Slave Revolt in Jamaica, 1831–32." *Comparative Perspectives on Slavery in New World Plantation Societies, Annals of the New York Academy of Sciences* 292 (27 June 1977): 41–62.

———. *The Development of Creole Society.* 1971. Kingston, Jamaica: Ian Randle, 2005.

———. "The Dream Sycorax Letter." *Black Renaissance / Renaissance Noire* 1, no. 1 (1996): 120–36.

Braziel, Jana Evans. *Artists, Performers, and Black Masculinity in the Haitian Diaspora.* Bloomington: Indiana University Press, 2008.

Brennan, Denise. *What's Love Got to Do with It? Transnational Desires and Sex Tourism in the Dominican Republic.* Durham, NC: Duke University Press, 2004.

———. "Women Work, Men Sponge, and Everyone Gossips: Macho Men and Stigmatized/ing Women in a Sex Tourist Town." *Anthropological Quarterly* 77, no. 4 (2004): 705–33.

Brice-Finch, Jacqueline. "Buxton Spice (Book Review)." *World Literature Today* 74, no. 1 (2000): 224.

Brodber, Erna. *Jane and Louisa Will Soon Come Home.* London: New Beacon Books, 1980.

Bryce, Jane. "Review of Oonya Kempadoo, *Buxton Spice* and Shani Mootoo, *Cereus Blooms at Night.*" *Wasafiri* 30 (Autumn 1999): 72–73.

Burnard, Trevor. *Master, Tyranny, and Desire: Thomas Thistlewood and His Slaves in the Anglo-Jamaican World.* Chapel Hill: University of North Carolina Press, 2004.

Bush, Barbara. *Slave Women in Caribbean Society, 1650–1838.* Bloomington: Indiana University Press, 1990.

Butler, Judith. *Bodies That Matter: On The Discursive Limits of "Sex."* New York: Routledge, 1993.

———. *Gender Trouble: Feminism and the Subversion of Identity.* 10th Anniversary Edition. New York: Routledge, 1999.

Calhoun, Cheshire. "Separating Lesbian Theory from Feminist Theory." *Ethics* 104 (April 1994): 558–81.

Calhoun, Craig, Edward LiPuma, and Moishe Postone. *Bourdieu: Critical Perspectives.* Chicago: University of Chicago Press, 1993.

Callahan, John F. *In the African-American Grain: Call-and-Response in Twentieth-Century Black Fiction.* Champaign: University of Illinois Press, 1989.

Camus, Albert. "Create Dangerously." In *Resistance, Rebellion, and Death*, trans. Justin O'Brien, 249–72. New York: Knopf, 1961.

Cantet, Laurent, dir. *Heading South.* With Charlotte Rampling, Karen Young, and Louise Portal. Soda Pictures, 2006.

Caribbean Gender and Trade Network. "The Impact of the Trade Liberalisation on Women's Livelihoods and Their Response: Beijing+10 Meets WTO+10—The Bird in the Hand." 8 February 2004. http:www.cafra.org/article.php3?id_article=346.

Carnegie, Charles V. "The Dundus and the Nation." In *Postnationalism Prefigured: Caribbean Borderlands*, 15–40. New Brunswick, NJ: Rutgers University Press, 2002.

Carr, Robert. "On 'Judgements': Poverty, Sexuality-Based Violence and Human Rights in 21st Century Jamaica." *Caribbean Journal of Social Work* 2 (July 2003): 71–87.

Cazenave, Odile. "Calixthe Beyala's Parisian Novels: An Example of Globalization and Transculturation in French Society." In "Women/Femmes," ed. Isabelle de Courtivron et al., special issue, *Sites: The Journal of 20th Century / Contemporary French Studies* 3, no. 2 (2000): 119–27.

———. "Écriture des sexualités dans le roman francophone au feminin." *Notre Librairie* 151 (July–September 2003): 58–65.

———. "Francophone Women Writers in France in the Nineties." In *Beyond French Feminisms: Debate on Women, Politics, and Culture in France, 1980–2001*, ed. Roger Célestin, Eliane Dalmolin, and Isabelle de Courtivron, 129–42. New York: Palgrave Macmillan, 2002.

———. "Le roman africain et antillais: Nouvelles formes d'engagement au féminin." In *Enseigner le monde noir: En hommage à Jacques Chevrier*, 499–513. Paris: Maisonneuve & Larose, 2007.

Césaire, Aimé. *Notebook of a Return to the Native Land.* Trans. Clayton Eshleman and Annette Smith. Middletown, CT: Wesleyan University Press, 2001.

———. *A Tempest.* Trans. Richard Miller. New York: Ubu, 1992.

———. *Une Tempête.* Paris: Seuil, 1969.

Channer, Colin. *Waiting in Vain.* New York: One World, 1998.

Chatterjee, Partha. *Nationalist Thought and the Colonial World.* Delhi: Oxford University Press, 1986.

———. *The Nation and Its Fragments.* Princeton, NJ: Princeton University Press, 1993.

Chávez-Silverman, Susana, and Librada Hernández. *Reading and Writing the Ambiente: Queer Sexualities in Latino, Latin American, and Spanish Culture.* Madison: University of Wisconsin Press, 2000.

Chevannes, Barry. *Rastafari: Roots and Ideology.* Syracuse, NY: Syracuse University Press, 1994.

Chin, Stacey-Ann. *The Other Side of Paradise: A Memoir.* New York: Scribner, 2009.

Chin, Timothy. "'Bullers' and 'Battymen': Contesting Homophobia in Black Popular Culture and Contemporary Caribbean Literature." *Callaloo* 20, no. 1 (1997): 127–41.

Christian, Barbara. "The Race for Theory." In *Making Face, Making Soul: Haciendo Caras; Creative and Critical Perspectives by Women of Color,* ed. Gloria Anzaldúa, 335–45. San Francisco: Aunt Lute, 1990.

Clarke, Cheryl. "The Failure to Transform: Homophobia in the Black Community." In *Dangerous Liaisons: Blacks, Gays, and the Struggle for Equality,* ed. E. Brandt. New York: New Press, 1999.

Clarke, Roberta. *Women in Trade Unions in Trinidad and Tobago.* IDP Women Working Papers, 17. Geneva: International Labour Office, 1993.

Cliff, Michelle. *Abeng.* New York: Crossing, 1984.

———. "Caliban's Daughter: The Tempest and the Teapot." *Frontiers: A Journal of Women's Studies* 12, no. 2 (1991): 36–51.

——. *The Land of Look Behind.* Ann Arbor, MI: Firebrand Books, 1985.

——. *No Telephone to Heaven.* New York: Vintage International, 1989.

Clifford, James. "A Politics of Neologism: Aimé Césaire." In *The Predicament of Culture: Twentieth-Century Ethnography, Literature, and Art,* 175–81. Cambridge, MA: Harvard University Press, 1988.

Cobham, Rhonda. "'Mwen Na Rien, Msieu': Jamaica Kincaid and the Problem of Creole Gnosis." *Callaloo* 25, no. 3 (2002): 868–84.

Cohen, William. B. "The Algerian War and French Memory." *Contemporary European History* 9, no. 3 (2000): 489–500.

Comins, D. *A Note on Emigration from India to Trinidad.* Calcutta: Bengal Secretarial Press, 1893.

Comvalius, Th. A. C. "Een der vormen van de Surinaamsche lied na 1863." *De West Indische Gids* 20, no. 22 (1939): 355–60.

Conde, Mary. "The Flight from Certainty in Shani Mootoo's *Cereus Blooms at Night.*" In *Flight from Certainty: The Dilemma of Identity and Exile,* ed. Anne Luyat and Francine Tolron, 63–70. Amsterdam: Rodopi, 2001.

Condé, Maryse. *Les belles ténébreuses.* Paris: Mercure de France, 2008.

——. *La colonie du nouveau monde.* Paris: Laffont, 1993.

——. *Desirada.* Paris: Mercure de France, 1997.

——. "Finalement, on va arriver à simplement dire: Je suis ce que je suis." Interview by Catherine Dana. In "Masculin/Féminin," special issue, *Africultures* 35 (February 2001): 19–25.

——. *Histoire de la femme cannibale.* Paris: Mercure de France, 2003.

——. *La migration des coeurs.* Paris: Lafrront, 1995.

——. "O Brave New World." *Research in African Literatures* 29 (Fall 1998): 2–7.

——. *Pays mêlé.* Paris: Hatier, 1986.

Cooper, Carolyn. "Lyrical Gun: Metaphor and Role-Play in Jamaican Dancehall Culture." *Massachusetts Review* 35, nos. 3–4 (1994): 145–78.

——. *Noises in the Blood: Orality, Gender, and the "Vulgar" Body of Jamaican Popular Culture.* London: Macmillan, 1993; Durham, NC: Duke University Press, 1995.

——. "Race and the Cultural Politics of Self-Representation: A View from the University of the West Indies." *Research in African Literatures* 27 (Winter 1996): 97–99.

——. "Slackness Hiding from Culture: Erotic Play in the Dancehall." In Cooper, *Noises in the Blood,* 136–73.

——. *Sound Clash: Jamaican Dancehall Culture at Large.* New York: Palgrave Macmillan, 2004.

Cornell, Drucilla. *At the Heart of Freedom: Feminism, Sex, and Equality.* Princeton, NJ: Princeton University Press, 1998.

——. *The Imaginary Domain: Abortion, Pornography, and Sexual Harassment.* New York: Routledge, 1995.

Cornell, Drucilla, and bell hooks. "The Imaginary Domain: A Discussion between Drucilla Cornell and bell hooks." *Women's Rights Law Reporter* 19, no. 3 (1998): 261–65.

Cowley, John. *Carnival, Canboulay, and Calypso: Traditions in the Making.* New York: Cambridge University Press, 1996.

Crenshaw, Kimberle. "Mapping the Margins: Intersectionality, Identity Politics, and Violence against Women of Color." *Stanford Law Review* 43, no. 6 (1991): 1241–99.

Crichlow, Warren. "Be Like Who? On Race, Role Models and Difference in Higher Education." In *Equity and How To Get It: Rescuing Graduate Studies,* ed. K. Armatage. Toronto: Inanna, 1999.

Crowley, Daniel J. "The Traditional Masques of Carnival." In *Trinidad Carnival: A Republication of the Caribbean Quarterly Trinidad Carnival Issue Volume 4, Numbers 3 & 4 of 1956,* 42–90. Port of Spain, Trinidad and Tobago: Paria, 1988.

Cruz, Angie. *Soledad.* New York: Simon & Schuster, 2001.

———. "Writing has to be Generous: An Interview with Angie Cruz." By Silvio Torres-Saillant. *Calabash: A Journal of Caribbean Arts and Letters* 2 (Summer–Fall 2003): 108–27.

Cruz-Malavé, Arnaldo, and Martin F. Manalansan IV. *Queer Globalizations: Citizenship and the Afterlife of Colonialism.* New York: New York University Press, 2002.

Cuarón, Alfonso. "Sexual Awakenings and Stark Social Realities: An Interview with Alfonso Cuarón." By A. G. Basoli. *Cinéaste* 27 (Summer 2002): 26–29.

———, dir. *Y tu mamá también.* Written by Alfonso Cuarón and Carlos Cuarón. DVD. English subtitles by Manuel Billeter. MGM Home Entertainment, 2002.

Dacres, Petrina, et al. "Discussion Forum." In "Caribbean Locales and Global Artworlds," ed. Annie Paul and Krista Thompson, special issue, *Small Axe,* no. 16 (2004).

Daley, Annette M. "Body and Soul: Religion and Caribbean Women." PhD thesis, University of Queensland, 2001.

Danticat, Edwidge. *Breath, Eyes, Memory.* New York: Random House, 1994.

Dash, Michael. "The Disappearing Island: Haiti, History, and the Hemisphere." Lecture delivered at New York University, 20 March 2004.

Davis, Angela. *Blues Legacies and Black Feminism.* New York: Random House, 1998.

Decena, Carlos Ulises. "Tacit Subjects." *GLQ: A Journal of Lesbian and Gay Studies* 14, nos. 2–3 (2008): 339–59.

De Certeau, Michel. *The Writing of History.* Trans. T. Conley. New York: Columbia University Press, 1988.

Delany, S. "Street Talk/Straight Talk." *Differences: A Journal of Feminist Cultural Studies* 3 (Summer 1991): 21–38.

Deleuze, Gilles, and Félix Guattari. *Qu'est-ce que la philosophie?* Paris: Minuit, 1991. Trans. Hugh Tomlinson and Graham Burchell as *What is Philosophy?* (New York: Columbia University Press, 1994).

Denizet-Lewis, Benoit. "Double Lives on the Down Low." *New York Times Magazine,* 3 August 2003, 28–33, 48, 52–53.

Diamond, Lisa. "Passionate Friendships among Adolescent Sexual-Minority Women." *Journal of Research on Adolescence* 10, no. 2 (2000): 191–209.

Donnell, Alison. "Sexing the Subject: Writing and the Politics of Caribbean Sexual Identity." In *Twentieth Century Caribbean Literature*, 181–250. New York: Routledge, 2006.

———. "The Spectacle of Deviance and the Staging of Difference: Sexual Identities in Shani Mootoo's *Cereus Blooms at Night*." Paper presented at the 21st annual conference on West Indian Literature, University of the West Indies, Cave Hill, 24–26 March 2002.

———. "What It Means to Stay: Reterritorialising the Black Atlantic in Erna Brodber's Writing of the Local." *Third World Quarterly* 26, no. 2 (2005): 479–86.

Doty, Alexander. *Making Things Perfectly Queer: Interpreting Mass Culture*. Minneapolis: University of Minnesota Press, 1993.

Douglas, Claude. *Homosexuality in the Caribbean: Crawling Out of the Closet*. St. Andrew, Grenada: Maryzoon, 2008.

Downes, Aviston. "Gender and Elementary Teaching Service in Barbados, 1880–1960: A Re-examination of the Feminization and Marginalization of the Black Male Theses." In E. Barriteau, *Confronting Power, Theorizing Gender*, 303–23.

Dracius, Suzanne. *L'autre qui danse*. Paris: Seghers, 1989.

———. *Rue Monte au ciel*. Fort-de-France, Martinique: Desnel, 2003.

ECLAC/UNIFEM. *Eliminating Gender-Based Violence, Ensuring Equality: ECLAC/ UNIFEM Regional Assessment of Actions to End Violence Against Women in the Caribbean*. ECLAC Series No. LC/CAR/G.764. 2003. http://www.eclac.org/ cgi-bin/getProd.asp?xml=/publicaciones/xml/0/38620/P38620.xml&xsl=/ portofspain/tpl-i/p9f.xsl&base=/socinfo/tpl-i/top-bottom.xslt.

Edmondson, Belinda. *Making Men: Gender, Literary Authority, and Women's Writing in Caribbean Narrative*. Durham, NC: Duke University Press, 1999.

Ehrenreich, Barbara, and Arlie Russell Hochschild. *Global Woman: Nannies, Maids, and Sex Workers in the New Economy*. New York: Henry Holt, 2006.

Emecheta, Buchi. *The Family*. Oxford: Heinemann, 1992.

Emmer, P. C. "The Meek Hindu: The Recruitment of Indian Indentured Labourers for Service Overseas, 1870–1916." In *Colonialism and Migration: Indentured Labour Before and After Slavery*. ed. P. C. Emmer, 187–207. Dordrecht, Netherlands: Martinus Nijhoff, 1986.

Eng, David L. *Racial Castration: Managing Masculinity in Asian America*. Durham, NC: Duke University Press, 2001.

Enloe, Cynthia. *Bananas, Beaches, and Bases: Making Feminist Sense of International Politics*. Berkeley and Los Angeles: University of California Press, 1990.

Epps, Brad, Keja Valens, and Bill Johnson González, eds. *Passing Lines: Sexuality and Immigration*. Cambridge, MA: Harvard University, David Rockefeller Center for Latin American Studies, 2005.

Eriksen, Erik. *Gandhi's Truth: On the Origins of Militant Non-Violence*. London: Faber & Faber, 1970.

Espín, Olivia. *Women Crossing Boundaries: A Psychology of Immigration and Transformations of Sexuality*. London: Routledge, 1999.

Espinet, Ramabai. *The Swinging Bridge*. Toronto: HarperCollins 2003.

Evans, David. *Sexual Citizenship: The Material Construction of Sexualities.* London: Routledge, 1993.

Evanson, Heather. "Crushed by His Love." *Sunday Sun* (Bridgetown, Barbados), 3 July 2005, 16A.

Faderman, Lillian. *Surpassing the Love of Men: Romantic Friendship and Love between Women from the Renaissance to the Present.* New York: Morrow, 1981.

Fanon, Frantz. *Black Skin, White Masks.* Trans. Charles Lam Markmann. New York: Grove, 1967.

Ferguson, Kathy. *The Man Question: Visions of Subjectivity in Feminist Theory.* Berkeley and Los Angeles: University of California Press, 1993.

Ferguson, Roderick A. *Aberrations in Black: Toward a Queer of Color Critique.* Minneapolis: University of Minnesota Press, 2004.

———. "Of Our Normative Strivings: African American Studies and the Histories of Sexuality." *Social Text* 23, nos. 3–4 (2005): 85–100.

Findlay, Eileen. *Imposing Decency: The Politics of Sexuality and Race in Puerto Rico, 1870–1920.* Durham, NC: Duke University Press, 1999.

Firmin, Anténor. *De l'égalité des races humaines: Anthropologie positive.* 1885. Montreal: Mémoire d'encrier, 2005.

———. *The Equality of the Human Races.* Trans. Asselin Charles. New York: Garland, 2000.

Fischer, Louis. *The Life of Mahatma Gandhi.* London: Cape, 1951.

"Fitting the Bill to a 'T.'" *Sun on Saturday* (Bridgetown, Barbados), 22 February 1997, *Pudding and Souse.*

Ford-Smith, Honor. "Ring Ding in a Tight Corner: Sistren, Collective Democracy, and the Organization of Cultural Production." In *Feminist Genealogies, Colonial Legacies, Democratic Futures,* ed. M. Jacqui Alexander and Chandra Talpade Mohanty, 213–58. New York: Routledge, 1997.

Foster, Robert J. "Making National Cultures in the Global Ecumene." *Annual Review of Anthropology* 20 (1991): 235–60.

Foucault, Michel. *The History of Sexuality.* Vol. 1, *An Introduction.* Trans. Robert Hurley. New York: Vintage, 1990.

———. "Truth and Power." In *Power/Knowledge: Selected Interviews and Other Writings, 1972–1977, by Michel Foucault,* ed. Colin Gordon, trans. Colin Gordon et al., 109–33. New York: Pantheon, 1980.

Francis, Donette. *Fictions of Feminine Citizenship: Sexuality and the Nation in Contemporary Caribbean Literature.* New York: Palgrave Macmillan, 2009.

———. "Uncovered Stories: Politicizing Sexual Histories in Third Wave Caribbean Women's Writing." *Black Renaissance/Renaissance Noire* 6, no. 1 (2004): 61–81.

Franco, Pamela. "The 'Unruly Woman' in Nineteenth-Century Trinidad Carnival." *Small Axe,* no. 7 (2000): 60–76.

Freeman, Carla. *High Tech and High Heels in the Global Economy: Women, Work, and Pink-Collar Identities in the Caribbean.* Durham, NC: Duke University Press, 2000.

Froude, James Anthony. *The English in the West Indies, or the Bow of Ulysses.* London: Longman's Green, 1888.

Frye, Marilyn. *The Politics of Reality: Essays on Feminist Theory.* New York: Crossing, 1983.

Fusco, Coco. "Hustling for Dollars: Jineterismo in Cuba." In Kempadoo and Doezema, *Global Sex Workers,* 151–66.

Gale, Derek. "Gays Deserve Equal Right." *Sun on Saturday* (Bridgetown, Barbados), 18 January 1997, 13.

Gallagher, Catherine, and Charles Laqueur. *The Making of the Modern Body.* Berkeley and Los Angeles: University of California Press, 1987.

Gandhi, M. K. "Abolition of Indentured Emigration." In Gandhi, *My Experiments with Truth,* 2:346–54.

———. *The Collected Works of Mahatma Gandhi.* 100 vols. Delhi: Publications Division, Ministry of Information and Broadcasting, Government of India, 1958–84.

———. "Indentured Labour." In Gandhi, *Collected Works,* 13:247–50.

———. "Indenture or Slavery?" In Gandhi, *Collected Works,* 13:146–48.

———. *My Experiments with Truth: An Autobiography.* Ahmedabad: Navajivan, 1968.

———. *Satyagraha in South Africa.* Vol. 3 of *Selected Works of Mahatma Gandhi,* ed. S. Narayan. Ahmedabad: Navajivan, 1969.

———. "Speech at Surat on Indenture." In Gandhi, *Collected Works,* 13:347–51.

———. "Speech on Indentured Labour at Bombay." In Gandhi, *Collected Works,* 13:130–34.

Garber, Marjorie. *Vested Interests: Cross-Dressing and Cultural Anxiety.* New York: Routledge, 1992.

Garner, Kerwin. "Mekking the Billing Issue Clear." *Investigator* (Bridgetown, Barbados), 23 May 1997, 9.

Garraway, Doris. *The Libertine Colony: Creolization in the Early French Caribbean.* Durham, NC: Duke University Press, 2005.

Gay, Judith. "'Mummies and Babies,' and Friends and Lovers in Lesotho." *Journal of Homosexuality* 11 (1985): 69–81.

"Gay Around the World." *Oprah Winfrey Show.* ABC. 24 October 2007.

Gerhart, Ann. "Terry McMillan's Epilogue to 'Groove' Affair Author Files for Divorce, Claiming Husband Is Gay." *Washington Post,* 29 June 2005, C01.

Gilkes, Al. "The 'Outside Woman' of the 90's." *Sun on Sunday* (Bridgetown, Barbados), 23 February 1997, 9A.

———. "Tough Being a Bajan Bill." *Sun on Sunday* (Bridgetown, Barbados), 2 March 1997, 9A.

Gill, Lyndon Kamal. "Transfiguring Trinidad and Tobago: Queer Activism, Erotic Subjectivity, and the Praxis of Black Queer Anthropology." Talk, W. E. B. DuBois Institute, Harvard University, 19 May 2010.

Gilroy, Beryl. *Steadman and Joanna—A Love in Bondage: Dedicated Love in the Eighteenth Century.* New York: Vantage, 1991.

Gilroy, Paul. *The Black Atlantic: Modernity and Double Consciousness.* Cambridge: Cambridge University Press, 1993.

———. *"There Ain't No Black in the Union Jack": The Cultural Politics of Race and Nation.* London: Routledge, 1995.

Ginsburg, Faye, Lila Abu-Lughod, and Brian Larkin. *Media Worlds: Anthropology on New Terrain*. Berkeley and Los Angeles: University of California Press, 2002.

Glave, Thomas. "Toward a Nobility of the Imagination: Jamaica's Shame." In "Genders and Sexualities," ed. Faith Smith, special issue, *Small Axe*, no.7 (2000): 122–26.

———, ed. *Our Caribbean: A Gathering of Lesbian and Gay Writing from the Antilles*. Durham, NC: Duke University Press, 2008.

———. "Whose Caribbean? An Allegory, in Part." *Callaloo* 27, no. 3 (2004): 671–81.

———. *Words to Our Now: Imagination and Dissent*. Minneapolis: University of Minnesota Press, 2005.

Glissant, Édouard. *Poetics of Relation*. Trans. Betsy Wing. Ann Arbor: University of Michigan Press, 1997.

Gobineau, Comte Arthur de. *Essai sur l'inégalité des races humaines*. 4 vols. Paris: Firmin-Didot, 1884.

Goldberg, Jonathan. *Sodometries: Renaissance Texts, Modern Sexualities*. Stanford, CA: Stanford University Press, 1992.

———. *Tempest in the Caribbean*. Minneapolis: University of Minnesota Press, 2004.

Golding, Bruce. Interview by Stephen Sackur. *Hardtalk*. BBC. 20 May 2008. http://news.bbc.co.uk/2/hi/programmes/hardtalk/7410382.stm.

Goldwert, Marvin. "Mexican Machismo: The Flight from Femininity." *Psychoanalytic Review* 72, no. 1 (1985): 161–69.

Goodison, Lorna. *To Us, All Flowers Are Roses*. Urbana: University of Illinois Press, 1995.

Gopaul, Roanna, Paula Morgan, Rhoda Reddock, and Roberta Clarke. *Women, Family and Family Violence in the Caribbean: The Historical and Contemporary Experience with Special Reference to Trinidad and Tobago*. St. Augustine, Trinidad and Tobago: Center for Gender and Development Studies, University of the West Indies, for the CARICOM Secretariat, 1994.

Gopinath, Gayatri. *Impossible Desires: Queer Diasporas and South Asian Public Cultures*. Durham, NC: Duke University Press, 2003.

Greaves, Gail-Ann. "Call-Response in Selected Calypsos of Political Commentary from the Republic of Trinidad and Tobago." *Journal of Black Studies* 29 (1998): 34–51.

Gregg, Veronica. "Yuh Know Bout Coo-Coo?" In *Questioning Creole*, ed. Verene A. Shepherd and Glen L. Richards, 148–64. Kingston, Jamaica: Ian Randle, 2002.

Gregory, Steven. *The Devil behind the Mirror: Globalization and Politics in the Dominican Republic*. Berkeley and Los Angeles: University of California Press, 2007.

Grewal, Inderpal, and Caren Kaplan. "Global Identities: Theorizing Transnational Studies of Sexuality." *GLQ: A Journal of Lesbian and Gay Studies* 7, no. 4 (2001): 663–79.

———, eds. *Scattered Hegemonies: Postmodernity and Transnational Feminist Practices*. Minneapolis: University of Minnesota Press, 1994.

Griffith, Janice. "Her Wicked Ways Telling." *Sun on Sunday* (Bridgetown, Barbados), 1 March 1997, *Pudding and Souse*, 11.

Gunkel, Henriette. *The Cultural Politics of Female Sexuality in South Africa.* New York: Routledge, 2010.

Gutzmore, Cecil. "Casting the First Stone: Policing of Homo/Sexuality in Jamaican Popular Culture." *Interventions* 6, no. 1 (2004): 118–34.

Halberstam, Judith Jack. "The First Cut Is the Deepest: Collage and Queer/Feminist Negation." Paper presented at the "What is Feminist Politics Now?" conference, Columbia University, New York, 19–20 September 2008.

Hall, Douglas. *In Miserable Slavery: Thomas Thistlewood in Jamaica, 1750–1786.* Kingston, Jamaica: University of the West Indies Press, 1998.

Hall, Stuart. "Cultural Identity and Diaspora." In *Diaspora and Visual Culture: Representing Africans and Jews,* ed. Nicholas Mirzoeff, 21–32. New York: Routledge, 2000.

———. "What is this 'Black' in Black Popular Culture?" In *Stuart Hall: Critical Dialogues in Cultural Studies,* ed. David Morley and Kuan-Hsing Chen, 466–75. London: Routledge, 1996.

———. "Who Needs 'Identity'?" In *Questions of Cultural Identity,* ed. Stuart Hall and Paul du Gay, 1–17. London: Sage, 1996.

———. "Worlds Apart." Pt. 3 of *Portrait of the Caribbean.* Ambrose Video Publishing, 1992.

Halperin, David. *One Hundred Years of Homosexuality: And Other Essays on Greek Love.* New York: Routledge, 1990.

Hammonds, Evelyn. "Black (W)holes and the Geometry of Black Female Sexuality." In *African American Literary Theory: A Reader,* ed. Winston Napier, 482–97. New York: New York University Press, 2000.

Hamri, Sanaa, dir. *Something New.* Universal Studios Home Entertainment, 2006.

Hannerz, Ulf. *Cultural Complexity.* New York: Columbia University Press, 1992.

Harper, Phillip Brian. *Are We Not Men? Masculine Anxiety and the Problem of African American Identity.* New York: Oxford University Press, 1993.

Hartman, Saidiya. *Lose Your Mother: A Journey along the Atlantic Slave Route.* New York: Farrar, Straus & Giroux, 2007.

———. *Scenes of Subjection: Terror, Slavery, and Self-Making in Nineteenth-Century America.* New York: Oxford University Press, 1997.

Haver, W. *The Body of This Death: Historicity and Sociality in the Time of AIDS.* Stanford, CA: Stanford University Press, 1996.

Hawley, John C., ed. *Postcolonial, Queer: Theoretical Intersections.* Albany: State University of New York Press, 2001.

Hayes, Jarrod. "Queer Resistance to (Neo-)colonialism in Algeria." In Hawley, *Postcolonial, Queer,* 79–97.

Heereral, Daryl. "Sexually abused girl murdered: Teen killed by relative after years of abuse." *Trinidad Express,* 25 June 2005. http:www.trinidadexpress.com/index.pl/article?id=8533470.

Heng, Geraldine, and Janadas Devan. "State Fatherhood: The Politics of Nationalism, Sexuality, and Race in Singapore." In Parker et al., *Nationalisms and Sexualities,* 343–64.

Hennessy, Rosemary. *Materialist Feminism and the Politics of Discourse*. New York: Routledge, 1993.

———. "Queer Visibility and Commodity Culture." *Cultural Critique* 29 (Winter 1994–95): 31–76.

Herskovits, Melville, and Frances Herskovits. *Suriname Folk-lore*. New York: Columbia University Press, 1936.

Higman, Barry. *Slave Population and Economy in Jamaica, 1807–1834*. Cambridge: Cambridge University Press, 1976.

Hill, Errol. *The Trinidad Carnival: Mandate for a National Theatre*. Austin: University of Texas Press, 1972.

Hoad, Neville. *African Intimacies: Race, Homosexuality, and Globalization*. Minneapolis: University of Minnesota Press, 2007.

Hoad, Richard. "This is War!! The Lowdown." *Weekend Nation* (Bridgetown, Barbados), 27 March 1997, 9.

Hoekstra, Dave. "Homewrecker with a Twist: In 'Bill' Ballad She Loses to the Other Man." *Chicago Sun-Times*, 16 January 1997.

Holton, Robert. "Globalization's Cultural Consequences." In *Annals of the American Academy of Political and Social Science: Dimensions of Globalization*, ed. Lois Ferleger and Jay R. Mandle, 140–52. Newbury Park, CA: Sage, 2000.

"Homosexuality Out of the Closet" (editorial). *Sunday Herald* (Kingston, Jamaica), 29 June–5 July 2003, 4A.

Hope, Donna P. *Inna Di Dancehall: Popular Culture and the Politics of Identity in Jamaica*. Kingston: University of the West Indies Press, 2006.

Horswell, Michael J. *Decolonizing the Sodomite: Queer Tropes of Sexuality in Colonial Andean Culture*. Austin: University of Texas Press, 2005.

Hoyte, Harold. "Not the Real Bill." *Daily Nation* (Bridgetown, Barbados), 24 March 1997, 9A.

Hulme, Peter. *Colonial Encounters: Europe and the Native Caribbean, 1492–1797*. 1986. New York: Routledge, 1992.

Immigration and Refugee Board of Canada. *Barbados: Treatment of Homosexuals, Including Protection Offered by the State and the Attitude of the Population*. 9 March 2007. http:www.unhcr.org/refworld/docid/469cd6a52.html (accessed 14 September 2009).

International Lesbian and Gay Association. http:www.qrd.org/qrd/world/americas/age-of-consent.americas (accessed July 1997).

Jay, Karla, and Joanne Glasgow, eds. *Lesbian Texts and Contexts: Radical Revisions*. New York: New York University Press, 1990.

Jefferson, Thomas. *Notes on the State of Virginia*. 1785. New York: Harper & Row, 1964.

Jenkins, Candice M. *Private Lives, Proper Relations: Regulating Black Intimacy*. Minneapolis: University of Minnesota Press, 2007.

Johnson, E. Patrick, and Mae G. Henderson, eds. *Black Queer Studies: A Critical Anthology*. Durham, NC: Duke University Press, 2001.

Johnson, Tina. "The Impact of Women's Consciousness on the History of the Present." *Social Justice* 17 (Summer 1990): 126–35.

Jones, Steve. "Bisexual-Themed 'Bill' Hits Big for Scott-Adams." *USA Today*, 22 January 1997. http:www.usatoday.com.life/enter/music/lenm606.htm.

Joyce, Mike. "Peggy Scott-Adams: Helping Yourself." *Washington Post*, 21 March 1997, 12.

Kaplan, Caren, Norma Alarcon, and Minoo Moallem, eds. *Between Woman and Nation: Nationalism, Transnational Feminisms, and the State.* Durham, NC: Duke University Press, 1999.

Kapur, Ratna. *Erotic Justice: Law and the New Politics of Postcolonialism.* London: Glasshouse, 2005.

———. "The Tragedy of Victimization Rhetoric: Resurrecting the 'Native' Subject in International/Post-Colonial Feminist Legal Politics." *Harvard Human Rights Journal* 15, no. 1 (2002): 1–38.

Keaton, Trica Danielle. *Muslim Girls and the Other France: Race, Identity Politics, and Social Exclusion.* Bloomington: Indiana University Press, 2006.

Kelly, John D. *A Politics of Virtue: Hinduism, Sexuality, and Countercolonial Discourse in Fiji.* Chicago: University of Chicago Press, 1991.

Kempadoo, Kamala. "Centering Praxis in Policies and Studies of Caribbean Sexuality." In Barrow, de Bruin, and Carr, *Sexuality, Social Exclusion, and Human Rights,* 179–91.

———. *Sexing the Caribbean: Gender, Race, and Sexual Labor.* New York: Routledge, 2004.

———, ed. *Sun, Sex, and Gold: Tourism and Sex Work in the Caribbean.* Lanham, MD: Rowman & Littlefield, 1999.

Kempadoo, Kamala, and Jo Doezema, eds. *Global Sex Workers: Rights, Resistance, and Redefinition.* New York: Routledge, 1998.

Kempadoo, Oonya. *Buxton Spice.* London: Phoenix House, 1998.

Khan, Aisha. "Journey to the Center of the Earth: The Caribbean as Master Symbol." *Cultural Anthropology* 16, no. 3 (2001): 271–302.

Kim-Puri, H. J. "Conceptualizing Gender-Sexuality-State-Nation: An Introduction." *Gender and Society* 19 (April 2005): 137–59.

Kincaid, Jamaica. *Annie John.* New York: Farrrar, Straus & Giroux, 1983.

———. *The Autobiography of My Mother.* New York: Farrar, Straus & Giroux, 1996.

———. *Lucy.* New York: Farrar, Straus & Giroux, 1990.

———. *My Brother.* New York: Farrar, Straus & Giroux, 1997.

———. *A Small Place.* New York: Farrar, Straus & Giroux, 1988.

King, J. L., and Karen Hunter. *On the Down Low.* New York: Harlem, 2005.

King, Katie. "There Are No Lesbians Here." In Cruz-Malavé and Manalansan, *Queer Globalizations,* 33–48.

Kingsley, Charles. *At Last: A Christmas in the West Indies.* 1871. London: Macmillan, 1910.

Klass, Morton. *East Indians in Trinidad: A Study of Cultural Persistence.* 1961. Prospect Heights, IL: Waveland, 1988.

Klein, Melanie. *Love, Guilt, and Reparation, and Other Works, 1921–1945.* London: Virago, 1988.

Ko, Dorothy. "Footbinding and Anti-footbinding in China: The Subject of Pain in the Nineteenth and Early Twentieth Centuries." In *Discipline and the Other Body: Correction, Corporeality, Colonialism,* ed. Steven Pierce and Anupama Rao, 215–42. Durham, NC: Duke University Press, 2006.

Kuntsman, Adi, and Esperanza Miyake. *Out of Place: Interrogating Silences in Queerness/Raciality.* London: Raw Nerve Books, 2008.

Kutzinski, Vera M. *Sugar's Secrets: Race and the Erotics of Cuban Nationalism.* Charlottesville: University Press of Virginia, 1993.

La Fountain-Stokes, Lawrence. "1898 and the History of a Queer Puerto Rican Century: Imperialism, Diaspora, and Social Transformation." In *Chicano/Latino Homoerotic Identities,* ed. David William Foster, 197–215. New York: Garland, 1999.

———. *Queer Ricans: Cultures and Sexualities in the Diaspora.* Minneapolis: University of Minnesota Press, 2009.

Lahens, Yannick. *La couleur de l'aube.* Paris: Sabine Wespieser, 2008.

Lamming, George. *Pleasures of Exile.* 1960. Ann Arbor: University of Michigan Press, 1991.

Lancaster, Roger N. "Subject Honor and Object Shame: The Construction of Male Homosexuality and Stigma in Nicaragua." *Ethnology* 28, no. 2 (1988): 111–26.

Laqueur, Thomas. *Solitary Sex: A Cultural History of Masturbation.* New York: Zone Books, 2003.

Lascelles, Angelo. "Take the high road on morals." *Daily Nation* (Bridgetown, Barbados), 12 July 2005, 10.

Laurence, K. O. *A Question of Labour: Indentured Immigration into Trinidad and British Guiana, 1875–1917.* Kingston, Jamaica: Ian Randle, 1994.

Lazarus-Black, Mindie. "The (Heterosexual) Regendering of a Modern State: Criminalizing and Implementing Domestic Violence Law in Trinidad." *Law and Social Inquiry* 28, no. 4 (2003): 979–1008.

———. "Law and the Pragmatics of Inclusion: Governing Domestic Violence in Trinidad and Tobago." *American Ethnologist* 28, no. 2 (2001): 388–416.

Leap, William L., and Tom Boellstorff. *Speaking in Queer Tongues: Globalization and Gay Language.* Urbana: University of Illinois Press, 2003.

Leiby, Richard. "The Torch Song That's Burning Up the Airwaves." *Washington Post,* 13 January 1997, D1.

Lewis, Jimmy. "Bill." Perf. Peggy Scott-Adams. *Help Yourself.* Miss Butch Records, 1996.

Lewis, Linden, ed. *The Culture of Gender and Sexuality in the Caribbean.* Gainesville: University Press of Florida, 2003.

Lionnet, Françoise. "Inscriptions of Exile: The Body's Knowledge and the Myth of Authenticity in Myriam Warner-Vieyra and Suzanne Dracius-Pinalie." In *Postcolonial Representations: Women, Literature, Identity,* 87–100. Ithaca, NY: Cornell University Press, 1995.

Lipkin, Arthur. *Beyond Diversity Day: A Q&A on Gay and Lesbian Issues in Schools.* Lanham, MD: Rowman & Littlefield, 2004.

———. *Understanding Homosexuality, Changing Schools*. Boulder, CO: Westview, 2001.

Lloyd, Moya. *Beyond Identity Politics: Feminism, Power and Politics*. London: Sage, 2005.

Lokaisingh-Meighoo, Sean. "Jahaji Bhai: Notes on the Masculine Subject and Homoerotic Subtext of Indo-Caribbean Identity." In "Genders and Sexualities," ed. Faith Smith, special issue, *Small Axe*, no. 7 (2000): 77–92.

Lord, Ndelamiko. "All One People." *Barbados Advocate*, 7 March 1997, *Hype Magazine*, 4.

Lorde, Audre. *Sister/Outsider: Essays and Speeches*. Freedom, CA: Crossing, 1984.

———. *Zami: A New Spelling of My Name*. Freedom, CA: Crossing, 1982.

Luibhéid, Eithne. *Entry Denied: Controlling Sexuality at the Border*. Minneapolis: University of Minnesota Press, 2002.

Luibhéid, Eithne, and Lionel Cantú Jr., eds. *Queer Migrations: Sexuality, U.S. Citizenship, and Border Crossings*. Minneapolis: University of Minnesota Press, 2005.

MacIntyre, Alasdair. "Epistemological Crises, Dramatic Narrative and the Philosophy of Science." *Monist* 60, no. 4 (1977): 453–72.

MacKinnon, Catharine. *Feminism Unmodified*. Cambridge, MA: Harvard University Press, 1987.

Mahabir, Noor Kumar. *The Still Cry: Personal Accounts of East Indians in Trinidad and Tobago during Indentureship (1845–1917)*. Ithaca, NY: Calaloux, 1985.

Manalansan, Martin F., IV. "Speaking in Transit: Queer Language and Translated Lives." In *Global Divas: Filipino Gay Men in the Diaspora*, 45–61. Durham, NC: Duke University Press, 2003.

Mangru, Basdeo. "The Sex Ratio Disparity and its Consequences under the Indenture in British Guiana." In *India in the Caribbean*, ed. David Dabydeen and Brinsley Samaroo, 211–30. London: University of Warwick for Hansib, 1987.

Marshall, Paule. "Brazil." In *Soul Clap Hands and Sing*, 131–75. New York: Atheneum, 1961.

Martí, José. "The Monetary Conference of the American Republics." In *José Martí: Selected Writings*, trans. Esther Allen, 304–10. New York: Penguin, 2002.

Martinez-Alier, Verena. *Marriage, Class, and Colour in Nineteenth-Century Cuba: A Study of Racial Attitudes and Sexual Values in a Slave Society*. 1974. Ann Arbor: University of Michigan Press, 1989.

Massad, Joseph Andoni. "Re-Orienting Desire: The Gay International and the Arab World." *Public Culture* 14, no. 2 (2002): 361–85.

Massiah, Joycelin. Preface to Tang Nain and Bailey, *Gender Equality in the Caribbean*, xii–xviii.

Matthews, Aaron, dir. *My American Girls: A Dominican Story*. Filmmakers Library, 2000.

Maurer, Bill. *Symbolic Sexuality and Economic Work: The Meanings of Gender and Eroticism in Dominica, West Indies*. East Lansing: Women in International Development, Michigan State University, 1990.

McClintock, Anne. *Imperial Leather: Race, Gender, and Sexuality in the Colonial Contest.* New York: Routledge, 1995.

McHenry, J. Patrick. *A Short History of Mexico.* Rev. ed. New York: Dolphin, 1970.

McMillan, Terry. *How Stella Got Her Groove Back.* New York: Viking, 1996.

Meighoo, Kirk. *Politics in a Half Made Society: Trinidad and Tobago, 1925–2001.* Kingston, Jamaica: Ian Randle, 2003.

Mendes, John. *Cote ce cote la.* Arima, Trinidad and Tobago: John Mendes, 1986.

Mercer, Kobena. "Decolonisation and Disappointment: Reading Fanon's Sexual Politics." In *The Fact of Blackness: Frantz Fanon and Visual Representation,* ed. Alan Read, 115–31. London: Institute of Contemporary Arts; Seattle: Bay Press, 1996.

Merry, Sally Engle. "Rights Talk and the Experience of Law: Implementing Women's Human Rights to Protection from Violence." *Human Rights Quarterly* 25, no. 2 (2003): 43–81.

Minow, Martha. "Surviving Victim Talk." *UCLA Law Review* 40 (1992–93): 1441–45.

Mintz, Sidney. "Enduring Substances, Trying Theories: The Caribbean Region as Oikoumene." *Journal of the Royal Anthropological Institute* 2, no. 2 (1996): 289–311.

Mohammed, Patricia. "The Future of Feminism in the Caribbean." *Feminist Review* 64 (Spring 2000): 116–19.

———. "Reflections on the Women's Movement in Trinidad: Calypsos, Changes, and Sexual Violence." *Feminist Review* 38 (Summer 1991): 33–47.

———. *Rethinking Caribbean "Difference": Feminist Review Issue 59.* New York: Routledge, 1998.

Mohanty, Chandra Talpade, Ann Russo, and Lourdes Torres, eds. *Third World Women and the Politics of Feminism.* Bloomington: Indiana University Press, 1991.

Monson, Ingrid. "Riffs, Repetition, and Theories of Globalization." *Ethnomusicology* 43 (Winter 1999): 31–65.

Moore, Lisa. "Something More Tender Still than Friendship: Romantic Friendship in Early Nineteenth Century England." *Feminist Studies* 18, no. 3 (1992): 499–520.

Mootoo, Shani. *Cereus Blooms at Night.* London: Granta, 1999.

———. *Out on Main Street.* Vancouver: Press Gang, 1993.

Morton, Sarah E., ed. *John Morton of Trinidad, Pioneer Missionary of the Presbyterian Church in Canada to the East Indians in the British West Indies: Journals, Letters and Papers.* Toronto: Westminster, 1916.

Mudimbe, Valentine. *The Invention of Africa: Gnosis, Philosophy, and the Order of Knowledge.* Bloomington: Indiana University Press, 1988.

Mullings, Beverly. "Globalization, Tourism, and the International Sex Trade." In K. Kempadoo, *Sun, Sex, and Gold,* 55–80.

Mulot, Stéphanie. "Je suis la mère, je suis le père!": L'enigme matrifocale." In "Relations familiales et rapports de sexes en Guadeloupe." PhD thesis, Écoles des Hautes Etudes en Sciences Sociales, Paris, 2000.

Muñoz, José Esteban. *Disidentifications: Queers of Color and the Performance of Politics.* Minneapolis: University of Minnesota Press, 1999.

Murdoch, Adlai. "Introduction: Departmentalization's continuing conundrum; Locating the DOM-ROM between 'home' and 'away.'" *International Journal of Francophone Studies* 11, no. 3 (2003): 307–25.

———. "Negotiating the Metropole: Patterns of Exile and Cultural Survival in Gisèle Pineau and Suzanne Dracius-Pinalie." In *Literature of Immigration in France*, ed. Susan Ireland and Patrice J. Proulx, 129–39. Westport, CT: Greenwood, 2001.

Murray, David A. B. "Between a Rock and a Hard Place: The Power and Powerlessness of Transnational Narratives among Gay Martinican Men." *American Anthropologist* 102, no. 2 (2000): 261–70.

———. *Opacity: Gender, Sexuality, Race, and the "Problem" of Identity in Martinique.* New York: Peter Lang, 2002.

Murray, Sonia. "Novelty Song Puts Singer on Comeback Trail." *Atlanta Constitution,* 14 March 1997, P5.

Nair, Supriya. "Expressive Countercultures and Postmodern Utopia: A Caribbean Context." *Research in African Literatures* 27 (Winter 1996): 71–88.

Nanda, B. R. *Gokhale: The Indian Moderates and the British Raj.* Delhi: Oxford University Press, 1977.

Niaah, Sonjah Stanley. *Dancehall: From Slaveship to Ghetto.* Ottawa: University of Ottawa Press, 2010.

———. "Making Space: Kingston's Dancehall Culture and its Philosophy of 'Boundarylessness.'" *African Identities* 2, no. 2 (2004): 117–32.

Nietzsche, Friedrich Wilhelm. *The Gay Science with a Prelude in Rhymes and an Appendix of Songs.* Trans. Walter Kaufmann. New York: Vintage, 1974.

Niranjana, Tejaswini. *Mobilizing India: Women, Music, and Migration between India and Trinidad.* Durham, NC: Duke University Press, 2006.

Nixon, Rob. "Caribbean and African Appropriations of *The Tempest.*" *Critical Inquiry* 13, no. 3 (1987): 557–78.

Noel, Peter. "Batty Boys in Babylon." *Village Voice,* 12 January 1993, 29–36.

"No Homos! Opposition to Gays in the Cabinet." *Sunday Herald,* 8 April 2006.

Nussbaum, Martha. *Cultivating Humanity: A Classical Defense of Reform in Liberal Education.* Cambridge, MA: Harvard University Press, 1997.

———. "Humanities and Human Capabilities." *Liberal Education* 87, no. 3 (2004): 38–45.

O'Callaghan, Evelyn. "'Compulsory Heterosexuality' and Textual/Sexual Alternatives in Selected Texts by West Indian Women Writers." In Barrow, *Caribbean Portraits,* 294–319.

———. "Settling into 'Unhomeliness': Displacement in Selected Caribbean and Caribbean Canadian Women's Writing." *Kunapipi* 26, no. 1 (2004): 182–95.

Ongiri, Amy Abugo. "We are Family: Black Nationalism, Black Masculinity, and the Black Gay Cultural Imagination." In "Queer Utilities: Textual Studies, Theory, Redagogy, Praxis," special issue, *College Literature* 24, no. 1 (1997): 280–94.

Padgett, Tim. "The Most Homophobic Place on Earth?" *Time,* 12 April 2006. http:www.time.com/time/world/article/0,8599,1182991,00.html.

Pantin, Archbishop Anthony. "The Church and the Homosexuals." *Sunday Guardian* (Port of Spain, Trinidad), 1 December 1985, 21.

Parker, Andrew, Mary Russo, Doris Sommer, and Patricia Yaeger, eds. *Nationalisms and Sexualities*. New York: Routledge, 1992.

Parkes, Henry Bamford. *A History of Mexico*. 3rd ed., rev. and enl. Boston: Houghton Mifflin, 1969.

Parris, G. Ricky. "African Views." *Barbados Advocate*, 21 May 1997, 7.

Pathak, Zakia, and Rajeswari Sunder Rajan. "Shahbano." *Signs: Journal of Women in Culture and Society* 14, no. 3 (1989): 558–82.

Patton, Cindy, and Benigno Sánchez-Eppler, eds. *Queer Diasporas*. Durham, NC: Duke University Press, 2000.

Paz, Octavio. "The Sons of La Malinche." In *The Labyrinth of Solitude*, 65–88. 1961. New York: Grove Press, 1965.

Pearse, Andrew. "Carnival in Nineteenth Century Trinidad." In *Trinidad Carnival: A Republication of the Caribbean Quarterly Trinidad Carnival Issue Volume 4, Numbers 3 & 4 of 1956*, 4–41. Port of Spain, Trinidad and Tobago: Paria, 1988.

Pépin, Ernest. "Quelle Guadeloupe voulons-nous?" *Le petit lexique colonial*, 23 January 2009. lepetitlexiquecolonial.blogspace.fr/149227.

Pineau, Gisèle. *L'âme prêtée aux oiseaux*. Paris: Stock, 1998.

———. *Caraïbes sur Seine*. Paris: Dapper, 1999.

———. *C'est la règle*. Paris: Thierry Magnier, 2001.

———. *Chair Piment*. Paris: Mercure de France, 2002.

———. *L'espérance-macadam*. Paris: Stock, 1995.

———. *L'exil selon Julia*. Paris: Albin Michel, 1994.

———. *La grande drive des esprits*. Paris: Le Serpent à Plumes, 1993.

Pollard, Velma. *Dread Talk: The Language of Rastafari*. Kingston, Jamaica: Canoe, 2000.

Poovey, Mary. *Uneven Developments: The Ideological Work of Gender in Mid-Victorian England*. Chicago: University of Chicago Press, 1989.

Powell, Patricia. *Me Dying Trial*. Oxford: Heinemann, 1993.

———. *A Small Gathering of Bones*. Oxford: Heinemann, 1994.

Prado, C. G. *Starting with Foucault: An Introduction to Genealogy*. 2nd ed. Boulder, CO: Westview, 2000.

Pratt, Mary Louise. *Imperial Eyes: Travel Writing and Transculturation*. New York: Routledge, 1992.

Price, Richard, and Sally Price. *Two Evenings in Saramaka*. Chicago: University of Chicago Press, 1991.

Provencher, Dennis. *Queer French: Globalization, Language, and Sexual Citizenship in France*. New York: Ashgate, 2007.

Puar, Jasbir. "Circuits of Queer Mobility: Tourism, Travel, and Globalization." *GLQ: A Journal of Lesbian and Gay Studies* 8, nos. 1–2 (2002): 101–37.

———. *Terrorist Assemblages: Homonationalism in Queer Times*. Durham, NC: Duke University Press, 2007.

Puri, Shalini. "Facing the Music: Gender, Race, and Dougla Poetics." In *The Caribbean Postcolonial: Social Equality, Post-Nationalism, and Cultural Hybridity*, 189–222. New York: Palgrave Macmillan, 2004.

———. "Race, Rape and Representations: Indo-Caribbean Women and Cultural Nationalism." *Cultural Critique* 36 (Spring 1997): 119–63.

Quiroga, José. *Tropics of Desire: Interventions in Queer Latino America.* New York: New York University Press, 2000.

Rahim, Jennifer. "The Operation of the Closet and the Discourse of Unspeakable Contents in *Black Fauns* and *My Brother.*" *Small Axe,* no. 20 (2006): 1–18.

Reddock, Rhoda. "Douglarisation and the Politics of Gender Relations in Trinidad and Tobago." In *Caribbean Sociology: Introductory Readings,* ed. Christine Barrow and Rhoda Reddock, 320–33. Kingston, Jamaica: Ian Randle, 2001.

———, ed. *Interrogating Caribbean Masculinities: Theoretical and Empirical Analyses.* Kingston, Jamaica: University of the West Indies Press, 2004.

———. "Men as Gendered Beings: The Emergence of Masculinity Studies in the Anglophone Caribbean." *Social and Economic Studies* 52, no. 3 (2003): 89–117.

———. "Social Mobility in Trinidad and Tobago, 1960–1980." In *Social and Occupational Stratification in Contemporary Trinidad and Tobago,* ed. Selwyn Ryan, 210–33. St. Augustine, Trinidad and Tobago: Institute for Social and Economic Research, University of the West Indies, 1991.

———. *Women, Labour and Politics in Trinidad and Tobago.* London: Zed Books, 1994.

———. "Women's Organizations and Movements in the Commonwealth Caribbean: The Response to the Global Economic Crisis in the 1980s." *Feminist Review* 59 (Summer 1998): 57–73.

———. "Women's Organizations in the Caribbean Community from the Nineteenth Century to Today." *Women in Action* 2 (1991): 12–15.

Red Thread Women's Development Programme. "'Givin' Lil' Bit fuh Lil' Bit': Women and Sex Work in Guyana." In K. Kempadoo, *Sun, Sex, and Gold,* 263–90.

Reece, Doug. "Scott-Adams Helps Herself to a Comeback." *Rolling Stone,* 15 February 1997, 10–12.

Reid-Pharr, Robert F. *Black Gay Man.* New York: New York University Press, 2001.

———. "Tearing the Goat's Flesh: Homosexuality, Abjection and the Production of a Late Twentieth-Century Black Masculinity." *Studies in the Novel* 28, no. 3 (1996): 372–94.

Renne, Denyse. "Bloody Easter Weekend: Tobago rocked by third murder." *Trinidad Guardian,* 29 March 2005. http:www.guardian.co.tt/archives/2005-03-29/news1.html.

Retamar, Roberto. "Caliban: Notes Towards a Discussion of Culture in Our America." In *Caliban and Other Essays,* trans. Edward Baker, 3–45. Minneapolis: University of Minnesota Press, 1989.

Rey, Terry. "Junta, Rape, and Religion in Haiti, 1993–1994." *Journal of Feminist Studies in Religion* 15, no. 2 (1999): 73–100.

Reynolds, Felisa. "'Almost the same, but not quite / Almost the same but not white': The Question of Literary Cannibalism." PhD diss., Harvard University, 2009.

Rhys, Jean. *Wide Sargasso Sea.* New York: Norton, 1966.

Rich, Adrienne. "Compulsory Heterosexuality and Lesbian Existence." *Signs* 5 (1980): 631–60.

Richards, Peter. "Coming Down Hard on Sex Offences." http://www.ips.org/rights/news/nup251299_02.htm (accessed before 2007).

Riggs, Marlon, dir. *Black Is / Black Aint*. With Essex Hemphill, Bill T. Jones, bell hooks, et al. California Newsreel, 1994.

Robinson, Tracy. "Beyond the Bill of Rights: Sexing the Citizen." In E. Barriteau, *Confronting Power, Theorizing Gender*, 231–61.

———. "Changing Conceptions of Violence: The Impact of Domestic Violence Legislation in the Caribbean." *Caribbean Law Review* 9 (1999): 113–35.

———. "Fictions of Citizenship: Bodies Without Sex: The Production and Effacement of Gender in Law." In "Genders and Sexualities," ed. Faith Smith, special issue, *Small Axe*, no. 7 (2000): 1–27.

———. "Gender, Feminism and Constitutional Reform in the Caribbean." In Bailey and Leo-Rhynie, *Gender in the 21st Century*, 592–625.

Rodríguez, Ileana. *House/Garden/Nation: Space, Gender, and Ethnicity in Post-Colonial Latin American Literatures by Women*. Trans. Robert Carr. Durham, NC: Duke University Press, 1994.

Rodríguez, Juana Maria. *Queer Latinidad: Identity Practices, Discursive Spaces*. New York: New York University Press, 2003.

Rodríguez, María Cristina. *What Women Lose: Exile and the Construction of Imaginary Homelands in Novels by Caribbean Writers*. New York: Peter Lang, 2005.

Rohlehr, Gordon. *Calypso and Society in Pre-Independence Trinidad*. Port of Spain, Trinidad and Tobago: Rohlehr, 1990.

Rolland, Romain. *Mahatma Gandhi*. Zurich: Rotapfel-Verlag, 1924.

Roper, Garnet. "The Church's Same Sex." *Sunday Herald* (Kingston, Jamaica), 29 June–5 July 2003, 4A.

Rosario, Nelly. *Song of the Water Saints*. New York: Pantheon, 2002.

Rose, Tricia. *Black Noise: Rap Music and Black Culture in Contemporary America*. Middletown, CT: Wesleyan University Press, 1994.

Ross, Leone. *All the Blood Is Red*. London: Angela Royal, 1996.

Ross, Marlon B. "Beyond the Closet as Raceless Paradigm." In E. Johnson and Henderson, *Black Queer Studies*, 161–89.

———. "In Search of Black Men's Masculinities." *Feminist Studies* 24, no. 3 (1998): 599–626.

Rowley, Michelle V. "Caribbean In/Humanities." Roundtable, Caribbean Studies Association, Port of Spain, Trinidad and Tobago, June 2006.

———. "Whose Time is It? Gender and Humanism in Contemporary Caribbean Feminist Advocacy." *Small Axe* 14, no. 1 (2010): 1–15.

"Rum Shops Here to Stay." *Private-eye*, 24 April 1997, 8.

Rupp, Leila. "Towards a Global History of Same-Sex Sexuality." *Journal of the History of Sexuality* 10, no. 2 (2001): 287–302.

Salih, Sara, ed. "Focus on Queer Postcolonial." Special issue, *Wasafiri* 50 (Spring 2007).

————. "'Our people know the difference, black is a race, jew is a religion, f*g**tism is a sin': Towards a Queer Postcolonial Hermeneutics." In "Focus on Queer Postcolonial," ed. Sarah Salih, special issue, *Wasafiri* 50 (Spring 2007): 1–5.

Sarkar, Tanika. "Hindu Wife, Hindu Nation: Domesticity and Nationalism in Nineteenth-Century Bengal." In *Hindu Wife, Hindu Nation: Community, Religion and Cultural Nationalism*, 23–52. Delhi: Permanent Black, 2001.

Saunders, Patricia. "Is Not Everything Good to Eat Good to Talk: Sexual Economy and Dancehall Music in the Global Marketplace." *Small Axe*, no. 13 (2003): 95–115.

Schultz, Vicki. "Life's Work." *Columbia Law Review* 100, no. 7 (2000): 1881–1964.

Scott, David. *Refashioning Futures: Criticism after Postcoloniality*. Princeton, NJ: Princeton University Press, 1999.

Scott, Joan Wallach. *The Politics of the Veil*. Princeton, NJ: Princeton University Press, 2007.

Scott, Lawrence. *Aelred's Sin*. London: Allison & Busby, 1998.

————. *Witchbroom*. London: Heinemann, 1993.

Seaga, Edward. "Social Riddles Rooted in Cultural Identity." *Jamaica Gleaner Online*, 15 May 2005. http:www.jamaica_gleaner.com/gleaner/20050515/lead/lead5.html.

Sedgwick, Eve Kosofsky. *Epistemology of the Closet*. Berkeley and Los Angeles: University of California Press, 1990.

————. "How to Bring Your Kids Up Gay." *Social Text* 9, no. 4 (1991): 18–27.

Seidman, Steven. "From Identity to Queer Politics: Shifts in Normative Heterosexuality and the Meaning of Citizenship." *Citizenship Studies* 5, no. 3 (2001): 321–28.

Shakespeare, William. *The Tempest*. London: Oxford University Press, 1994.

Sharpe, Jenny. *Ghosts of Slavery: A Literary Archaeology of Black Women's Lives*. Minneapolis: University of Minnesota Press, 2003.

Sheller, Mimi. *Citizenship from Below: Erotic Agency and Caribbean Freedom*. Durham, NC: Duke University Press, forthcoming.

————. *Consuming the Caribbean: From Arawaks to Zombies*. London: Routledge, 2003.

————. "Work That Body: Sexual Citizenship and Embodied Freedom." In *Constructing Vernacular Culture in the Trans-Caribbean*, ed. Holger Henke and Karl-Heinz Magister, 345–76. Lanham, MD: Lexington Books, 2008.

Shepard, Todd. *The Invention of Decolonization: The Algerian War and the Remaking of France*. Ithaca, NY: Cornell University Press, 2006.

Shewcharan, Narmala. *Tomorrow Is Another Day*. Leeds, UK: Peepal Tree, 1994.

Shin, Andrew, and Barbara Judson. "Beneath the Black Aesthetic: James Baldwin's Primer of Black American Masculinity." *African American Review* 32, no. 2 (1998): 246–61.

Silvera, Makeda. "Man Royals and Sodomites: Some Thoughts on the Invisibility of Afro-Caribbean Lesbians." In *Piece of My Heart: A Lesbian of Colour Anthology*, ed. Makeda Silvera, 14–26. Toronto: Sister Vision, 1991.

Silverstein, Paul. *Algeria in France: Transpolitics, Race, and Nation*. Bloomington: Indiana University Press, 2004.

Sinfield, Alan. "Diaspora and Hybridity: Queer Identities and the Ethnicity Model." In *Diaspora and Visual Culture: Representing Africans and Jews,* ed. Nicholas Mirzoeff, 95–114. New York: Routledge, 2000.

Singh, Jyotsna G. "Caliban versus Miranda: Race and Gender Conflicts in Postcolonial Rewritings of *The Tempest.*" In *Feminist Readings of Early Modern Culture,* ed. Valerie Traub, M. Lindsay Kaplan, and Dympna Callaghan, 191–209. Cambridge: Cambridge University Press, 1996.

Sinha, Mrinalini. "Gender in the Critiques of Colonialism and Nationalism: Locating the 'Indian Woman.'" In *Feminism and History,* ed. Joan Wallach Scott, 477–504. Oxford: Oxford University Press, 1996.

Skelton, Tracey. "Boom, Bye, Bye": Jamaican Ragga and Gay Resistance." In *Mapping Desire: Geographies of Sexualities,* ed. David Bell and Gill Valentine, 264–83. London: Routledge, 1995.

Smith, Barbara. "The Truth That Never Hurts: Black Lesbians in Fiction in the 1980s." In Mohanty, Russo, and Torres, *Third World Women and the Politics of Feminism,* 101–29.

Smith, Faith. *Creole Recitations: John Jacob Thomas and Colonial Formation in the Late Nineteenth Century.* Charlottesville: University of Virginia Press, 2002.

———. "Crosses/Crossroads/Crossings." *Small Axe,* no. 24 (2007): 130–38.

———, ed. "Genders and Sexualities." Special issue, *Small Axe,* no. 7 (2000).

———. Preface to "Genders and Sexualities," ed. Faith Smith. Special issue, *Small Axe,* no. 7 (2000): v–vii.

———. "'You Know You're West Indian If . . .': Codes of Authenticity in Colin Channer's *Waiting in Vain.*" *Small Axe,* no. 10 (2001): 41–59.

Somerville, Siohban. "Queer History of Naturalization." *American Quarterly* 57, no. 3 (2005): 659–75.

———. *Queering the Color Line: Race and the Invention of Homosexuality in American Culture.* Durham, NC: Duke University Press, 2000.

Sommer, Doris. *Foundational Fictions: The National Romances of Latin America.* Berkeley and Los Angeles: University of California Press, 1991.

Spillers, Hortense. "Mama's Baby, Papa's Maybe: An American Grammar Book." *Diacritics* 17, no. 2 (1987): 64–81.

Spivak, Gayatri. "Can the Subaltern Speak? Speculations on Widow Sacrifice." In *Marxism and the Interpretation of Culture,* ed. Cary Nelson and Lawrence Grossberg, 271–316. Urbana: University of Illinois Press, 1988.

Springfield, Consuelo López. *Daughters of Caliban: Caribbean Women in the Twentieth Century.* Bloomington: Indiana University Press, 1997.

"Spurned lover jailed for 10 years." *Daily Nation* (Bridgetown, Barbados), 1 July 2005, 12.

Stephen, Henri J. M. *Winti: Afro-Surinaamse religie en magische rituelen in Suriname en Nederland.* Amsterdam: Karnak, 1985.

Stephens, Michelle Ann. *Black Empire: The Masculine Global Imaginary of Caribbean Intellectuals in the United States, 1914–1962.* Durham, NC: Duke University Press, 2005.

Stockton, Kathryn Bond. *Beautiful Bottom, Beautiful Shame: Where "Black" Meets "Queer."* Durham, NC: Duke University Press, 2006.

Stoler, Ann. *Carnal Knowledge and Imperial Power: Race and the Intimate in Colonial Rule.* Berkeley and Los Angeles: University of California Press, 2002.

———, ed. *Haunted by Empire: Geographies of Intimacy in North American History.* Durham, NC: Duke University Press, 2006.

———. *Race and the Education of Desire: Foucault's "History of Sexuality" and the Colonial Order of Things.* Durham, NC: Duke University Press, 1995.

Stout, Noelle M. "Feminists, Queers and Critics: Debating the Cuban Sex Trade." *Journal of Latin American Studies* 40 (2008): 721–42.

Sullivan, Kevin Rodney, dir. *How Stella Got Her Groove Back.* Twentieth-Century Fox, 1998.

Summers, Martin. *Manliness and Its Discontents: The Black Middle Class and the Transformation of Masculinity, 1900–1930.* Chapel Hill: University of North Carolina Press, 2004.

Tang Nain, Gemma, and Barbara Bailey, eds. *Gender Equality in the Caribbean: Reality or Illusion.* Kingston, Jamaica: Ian Randle, 2003.

Taylor, Lynette. "Crossing the Line." *Sunday Advocate* (Bridgetown, Barbados), 20 April 1997, *Lifestyle*, 3.

Taylor, Timothy D. *Global Pop: World Music, World Markets.* Routledge: London, 1997.

Tharu, Susie, and K. Lalita. "Empire, Nation and the Literary Text." In *Interrogating Modernity,* ed. Tejaswini Niranjana, P. Sudhir, and Vivek Dhareshwar, 199–219. Calcutta: Seagull Books, 1993.

———. *Women Writing in India, 600 BC to the Present.* Vol. 2, *The Twentieth Century.* New York: Feminist Press, 1993.

Thomas, Bonnie. *Breadfruit or Chesnut? Gender Construction in the French Caribbean Novel.* Lanham, MD: Lexington Books, 2006.

Thomas, Deborah A. *Modern Blackness: Nationalism, Globalization, and the Politics of Culture in Jamaica.* Durham, NC: Duke University Press, 2004.

———. "Public Bodies: Virginity Testing, Redemption Songs, and Racial Respect in Jamaica." *Journal of Latin American Anthropology* 11, no. 1 (2006): 1–31.

Thomas, J. J. *Froudacity: West Indian Fables by J. A. Froude.* 1889. London: New Beacon Books, 1969.

Thomas, Nigel H. *Spirits in the Dark.* Oxford: Heinemann, 1993.

Thomas, Norman "Gus." "Another woman murdered in Antigua." *Caribbean Net News,* 16 November 2004. http:www.caribbeannetnews.com/2004/11/16/murder.htm.

Thompson, Krista A. *An Eye for the Tropics: Tourism, Photography, and Framing the Caribbean Picturesque.* Durham, NC: Duke University Press, 2006.

Tikasingh, G. I. M. "The Establishment of the Indians in Trinidad, 1870–1900." PhD thesis, University of the West Indies, St. Augustine, Trinidad and Tobago, 1975.

Timothy, Helen Pyne. "About the Name." *MaComère* 5 (2002): ix.

Tinker, Hugh. *A New System of Slavery.* London: Hansib, 1993.

Townsend, Robert, and Jeffrey Chernov. *Raw.* Paramount Pictures, 1987.

Trexler, Richard C. *Sex and Conquest: Gendered Violence, Political Order, and the European Conquest of the Americas.* Ithaca, NY: Cornell University Press, 1995.

Trinidad and Tobago. "Bill: An Act to repeal and replace the laws of Trinidad and Tobago relating to sexual crimes, to the procuration, abduction and prostitution of persons and to kindred offences, 1984." Draft. Copy in possession of Yasmin Tambiah.

———. *Bill: An Act to repeal and replace the laws of Trinidad and Tobago relating to sexual crimes, to the procuration, abduction and prostitution of persons and to kindred offences.* Port of Spain, Trinidad: Government Printery, 1985.

———. *Bill: An Act to repeal and replace the laws of Trinidad and Tobago relating to sexual crimes, to the procuration, abduction and prostitution of persons and to kindred offences.* No. 2. Port of Spain, Trinidad: Government Printery, 1986.

———. "Commentary on the Sexual Offences Bill." 1984. Copy in possession of Yasmin Tambiah.

———. "Equal Opportunities Act." *Trinidad and Tobago Gazette* 39, no. 208, Legal Supplement Part A, 27 October 2000. http:www.ttparliament.org/bills/acts/2000/a2000-69.pdf.

———. *Sexual Offences Act 1986, Republic of Trinidad and Tobago, Act No. 27 of 1986.* Port of Spain, Trinidad: Government Printery, 1986.

———. "Verbatim notes from the debates of the House of Representatives and the Senate, Republic of Trinidad and Tobago, 1986." Port of Spain, Trinidad: Government Printery, 1986.

Trotman, David V. "Women and Crime in Late Nineteenth Century Trinidad." *Caribbean Quarterly* 30, nos. 3–4 (1984): 60–72.

———. "Women and Crime in Late Nineteenth Century Trinidad." In *Caribbean Freedom: Society and Economy from Emancipation to the Present,* ed. Hilary Beckles and Verene Shepherd, 251–59. Kingston, Jamaica: Ian Randle, 1993.

Trotz, Alisa. "Between Despair and Hope: Women and Violence in Contemporary Guyana." *Small Axe,* no. 15 (2004): 1–20.

Trouillot, Michel-Rolph. "The Caribbean Region: An Open Frontier in Anthropological Theory." *Annual Review of Anthropology* 21 (1992): 19–42.

———. "Les pays pauvres et l'ogre." *Le Monde,* 1 February 2009.

———. *Silencing the Past: Power and the Production of History.* Boston: Beacon, 1995.

———. *State Against Nation: The Origins and Legacy of Duvalierism.* New York: Monthly Review Press, 1990.

Turino, Thomas. "Are We Global Yet? Globalist Discourse, Cultural Formations and the Study of Zimbabwean Popular Music." *British Journal of Ethnomusicology* 12, no. 2 (2003): 51–79.

"Uncle Sam Wags His Finger." *Economist,* 4 January 1997, 44–66.

UNIFEM. "Child Support, Poverty and Gender Equality in the Caribbean: A Research Proposal." Unpublished. 2004.

United Kingdom. Home Office and Scottish Home Department. *Report of the Committee on Homosexual Offences and Prostitution*. London: HMSO, 1957.

U.S. Department of Justice, Office for Victims of Crime. "State Legislators' Handbook for Statutory Rape Issues." http:www.ojp.usdoj.gov/ovc/publications/infores/statutoryrape/handbook/statrape.pdf (accessed 16 September 2009).

Vaissière, Pierre de. *Saint-Domingue: La société et la vie créole sous l'Ancien Régime (1629–1789)*. Paris: Perin en cie, 1909.

Van Lier, Rudolph. *Tropische Tribaden*. Dordrecht, Netherlands: Foris, 1986.

Voorhoeve, Jan, and Ursy Lichtveld. *Creole Drum: An Anthology of Creole Literature in Suriname*. New Haven, CT: Yale University Press, 1970.

Walcott, Rinaldo. "Queer Texts and Performativity: Zora, Rap and Community." In *Queer Theory in Education*, ed. W. Pinar, 133–45. Mahwah, NJ: Lawrence Erlbaum Associates, 1998.

Walker, Alice. *The Color Purple*. London: Women's Press, 1982.

Warner, Michael, ed. *Fear of a Queer Planet: Queer Politics and Social Theory*. Minneapolis: University of Minnesota Press, 1993.

Warner-Vieyra, Myriam. *Femmes échouées*. Paris: Présence Africaine, 1988.

———. *Juletane*. Paris: Présence Africaine, 1982.

———. *Le quimboiseur l'avait dit*. Paris: Présence Africaine, 1980.

Webber, A. R. F. *Those That Be in Bondage: A Tale of Indian Indentures and Sunlit Western Waters*. Georgetown, Guyana: Daily Chronicle, 1917.

Weekly Compilation of Presidential Documents, 19 May 1997, 699–705.

Weeks, Jeffrey. *Invented Moralities: Sexual Values in an Age of Uncertainty*. New York: Columbia University Press, 1997.

Wekker, Gloria. "'Girl, It's Boobies You're Getting, No'? Creole Women in Suriname and Erotic Relationships with Children and Adolescents." *Paidika: The Journal of Paedophilia* 2, no. 4 (1992): 43–48.

———. *Ik ben een gouden munt: Subjectiviteit en Seksualiteit van Creoolse Volksklasse Vrouwen in Paramaribo*. Amsterdam: Feministische Uitgeverij Vita, 1994.

———. "Of Mimic Men and Unruly Women: Social Relations in Twentieth Century Suriname." In *Twentieth-Century Suriname: Continuities and Discontinuities in a New World Society*, ed. Rosemarijn Hoefte and Peter Meel, 174–97. Kingston, Jamaica: Ian Randle; Leiden: KITLV, 2001.

———. *The Politics of Passion: Women's Sexual Culture in the Afro-Surinamese Diaspora*. New York: Columbia University Press, 2006.

———. "What's Identity Got to Do With It?" In *Female Desires*, ed. Evelyn Blackwood and Saskia E. Wieringa, 119–35. New York: Columbia University Press, 1999.

Weller, Judith Ann. *The East Indian Indenture in Trinidad*. Rio Piedras: Institute of Caribbean Studies, University of Puerto Rico, 1968.

West, Cornell. *Race Matters*. Boston: Beacon, 1993.

West, Robin. "The Difference in Women's Hedonic Lives: A Phenomenological Critique of Feminist Legal Theory." *Wisconsin Women's Law Journal* 15, no. 1 (2000): 149–215.

"William Is That You?" *Barbados Advocate,* 15 March 1997, *Lifestyle,* 16–17.

Williams, Petre. "Phillips offers help to families of girls raped and murdered." *Jamaica Observer,* 5 July 2005. http:www.jamaicaobserver.com/news/html/20050704t210000-0500_83617_obs_phillips_offers_help_to_families_of_girls_raped_and_murdered.asp.

Wilson, Elizabeth. "Le voyage et l'espace clos—Island and Journey as Metaphor: Aspects of Woman's Experience in the Works of Francophone Caribbean Women Novelists." In *Out of the Kumbla,* ed. Carole Boyce Davies and Elaine Savory Fido, 45–57. Trenton, NJ: Africa World, 1990.

Wilson, Peter J. *Crab Antics: A Caribbean Study of the Conflict between Reputation and Respectability.* New York: Waveland, 1973.

Wiltshire, Stedson. "In De Tail." Bayfield Records, 1997.

Wittig, Monique. "One is Not Born a Woman." *Feminist Issues* 1, no. 2 (1981): 47–54.

The Wolfenden Report: Report of the Committee on Homosexual Offences and Prostitution. New York: Stein and Day, 1963.

Wynter, Sylvia. "Beyond Miranda's Meanings: Un/silencing the Demonic Ground of Caliban's Woman." In *Out of the Kumbla: Caribbean Women and Literature,* ed. Carole Boyce-Davies and Elaine Savory-Fido, 355–72. Trenton, NJ: Africa World, 1990.

———. "1492: A New World View." In *Race, Discourse, and the Origin of the Americas: A New World View,* ed. V. Lawrence and R. Nettleford, 5–57. Washington, DC: Smithsonian Institution Press, 1995.

Yelvington, Kevin A. "The Anthropology of Afro-Latin America and the Caribbean: Diasporic Dimensions." *Annual Review of Anthropology* 30 (2001): 227–60.

Young, Robert J. C. *Colonial Desire: Hybridity in Theory, Culture, and Race.* New York: Routledge, 1995.

Younge, Gary. "Troubled Island." *London Guardian,* 27 April 2006. http:www.guardian.co.uk/print/0,,329466084111157,00.html.

Notes on Contributors

VANESSA AGARD-JONES is a PhD candidate in New York University's doctoral program in anthropology and French studies; her dissertation project focuses on sexual politics in Martinique. She is co-editor with Manning Marable of *Transnational Blackness: Navigating the Global Color Line* (Palgrave Macmillan, 2008).

ODILE CAZENAVE, Professor of French Studies at Boston University, is the author of *Femmes rebelles: Naissance d'un nouveau roman africain au féminin* (1996, translated into English as *Rebellious Women*, 1999) and *Afrique sur Seine: Une nouvelle génération de romanciers africains à Paris* (2003, translated as *Afrique sur Seine: A New Generation of African Writers in Paris*, 2005). She has published and coauthored numerous texts on women writers, displacement, and globalization.

MICHELLE CLIFF was born in Kingston, Jamaica, and is the author of *EVERYTHING IS NOW, If I Could Write This in Fire*, and the acclaimed novels *Abeng, No Telephone to Heaven*, and *Free Enterprise*. She lives in California.

SUSAN DAYAL is a Trinidadian artist who works mainly in wire. Her sculptures use the female torso, in the form of the corset, as a starting point to explore notions of femaleness, stereotype, and role-play.

ALISON DONNELL is a Reader in English Literature at the University of Reading, United Kingdom. She is the author of *Twentieth Century Caribbean Literature* (Routledge, 2006) and is coeditor (with Michael Bucknor) of *The Routledge Companion to Caribbean Literature* (2011).

DONETTE FRANCIS is an Associate Professor in the Department of English at Binghamton University. She recently published *Fictions of Feminine*

Citizenship: Sexuality and the Nation in Contemporary Caribbean Literature (Palgrave, 2010).

CARMEN R. GILLESPIE is a Professor of English and Creative Writing at Bucknell University. She is the author of the books *A Critical Companion to Toni Morrison* (2007) and *A Critical Companion to Alice Walker* (2011) as well as the poetry collection *Jonestown: A Vexation* (2011). In 2010 she was named one of *Essence Magazine*'s forty favorite poets.

ROSAMOND S. KING, PhD, is a critical and creative writer and performer. Her scholarship, which focuses on sexuality and performance in the Caribbean and Africa, has been widely published. She is an Assistant Professor at Brooklyn College.

ANTONIA MACDONALD-SMYTHE is a Professor at St. George's University, Grenada. She writes on contemporary Caribbean women writers and more recently on Derek Walcott. She is the author of *Making Homes in the West/Indies.*

TEJASWINI NIRANJANA is a Senior Fellow at the Centre for the Study of Culture and Society, Bangalore, India. Her publications include *Mobilizing India: Women, Music and Migration between India and Trinidad* (Durham, NC, 2006) and *Siting Translation: History, Post-structuralism and the Colonial Context* (Berkeley and Los Angeles, 1992).

EVELYN O'CALLAGHAN is Professor of West Indian Literature in the Department of Language, Linguistics and Literature at the University of the West Indies–Barbados. She has published extensively on West Indian literature, particularly by women, and edited the nineteenth-century Caribbean novel *With Silent Tread,* by Frieda Cassin.

TRACY ROBINSON is a Senior Lecturer in the Faculty of Law, University of the West Indies, Cave Hill Campus, where she teaches courses on family law, gender and the law, constitutional law, and human-rights law.

PATRICIA J. SAUNDERS is an Associate Professor of English at the University of Miami, Coral Gables. She is the author of *Alien-Nation and Repatriation: Translating Identity in Anglophone Caribbean Literature* (2007) and coeditor of *Music. Memory. Resistance: Calypso and the Caribbean Literary Imagination* (2007). Her book *Fusion and Con/Fusion: Sexuality and Consumerism in Caribbean Popular Culture* is forthcoming.

FAITH SMITH teaches at Brandeis University. She is the author of *Creole Recitations: John Jacob Thomas and Colonial Formation in the Late Nineteenth-Century Caribbean* (2002) and edited "Genders and Sexualities," a special issue of *Small Axe* (2000).

YASMIN TAMBIAH has been a Research Fellow at the International Centre for Ethnic Studies, Colombo, Sri Lanka, and a Research Associate of the Centre for Feminist Legal Research, New Delhi, India. Currently she is an Honorary Associate in the Department of History, University of Sydney, Australia.

OMISE'EKE NATASHA Tinsley is an Assistant Professor of English at the University of Minnesota. Her book *Thiefing Sugar: Eroticism between Women in Caribbean Literature* (2010) traces how Dutch-, French-, and English-language writers queer traditional tropical-landscape-as-female-beloved metaphors to imagine a poetics of decolonization.

RINALDO WALCOTT is an Associate Professor at the Ontario Institute for Studies in Education and the Institute for Women's and Gender Studies at the University of Toronto. He is working on a book manuscript titled "Black Diaspora Faggotry: Frames, Readings, Limits."

M. S. WORRELL teaches philosophy at Long Island University Brooklyn Campus. He is interested in epistemological questions about self-identity and their relation to race, sexuality, and gender studies.

Index